The Minister's Instruction Manual

A How-To Manual for Pastors, Missionaries, and Lay Leaders

By
Dr. Mel Brown

Dedication

This manual is dedicated to the most important people in my life.

To my wife Barbara, who has shared so many of the things experienced and taught in this book and who has been a diligent filter for my thoughts and words expressed in print

To my daughter Lori, a teacher, who has been my editor and typist for much of this process

To my son Timothy, an attorney, who has read the manuscript and made many helpful suggestions and contributed to the section on critical thinking

To my daughter Cheryl, a doctor, who has shared her medical expertise with me and has answered my numerous questions related to physiology and medicine

To my grandchildren who have brought unlimited joy and delight to my life

To my father Floyd Brown whose thirst for knowledge and insatiable curiosity about all things provided me with an example of diligent study

To my mother Mamie Brown whose love and service to Christ provided the inspiration for my spiritual journey

To my many teachers who have provided a foundation of knowledge upon which my ministry rests

Finally, to the people of my three congregations, especially the Edgewood Baptist Church in Rock Island, Illinois, where I have spent the last forty years ministering and sharing with them the unsearchable riches of Christ

With love to all of them, I dedicate this book.

Acknowledgements

This manual is the product of the efforts of many people. It is with grateful appreciation that I acknowledge their contributions.

Amy Smith, a former intern, took extensive notes during our weekly training sessions and began the process of committing the material to writing. She also integrated the nearly eight-inch stack of reading materials that were used in the training. A former Catholic, she produced the section on witnessing to Catholics.

Tracy Mingo, a former intern, expanded the material through additional note taking and continued the integration of the educational materials.

Lani Joyce, a former intern, developed some of the graphics used to illustrate a number of the key concepts presented.

Ed Kuriscak, Edgewood Associate Pastor, contributed to the sections on attitude and self-esteem.

Timothy Green, Edgewood Associate Pastor, contributed to the sections on counseling, grief counseling, and valid meetings.

Sheila Kuriscak, Edgewood's Christian Education Director, contributed to the section on Children's Ministry together with my daughter, Lori Kimmel.

Craig Stevenson, Edgewood's current youth pastor, Ed Kuriscak, and former youth pastor Dan Watson contributed to the Youth Ministry section.

My wife, Barbara, and daughter, Lori, edited the manuscript and made many helpful suggestions during the process.

The former interns have been a blotter soaking up the knowledge represented in the materials presented here and a mirror reflecting the principles and practices that they learned. They are impacting the unreached for the glory of God at home and abroad. Their actions, reactions, and suggestions have been vital to the success of the internship program and this manual. Without their contributions and invaluable assistance, this manual would never have been published.

The Minister's Instruction Manual
A How-To Manual for Pastors, Missionaries, and Lay Leaders by Dr. Mel Brown

Guidance House Publishing
3109 29th Street
Moline, IL 61265 U.S.A.

Unless otherwise indicated, Scripture quotations used in this book are from the Holy Bible, King James Version.

First Edition, 2009.

Table of Contents

General Introduction and Methodology

The compilation of this manual began over ten years ago when I began teaching young people chosen to participate in Edgewood's Missionary Intern Program ultimately preparing them for success in the ministry. Although they were well prepared theologically, I realized there was more they could learn to better prepare them to handle the unique difficulties they would face in their ministries. I was able to share with them the insights, wisdom, and practical lessons I had learned from my forty-plus years of experience as a pastor. After hearing about the success with our Missionary Intern Program, many people have requested the information contained within this manual. I pray that you will find it beneficial in your ministry.

The training of the interns involved extensive personal instruction, participation in numerous areas of ministry, considerable reading, mentoring by the Edgewood staff, and personal coaching in the skills required in ministry.

Two years were necessary for teaching and training to prepare them for future service as Christian leaders. Our intent was not merely to produce future missionaries and pastors but outstanding servants of the Lord who would make a major impact on others as they served in various parts of the world. Our purpose was not to produce players but champions for Christ, fully equipped and ready to face the challenges of ministry.

For a more detailed description of our methodology of the intern training, see "General Information and Methodology of Intern Training" in the appendix.

Disclaimer

This book is designed to provide information for pastors, missionaries, and lay pastors about a variety of topics deemed important to the pastoral process. It is offered with the understanding that the publisher and author are not engaged in rendering legal, accounting, medical, psychological, or other professional services. If legal or other expert assistance is required, the services of a competent professional should be sought.

It is not the purpose of this manual to print all of the information that is otherwise available to ministers, but instead to complement, amplify, and supplement other texts. You are urged to read all the available material, learn as much as possible about ministry, and tailor the information to your individual needs.

Every effort has been made to make this manual as complete and accurate as possible. However, there may be mistakes, both typographical and in content. Therefore, this text should be used only as a general guide and not as the ultimate source of information.

The purpose of this manual is to educate and inform. The author and Guidance House Publications shall have neither liability nor responsibility to any person or entity with respect to any loss or damage caused, or alleged to have been caused, directly or indirectly, by the information contained in this book.

It is the fervent hope of both the author and publisher that the material contained in this book will enhance your ministry and lead to increased effectiveness as a servant of Jesus Christ.

Part One
Personal Preparation

Introduction
Personal Preparation

When I arrived at my first full-time church, I came with my eight years of collegiate educational preparation and the experience of pastoring two smaller part-time churches. I thought I was reasonably well prepared for what I was to experience in the pastorate. Immediately I was faced with problems for which I was inadequately prepared. Some were people's personal problems which were both serious and urgent—a suicidal mother, a young man with homosexual urges, and an older couple with gross marital problems. Some involved church-wide conflicts involving deep divisions within the congregation. I spent much time seeking advice from others with more knowledge and experience about the situations and problems. As a result of my circumstances, I was determined to learn everything I could. I only wish my personal preparation had included access to the material contained in this manual as I started my ministry.

The ultimate personal preparation comes from God through His shaping of both our life message and ministry as He makes us conformable to the image of Jesus Christ (Romans 8:29). This manual is produced by a Baptist minister and consequently reflects Baptist beliefs of 1) the priesthood and individual soul liberty of every believer who has the God-given right to interpret the Bible for himself and 2) the autonomy of the local church which exercises the right to conduct its own affairs without interference from any outside source. Therefore, it is presented with the conviction that it is not our duty to tell you what to do or how to conduct your ministry but rather to offer ideas which may prove helpful as you carry out your own God-ordained ministry.

Genuine Spirituality

Have you ever met someone or heard them speak and felt an overwhelming conviction that they were closely in touch with God? Was there something about their person that powerfully impacted you? Several people have so impressed me that contacts with them have helped shape my life and have given me a greater desire to know God better and walk more closely with Him.

Dr. Peter Connolly was one of those men and his story is included later in this section. To be close to him was to feel closer to God because Christ shined brightly through his life illuminating his words and actions. His life was like a magnet drawing me nearer to Christ.

Dr. George Gardner told of having a well-known preacher as a guest speaker in his church and entertaining him in his home. After spending time as a family with this man, his wife remarked, "I feel like I have been in the presence of Jesus Christ today." Dr. Gardner agreed that he felt the same way. That should be our desire, to be so genuinely spiritual, so close in our walk with Jesus Christ, that His presence shines through us making Him more real to those around us and drawing them to be more like Him as well.

Genuine Spirituality

The word spirituality is derived from the word *spirit* which is the Hebrew word *ruach* in the Old Testament and the Greek word *pneuma* in the New Testament. It is associated with sacredness, spiritual values, the supernatural, God consciousness, the devotional, purification, and spiritual depth and understanding.

Spirituality is then related to the Spirit. The spirit of man is dead toward God before encountering Christ through faith, but it is quickened or made alive as a result of that encounter (Ephesians 2:1). When man's spirit becomes alive, it opens a whole new realm in him. This is the new birth (John 3:3).

Four significant events take place when we are born again: we are regenerated or spiritually reborn and changed by God (Titus 3:5), indwelt by the Holy Spirit who produces a new nature within us (Romans 8:11; 2 Corinthians 5:17), baptized into the body of Christ (1 Corinthians 12:13), and sealed with the Holy Spirit unto the day of redemption (Ephesians 4:30). We are then in Christ and Christ is in us through the indwelling presence of the Holy Spirit (Galatians 2:20; Colossians 1:27; 2 Corinthians 13:5; Acts 2:33). The Spirit now bears witness with our spirit that we are the children of God (Romans 8:9, 10, 16).

Occurs at Salvation

Regeneration
Indwelling of Holy Spirit
Baptism of Holy Spirit into body of Christ
Sealing by Holy Spirit until day of redemption

The In-Christ Principle

Our vital union with Christ is a picture of Christ being in the Father and the Father in Him (John 14:10, 11, 20). Christ said that His authority and works came from the Father within Him. Similarly our spiritual works must flow from God within us (John 14:12). Every provision necessary for success in our spiritual life has been made through our two-fold vital union with Christ. Since we are both in Christ and have Christ in us we are complete and entire lacking nothing. When at salvation the Spirit places us in Christ we have positions and privileges beyond our natural comprehension. By being placed in the sphere of Christ, He supplies to us every resource imaginable to meet our needs. Consider these positions and privileges we have in Christ which are only representative of all available to us.

Justification	Sanctification
Newness of life	Completeness
Glorification	Godliness
Blessedness	Truth
Freedom	Fellowship with God
Redemption	Freedom and liberty
Hope	Grace
Alive unto God	Power
Victory	A new creation
Reconciliation	Security
Devotion	Love
Faith	Intimacy
Trust	The mind of Christ
His promises	Immortality
Consolation	Strength
The love of God	Faithfulness
One body in Christ	Wisdom
Heirs with Christ	Joy
Maturity	Salvation
Will of God known	Confirmation of covenant
Boldness	Forgiveness

There are about 130 biblical references to being in Christ or variations such as *in Christ Jesus* or *in Him*. Clearly this is an important concept for our spiritual understanding and Christ-like living.

Contemplate that the spiritual qualities of Christ are readily available to us because we are in Christ; they are already present within us in Christ. We need only to let Christ express them through us. The fruit of the Spirit is love, joy, peace, longsuffering, gentleness, goodness, meekness, temperance, and faith (Galatians 5:22, 23). Not allowing Christ to live and express His life through us will bring certain failure in our spiritual lives.

Picture putting a needle into a bowl of water. The moment you drop the needle into the water it sinks to the bottom, but if you push the needle through a piece of cork and then drop it into the water, it does not sink but

floats. Putting the needle inside the cork allows the buoyant qualities of the cork to operate on the needle. It is by understanding our position of being in Christ and allowing that connection to counteract our natural ungodly inclinations that we rise above and conquer our sinful desires.

Vitality of Spiritual Nature

Feeding our spiritual nature should be an ongoing process of communing with God. **God's Word** is described in the Bible as living; it is the only life-giving book (John 6:63). It is inspired of God and is profitable in our lives for doctrine, reproof, correction, and instruction in righteousness (2 Timothy 3:16; Hebrews 4:12). We must use Scripture, read, study, memorize, and apply it to our lives. Dr. Tom Malone suggested reading God's Word until our heart burns within us. Have you experienced what He meant by letting God's Word so warm your heart?

Meditation is the process of contemplating God's Word, His works, and His attributes. This can be illustrated by the process of rumination which occurs in cows. When a cow eats, food is deposited into one of its four stomachs. Later it brings the food up out of its stomach, chews it some more, and swallows it again. The process of chewing its cud is repeated many times. This illustrates how we are to practice meditation on God's Word. We should let it flood our mind, then bring it back to mind again and again considering how to apply it to our lives. This meditation on the Scripture carries a promise from God for success and prosperity (Joshua 1:8).

We are also instructed to pray without ceasing (1 Thessalonians 5:17). Some say it is impossible to fulfill this command because of our busy schedules and hectic life styles. The concept of **prayer** is clarified by the meaning of the words *without ceasing*. The Greek word meaning used here is of a cough. We don't cough nonstop day and night, rather we cough intermittingly throughout the day. Praying without ceasing then means as we go through a day, we periodically engage in prayer. When you talk to someone on the phone, pray for him. When you meet with someone, pray for him. When people cross your mind, pray for them. When you face a problem, pray about it. In this way you pray throughout the day, praying without ceasing.

Have you ever spent an entire hour in prayer? If so, did it seem like one big list of requests? Try to approach prayer not as just a time of supplication and intercession but as a time of intimate fellowship with God. If you don't think you can spend an hour daily in prayer, try scheduling an hour or two into your weekly calendar just as if it were an important meeting and see what amazing things will begin to happen. There is a guide to spending an hour with God on the following page.

George Müller was one of the giants of the Christian faith, especially in the practice of prayer and applied faith. He supported several orphanages in England without ever asking any person for a penny, or in his case, a pound. He had vowed that he would prove the faithfulness of God in answering prayer by taking all of his needs to God and God alone. His biography is filled with inspiring, almost unbelievable incidents of miraculous answers to his prayers. During his life he experienced fifty thousand specific answers to prayer, housed over ten thousand orphans in five orphanages, received over seven million dollars in answer to prayers, supported hundreds of missionaries and a number of schools for children of all ages, and engaged in many Christian publishing endeavors.

He read the Bible through more than 200 times, most of them on his knees. Müller practiced prevailing prayer following these conditions:

1. To ask for those things and those things only that, when given to us, are for the glory of God; to pray in accordance with His will, with godly motives, and not seek any gift which would be consumed upon our own lusts

2. To ask in the name of the Lord Jesus on the basis of His merits and worthiness, our entire dependence being on the mediation of our Savior as the only grounds upon which to claim any blessing

3. To believe that God is able and willing to give us what we ask; to have faith in His Word and its promises as confirmation of His oath

4. To separate ourselves from all known sin (Scripture teaches that if we regard iniquity in our hearts, He will not hear us.)

5. To determine to pray and continue to pray until the blessing is granted without fixing a time limit; to look for and expect an answer until it is received (Patience must be exercised as we wait upon God and his answers, then our souls will be refreshed and invigorated.)

The brief testimony included in this section is a powerful presentation of Müller's practice of a genuinely spiritual life. The reading of biographies of men and women of God is one of the best ways to encourage spiritual growth by gleaning important lessons from their lives.

> *The greatest spiritual challenge is not merely knowing God's Word, it is living it.*

Spending One Hour With God

Simplify your life in order to spend one hour each day with God in prayer. We enter needlessly and become too involved in the affairs of the world. Being so occupied, there is no desire, no zeal, and no power for intimate fellowship with God. God can only work perfectly when we cease our struggles, abide in Him, and expect Him to work in and through us. Spend approximately five minutes on each of these.

Praise — Focus on who God is and His attributes such as His omnipotence, omniscience, faithfulness, love, holiness, goodness, and mercy. Focus on the names of God (Psalm 34:1-3; Psalm 35:27-28; Psalm 104; Psalm 139:14).

Thanksgiving — Dwell with gratitude on what God has done. Be mindful of the blessings in your life: health, strength, family, freedom, daily provisions, and spiritual benefits (Psalm 26:7; Psalm 100:2-5; Philippians 4:6; Colossians 4:2).

Worship — Listen to or sing music that evokes honor and reverence for God (2 Samuel 22:47; Psalm 66:1-2; Psalm 95:1-7).

Read — Read selected passages from the Bible seeing these as God's own words. As you read, it is as if God Himself is speaking them anew to you.

Reflect — Personalize the Psalms. Example from Psalm 23: The Lord is my shepherd and as such He cares for me and sees that I have food, water, and rest; He keeps me safe and in His care I am content.

Meditation — Contemplate who He is in your life and all He has done for you (Joshua 1:8; Psalm 1:1-8; Psalm 63:5-6).

Silence and Listening — Quiet your heart and mind before God. Anticipate hearing His voice. View silence as an attitude of stillness and waiting before God (2 Samuel 3:10; Psalm 37:7,34; Psalm 46:10; Psalm 62:5; Isaiah 30:15).

Confession — Ask God to search your heart and reveal any sinful way in you, then admit failures, seek forgiveness of sins, and commit to change with God's power (Psalm 51:10-11; Psalm 139:23-24; Romans 4:7-8; Hebrews 8:12; 1 John 1:9).

Intercession — Pray for others and their needs: guidance, health, salvation, comfort, and growth (Colossians 1:9-12; 4:2,12; 1 Timothy 2:1-2; James 5:16).

Petition — Pray for the wisdom to become the kind of person God wants you to be (Psalm 34:4; Matthew 7:7; Philippians 4:6-7, 19; James 4:2; 1 John 5:14).

Promises — Claim God's promises and thank Him for fulfilling those promises in your life (1 Kings 8:56; Jeremiah 29:11-13; 2 Peter 1:4).

Praise — Focus again on God and praise Him for what He is going to do in your life today (Psalm 22:3; Psalm 50:23; Psalm 63; Psalm 150:1-6).

Be sure to take time in prayer, to dwell at the footstool of the throne of God and the Lamb, from which flow the river of life. ~Andrew Murray

Soul Nourishment First

From the *Autobiography of George Müller*

It has pleased the Lord to teach me a truth, the benefit of which I have not lost for more than fourteen years. The point is this: I saw more clearly than ever that the first great and primary business to which I ought to attend every day was to have my soul happy in the Lord. The first thing to be concerned about was not how much I might serve the Lord, or how I might glorify the Lord, but how I might get my soul into a happy state, and how my inner man might be nourished.

I saw that the most important thing I had to do was to give myself to the reading of the Word of God — not prayer, but the Word of God. And here again, not the simple reading of the Word of God so that it only passes through my mind just as water runs through a pipe, but considering what I read, pondering over it, and applying it to my heart. To meditate on it, that thus my heart might be comforted, encouraged, warned, reproved, instructed. And that thus, by means of the Word of God, whilst meditating on it, my heart be brought into experimental communion with the Lord.

I began therefore to meditate on the New Testament from the beginning, early in the morning. The first thing I did, after having asked in a few words the Lord's blessing upon His precious Word, was to begin to meditate on the Word of God, searching as it were into every verse to get blessing out of it.

When we pray, we speak to God. Now, prayer, in order to be continued for any length of time in any other than a formal manner, requires, generally speaking, a measure of strength or godly desire, and the season, therefore, when this exercise of the soul can be most effectively performed is after the inner man has been nourished by meditation on the Word of God, where we find our Father speaking to us, to encourage us, to comfort us, to instruct us, to humble us, to reprove us.

By the blessing of God, I ascribe to this mode the help and strength which I have had from God to pass in peace through deeper trials, in various ways, than I had ever had before.

How different, when the soul is refreshed and made happy early in the morning, from what it is when, without spiritual preparation, the service, the trials, and the temptations of the day come upon me.

1841, May 9

Confession is a vital part of living a victorious Christian life (1 John 1:9). It means agreeing with God. Confession then is not merely repeating words to God asking Him to forgive our sins, but it involves seeing our sins from His point of view, feeling about them the same way He does, admitting, and forsaking them (Proverbs 28:13). One well-known Christian leader used to write his sins on a piece of paper, confess each one to God, tear the list into tiny pieces, and flush them down the commode washing them away. Claim this promise of forgiveness, *The blood of Jesus Christ cleanses us from all sin* (1 John 1:7).

Praise and thanksgiving should be a vital and constant part of our lives. If you want access to God's presence, then just begin praising the Lord, thanking God for who and what He is. It is very important to God to hear from us and it should be very important to us to spend time with Him. Thanksgiving is a companion to praise. It is counting our blessings and expressing appreciation and gratitude for all He has done, is doing, and will do in our lives.

The greatest spiritual challenge is not merely knowing God's Word, it is living it and putting it into practice in our lives (James 1:22). This is a full-time job that will last a lifetime. The Christian life is about receiving, giving, doing, becoming, and being. All are part of the process. We are both passive and active participants in the process.

Genuine Spirituality Blueprint

God has provided the means for our living a victorious Christian life. The book of Romans shows an important difference between sins and sin. Sins usually refer to individual transgressions whereas sin refers to the sinful nature with its moral weakness and susceptibility to sinfulness. It is essential to know that Christ provided for our victory over both sins and sin.

In Romans chapters five through eight, the formula is carefully laid out. Chapter five shows us we are justified and made righteous before God through the finished work of Jesus Christ. By faith, receiving Christ as our Lord and Savior, we are justified before God, declared righteous or right with God through the finished work of Jesus Christ (Romans 5:1). In Romans chapter six, three key words place us on the path to victory over sin.

1. Know

We are to realize with absolute certainty that Christ's death, burial, and resurrection have provided all that is necessary to ensure spiritual victory. The same power of God that raised Jesus Christ from the dead is now available to us because Christ is in us and we are in Christ.

2. Reckon

We are to count ourselves to be dead unto sin and alive unto God. Sin's power over us is broken. A good illustration of this is the working of a clutch when you drive an automobile with a manual transmission, commonly called a stick shift. The power of the engine flows to the wheels of the car through the clutch assembly and the transmission. When you depress the clutch, it disengages the engine from the drive train of the car. When the clutch is released, it reengages the engine's power to the car's drive train. It is by the power of God that we can reckon our ability through Christ to disengage the power of sin in our lives. When you are tempted, simply imagine the power of Christ at your disposal and depress the spiritual clutch allowing Christ to disengage you from the power of that sin in your life.

3. Yield

We are to yield to Christ so that His power flows through us. It is not our strength or ability which gives us victory.

It is depending upon His strength, His presence, and His power. When we realize our inability and yield ourselves to His divine influence and control in any temptation, His power is made available to and through us. This principle is further amplified in Romans.

Dr. A. T. Pierson, a godly man of yesteryear, told of having a dream that profoundly impacted his spiritual life. He dreamed that the Lord Jesus appeared before him. Pierson held in his hand a large ring of keys. The Lord asked for all of the keys on the ring, each one representing a different area of Pierson's life. He carefully considered all it would mean to give each key to the Lord, including giving up control of that area. Dr. Pierson had an amazing revelation of what it would mean to yield all to Jesus Christ. He pondered the thought of giving the Lord control of every area of his life. In the dream he slipped two or three keys off the ring and presented the rest of the keys to the waiting Lord Jesus. As the dream continued, he pictured Christ sorrowfully holding the ring of keys, carefully examining them, and then returning them to him. Christ said, "Arthur, if you can't trust me with all the keys, you can't trust me with any of them." Yielding all is what it means to be filled with the Holy Spirit.

In Romans chapter seven, after showing us our deliverance from the effects of the law through Christ, Paul focuses on the continuing power of the old nature. The old nature never changes and never improves. It is possible to sin, given the right circumstances, at any time in our Christian life. We are warned, *Let him that thinketh he standeth take heed lest he fall* (1 Corinthians 10:12). Paul tells us that the things he wanted to do he found himself not doing, and the things he didn't want to do he found himself doing. He finally exclaims, *Oh wretched man that I am! who shall deliver me from the body of this death* (Romans 7:24)? This is probably a picture of dragging a dead corpse with him wherever he went. The old nature is such a weight, always ready to drag us down.

In Romans chapter eight, we are taught that God's presence dwelling within us in the person of the Holy Spirit supplies us with the power for victorious living. Trying to live the Christian life in your own strength is like a pilot not availing himself of the power of the jet engines of his plane. Regularly some of the strongest men in the world assemble to compete in the World's Strongest Man Contest. The participants must perform difficult feats which test their physical strength. One such task was to pull a jet airplane down a runway from a standing start using only their brut strength. That is a good example of how many attempt to live their Christian lives when facing trials and temptations in their own strength. Compare that to sitting in the plane at the end of the runway, listening to the jet engines accelerate, then sending the plane down the runway to a speed of approximately 150 mph before becoming airborne. The continuing thrust of power from the engines takes the plane soaring up to 600 mph. The jet engines are a picture of the power of Christ at our disposal. The jet engines engage and we soar to victory.

Since Romans seven teaches us that sin's potential power will always be present in our lives, we must learn to walk in the Spirit so that we will not fulfill the lusts of the flesh (Romans 13:14). Note that the verse does not say that we will not have lusts or desires of the old nature but rather promises we will not fulfill them. In early days some people attempted to fly using homemade wing-like contraptions as they stood upon a high place. When they leaped into the air they soon discovered that, in spite of the feverish flapping of their arms, they quickly fell to the ground. Yet when a plane flies, it counteracts the law of gravity. It's not that the law of gravity is not present and at work, it is that the law of propulsion is counteracting it. The powerful thrust of the plane's engines counteracts the law of gravity. If the engines of the plane fail, the law of propulsion is discontinued and the law of gravity takes over, with the plane crashing to the earth. Walking in the Spirit by availing ourselves of God's power counteracts the pull of the old nature and helps us to soar to new heights in Christ.

We are taught in John Chapter 15 to abide in Christ. The Greek word for abide (*meno*) denotes a plant with its root system abiding in the ground. The roots abide in the ground and the ground abides on the roots. Sap flows upward to nourish the branches and produce fruit. Abiding in Christ can also be illustrated by a baby in the mother's womb. The umbilical cord enables blood carrying oxygen and nutrients to flow to the baby and the baby's blood to return to the mother. Our relationship with and dependence upon Christ is like the umbilical cord. Abiding in Christ is exchanging His life for our lives moment by moment so that the presence, character, power, and strength of Christ becomes ours and will produce in us the fruit of the Spirit. It is characterized by our complete dependency upon Him.

The practical steps to walking in the Spirit involve renewing our mind with God's Word, appropriating it to our life situations, and calling out to God in prayer for our needs and the needs of others. Fill the mind with godly thoughts, things true, lovely, honest, pure, and of good report (Philippians 4). This is the book of Romans formula for victorious Christian living.

Holy Spirit Empowered Ministry

Ministry is much more than performing various tasks and duties. Service to the Lord should be performed under the influ-ence of the Holy Spirit. Ephesians 5:18 says, *And be not drunk with wine wherein is excess, but be filled with the Spirit.* When someone is intoxicated he is under the influence of alcohol, so the comparison is when he is under the influence of the Holy Spirit. All of his thoughts, words, and actions are under the influence of the Spirit of God. Hence the saying, "If there is a work done for God, God must do the work."

Ministry can be performed in our own wisdom, strength, and ability or performed under the direction, control, and influence of the Holy Spirit. Paul had that in mind when he wrote, *For I have received of the Lord that which also I delivered unto you* (1 Corinthians 11:23). Knowing the importance of practicing what he preached, he warned, *For I will not dare to speak of any of those things which Christ hath not wrought by me...*(Romans 15:18). The filling of the Spirit is allowing the Holy Spirit to influence all areas of our lives. Walking in the Spirit is a moment by moment experience. It is God-consciousness demonstrated by Jesus relying on His Father's presence and power in His life.

Scripture says, *If any of you lack wisdom, let him ask of God*, then promises that God will give it liberally (James 1:5). Many of our spiritual needs are portrayed in Scripture as being supplied simply by our asking and depending on the Lord.

The Importance of Discipline

In order to walk closely with the Lord Jesus Christ and grow in our spiritual life, it is imperative to develop and exercise spiritual disciplines. The word *disciple* is associated with *discipline*. A disciple is literally a disciplined one. Our daily walk with the Lord must include time set aside with Him and for Him. Spiritual discipline gives meaning and fulfillment to our lives. We see Jesus as the ultimate spiritual example, but what we often fail to realize is that Jesus practiced a series of disciplines in his relationship with His heavenly Father. Consider some of the disciplines that Christ practiced.

1. Solitude

The Lord Jesus regularly left the disciples, withdrew to a private place, and spent time alone with the heavenly Father. If we are going to walk in the Spirit, we must take time or make time to be alone with God. This will involve setting priorities and putting God at the top of the list.

2. Silence

Scripture tells us to *Be still, and know that I am God...* (Psalm 46:10). With our often busy, hectic schedules, it is important to slow down, get off the treadmill of constant activity, and quiet our hearts before God. Most people report this is the hardest discipline for them to practice, bringing the heart, mind, lips, emotions, and body to a quiet rest. As in Psalm 23, we need to lie down in the green pastures beside the still waters alone with the Shepherd.

3. Surrender

To yield ourselves without reservation is what God requires as in Romans 12:1 which says, *I beseech you therefore, brethren, by the mercies of God, that ye present your bodies a living sacrifice, holy, acceptable unto God, which is your reasonable service.* When an animal was brought for sacrifice, it was tied in place to prevent its jumping off the altar. We as human beings can put ourselves on the altar of surrender and take ourselves off again. God asks us to be living sacrifices and through our daily living to surrender our wills to Him moment by moment.

4. Sacrifice

Sacrifice involves giving up something for the sake of another. Christ said that all of the law and the prophets hinged on the commandments to love the Lord our God with all of our heart, soul, strength, and mind and to love our neighbor as ourselves. When we give up our time, treasure, and plans to God and serve others, we practice the discipline of sacrifice. This is undoubtedly what Christ meant when He told us to deny ourselves, take up our cross, and follow Him.

5. Purity

Purity comes from purging our lives of the sinful things which are dishonoring to God including both the sins of commission and omission. The goal is to be Christ-like in word, thought, and deed. It is to follow in His footsteps of a righteous life. It is the discipline of choosing in every situation to do what is right.

6. Worship and Praise

Psalm 22 tells us that God inhabits the praises of His people. If we want to enter God's presence, there is no better way than doing so through the act of praise. The model prayer begins and ends with praise to God. Praise is acknowledging God's worthiness. Thanksgiving is acknowledging God's blessings in our lives. The most oft repeated commandment in scripture is *Praise Ye the Lord*. Practicing the discipline of praise, worship, and thanksgiving is absolutely necessary for a genuinely spiritual life. An attitude of gratitude expressed to God is paramount in importance.

7. Study

We are to hide God's word in our hearts (Psalm 119:11) and renew our minds with it. This can only be accomplished by disciplining ourselves to spend time in the Word. Reading, studying, and memorizing God's Word are necessary to fuel our spiritual walk. Consider the lady who attempted to read a book and found it to be boring and uninteresting. After meeting the author, dating, and falling in love with him, she returned to the same book and found it to be interesting and appealing. The change occurred because she fell in love with the author. If we love the One who wrote the Bible, we will surely care more about what He wrote. It is not enough to merely fill our minds with scriptures, we must apply the principles to the daily activities of our lives. This is what James meant when he said we should not be a hearer of God's Word only but a doer (James 1:23).

8. Prayer

Prayer is our lifeline to God and should be as natural as breathing. We inhale by taking in God's word; we exhale by pouring ourselves out to Him in prayer. Genuine prayer time should involve praise and thanksgiving (exalting God), confession (acknowledging our sinful ways and asking for forgiveness), intercession (praying for others and their needs), and petition (praying for our own needs). With little prayer comes little power. With more prayer comes more power. With much prayer comes much power.

9. Fellowship

Believers need each other for support, strength, encouragement, and accountability. It is a relationship based on commonality. The Bible has much to say about fellowship both with God and with others. During the darkest hours of His life, Jesus craved fellowship and sought the companionship of Peter, James, and John (Matthew 26:36-46).

10. Service

Serving the Lord is ministering to others on His behalf. If love is meeting the needs of others, then we serve in love by meeting another's needs. We become His hands, His feet, and His mouth. Every member is to be a minister through acts of service for our Lord.

This list of disciplines is not exhaustive, but each of the disciplines mentioned is necessary to live a Christ-like life. What we do with God determines what God does with us.

Model of Genuine Spirituality

Fortunate are we who have had godly mentors who have shown the way. Such a man was Dr. Peter Connolly, evangelist, author, teacher, and theologian. One of the most valuable lessons he taught was the pathway to genuine spirituality. The apostle Paul said, *If ye then be risen with Christ, seek those things which are above...*(Colossians 3:1a). If a message prepared in the mind reaches the mind, a message prepared in the heart reaches the heart, and a message prepared in the life reaches the life, Dr. Connolly's message was prepared in his life and consequently influenced the lives of so many.

> *If there is a work to be done for God, then God must do the work through us.*

Dr. Connolly experienced a complete life change through a dramatic encounter with Christ. He yielded to the call to service and experienced a rewarding ministry. Some called him the Billy Graham of the British Isles. A testimony of another Christian leader that Dr. Connolly heard speak had a marked impact on his life. The speaker told of meeting an evangelist who had also been living a routine normal Christian life with its ups and downs until his life and ministry were literally transformed by being filled with the Spirit. When Peter Connolly heard this message, he vowed that he would settle for nothing less than to experience Christ's best in his spiritual life. Dr. Connolly described his personal quest in three phases related to this relationship with the Holy Spirit.

The first phase he called **Not Always** which referred to the Old Testament occurrences when the Spirit of God came upon or anointed people at various times in different ways for specific tasks. He analogized that this had been his experience with God. There were times of spiritual refreshment and power, but the lack of continuity resulted in an uneven spirituality. His spiritual power was *sometimes*, but *not always*.

The second phase he called **Not Yet**, which referred to the New Testament status of the disciples while with Christ but the Holy Spirit was not yet possessed by them, ...*for the Holy Ghost was not yet given; because that Jesus was not yet glorified* (John 7:39b). He acknowledged that today believers receive the Holy Spirit at salvation, unlike the disciples who later received the Spirit of God when Jesus breathed on them and said, ...*Receive ye the Holy Ghost* (John 20:22b). He used the *not yet* expression to illustrate this stage of his journey toward a closer relationship with Christ. Since he desired Christ to control and influence every area of his life, he gradually surrendered possessions, family, future, desires, career, and choices to the complete rule of God. He stated that his pursuit was continuous and laborious as God revealed unyielded things. He struggled but let them go, choosing to be under the Lord's control. It was the pursuit of "Not I but Christ." God singled out things he never would have thought of and kept them before him until he released his hold and gave them over to God.

One night while deep in prayer after an eight-month quest, he experienced the full-ness of the presence of God in a way that would alter his relationship with Christ immeasurably. God filled his life in such a way that he compared it to the testimony of Finney, Wesley, and Moody. He described the experience "...as if he could see through the eyes of God" and added that from that day on, his life and ministry would never be the same. God possessed him in a new way. God's presence and power were evident in all areas of his life.

The third phase was **Walking in the Spirit**. He developed the daily practice of yielding all to God, practicing spiritual disciplines, abiding in Christ, and allowing Christ to live and flow through his life. To be near Peter Connolly was to be nearer to Christ. His testimony was a clear call to "Follow me as I follow Christ."

D. L. Moody was challenged by Butcher Varney when he said that the world had yet to see what God could do with a man who was totally surrendered to Him. Moody accepted the challenge and said, "I will be that man." The pursuit and accomplishment of that challenge is genuine spirituality.

Spiritual Dichotomy: Charts

Jesus said all the law and the prophets rested on the commandment to love the Lord our God with all our heart, soul, strength, and mind and to love our neighbor as ourselves (Matthew 22:37-40). Genuine spirituality flows from these roots and fulfills this commandment with the fruit of the Spirit evidenced in our lives. The lack of genuine spirituality flows from disobedience to the root requirements. Read the charts (*Lack of Spirituality* on page 26 and *Genuine Spirituality* on page 27) from the bottom up.

No good thing will He withhold from them that walk uprightly.   ~Psalm 84:11

So live that when people get to know you, they will get to know God better.

~Unknown

You are writing a gospel, a chapter each day,
By the deeds that you do and the words that you say.
Men read what you write, whether faithful or true,
Just what is the gospel according to you?   ~Unknown

Is God using you as much as He can but not all He could?
Increase your usability.   ~Vance Havner

Nothing lies beyond the reach of prayer
because nothing lies beyond the reach of God.   ~Unknown

His greatest spiritual asset was his unwavering awareness of the actual presence of Jesus. Nothing sustained him as much as the realization that Jesus was always actually present with him. This realization was totally independent of his own feelings, his own worthiness, and his perceptions as to how Jesus would demonstrate His presence. Christ was the center of his thoughts; whenever his mind was free from other matters, it would turn to Christ. Whenever he was alone, no matter where he was, he would talk aloud to Christ as easily and naturally as to any human friend. That is how very real Jesus' actual presence was to him.   ~ Charles Trumbull of Dr. John Douglas Adams

If Jesus Christ be God and died for me, then no sacrifice can be too great for me to make for Him.   ~C. T. Studd

Expect great things from God; attempt great things for God.

~William Carey

Clay has no plan of its own, no aspirations for service, no reluctance to perform its given task. It is just clay—moldable, pliable, totally submissive to the will of the Master. Allow Him to shape you into the person He wants you to be … like clay.   ~Blackaby and Blackaby

He is no fool who gives up what he cannot keep to gain that which he cannot lose.   ~Jim Elliot

Christ-likeness is a journey...not a destination.   ~Charles Swindoll

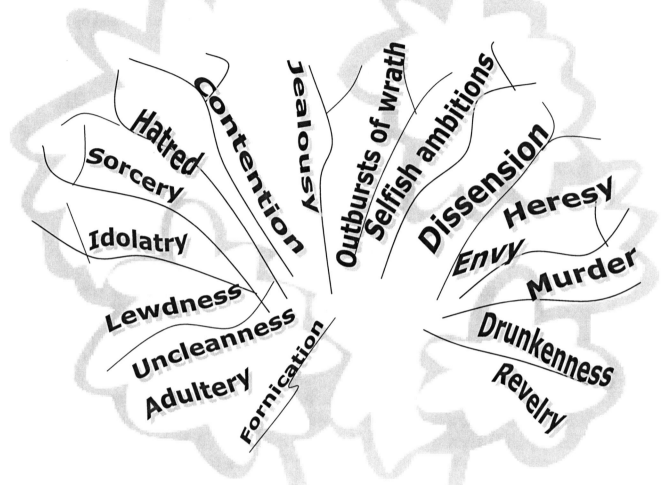

Lack of Spirituality
Fruit of the Flesh

Jealousy
Contention
Hatred
Sorcery
Idolatry
Outbursts of wrath
Selfish ambitions
Dissension
Heresy
Envy
Murder
Lewdness
Uncleanness
Fornication
Adultery
Drunkenness
Revelry

OUR OWN WAY
Isaiah 53:6

MISSING THE MARK
Romans 3:23

OUR OWN RIGHTEOUSNESS
Romans 3:10

WORLD

FLESH

DEVIL

THE WORLD IN YOU

YOU IN THE WORLD

Lack of love for the Lord.

Romans 3: 10, 23
Matthew 22:37-39

Love yourself above others.

ROOTS-**Lack of obedience to commandments on which all laws & prophets are based.**

Graphics by Lani Joyce, Missionary

26

Genuine Spirituality
Fruit of the Spirit

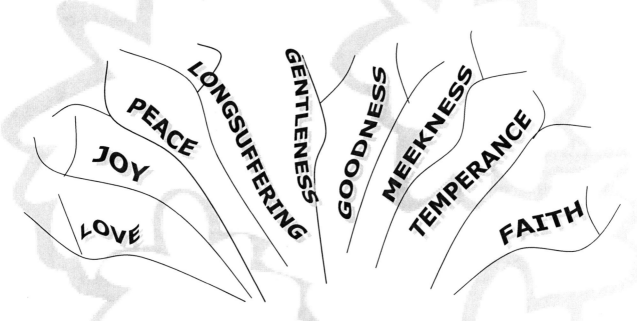

LOVE
JOY
PEACE
LONGSUFFERING
GENTLENESS
GOODNESS
MEEKNESS
TEMPERANCE
FAITH

Galatians 5:22-23

KNOW
That Christ has made victory possible.

COUNT
On the power of His death, burial, & resurrection.

YIELD
Yourself completely moment by moment to Him. Let His presence & power flow through you.
Romans 6-8

CHRIST IN YOU

YOU IN CHRIST

FILLED WITH THE SPIRIT

WALK IN THE SPIRIT

Matthew 22:37-39

Love the Lord with all your heart, mind, soul, & strength.

Love your neighbor as yourself.

ROOTS-On these commandments all of the laws & prophets are based.

Personal Preparation

Recommended Scripture References

In harmony with God, Psalm 2:7-8, John 11:41-42
Fervent prayer, Psalm 3:4-5
Separated, Psalm 4:3
Morning prayer, Psalm 5:1-3
Picture of holy life, Psalm 15:1-5
Preparation for worship, Psalm 24:3-5
Dwelling with the Lord, Psalm 27:4
Worship, Psalm 29:2
Commitment to the Lord, Psalm 31:5
Resting in the Lord, Psalm 37:7
Longing desire, Psalm 73:25
Godly man, Psalm 86:2-15
Answered prayers, Psalm 91:14-16
In stillness of soul, Isaiah 30:15
Search with all your heart, Jeremiah 29:11-13
Great and mighty answers, Jeremiah 33:3
Blessed are those who hunger, Matthew 5:6; Luke 6:21
Reconcile with brother, Matthew 5:23-24
Pray in secret, Matthew 6:6-8
Ask, seek, find, Matthew 7:7
Father gives good gifts, Matthew 7:11
Counting the cost, Matthew 8:19-21
Losing life to find it, Matthew 10:39, Mark 8:35
Agreeing prayer, Matthew 18:19-20
Mountain moving faith, Matthew 21:21-22
Pray in faith, Mark 11:22-26
Conviction of sin in presence of Jesus, Luke 5:8
All night prayer, Luke 6:12-13
Pray and not faint, Luke 8:1-14
Daily decision, Luke 9:23
Don't look back, Luke 9:62
Intercession, Luke 11:5-8
Expectant prayer, Luke 11:22-23
God's kingdom within, Luke 17:20-21
Persevering, Luke 18:1-8
Alone in prayer, Luke 22:40-44
Abide then ask, John 15:7, 16; 16:23-24

Sanctified by the Word, John 17:17
Devoted to prayer, Acts 6:4
God-given righteousness, Romans 1:17
Life in Christ, Romans 6:4
Freedom from sin, Romans 6:14
Spirit makes intercession, Romans 8:6-28
Secret to holiness, Romans 12:1-2
Christian living, Romans 13:12-14
Real spirituality, Romans 14:17-18
Discerning spirituality, Romans 16-19
Christ's righteousness, 1 Corinthians 1:4-9
Pursuit of holiness, 1 Corinthians 3:16-7;6:19-20, 2 Corinthians 3:7-8, 2 Corinthians 7:1
Winning the race, 1 Corinthians 15:30-31
Fragrance of good sacrifice, 2 Corinthians 2:15; Ephesians 5:1-2
Crucified with Christ, Galatians 2:20
Enduring commitment, Galatians 5:16
Fruit of the Spirit, Galatians 5:22
Growth toward maturity, Ephesians 6:10
Pray at all times, Ephesians 6:18
In everything pray, Philippians 4:6-7
Mindset and lifestyle, Philippians 4:8-9
Knowledge of God's will, Colossians 1:9-12
Christ–centered life, Colossians 3:1-17, 1 Thessalonians 4:1-8
Thanksgiving, Colossians 4:2-4
Pray without ceasing, 1 Thessalonians 5:17
Holy Spirit and impact of Scripture, 2 Thessalonians 2:13
Everlasting commitment, 2 Timothy 1:12
Paul's sacrifice to help others, 2 Timothy 2:10
Don't grow weary, Titus 2:11-12, Hebrews 2:10
Pleasing God, Hebrews 11:5; 1 Peter 4:19
Live soberly and righteously, Hebrews 12:11, James 3:17-18
Pursuit of holiness, James 4:7-10; 1 Peter 1:1-2, 1:14-16, 1:22, 2:1, 3:9
Provision for cleansing, 1 John 1:7-10, 3:1-3

Attitude and Thought Life

Attitude is the expression of the real you, the person you have become. Your environment, your past, family, friends, and education are some of the contributing factors. Many things influence your feelings about yourself—your self-image, your accomplishments, your status in life, your level of success in your profession, in marriage and child rearing, in finances, and whether you have a personal sense of peace and contentment in your current stage of life. Attitudes can be shaped by crises and other occurrences which bring abrupt and radical changes to our lives.

Attitudes are Important

Attitudes are important because they affect your actions, feelings, and choices. Having a can-do attitude prods one to success or to completion of a task. The opposite is accomplished by the person who maintains a poor self-concept, doubts himself, and is tentative and indecisive. Ultimately, good attitudes affect your life positively and poor attitudes affect your life negatively.

Attitudes are important because they determine with which frame of mind you will meet every duty or challenge that will be encountered in your daily routine. Paul learned how to abound and how to be abased, to be full or hungry, to be needy or to have plenty. He had learned to keep a right attitude whatever he encountered (Philippians 4:11-13). The person with an attitude that says, "I am unsure," "I can't," or "I will fail again," has already condemned himself to failure.

Attitudes are important because they provide the opportunity to build strong relationships with family members, friends, coworkers, and acquaintances. A positive attitude draws others to you for friendship or to learn from you. A good attitude is like a magnet drawing people toward you so that you can then point them to your Lord. Attitudes with which one accepts a job, project, position, or task determines how well, how quickly, and how efficiently the assignments will be completed.

A good attitude can turn a crisis into something positive which may even be seen as a blessing. The attitude of those experiencing loss from a natural disaster, death of a child, financial reversals, or the diagnosis of a terminal disease will be manifested by either calmness, acceptance, and peace or anxiety, bitterness, and anger.

One's personal attitude colors how he sees things that happen to him as well as his view of facts. The positive person looks for what is good and wholesome, looks for a good outcome, and looks for the best in others. The one with a negative attitude comes looking for what is wrong with the world, sees the faults and flaws in others, expects the worst, and expects to fail. Do you see the cup as half full or half empty?

The Christian attitude should be that in Christ, I can do anything with His power, presence, wisdom, and guidance. In Christ, I can cope with loss or disappointment. This attitude is developed only through an intimate relationship with Jesus Christ. It is understood that God is all that we need. He can change us into the person He has always planned for us to be and to change our thoughts and attitudes permanently. Just because you are a Christian doesn't ensure your attitude is positive.

Attitudes are often caught rather than taught. The people often mirror the pastor's attitude; they are the flock that is following. Employees in a company, clerks in a store, or workers in a restaurant usually reflect the attitude of a leader or owner. As leaders you set the tone for your group, organization, or church. Every place has a personality of its own, usually reflective of the person in charge.

Jesus gives us the best example of having the right attitude and thinking. See the section entitled "Thinking Patterns of Jesus" (page 34). Paul is an excellent example of how one can change. He first was a man of arrogance and pride radically seeking the murder of believers. His attitude after his life was changed by Christ demonstrated humility, self-sacrifice, reliance on God, and acceptance of God's leadership. Study the lives of Daniel, Nehemiah, Joshua, and Caleb for examples of how good attitudes can positively affect your life.

Why Do We Have Bad Attitudes?

Wrong attitudes will be evidenced by poor family relationships, inability to get along with people, conceptualization of people as being only bad, cynicism, failure to spend time with God, failure to let go of hurts or injuries, lack of control over emotions, and allowing oneself to play the perpetual victim thinking that the world owes him.

> *Attitude determines outlook and altitude.*

Where do these bad attitudes come from? The simple answer is that they are a result of our sinful nature. The tendency is to gravitate toward the negative; if we are surrounded with negative attitudes, it will affect our outlook. Bad attitudes are contagious! These attitudes can be a pattern of thinking learned at an early age. Being hurt or disappointed may contribute to attitude problems. Failure, criticism, or comparison to others lead to negative attitudes. When we get our eyes off of what is important and

value wrong things, our attitudes will slip. These are the patterns that lead to negativity and developing an unhealthy way of thinking. If we fail, we tend to perceive ourselves as total failures. If we constantly dwell on the negative, our thinking will be distorted.

Stinking Thinking

Certain patterns of thinking can destroy one's attitude. Recognizing these destructive patterns of stinking thinking and eliminating them will positively change one's attitude. The following patterns were identified by David Burns.[1]

♦ All or Nothing
One thinks either in extremes or in black and white categories. If his effort isn't perfect, he sees himself as a total failure. Example: Eating something not on his diet means he is such a failure it is no use trying to diet at all.

♦ Overgeneralization
One thinks that a negative event leads to a total pattern of negatives and defeat. Example: Being turned down for a date means he will never have a girlfriend.

♦ Negative Mental Filter
One obsesses over a negative detail so completely it colors the whole world like looking through dark colored glasses. Example: A teenager thinks the acne on his face means he is totally unacceptable and everyone else will see him that way.

♦ Disqualifying the Positive
One ignores or minimizes positive experiences as if they have no importance. Example: A student does well on a test and thinks it doesn't matter because it was an easy test, that everybody else did well, or that it was a fluke.

♦ Jumping to Conclusions
One automatically assumes the negative

even though no evidence supports it. Examples: A person assumes how others feel as if he can read minds. He predicts bad outcomes as if he is a fortune teller.

♦ Magnification and Minimization
One exaggerates and overblows the positive characteristics and accomplishments of others while undervaluing and understating his own, often catastrophizing by imagining the worst outcome or making a mountain out of a molehill. Example: A wife thinks her husband doesn't like her cooking and sees herself as a poor cook because he compliments a co-worker's cooking when she brought a dish for lunch at work.

♦ Emotional Reasoning
One allows negative feelings and emotions to determine his reality and decisions. Example: A person has feelings of inferiority or inadequacy and refuses to apply to an academic program because he feels like he is stupid.

♦ Should Statements
One has rigid, man-made rules he thinks he must follow or be overwhelmed by guilt. These rules become the controlling *shoulds* of his life. Example: The Pharisees established a whole list of these man-made rules and insisted others must follow them. When Jesus violated them they utterly condemned Him.

♦ Labeling
One assigns a negative label to oneself or others for some shortcoming or characteristic; terms like loser, moron, and jerk are used. Example: A person makes a mistake at work and thinks he is a loser or an idiot. A person may also assign these negative qualities to those around him.

♦ Personalization
One takes things personally by attributing causation to himself for something which isn't. Example: A child thinks because he had angry feelings toward a friend, he caused the friend to become seriously ill.

Attitude Adjustment Tips

One must make a conscious choice to change his attitude and to seek God's power in doing so. Romans 12:2 reminds us that we need to renew our minds.

♦ Adjust your expectations. When you are realistic about expectations concerning things over which you have no control, you are less likely to be disappointed.

♦ Identify which stinking thinking pattern you are following. Challenge and correct it with right thinking. It may prove helpful to chart these patterns and note when and how you successfully counteracted them.

♦ Try to find humor in negative situations. Have a laugh and move on.

♦ Don't take things personally or too seriously. Learn to laugh at yourself.

♦ Give up your rights. You do not need to have your own way all the time.

♦ Work at developing an attitude of gratitude; be content with what you have.

♦ Practice stress release management: exercise, thought stopping, and stress outlets.

♦ Separate your self-worth from performance. Do your best; don't try to be perfect.

♦ Practice choosing right words, books, entertainment, companions, and actions.

♦ Restore troubled relationships if possible through reconciliation, forgiveness, forbearance, and freeing yourself from the past.

♦ When attitude is out of control, get counseling.

♦ Use appropriate attitude vitamins: scripture verses, encouraging sayings, positive thoughts, and biblical meditation.

Biblical Attitude Questions

Is my attitude the attitude that Christ would have? (Philippians 2:5)

Do I have faith that will conquer my fears? (Matthew 21:21)

Do I believe that I can do all things through Christ, even changing my attitude? (Philippians 3:13-14)

Am I letting worry about tomorrow keep me from today's blessings? (Matthew 6:34)

Am I thinking the right thoughts? (Philippians 4:8)

Am I developing good habits? (Deuteronomy 6:5-9)

Am I choosing the right attitude instead of the wrong attitude? (Proverbs 3:31)

Do I have a friend that can help me have a good attitude? (Deuteronomy 32:30)

Are my friends keeping me from having a good attitude? (James 4:4)

Do I have someone to look up to that has a good attitude? (Philippians 4:9)

Can I learn from the mistakes I make? (John 8:11)

Am I ready to learn more? (Luke 11:1)

Am I feeding myself from God's Word daily? (2 Timothy 3:16-17)

Do I make my attitude a matter of daily prayer? (James 5:16)

Discouragement

Peace I leave with you, my peace I give unto you: not as the world giveth, give I unto you. Let not your heart be troubled, neither let it be afraid (John 14:27).

In your Christian walk, you will certainly meet with discouragement. Moses did. Elijah did. We will be no exception. When we are discouraged, we lose confidence in ourselves, in others, even in God. Practically speaking, how should we deal with discouragement?

Consider what discourages you. Read the following list. Honestly face your problem area.

Criticism
Dealing with people
Finances
Family problems
Health
Wasted or mismanaged time
Failure
Unmet expectations

Consider a practical approach to handle discouragement. What should I do?

♦ Read good books on adjusting and maintaining a positive attitude.

♦ Ask yourself if the situation is as bad as it seems. Gain a proper perspective. Make a list of what is discouraging you.

♦ Ask yourself, "What have I learned about discouragement that can help me?"

♦ Evaluate the situation.

♦ Determine whether the discouragement is from a personal attack or not.

♦ Ask yourself, "Will it really kill me?"

♦ Secure a mentor or counselor. Scripture says *Where no counsel is, the people fall: but in the multitude of counselors there is safety (Proverbs 11:14)*.

♦ Be positive and optimistic.

♦ Be systematic in evaluating the situation.

♦ Break the situation down into more manageable pieces.

♦ Face the discouragement. Don't be intimidated.

♦ Look to others who have been in similar situations for advice.

♦ Seek to be around uplifting people who demonstrate positive attitudes. Limit your time with those who are overly negative as they can contaminate your attitude.

What shouldn't I do?

- Ruminate
- Worry excessively
- Gossip
- Become irritable
- Bottle things up
- Become full of pride
- Try to get even
- Have self-pity
- Develop low self-esteem
- Magnify the problem by putting off dealing with it

Verses to combat discouragement:

God is with you, 1 Chronicles 28:20
God hears and answers, Psalm 34:17; 37:1-4; 40:1-3; 55:22; 121:1-8
He brings joy, Isaiah 12:1-6
Help from God's right hand, Isaiah 41:13
Don't worry, Matthew 6:34
Hope of heaven, John 14:1
God of hope, Romans 15:13
Able to bear it, 1 Corinthians 10:13
Daily renewal, 2 Corinthians 4:16-18
Peace of God, Philippians 4:6-7, 10-13
Promise never to leave us, Hebrews 13:5
A living hope, 1 Peter 1:3-5
Love casts out fear, 1 John 4:18

Frustration and Disappointment

The ministry is people-oriented. Because people are sinners, all ministers will at certain times grapple with frustration and disappointment. It would be easy to insulate ourselves from these feelings if we developed less than tender hearts, but this is not what God wants us to do. We need to have a tender heart and a thick skin – not the reverse.

How then should we handle frustration and disappointment?

- You have a choice. Realize that you can choose how you will feel as well as how you will react.

- Expect and accept that these things will happen even in the ministry.
- Realize these feelings are normal, natural, and human.
- Realize nothing can get you down unless you allow it to pull you down. You cannot always control what happens to you, but you can control your reaction to it.
- Expect the zenith of these feelings to last one to three days.
- Talk it out with a trustworthy partner.
- Put it in God's hands ...*Avenge not yourselves, but rather give place unto wrath: for it is written, Vengeance is mine; I will repay, saith the Lord* (Romans 12:19).

Antidotes for Discouragement

Spiritually

Pray about the situation. Someone facetiously said, "Why pray when you can worry?" We often find it easier to worry than to pray.
Turn the situation over to God.
Stand upon God's promises.
Confess any sin that may be hindering or discouraging you. Deal with the sin.
Think God's thoughts.
Seek out spiritual advice.

Emotionally

Talk about the situation and find a confidential support system.
Process other negative emotions that you might have such as anger, anxiety, and confusion.
Guard your heart from allowing negative emotions to become deep-rooted.
Realize 92% of those things you are worrying about won't happen or are things over which you have no control. Only 8% are legitimate worries.[2]

Mentally

Approach situations from a proper perspective.

Don't allow one problem to influence other areas of your life.
Check your expectations.
Think of things that encourage you.
Dwell on the positive more than negative.
Try to see humor in the situation.
Follow these suggestions:
  Remain optimistic seeing the bright side of life.
  Remain hopeful working vigorously to a solution.
  Remain confident in God's abilities.

The Thinking Patterns of Jesus

These are the ways Jesus <u>did not</u> think. He...

♦ Did not worry and become preoccupied with certain thoughts and have trouble getting them out of His mind.

♦ Did not dwell on the negative and overlook the positive.

♦ Did not dwell on the past.

♦ Did not live fearfully minded.

♦ Did not take things personally or have trouble putting them behind Him.

♦ Did not make mountains out of molehills.

♦ Did not distort the truth.

♦ Did not look at people through rose-colored or dark-colored glasses.

♦ Did not avoid life's difficulties and responsibilities.

♦ Did not get down on himself.

♦ Did not think of a single negative event as a continuing pattern of defeat. He looked beyond the cross to His ultimate triumph.

♦ Did not dwell on material things thinking that more money or possessions would bring happiness or fulfillment.

These are the ways Jesus <u>did</u> think. His thinking was filled...

♦ With humility, respect, equality, and balance.

♦ With gratefulness, appreciation, and thanksgiving.

♦ With the Word of God as He had knowledge, understanding, and insight into the scriptures applying them to life's situations.

♦ With obedience to the will of God seeking His Father's guidance and following His purpose.

♦ With worshipful thoughts of God, praise, reverence, adoration, and rejoicing.

♦ With trust, faith, commitment, convictions, and courage to act.

♦ With forgiveness, reconciliation, mercy, patience, and without vengeance.

♦ With insight into prophecy and facing the future with confidence and hope.

> *For as he thinketh in his heart, so is he.*
> *Proverbs 23:7a*

♦ With the reality of eternity.

♦ With love, compassion, helpfulness, kindness, gentleness, hospitality, caring, serving, living by the Golden Rule, meeting needs, and wisdom in dealing with people, opposition, and conflict.

♦ With a desire to live His life demonstrating a personal relationship with God.

♦ With the desire to share His faith with others, using their needs to begin a discussion of spiritual matters.

- With thoughts of the kingdom: the Father's rule in His life, living by its principles, and building His life on it as a foundation.

- With prayer being aware of His Father's presence and ability to meet His needs and provide spiritual power.

- With the maintenance of a constant right relationship with His father.

- With peace and contentment.

Attitude Formulas

High expectations with lower than expected results leads to discouragement and dissatisfaction.

Low expectations with higher than expected results leads to encouragement and satisfaction.

Thus, keep your expectations realistic.

Whatever you hold in your mind will tend to occur in your life.

If you continue to believe as you always have believed, you will continue to act as you have always acted.

If you continue to act as you have always acted, you will continue to get what you've always gotten.

If you want different results in your life or your work, all you have to do is ...

change your mind.

~Author Unknown

Recommended Scripture References

Haughty attitude, 1 Kings 12:13-14
Pagan king's attitude changed, Ezra 1:1-4, 7-8, 5:8-6:12; 7:13-26
Attitude of authority, Nehemiah 5:14-18
Optimistic outlook, Job 1:21-22
Willingness to listen, Job 6:24
Joy from the Lord, Job 8:21
Thoughts acceptable to God, Psalm 19:14
Hopeful, Psalm 31:24
New spirit, Psalm 51:10
God knows our thoughts, Psalms 94:11, 139:1-4
Attitude of rejoicing, Psalm 118:24
Thought on my way, Psalm 119:59
Heart wellspring of life, Proverbs 4:23
Happy countenance, Proverbs 15:13; 17:22
God hates wicked thoughts, Proverbs 15:26; Matthew 9:4; 15:19
Heart attitude, Proverbs 23:7a
Thoughts known to God, Ezekiel 11:5
Love neighbor as self, Matthew 5:38-48
No worry about tomorrow, Matthew 6:34
"Golden Rule", Matthew 7:12
Kingdom of Heaven, Matthew 19:14
Thoughts of heart revealed, Luke 6:8, Hebrews 4;12
Humility, Luke 7:6-7
Noble attitude, Acts 17:11
Conflict between natures, Romans 7:21-25, 8:6-9
Be transformed, Romans 12:2-3
Bless when persecuted, Romans 12:14
Refuse impure thoughts, Romans 13:14
Tolerance, Romans 14:1-8
In the image of the Lord, 2 Corinthians 3:18
Serving others, 2 Corinthians 4:5
Acceptance, 2 Corinthians 7:2
Repentant attitude, 2 Corinthians 7:10-13
Perseverance, Galatians 6:9
Thinking darkened, Ephesians 4:17
Will rejoice, Philippians 1:18
Christ-like attitude, Philippians 2:3-8
Do everything with right attitude, Philippians 2:14
Thought determines attitude, Philippians 4:8-9
Contentment, Philippians 4:11-13
Seek things above, Colossians 3:1-12
Joyful, prayerful thanksgiving, 1 Thessalonians 5:16-18
Be kind, not quarreling, 2 Timothy 2:24
Defined mind and conscience, Titus 1:15
Fixed thoughts, Hebrews 3:1
Word of God reveals thoughts of heart, Hebrews 4:12
Attitude toward God's discipline, Hebrews 12:5-11
Trials work patience, James 1:2-6
Eliminate negative thought patterns, 1 Peter 2:1
Rejoice in suffering, 1 Peter 4:12-16

Moral Purity

Purity is an area where ministers are extremely vulnerable to Satan's attacks. Twelve percent of ministers admit to committing adultery and twenty-three percent admit to improper relationships with members of the opposite sex.[1] Abide by the "Sexual Ten Commandments" on the following page to maintain moral purity and to prevent the questioning of your integrity. An ounce of prevention is worth a pound of cure because the consequences are great. What does it take a lifetime to build but a moment to destroy? The answer is your reputation and with it your testimony for Christ. Smart pastors avoid temptation. If you are ever in a position of temptation, act like Joseph, who ran away as fast as possible, instead of David, who ran head-long into it. It is a good idea to commit the "Sexual Ten Commandments" to memory and make them a way of life.

Always be mindful that Christ is with you whatever you do and carefully count the cost of your decisions. There is pleasure in sin for a season (while you are sowing), but the ultimate payoff is painful (while you are reaping.)

And hereby this we do know that we know Him, if we keep His commandments. He that saith, I know Him, and keepeth not His commandments, is a liar, and the truth is not in him. But whoso keepeth His Word, in him verily is the love of God perfected....
1 John 2:3-5

Remember to pray without ceasing concerning moral purity as if everything depends upon God, and work on these things as if everything depends on you. *I can do all things through Christ which strengtheneth me.* Philippians 4:13

Recommended Scripture References

Leisure time, 2 Samuel 11:1-5
David rebuked, 2 Samuel 12:1-4
Discipline required in avoiding lust, Job 31:1
Purity brings God's blessing, Psalm 18:20-21
Whiter than snow, Psalm 51:7
Cleansed heart, gift from God, Psalm 51:10
Lust in heart, Proverbs 6:24-25; Matthew 5:28
Immorality of heart and mind, Matthew 5:27-28
Through morality no salvation, Matthew 19:16-26
Needing the Great Physician, Mark 2:17; 10:17-20
Law in heart affects action, Romans 2:14-15
Blind leading the blind, Romans 2:17-18
Defeating immoral conduct, Romans 13:14
Bad company, 1 Corinthians 5:9-11
Conquest of immorality condemned, 1 Corinthians 6:9-10, 9:27
Temple of the Holy Spirit, 1 Corinthians 6:13-19
Evil company corrupts good morals, 1 Corinthians 15:33
New birth, 2 Corinthians 5:17
Holy Spirit purifies, Galatians 5:16
Fruit of the Spirit, Galatians 5:22-23
Unwholesome talk, Ephesians 4:29
Imitators of Christ, Ephesians 5:1-3
Flee immorality, Colossians 3:5-10, 2 Timothy 2:22, James 1:13-15
God's law written in the heart, Hebrews 8:10
Be ye holy, 1 Peter 1:13-16
Purified by obeying His word, 1 Peter 1:22
Character growth, 2 Peter 1:5

I Thou shalt accept that this will be an ongoing temptation in your life. It is a manifestation of the flesh which will never change. Maintaining a fresh intimate relationship with the Lord will help you make right choices.

II Thou shalt walk closely with the Lord at all times to experience His promise to walk in the Spirit and not fulfill the lust of the flesh (Galatians 5:16).

III Thou shalt avoid all sexual temptation by never being alone with a person of the opposite sex in any potentially compromising situation. Thou shalt not visit the opposite sex alone at home or counsel the opposite sex alone at the office unless other people are present in the office environment and glass permits visual access. Never go to lunch with or give the opposite sex a ride home when you are alone.

IV Thou shalt make a covenant with your eyes to not look lustfully upon a person of the opposite sex.

V Thou shalt think of every person as your brother or sister and treat him or her as such.

VI Thou shalt keep your mind clean by not dwelling on lustful things. Remember you can't always stop a bird from lighting on your head, but you can keep him from building a nest there.

VII Thou shalt not flirt with anyone of the opposite sex. Thou shalt not kiss any attendee of the opposite sex.

VIII Thou shalt remember that no unbiblical sexual relationship will increase your self-esteem but will only make it worse. Thou shalt not discuss your marriage problems with an attendee of the opposite sex.

IX Thou shalt flee any and all situations that involve sexual temptation. Thou shalt not answer cards, letters, or emails from the opposite sex that have any personal or sexual connotation. Make your secretary your protective ally.

X Thou shalt make yourself accountable to someone who will ask you the tough questions about your thoughts, actions, and activities. This accountability will be a life-long process.

Sexual Ten Commandments

Organization and Goal Setting

Balancing Life's Important Areas

Each of us has seven key areas in our lives. We must find time to manage and appropriately balance them. This is no easy task because we frequently tend to give extensive time and attention to some areas and consequently neglect others. Picture each of the seven as a part of a mobile like those placed over a baby's bassinet. When all seven components of the mobile are properly distributed, the mobile is not lopsided, it is in balance. A godly man must keep his relationships with God, family, and friends in balance appropriating each the proper amount of time and attention. Other areas entering into the equation include personal time for pleasurable and relaxing activities, care for health and physical well-being through rest and exercise, management of finances, and activities related to career and work schedules.

Balancing Life's Seven Important Areas

God – Spiritual
Family – Parental and Marital
Social – Friends
Self – Personal Time
Physical – Health and Welfare
Financial – Bills and Investments/
Giving and Spending
Employer – Occupational

Balance-Check Questions

The seven important areas listed above must be balanced when organizing and planning for personal goal setting. The following are some questions to help you determine whether you are out of balance. This will be an on-going process for life.

- Have I emphasized some areas too much?
- Have I neglected some areas?
- If so, which areas?
- Why?
- Where do I feel the most pressure?
- What specific things can I do to correct the imbalance?
- What if I don't?
- Am I willing to pay the price?

The Struggle for Balance

1. What are the areas that need to be balanced in my life?
2. What is my purpose?
3. Have I incorporated them in a clear statement?
4. What are my objectives?
5. What are my specific goals?
6. Does my schedule reflect my purposes, objectives, and goals?
7. Are my goals SMART goals? (This is covered later.)
8. What are my short-term goals?
9. What are my long-term goals?
10. What are the things I want to be?
11. What are the things I want to do?
12. What are the things I want to have?
13. Who are the people I want to help?

Personal Daily Planner and Informational System

The achievement of your goals is based largely on your ability to make and keep appointments and to reach project deadlines. You may find an organizer system at an office supply store or you may want to create one to fit your work and style.

This is an area in which people continually struggle, both personally and professionally. Since it is so critical to your success in achieving both personal and professional goals, it would be worth the time and investment to take a class or seminar such as one offered by the Franklin Covey International Institute or to spend time teaching yourself how to get organized. There are many good books written on the subject.

How to Use a Personal Organizer

Regardless of what organizational system you choose to use, whether on paper or computer, these elements should be part of your system:

1. A monthly calendar in which you will record all of your scheduled events — This becomes a card catalog in your organizational library.

2. A yearly calendar for an overview of the whole year

3. A section tied to your monthly calendar where you will log significant points of conversations, phone call results, thoughts, and ideas — This information should be connected to your monthly calendar by recording the date on the page on which the notes were written. When you record an appointment or something to do on a future date you can go back to that journal entry and refresh your memory.

4. A to-do list for each day prioritized by urgency and importance — Always work on the top priority items as you proceed down your list. Check off your finished tasks and carry them over if necessary. If you decide an item is so unimportant you don't need to do it, drop it from the list.

5. A list of things in the front of your planner to be reviewed daily

   ♦ The seven areas of your life which need to be kept in balance

   ♦ Your mission statement
   ♦ Your list of objectives
   ♦ Your SMART goals
   ♦ Your project pages

6. A section for meetings with a separate page for each upcoming event that includes things to remember, subjects to be discussed, items needed, people to contact, and important notes — Also include location, date, and time for each meeting.

7. An address and phone section containing lists of addresses, phone numbers, and e-mail addresses of the important people in your life and ministry

8. A study section for notes where you can jot down ideas and points from materials you are reading or reviewing

9. A section for recording ideas, facts, statistics, notes, illustrations, and outlines for your sermons

No plan will work if you don't consistently use it every day. Set aside a few minutes for planning and review every day.

Time Management Mistakes

Avoid these time-wasters that decrease productivity:

1. Doing an employee's job for him
2. Doing tasks that can be handled by someone with less responsibility
3. Spending a disproportionate amount of time on a favorite or pet project
4. Unnecessarily repeating instructions
5. Saying yes to every request or task

Prioritization

Handle tasks in the following order.

1. High importance/High urgency
2. High importance/Low urgency
3. Low importance/High urgency
4. Low importance/Low urgency

Personal Organization Top Ten List

1. Set priorities.
2. Place priorities on calendar.
3. Allow time for the unexpected.
4. Do projects one at a time.
5. Organize your workspace.
6. Work according to your temperament.
7. Use your driving time for light work and growth.
8. Develop systems that work for you.
9. Always have a plan for those minutes between meetings.
10. Focus on results and not the activity.

Goal-Setting and Achievement

Nehemiah fasted and prayed for four months before requesting leave of King Artaxerxes to go to Jerusalem, which was un-walled and under-protected. During this time God gave Nehemiah a vision of a vibrant Jerusalem protected by strong walls. However, the vision alone would not cause the wall to be built. Nehemiah had to set a plan in motion to accomplish the task of rebuilding the wall. He surveyed, recruited, divided the job into sections, and set guards to protect the work. In other words, he established objectives and goals while considering resources and obstacles.

What has God laid on your heart to accomplish in your personal life and ministry? How will you make your vision a reality? It will require more than prayer and hard work. It will require a realistic plan of action.

Regardless of the nature of the vision or mission, putting it in your mission statement with supporting objectives and goals is a proven way to bring your vision to fruition. If you fail to plan, you plan to fail. This section on goal setting will not take long to read but will require a great deal of thought. The real

value of this information will become evident as you develop a personal planning system that works for you.

Mission Statement

Start this process by thinking through a personal mission statement and work upward from there. It is the base from which you will work. A mission statement should express your reason for being, your purpose in life, and your purpose in ministry.

Example of a personal mission statement:

To bring honor and glory to the Lord Jesus Christ in all that I am, say, and do.

The goal-setting process can be summarized graphically above.

Objectives

An objective is something toward which effort is directed. Each objective should be like an arrow pointing directly to the goal. In other words, accomplishing an objective should be one component of the entire mission.

Consider objectives that will best fulfill the mission. It is important for your personal health and the health of your organization to have balanced objectives ensuring all areas are included and no area is neglected.

Example of Personal Objectives

1. To reach others and help them grow in the Lord
2. To make the church grow and meet the needs of its people
3. To build strong relationships with my family and friends
4. To achieve financial security and share resources with others
5. To share my knowledge with the widest possible audience within God's will
6. To enjoy life and maintain good physical and mental health
7. To accomplish continuing personal growth and to establish and maintain these priorities
8. To maintain balance among the seven roles in my life
9. To spend time daily in the Word and in prayer to maintain a strong personal relationship with the Lord
10. To make the most of every day having an attitude of gratitude and of appreciation to God and others

SMART Goals

Set specific goals that will help you achieve your objectives.

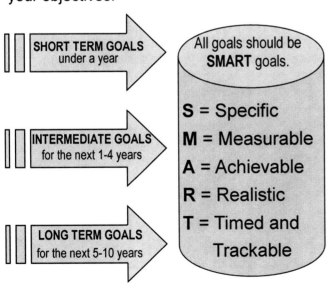

SHORT TERM GOALS
under a year

INTERMEDIATE GOALS
for the next 1-4 years

LONG TERM GOALS
for the next 5-10 years

All goals should be **SMART** goals.

S = Specific

M = Measurable

A = Achievable

R = Realistic

T = Timed and Trackable

Examples of Personal SMART Goals

It is easy to think of specific SMART goals to fulfill objectives involving physical things like building a garage, getting the office organized, or getting into shape. Developing SMART goals for intangible objectives can be more difficult. How would the following SMART goal map out for you?

To honor and glorify the Lord Jesus Christ in all I am, say, and do.

Prayerfully consider ways in which you currently do and do not glorify God in your being, speech, and actions. As the Holy Spirit convicts your heart of deficient areas, make a SMART goal to match. For example, if you find that you are constantly negative or complaining, you could make similar SMART goals as below.

Example of Personal SMART Goals: Negativity and Complaining

1. I will identify and study three scripture passages that teach about a complaining heart and the dangers of an unruly tongue. I will select several verses on thankfulness.

2. I will plan to commit to memory one passage a week for three weeks.

3. I will meditate upon scripture first thing in the morning, during devotional time, during daily duties, and when the mind is not occupied with specific tasks.

4. I will keep a memo pad in my pocket and throughout the month record instances when I complain or become negative and evaluate the results each evening.

5. I will consider solutions to the problems that constantly cause frustration or elicit complaints. (An example might sound like this concerning a problematic computer. Should new utility software be purchased or should the machine be serviced or replaced?)

S pecific

I will carefully think before I speak eliminating each negative comment and reframing it into a positive comment.

When I am tempted to complain, I will replace the complaint with a thoughtful expression of gratitude.

M easurable

I will post and tally each time I am positive or not positive in my speech.

A chievable

I can do all things through Christ who strengthens me (Philippians 4:13). This specifically includes correcting my negative and complaining attitudes and speech patterns.

R ealistic

I have watched my grandfather change his attitudes and speech patterns from that of a curmudgeon to being a positive person who delighted those he was around in his later years. If he could change his attitudes and speech patterns so completely at eighty years of age, it is realistic for me to believe I can do so in my lifetime.

T imed and Trackable

I will work toward this goal each day by tallying incidents of positive versus negative expressions. Assessment of success will come by comparing the total positives to the total negatives at the end of each day. The daily chart tallies will be recorded toward weekly totals. I will continue for the period throughout the month of June. I will repeat the process each month as needed. I will track the results of the ratio of positives to negatives and continue until the ratio is at least twelve positives to one negative for each assessment period.

Trackability means you can assess progress to make sure you are on course and succeed-

ing. Having a timeframe for the goal provides incentive and promotes concentrated effort. Are you a goal setter? What are your personal goals, your organizational goals, and goals for your followers?

Develop Project Worksheets

Make your goals a reality by breaking them down into individual, manageable projects. Project planning is useful for personal as well as professional goal achievement. Use a worksheet that suits your style and thinking pattern.

In planning and performing any project, it is important to anticipate and prepare for obstacles which will hinder the progress of the project.

It is recommended that trackable progress be processed by use of a Gantt chart developed as part of your project worksheets. A sample is included on page 44 for explanation and example. This Gantt chart was part of a project to temporarily move worship services from the church sanctuary to the multipurpose facility during a remodeling project.

The $10,000 Idea

A consultant was called into a company to give suggestions on turning the company around during a time of financial troubles. After extensive evaluation, he gave only one recommendation. Each employee was to begin every day by making a complete list of tasks ranking them by priority. They were then instructed to work on priority 1 until finished and then priority 2 and on through the list. The CEO thought the expert evaluation sounded too simple and was reluctant to pay the $10,000 fee. The consultant said to try out his suggestion and pay him only if it turned out to be worthwhile advice. A short time later, the consultant received a check for $10,000 in the mail.

Mind Mapping Technique

The *Mind Mapping Technique* provides a form of systematic brain storming to assist in the generation and organization of ideas. It is based on research regarding how the brain works through association and relationship of ideas. For many it provides valuable assistance in the generation of helpful ideas. In this technique the **quantity** of ideas is first in importance. You generate many ideas and cull unwanted ones later. You can then develop various stems and branches to determine the usability and feasibility of the idea. Discard any which are irrelevant. Among those who have used this technique, fifty percent report more effective results. Here are the steps for using this technique.

1. Identify the issue or problem. Place it in the center of the page and draw a circle around it.

2. Brainstorm all aspects of the problem and draw your thoughts and ideas as stems radiating from the circle.

3. Continue brainstorming and analyzing each thought and idea adding each as branches to your stems.

4. Use a different color for each stem and its respective branches. Some report that the use of separate colors improves both idea production and retention. Others find that the coloration of the separate stems and branches make little difference. Try it to see what works for you.

5. Review the finished product and add other ideas or perform further branching of ideas if they develop.

6. Examine the whole and its parts for interrelationships, feasibility, and usability.

Monitor Progress

Monitor the performance especially as it reaches the project milestones and provide any midcourse adjustments as necessary. As previously mentioned, a Gantt chart is ideal for this purpose.

Wrap-up

Provide final feedback and wrap up the project upon its completion.

Recommended Scripture References

Eyes on God's goals, not world's, Psalm 25:15
Blessedness for full obedience, Psalm 119:1-5
Move straight ahead, Proverbs 4:25-27
Harvest crops in season, Proverbs 10:5
Reward diligence, Proverbs 12:11; 22:29
Wise man plans, Proverbs 13:16
Man's plans, God's purposes, Proverbs 16:1,19:21
Man's plans, God's counsel, Proverbs 19:21
Goal oriented follow through with plan, Isaiah 32:8; Jeremiah 32:38-39
Self-centered plans, Jeremiah 45:4-5
Parable of talents, Matthew 25:14-30
Choosing twelve apostles, Mark 3:13-19
Paralytic let down from roof, Luke 5:17-26
The setting for a miracle, Luke 9:14-15
Counting cost before construction, Luke 14:28-30
Soul winning the Lord's one goal, Luke 19:10
Goal to do the Father's will, John 5:30
Actions follow knowledge, John 13:17.
Welfare for widows arranged, Acts 6:1-4
In unity, serve the Lord, 1 Corinthians 1:10
Church activities organized, 1 Corinthians 12:28-31
Planning journey, 2 Corinthians 1:15-17
Aim for perfection, 2 Corinthians 13:11
Fitly framed together, Ephesians 2:21
Diversity of gifts, Ephesians 4:11-13
Make the most of every opportunity, Ephesians 5:15-16; Colossians 4:5
Preparation to serve, Ephesians 6:15
Supreme goal to serve Christ, Philippians 3:7-11
Order and steadfastness ordained, Colossians 2:5
Plan for Christian lifestyle, 1 Thessalonians 4:11-12
God's pleasure fulfilled, 2 Thessalonians 1:11
Unwise motivation toward wealth, 1 Timothy 6:9-10
Purpose in life, 2 Timothy 3:10
Ordaining elders brought order, Titus 1:1-5
God orders all things, Hebrews 1:3
Do not be lazy, Hebrews 6:11-12
Put teaching into action, James 1:22-25
Holy living brings God's favor, James 4:7-10
Unknown tomorrows, James 4:13-16
Salvation planned before creation, 1 Peter 1:18-20

Gantt Charts

Gantt Charts are long-range time-on-task graphic organizers. This technique is used when:
- planning to show the actual calendar time spent on each task.
- scheduling work for individuals (to control the balance between time spent on various tasks).
- planning work for several people to ensure that those people who must work together are available at the same time.
- tracking progress of work against the scheduled activities.
- describing a regular process to show who does what and when.
- communicating the plan to other people.

Gantt Chart Project	August		September				October					November				December				
	20	27	3	10	17	24	1	8	15	22	29	5	12	19	26	3	10	17	24	31

Physical Properties Preparation

Determine placement of chairs

Decorate room for class

Program Preparation

Determine sermon topics & materials

Prepare detailed schedule for service formats

Process Preparation

Prepare people for class with vision casting

Organize refreshments including coffee and donuts

Follow-up Preparation

Contact all possible prospects

Take interested couples out to dinner

Evangelism

Cast vision for networking

Teach friendship evangelism

Worship

Model worship in church

Create relevant teaching in worship

Service

Emphasize service as the ultimate aim

Give opportunities in class to serve

Fellowship

Create a list of possible activities

Personal time w/each couple

Discipleship

Seek resources for relevant teaching

44 Model personal time/faithfulness

Personal Organization and Goal-Setting Worksheet

Mission Statement _____
_____
_____
_____

Objectives _____
_____
_____
_____
_____
_____
_____
_____
_____
_____
_____

SMART Goals _____
_____
_____
_____
_____
_____
_____

Project List (Transfer each to project worksheet) _____
_____
_____
_____
_____
_____
_____

Monitoring

Project #1
Prepare Gantt Chart and Review Weekly

Project #2
Prepare Gantt Chart and Review Weekly

Project #3
Prepare Gantt Chart and Review Weekly

Project #4
Prepare Gantt Chart and Review Weekly

Project #5
Prepare Gantt Chart and Review Weekly

Project #6
Prepare Gantt Chart and Review Weekly

Project #7
Prepare Gantt Chart and Review Weekly

Wrap Up

Project #1

Summary _____
_____
_____
_____
_____
_____

Project #2

Summary _____
_____
_____
_____
_____
_____

Project #3

Summary _____
_____
_____
_____
_____
_____

Project #4

Summary _____
_____
_____
_____
_____
_____

Project #5

Summary _____
_____
_____
_____
_____
_____

Project #6

Summary _____
_____
_____
_____
_____
_____

Project #7

Summary _____
_____
_____
_____
_____

PROJECT WORKSHEET

_____   _____   _____
          Title   Date Established   Deadline

Goal and purpose of project

_____

_____

_____

_____

Mind map

Action plan

Rank	Things to Do	By Whom	By When
____	_____	_____	_____
____	_____	_____	_____
____	_____	_____	_____
____	_____	_____	_____
____	_____	_____	_____
____	_____	_____	_____
____	_____	_____	_____
____	_____	_____	_____
____	_____	_____	_____
____	_____	_____	_____
____	_____	_____	_____
____	_____	_____	_____

Required resources (materials, supplies, personnel, helps)

_____

_____

_____

Obstacles and plan to overcome them

_____

_____

Notes / Communications

_____

_____

PROJECT WORKSHEET (Example)

<u>Financial Stewardship</u>   _____   _____
       Title   Date Established   Deadline

Goal/Purpose of Project
To motivate every member of the church to understand and practice stewardship faithfully.

Mind Map (see below)

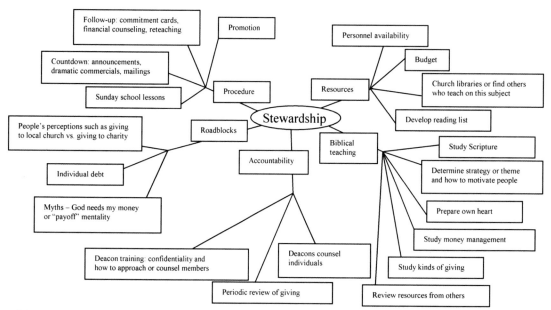

Action Plan

Rank	Things to Do	By Whom	By When
____	Prepare heart, study, determine theme	Pastor and staff	6-12 months in advance.
____	Review other resources	Staff	6-12 months in advance
____	Check personnel available/vacations	Pastor	6-12 months in advance
____	Develop budget	Pastor and trustees	6-12 months in advance
____	Check church library resources	Staff	6-12 months in advance
____	Choose head of promotion	Pastor	3-6 months in advance
____	Develop promotion committee	Pastor and head of com.	3-6 months in advance
____	Meet with promotion committee	Head of committee	3-6 months in advance
____	Develop Sunday school lesson plan	Children's minister	3-6 months in advance
____	Reteach/Financial counseling	Pastor and SS teachers	2 weeks after
____	Announcements, drama, letters	Staff/drama team	1 month
____	Investigate stats on debt, research myths	Pastor	6-12 months in advance
____	Brainstorm roadblocks	Pastor and staff	6-12 months in advance
____	Develop deacon approach/accountability	Pastor	3-6 months in advance
____	Develop tithing report/periodic review	Financial Manager	3-6 months in advance

Required Resources (materials, supplies, personnel, helps)
Special speaker? Study guide books for everyone? Financial software needs? Time requirements for financial manager?

Obstacles and Plan To Overcome Them
Complaints of too much talk about money (Show how Jesus talked more about money than other subjects.)

Notes / Communications
Consider discussion of faith promise giving.

Self-Esteem

Self-Esteem Basics

There are three related terms associated with our representation of ourselves.

Self-esteem—How we feel about ourselves
Self-image—How we see ourselves
Self-concept —How we think about
ourselves

All of these are formed by various critical factors. We determine how we feel about ourselves by how people have treated us and reacted to us. Repeatedly being called names or teased about physical or emotional characteristics as well as other defining moments can leave a lasting negative impression which may persist for a lifetime. We compare ourselves to others and make a decision as to our value. The Bible tells us not to compare ourselves with others because each of us is uniquely created by God (Psalm 139:15-16; 2 Corinthians 10:12). Thinking we are better than others or less valuable than others are both sinful attitudes. Our body-image, how we view ourselves physically, plays a major part in determining our self-esteem.

For example, an impressionable teenage girl is walking down a street when a car filled with older boys slowly pulls up beside her. They make fun of her, the size of her nose, the shape of her head, her hairstyle, and her acne. She is devastated by their attacks. Incorporating their comments into the image of herself, she then considers herself ugly and unattractive for years to come. As unreasonable as it is to give that much importance to these comments, she integrates them as if they were the truthful pronouncement of some expert on beauty.

Another example is of a young man who grows up in the home of an alcoholic father who becomes abusive and critical when he has had too much to drink. From the time his son was a little boy he would verbally attack him with comments like, "You will never amount to anything! You can't do anything right! How dumb can you get?" He was regularly called names like moron, stupid, imbecile, and fool. The boy grew up internalizing these attacks on his self-image and saw himself as worthless.

Many of our impressionable experiences are related to the unscriptural practice of comparing ourselves to others. We compare ourselves to siblings, classmates, friends, and even television, movie, and sports stars. These comparisons are made on the basis of how we look, intelligence, athletic ability, and popularity. Such comparisons frequently damage our self-esteem.

Twin boys were in the same classroom in elementary school, one consistently making better grades than the other. The teacher and principal approached the parents and recommended that the excelling twin skip a grade, possibly two grades, for the next school year. They suggested that the other brother continue to the next grade without skipping. The parents refused. The twin, who was to be passed over, learned of the recommendation, making him fully aware of his brother's better performance in school. Comparing himself, he felt unintelligent not realizing that grades in school are only determined in small part by one's mental acumen. Study skills and habits, motivation, and other factors are all important variables in determining academic performance. When the boys were tested as teenagers, both had an identical IQ in the superior range. It was only after being convinced that he was intelligent rather than unintelligent that the second twin began to excel academically.

We tend to act in accordance with our self-image. If we see ourselves as capable in certain areas, we tend to act like we are capable in those areas. If we see ourselves as incapable, we tend to act like we are incapable. Many with strong feelings of inadequacy don't even try or only give a half-hearted effort.

High self-esteem and pride are not synonymous. Pride is viewing ourselves as being superior to others whereas healthy self-esteem includes a humility with God-given confidence and assurance.

Our body image, especially as a teenager, can be an all-important shaper of our self-image for years to come, even if we change our body over time. If we see ourselves as fat or clumsy, we may continue to *feel* clumsy or fat even if we have changed our weight or coordination. Skinny, heavy, or moderately built people tend to see themselves according to their body style and may assign certain negative characteristics to themselves if they are out of the norm. This can have a profound effect on self-image.

There are no worthless people to God. Inferiority is a discouraging sense of being worthless or of less value in comparison to others. Job and Paul refused to be intimidated by the attempts of others to make them feel inferior (Job 12:3, 13:20; 2 Corinthians 11:5, 12:11). Jesus valued those who were counted of lesser value, such as lepers, publicans, and Samaritans. Believers are to encourage those who feel inferior (Luke 14:13; Romans 12:16; Hebrews 12:12-13). Jesus said that the things the world holds most valuable, God hates (Luke 16:15). We all need to take a careful retrospective inventory of those things which have negatively influenced our self-image and no longer allow them to impact our thoughts, actions, and future. Many of the perceptions about ourselves are inaccurate and overly negative. Some of the world's greatest leaders, athletes, and performers have overcome great obstacles through sheer determination and hard work. If you think you can, you have a good chance

of doing so. If you think you can't, you probably won't.

Self-Esteem and Ministry

If we have a poor self-image, it will limit us in ministry. We may try to compensate for a poor self-image by either being arrogant or overly complacent. Both situations will cause us to struggle as we relate to others. We must see that we have value in God's eyes and for that reason should esteem ourselves as His creation.

We are important to God and should have healthy self-esteem because:

1. He created us to be special, different from every other person on earth; we know we are fearfully and wonderfully made (Genesis 1:26-27).

2. We are His children, bought with the greatest price God could pay, the precious blood of Jesus (John 1:12-13).

3. We are the object of His love (John 3:16).

4. He is preparing a place for us in heaven and will be with us throughout all eternity (John 14:1-3).

5. We are blessed with every spiritual blessing in the heavenlies (Ephesians 1: 3).

6. We were chosen before the foundation of the world to be holy and blameless before Him (Ephesians 1: 4).

7. We were adopted as sons and daughters, as joint heirs with Jesus Christ, now and in the future (Ephesians 1:5).

8. We are in Christ and have Christ in us (Ephesians 1: 7).

Ways to build your biblical self-esteem:

1. Realize who you are in Christ.

2. Do not compare yourself to others.

3. Learn to laugh at yourself and overcome

your mistakes.

4. Be realistic in expectations of yourself.

5. Don't label yourself negatively.

6. When you fail, confess it to God and then live in His forgiveness (1 John 1:9).

Recommended Scripture References

Made in God's image, Genesis 1:26
Grateful stranger, Ruth 2:10
Grateful appreciation, 2 Samuel 9:1; 10:2
Respect for those older, Job 32:4
The Shepherd loves and cares for his sheep, Psalm 23
No appreciation for prior blessings, Psalm 78:9-18
Mercy and forgiveness from God as a father, Psalm 103:10-13, 52:2

Nation lacks appreciation, Psalm 106:1-43
Loving esteem, Song of Songs 5:10-16
God rewards according to our ways, Jeremiah 17:9
Asking for undeserved honor, Mark 10:35-45
Grateful for forgiveness, Luke 7:39-50
Ten lepers healed, one thankful, Luke 17:12-18
Jesus says, "You are mine," John 17:9-11, 22, 33
Cornelius' respect for Peter, Acts 10:25-26
He intercedes for us, Romans 5:1, 8:26-27
Gifts given by the Holy Spirit, 1 Corinthians 12:4, 11
God made us a new creation, 2 Corinthians 5:17, 21
Fruit of the Spirit ours through Christ, Galatians 5:22-23
Gifts from God, Ephesians 2:8-9
We are reconciled, Colossians 1:21-22
Appreciate pastors, teachers, others, 1 Thessalonians 5:12-13, 1 Timothy 5:17; 1 Peter 2:17
God's love for us, sent His Son, 1 John 4:9-10, 1:9

Handling Criticism

You cannot be in the ministry and not experience criticism. The Lord Jesus Christ was God and, as such, was perfect. Everything that He said and did was always right. Yet they crucified Him. What chance do you think you have of avoiding criticism?

Inappropriately handling criticism can lead to considerable emotional pain, self-doubt, and even feelings of failure. The typical pastor leaves a church because of the criticism and opposition of as few as one or two people. Here are some helpful facts and suggestions about criticism, which if taken to heart, can make a world of difference in the effectiveness of your ministry.

> *You cannot be in the ministry and not experience criticism.*

1. Understand the difference between constructive and destructive criticism. To determine whether it is constructive or destructive, ask the following questions:

    How is it given? Are they giving you the benefit of the doubt or are they being judgmental?

    When is it given? Is this done in public or in private?

    Why is it given? Are they expressing their personal hurt or are they truly concerned for your well being?

    Who is giving it? What is their relationship to you? Does their opinion matter to you?

2. Disregard caustic criticism, but use constructive criticism for your personal benefit and growth.

3. Develop a third party perspective. To avoid becoming defensive, focus on the content of the criticism from a detached, objective viewpoint instead of a subjective personal one.

4. Watch your attitude toward the critic.

    For even hereunto were ye called, because Christ also suffered for us, leaving us an example, that ye should follow His steps; who did no sin, neither was guile found in His mouth; who, when He was reviled, reviled not again; when He suffered, He threatened not, but committed Himself to Him that judgeth righteously.

    1 Peter 2:21-23

5. Realize that Jesus Christ, who was perfect, was often criticized for associating with sinners. He was called a glutton and a winebibber.

6. Develop a thicker skin to avoid an inappropriate reaction based on emotion rather than reason.

7. Walk closely with Christ to access His strength and wisdom.

8. Follow the LEAD formula when dealing with criticism.

    L isten with objectivity.

    E valuate the criticism. Is there any truth to it? How can I use it to better myself or further my purpose?

    A ssess what changes need to be made.

    D ecide what actions to take.

9. See criticism as a means to improve or even to excel. Note that only the mediocre are always at their best.

    For I know that this shall turn out to my salvation through your prayer, and the supply of the Spirit of Jesus Christ, according to my earnest expectation and my hope, that in nothing I shall be ashamed, but that with all boldness, as always, so now also Christ shall be magnified in my body, whether it be by life or by death.

    Philippians 1:19-20

Recommended Scripture References

God does not tolerate slander, Psalm 101:5
Proud lied against me, Psalm 119:69
Not offended by criticism, Psalm 119:165
The Lord will vindicate, Psalm 135:14
Accepting rebuke, Psalm 141:5
Fool unable to take criticism, Proverbs 9:8a
Slanderous mouths injure neighbor, Proverbs 11:9
Reaction to criticism, Proverbs 15:32, Job 16:1-5
Faithful are the wounds of a friend, Proverbs 27:6, 9
Rebuke better than flattery, Proverbs 28:23
Criticism refused, Proverbs 29:1
Result of criticizing others, Matthew 7:1-5, James 4:11
Slander against Jesus, Matthew 11:18-19
Jesus and critics, Matthew 21:23-27; Mark 14:53-62

Jesus taunted on the cross, Matthew 27:39-44
Looking to criticize, Mark 3:1-6, Luke 20:1-8
Rejoice when insulted for faith, Luke 6:22-23
Jesus persecuted, John 5:16
Criticizing others, guilty yourself, Romans 2:1
God is the only judge, Romans 8:33
Judging others, Romans 14:13
Don't be a stumbling block, Romans 15:1-3
Clear conscience, 1 Corinthians 4:3-4
Don't be judged by food and drink, Colossians 2:16
Know how to answer, Colossians 4:6
Live above criticism, Titus 2:8
Be humble, you were once as they, Titus 3:1-3
Don't say cruel things, James 3:1, James 4:11

> *The Lord Jesus Christ was God and, as such, was perfect. Everything that He said and did was always right. Yet they crucified Him. What chance do you think you have of avoiding criticism?*

Critical Thinking

Logic and Persuasion

The capacity of human beings to think intelligently and logically to discover truth is an important gift of God. In Isaiah 1:18 God invites us to reason with Him. Human reason is limited in its ability to arrive at a comprehensive knowledge of God, hence the reason for divine revelation. In the time of Isaiah, God reasoned with His people who were rebelling against Him. The apostle Paul used human reason to point people to God (Act 17:2-4; Romans 2:14-15). Believers are told to give reasons for their faith (1 Peter 3:15). We should not blindly follow others without reason or reflection but should follow the example of the Bereans searching the Scripture to see if these things are right (Acts 17:11).

Some of history's greatest biblical scholars reached a point in their lives where they began to closely examine the things they had heard and had been taught and to critically evaluate them in the light of scriptural analysis. Many concluded that some of the ideas they held, having blindly received from others, were wrong.

Critical analysis requires thorough, detailed, and skillful thinking and a deep understanding of the underlying issues. There is no substitute for the difficult and demanding work necessary to carefully read, review, analyze, challenge, anatomize, and resolve definitions, premises, arguments, and conclusions. The following methods are invaluable instruments in the pursuit of truth. Henry Ford said, "Thinking is the hardest work there is, which is probably the reason so few engage in it."

Steps for Performing Analysis

♦ Make sure the definition of every term is specific and accurate.

♦ Identify any prior assumptions, inappro-

priate value judgments, or unresolved conflicts.

♦ Examine cause and effect relationships. For every cause look for effects and for every effect look for causes.

♦ Follow the six serving men analysis— Who? What? When? Where? How? Why?

♦ Use the why analysis for each premise and conclusion. Keep asking, Why? Why? Why?

♦ Develop analogies for important concepts. When the apostle Paul wanted to explain the spiritual gifts given by the Holy Spirit in the body of Christ, he compared them to parts of the human body which all work together (Romans 12).

♦ Try to both compare and contrast each major concept.

♦ Consider the opposites; then process the thesis, antithesis, and synthesis. A thesis is a proposition which is offered. The antithesis is the opposite position to what has been offered. A synthesis is the combination of the elements of both into a higher or more comprehensive truth.

♦ Use argument by example and counterexample if possible. This is sometimes referred to as the immunization effect. If you were teaching a group of intellectual students about atheistic organic evolution and creation, as taught in Genesis, you could proceed as follows:

1. Present the arguments for atheistic organic evolution as they would be presented by its proponents.

2. Counter those arguments with a point by point refutation and teaching of the principles found in the book of Genesis.

3. Present the counterarguments that the atheistic organic evolutionist would have presented in part two and then

provide the answers as a counter argument. In other words, counter-argue the counterargument. This process immunizes the learner against the arguments at each level which will be presented against the position you are teaching.

- Check the logic used by both inductive (specific to general) and deductive (general to specific) procedures.
- Challenge each premise.
- Examine and challenge evidence.
- Challenge misleading or deceptive statistics.
- Look for exceptions.
- Ask critical questions.
- Examine for omitted critical information.
- Generate other possible conclusions.
- Review material for presence of logical fallacies.

Persuasion can be accomplished by the use of logical argumentation. The following points are intended to provide the reader with a basic understanding of the principles and means of effective argumentation.

Argument Defined

argument: any group of propositions of which one is claimed to follow logically from the others

For our purposes the normal sense of argument, someone yelling at another person who took his parking spot at the mall, is not termed an argument. By argument we mean a demonstration or a proof of some statement. For example, the doorbell just rang, therefore someone is at the door.

Essential Parts of an Argument

Premise: A proposition which gives reasons, grounds, or evidence for accepting some other proposition.

Conclusion: A proposition which is purported to be established on the basis of other propositions.

Process of Drawing a Conclusion

Consider the following example of an argument:

All men are mortal.
Socrates is a man.
Therefore, Socrates is a mortal.

As you read the passage from which you would like to draw a conclusion and come to understand it, you are undergoing a psychological process called making an inference. An inference is the reasoning process by which a logical relation is understood. If an argument is properly constructed, the premises, taken together, will compel the listener or reader to infer that the conclusion is true.

Here we can infer that Socrates is indeed a mortal, provided it is true that all men are mortal and Socrates is a man.

Validity and Soundness

An argument is valid if the conclusion logically follows from the premises. The test for validity is as follows: If we assume that the premises are true and the conclusion logically follows from the premises that are assumed to be true, then the argument is valid. A valid argument is an argument that is composed in a manner that establishes an absolute logical relationship between the premises and conclusion.

The fact that an argument is valid cannot by itself assure us that any of the statements in the argument are true; this fact only tells us that the conclusion must be true if the premises are true.

An argument is sound if the argument: (1) is valid and (2) contains premises that are true. Obviously, the conclusion is true as based on the definition of validity. The test for soundness is as follows: the argument is valid, as stated above, and the premises of argument are all true.

There are two steps to evaluating the truth of a premise. First, identify the type of evidence being used as a premise. Types of evidence may include observation, information from books or newspapers, statements made by an expert, statistics, and scientific data. Second, in order to assess the evidence being offered, consider the following:

- Did the observer have the ability to accurately perceive (see, hear, feel)?

- Is the observer able to accurately remember?

- Does the observer have any bias that might influence his perception?

- Does the observer have a motive to be less than honest?

- Is the account of the observer consistent with other evidence you know to be true?

- What is the nature of the publication?

- Who is the writer and what kind of reputation does he have?

- Is the writer stating opinion or fact?

- If the writer is stating opinion, what is its basis?

- Does the writer have some sort of bias or prejudice?

- Who is the expert?

- What is the expert's training? Education? Credentials?

- What is the expert's scope of expertise?

- Do other experts agree?

- What is the source of any statistics?

- Are the statistics accurate?

- Who conducted the scientific study?

- Was it properly conducted?

- Was the study replicated?

Fallacies and Common Logic Errors to Avoid

Ad hominem (Latin meaning *against the person*): An attempt to discredit an argument by attacking the person making it
> *Example:* Bill says that drinking alcohol will harm my health. Bill, however, is a convicted felon.

Post Hoc or Ergo Prompter Hoc (Latin meaning "after this therefore because of this"): Incorrect assertion that one event caused another
> *Example:* After I washed my car, it began to rain. Therefore, the washing of the car caused it to rain.

False Generalization: A conclusion based on limited observations
> *Example:* These two bad drivers are from Iowa. Therefore, all Iowa drivers are bad drivers.

Red Herring: Diverting the attention of the reader or listener by changing the subject to some totally different issue
> *Example:* The movie is better than the book. More movie tickets were sold this year than last year.

Appeal to the masses: Claiming that a proposition is true because a majority of others believe it to be true
> *Example:* A majority of people believe that Channel 5 News is the best. Therefore, Channel 5 News is the best.

Begging the Question: Deriving a conclusion from a premise that presupposes the conclusion
> *Example:* The verdict must be correct because it was decided in a court of law. The second part presupposes that decisions made in a court of law are always correct.

False Dilemma: Presenting too few choices and implying that a choice must be made between these limited choices

Example: Either you are going to purchase this car or you are going to walk to work.

Straw Man: Attributing an easily refuted position to an opponent, one that the opponent does not endorse, and then proceeding to attack that position believing that the attack undermines the opponent's actual position

Example: Bill believes we should spend less for defense. However, if we do not have any defense, we will be helpless if attacked.

Faulty Cause: Having a wrong cause and effect connection—a particular cause does not produce the stated specific effect because of an assumed incorrect association

Example: The number of fatal auto accidents increases in hot weather because of increased temperatures of the pavement surfaces. The actual cause is increased consumption of alcohol among drivers during hot weather.

Faulty Analogy: Assuming that things are alike in some ways they must be alike in all

Example: Because Bill and Bob are both Irish they must also have bad tempers and both be Catholic.

Slippery Slope: Thinking in a direction which produces a fallacy that some event must inevitably follow another—the series of steps between one event and another not substantiated

Example: If we permit Joe to go home early from work today then all other employees will want to go home from work early.

Appeal to Ignorance: Making an argument that something must be true because no one can prove otherwise

Example: You cannot prove that God exists, therefore He must not.

Appeal to Authority: Citing an authority to prove something must be right even though the authority may be wrong (The fact that an authority believes a certain proposition does not automatically make it so.)

Example: Dr. Jones says that smoking cigarettes is not harmful to you.

For an example of the application of the principles of critical thinking presented in this section, study the material contained in the Appendix B, "Why Bad Things Happen to Good People."

Recommended Scripture References

Bible centered thinking, Psalm 1:2
Examination of heart, Psalm 26:2; Jeremiah 17:10
God knows man's thoughts, Psalm 94:11
Evaluated my way, God's way, Psalm 119:59
Thoughts determine path taken, Proverbs 4:23
My way is higher, Isaiah 55:8-9
God's law in mind, heart, Jeremiah 31:33
Call upon Me, I'll answer, Jeremiah 33:3
Wicked thought, Matthew 9:4
Evil thoughts, Mark 7:20, 24
Good from good, evil from evil, Luke 6:45
Thinking Spirit controlled, Romans 8:6-8
Mind renewal, Romans 12:2-3
Mature thinking, Philippians 3:15
Think on these things, Philippians 4:8
Ask God's will for you, Colossians 1:9-14
Have full riches of complete understanding, know God, Colossians 2:2-3
Avoid hollow and deceptive philosophy, Colossians 2:8
Set affection on things above, Colossians 3:1-2
Word of God dwells in you, Colossians 3:16
Known scripture from childhood, 2 Timothy 3:15
Thoughts of the heart revealed, Hebrews 4:12
Minds ready for action, I Peter 1:13
Perfected character, 2 Peter 1:5-9

Vision

Where there is no vision, the people perish.
Proverbs 29:18

Why do 80-90% of new businesses fail? According to Michael E. Gerber in the book entitled *The E-Myth*[1], a new enterprise requires the following: a visionary, an organizer, and a technician. Some businesses start with a great idea (a vision), but there is no one to manage it (an organizer) or make it happen (a technician). The same three elements carry over in the functioning of a church if it is to reach its full potential.

The Pastor as Visionary

The pastor must be the visionary. He must have a clear idea of where the church should go. The pastor and church leadership are the organizers determining how to make the vision a reality. There must be technicians in the church to carry out the vision and organizational plans. These would include such people as associate pastors, board members, Sunday school teachers, janitors, trustees, ushers, and other volunteers. Churches operating without vision and planning fail because they have failed to plan. Such churches will never reach their potential.

It is solely the leader's responsibility to get before God and discern the direction of the Holy Spirit. The pastor must see a preferred future for the church, develop the vision, communicate that vision, and successfully persuade and influence the church membership to wholly commit to it. Good leadership is necessary to influence others and accomplish goals that make a vision reality. If there is no clear vision, no leadership direction, the church will languish.

Definition of Vision

A clear mental image of a preferable future imparted by God based upon an accurate understanding of God, self, and circumstances

Characteristics of Vision

- Inspired
- Change-oriented
- Challenging
- Empowering
- Long-term
- Customized and detailed
- People-oriented
- Optimistic revealing a promising future

Capturing God's Vision

You should know yourself and the reason you are in the ministry. You should identify your foundation, including your values, attributes, assumptions, and expectations which provide the framework for your ministry. You should know your environment, including your community, colleagues, congregation, and your competition (television, sleeping late, golf). You should know God, study His Word, fast, and assess your prayer life. Finally, you should verify your vision and periodically reassess its nature and direction.

Vision Killers

- Tradition – We've always done it that way
- Fear – Only Joshua and Caleb were not afraid to enter the Promised Land
- Stereotypes – These are connotations regarding denominational labels
- Complacency – This is a satisfaction with "us four and no more" or "we and not thee"
- Fatigue – It is easier to leave things as they are
- Short-term thinking – This parking lot is adequate for our needs right now

Start Communicating Vision

♦ Identify your target audience.

♦ Find their affinity. Discover what aspirations, goals, interests, needs, or dreams they have in common.

♦ Prepare to make an effective presentation of the vision.

♦ Write a brief vision message. Use creativity, metaphors, symbols, and stories.

♦ Be positive and optimistic. Don't say *try*, say *will* and *are*.

♦ Use other methods to share your vision. These include sermons, printed materials, letters, lessons, and meetings. See vision casting sermon outline below.

The following gives the points of a sermon presented in which a vision was cast for the entire congregation. Current church statistics were presented to show the need for a comprehensive plan to expand the church. Vision casting sermons are presented annually or more often as needed to facilitate growth and to prepare the people for change. The vision casting must be reinforced periodically. This reorganization plan will grow the church from 600 to 1,000 people.

Breaking Growth Barrier Ideas

Approximated church attendance in North America in the late 1990s:

60% of the churches averaged 80 people
27% of the churches averaged 200 people
6% of the churches averaged 400 people
4% of the churches averaged 600 people
2% of the churches averaged 800 people
1% of the churches in America averaged 1,000 people or more in attendance

Our church is currently at a growth barrier and must do the following to break through it and better fulfill the Great Commission to reach more of our community for our Lord and Savior Jesus Christ.

Grow existing groups or classes larger. Find a hook to get others interested.

Add additional staff members. There should be one staff member per 100-150 people.

Reorganize. Start new classes and provide more opportunity for congregation to connect through evangelism, fellowship, assimilation, and teaching.

Start a Lay Pastor Program to provide additional training and ministries to overcome the needs and care barrier of the church.

Establish new ministries. Example: Edgewood Institute of Theology, 101-401

Establish small groups, like 20:20 groups, growing bigger and smaller at the same time.

Expand opportunities for worship which may involve multiple services offering options and opportunities.

Concentrate on equipping and training team leaders.

Expand quality outreach events, including sports banquets, harvest programs, topics of interest series, and vacation Bible schools.

Implement a Hispanic outreach ministry.

Four Parts to your Vision
(Sermon Outline)

These four parts are essential in making any vision a reality.

1. Developing the vision
2. Creatively and redundantly casting the vision
3. Helping the people own the vision
4. Maintaining the vision

Developing and Presenting the Vision (worksheet sample follows)

1. Seek God and His leadership asking what He wants of you.

2. Examine yourself by asking what are your spiritual gifts, natural abilities and talents, temperament, passions, desires, previous experiences, leadership styles, and philosophies of ministry?

3. What is the culture, congregation, and capacity?

4. Who else is fulfilling similar visions and what can you learn from them?

5. Write a vision statement. What do you believe God wants to see happen? What do you see as the finished product?

6. Write a mission statement which is goal and objective oriented. What will be your vision development and implementation?

7. Write a comprehensive plan including: values, purpose, priorities, goals, objectives, strategies, slogan, performance measures, and sources of accountability.

8. How will this vision be cast? By whom? When? How often? In what ways?

9. What are the anticipated obstacles and hindrances? How will they be handled, averted, and overcome?

10. How will this process be repeated in individual lives and in the congregation?

11. How can you make others own the vision creating a personal connection to it?

12. See in your mind's eye as if you and others are watching two television screens. On the left screen, see potential obstacles and hindrances which will prevent you from fulfilling your vision. Then consider each obstacle's solution and see yourself overcoming those hindrances. On the right screen, see yourself step-by-step successfully fulfilling your vision. This has proven to be a powerful combination in helping turn your vision into reality.

Being a visionary is critical for the leader in any organization, but without strong leadership even the best vision will not come to fruition. Leadership enables one to communicate the vision and make it a reality. Although leadership may not come to you naturally, consider that leaders are made, not born.

Jesus chose ordinary men and spent several years turning them into leaders. Many leaders warn that it is easy to underestimate the required repetitiveness to help their followers own the vision. Successful vision casting must be performed repeatedly and continuously in a variety of ways.

Recommended Scripture References

Eyes that see, ears that hear, Deuteronomy 29:2-3
I will guide you, Proverbs 4:7
Lack vision of future, Ecclesiastes 3:22
Vision of great expansion, Isaiah 54:2-3; Micah 7:11
Vision comes to nothing, Ezekiel 12:22-25
Hear the word of the Lord, Ezekiel 13:1-23
Things to come, Daniel 7:1, Daniel 10:7
Amazed at what God does, Habakkuk 1:5
Emmaus road, Luke 24:13-27
Gave directions, Acts 10:9-16
Eye hath not seen, 1 Corinthians 2:9
Look to fulfillment of purpose, Ephesians 1:8
Heart opened to see future, Ephesians 1:18-19
Lord will give insight, 2 Timothy 2:7

Vision Worksheet

Seek God and His leadership.   What is my God-given vision?

_____

_____

_____

Examine your culture, congregation, and capacity. What is God's unique vision for my ministry?

_____

_____

_____

What others are fulfilling similar visions? What can I learn from them?

_____

_____

_____

Write a vision statement. What do I believe God wants to see happen? What is my preferred persuasion for the future? Is it a clear and challenging picture of my ministry's future? What do I see as a finished product? What is supposed to be accomplished?

_____

_____

_____

Seek God and His leadership. What is my God-given vision?

_____

_____

Write a comprehensive plan. (See section on Strategic Planning.)

_____

_____

_____

How will this vision be cast? By whom? When?

_____

_____

How can others be helped to own the vision with support and enthusiasm?

_____

_____

Personal Preparation

What are the necessary tools for casting and implementation?

_____

_____

How can the picture be painted and articulated from leader to other leaders and followers?

_____

_____

_____

How will people be selected to become leaders who will be nurtured and developed to follow the vision and perpetuate it? How will they be mentored?

_____

_____

_____

Which of these will I use in vision casting: Sermons? Word pictures? Stories? Analogies? Metaphors? Profiles? Hero examples? Slogans? Lessons? Examples? Exposure to those who are doing it? Rewards? Printed materials? Other ideas?

_____

_____

_____

Anticipate development and change. What are the expected obstacles, hindrances, and resistances to change? How will they be headed off or overcome?

_____

_____

_____

What are strategies for handling changes resulting from the vision, including outreach, mobilization, motivation, and assimilation?

_____

_____

_____

How will this process be repeated within individual lives and within the congregation? How can I be creatively redundant in casting the vision so that it will be constantly before my people (weekly, bi-weekly, monthly)?

_____

_____

_____

How will I know if they own it?

_____

_____

Leadership

Although this is a section entitled *Leadership*, the entire contents of this manual are all necessary to equip one for leadership. This section's goal is to show ways to become an extraordinary leader.

Leadership is influence. It is getting others to do what needs to be done and getting them to want to do those things. It is encouraging, equipping, motivating, and allowing others to be the best they can be. Leadership is not simply telling others what to do, which is a common misconception. Leadership skills are not adequately taught in many Bible colleges and seminaries. If lacking in this area, the minister must then learn leadership principles and develop personal leadership skills to become a successful pastoral leader. When you look at the calling of God upon many of the men of the Bible, it was clearly a call to the leadership of God's people. One of the major purposes of this instructional manual is to provide help in acquiring these leadership skills.

For a leader to be truly leading, someone must be following. What would motivate someone to follow you? Which of these describe you?

Personal Characteristics of a Successful Leader

Visionary	Clear communicator
Achieving	Self-controlled
Positive	Loyal
Approachable	Inspiring
Broad-minded	Straight-forward
Caring	Courageous
Dependable	Competent
Cooperative	Ambitious
Intelligent	Independent
Fair-minded	Persistent
Supportive	Credible
Honest	Innovative
Mature	Creative
Determined	Decisive

Why People Follow

You <u>know</u> something they want or need to know.

You <u>have</u> something they want or need to have.

You <u>are</u> something they want or need to be.

You <u>can do</u> something they want or need to do.

You <u>are going</u> somewhere they want to go.

Effective leadership begins with the leader himself. That leader must have qualities that make others want to follow. What qualities make others want to follow you? In leadership, to whom do you look for guidance? Which abilities do they possess? Which do you possess?

It is important to note that the previous list of traits in the spectrum of leadership, while important, does not tell the whole story about leadership and successful leaders. Jesus Christ told His disciples 2000 years ago, *But he that is greatest among you shall be your servant* (Matthew 23:11). This is the principle of servant leadership.

It was illustrated when George Washington was at Valley Forge training his army with the help of Baron VonSteuben of Germany. VonSteuben instructed that a leader must pay great attention to the health of his men, work toward resolving legitimate complaints, and show that he is keeping their best interests at heart. When the leader cares for those who follow, they in turn are more likely to care about the leader and his leadership. They work together to accomplish a common goal. The practice of servant leadership should permeate every aspect of Christian leadership.

A leader is one who knows the way, goes the way, and shows the way.
~ John C. Maxwell

Leadership Style	Definition	Application
Laissez-faire	Minimum direction with maximum freedom; anything goes	Social gatherings, fellowship
Democratic	Group participation and decision-making	Business meetings, voting in new leaders
Bureaucratic	Management is by the book	Legal issues, trials, governance
Autocratic	One-man rule; dictator	Emergencies
Theocratic	God leads, guides, and directs	Strategic planning, future plans
Benevolent	Father-like concern	Guidance, relationship building, and correction

Leadership Styles

You have probably seen many different leadership styles used by your parents, teachers, pastors, and bosses. Which styles do you respond to best? Which approach should you use in your ministry? The styles above are found in Scripture. Discern which style to use by the situation. Flexibility is the key.

Leaders are Influential

Influence is the number one area in which a leader must excel in order to be successful. Everyone influences someone even if he does not realize how much. As influence is not an inherited skill, we can develop the ability to influence others through credibility.

Credibility

It is important to understand the origin of credibility which is the root of influence. Credibility is based on:

Ethos – who you are.

Logos – what you say and do, both past and present.

Pathos – your commitment and passion.

Enhance Credibility with Others

Maintain good credentials and reputation. Keep growing in your skills and abilities through personal study or more formalized training such as self-study, college courses, and seminars. Be above reproach especially in matters of marital fidelity and financial accountability.

Provide precise and accurate information. Example: If you are going to build a new parking lot, submit multiple quotes and detailed plans to your board enabling them to make an informed decision.

Always be believable. Do not give anyone cause to doubt your word. Keep appointments, honor commitments, and be accurate in your accounting.

Use testimonials and documentation. Use the reliable testimony of another to back up your credibility like a doctor's second opinion or expert testimony in a trial.

Have the best interests of others at heart. If you show genuine interest through your comments, questions, and eye contact, others will be more likely to trust what you have to say.

Clearly meet the standards of the perceptions of others. Mean what you say and say what you mean.

Be trustworthy. Actively demonstrate dependability in all areas. Show yourself worthy of confidence.

Fatal Flaws of a Leader

The following are characteristics which result in poor leadership. If any of these have become part of your leadership style, they must be addressed and corrected with diligent effort.

- Does not produce results
- Lacks people skills
- Possesses poor understanding of people
- Has few committed followers
- Is not developing new followers
- Lets problems fester unresolved
- Lacks imagination and innovation
- Has serious unresolved personal problems
- Is apathetic about current situation
- Lacks organization and discipline
- Passes the blame; refuses to take personal responsibility
- Does not control his temper
- Refuses to take carefully considered risks; always plays it safe
- Rules by intimidation
- Is insecure and defensive
- Remains inflexible
- Has no team spirit
- Resists change
- Does not learn from own mistakes
- Lacks genuine integrity
- Has no vision
- Is without goals and direction
- Is not continually growing and learning
- Has minimal passion and commitment
- Is not developing leadership skills

The Extraordinary Leader

Research by John Zenger and Joseph Folkman on those judged to be extraordinary leaders revealed these findings.[1] The five traits of the extraordinary leader are:

Character and integrity

The leader must be above reproach in all areas (Titus 1:2-5).

Personal competence

The leader must have intellectual, emotional, technical, and spiritual capabilities.

Focus on results

The leader works diligently toward the accomplishment of the goal.

Interpersonal skills

The leader must be able to communicate with people in clear, confident, and purposeful ways in order to direct them toward success.

Leading organizational change

The leader must be able to motivate others to change in order to achieve desired success.

> *When a leader stops learning, he stops leading.* ~ Unknown

Each of these traits can be pictured as poles of a tent providing the support that allows it to stand on its own. The entire structure is then secure when all five poles are properly placed providing strength and stability to the tent.

Great leaders make a immense difference in organizations compared to good leaders. Only the top ten percent of people in leadership positions could be considered truly extraordinary leaders. The top thirty percent of leaders have the ability to seriously impact the commitment of the followers. Seven of ten leaders cannot effect change as they are lacking proficiency in the five traits of the extraordinary leader.

Tests based on an inventory of the five traits show that a truly great leader must posses at least three of the five in order to effect change in the people of the organization. Obviously, the goal would be to work diligently in acquiring or strengthening these leadership skills in all five areas. It is better to have developed strengths from each of the five areas rather than from only one or two.

Am I an Extraordinary Leader?

These sixteen competencies combine to give a profile of the successful leader.

- Do I have character and integrity?
- Am I personally capable and professionally competent?
- Am I a proficient problem solver?
- Am I creative and innovative?
- Am I willing to be a learner, implementing what I have learned?
- Can I take projects to completion?
- Can I use my performance to set the bar for those around me?
- Do I realize that I am ultimately responsible?
- Do I possess strong interpersonal skills?
- Am I able to provide inspiration and motivation to better performance?
- Do I recognize the importance of developing and maintaining personal relationships with those around me?
- Do I work diligently to ensure the success of the people around me?
- Do I set up an atmosphere of cooperation, collaboration, and teamwork?
- Can I effectively organize to achieve goals and objectives for myself and can I help others do the same?
- Can I gain effective support for my cause?
- Am I a good representative from the inside of my organization to the outside world?

Integrating Leadership Process

If leadership is about making things happen, then leadership involves three important roles. First is the role of the **visionary**, the entrepreneur. The second is the role of the **organizer**, the one making it happen by transforming the vision into reality through the organization and management process. This includes recruiting, training, and overseeing the producers (the people doing the work). The final role is the **producer**, who successfully transforms the vision into reality.

Leaders Strive for Constant Success

Influencing others
Setting priorities
Solving problems
Casting vision
Building people
Creating and maintaining a winning attitude
Making good decisions
Sustaining unity
Establishing synergy
Creating positive change
Developing other leaders
Developing self
Creating and managing momentum
Accomplishing results
Improving interpersonal skills

All three roles are equally important. The leader must ensure the vision is caught by others, is strategically planned, and is properly implemented and performed. Many ministers do not see themselves as leaders because it is not one of their preferred areas of responsibility compared to preaching, teaching, and shepherding the flock. If the minister is not capable in all three areas of the leadership process, it is essential that others be recruited who are capable and in combination can guarantee that all three responsibilities are covered.

One Christian leader lamented that, after spending a number of years conducting seminars to help pastors develop leadership skills, he found that many simply lacked the desire to fulfill the three functions of leadership. An example is a minister who talked about his role as a visionary and described himself as a concept-oriented person. He often came up with great ideas for church programs but somehow they never became reality. It was only after a member of the congregation, who had been a union organizer, retired and offered his assistance in the Lord's work that things began to happen. The former union organizer would take the concepts shared by the pastor, break them down into segments, organize the necessary programs and people to be involved, and then see that they were properly equipped and monitored as the program was implemented. The minister later commented that it was the combination of the two fulfilling the three roles of seeing, planning, and doing that got the job done. Are you a visionary? An organizer? A producer?

Leadership Tips [2, 3]

Leadership is about passion. Those who are passionate tend to attract others who also are passionate. Without passion for what you are doing, leadership is flat and ineffective. Channel your passion and make it work for you.

Leaders are tenacious. They simply refuse to give up. When setbacks and problems occur, leaders view them as opportunities to make the situation better. Whatever it takes, they do. Take *quit* out of your vocabulary and realize that projects may fail but the only failure is he who quits. You can fail without being a failure.

Leaders handle stress. Since leaders experience many pressures, some particularly strong, it is essential to learn to manage the stress in your life so that it does not become debilitating or cause burnout. Learn the secrets of successful stress management and practice them daily.

Leaders attract good ideas. They look for them everywhere. They seek them out. Though they often have many great ideas of their own, they are not afraid to borrow from others. Albert Einstein said, "The secret of creativity is how well you conceal your sources." Seek good ideas from others and use them when appropriate.

Leaders practice complexity through simplicity. Simplify. Simplify. Simplify. The profound can be wrapped in simplicity. Jesus Christ was the most profound leader and teacher, yet His ministry was clothed in simplicity. Reduce a complex thing into its simplest form.

Leaders understand the necessity of change. Although the message of the Gospel must never change, our methods must. Refusal to change is planned obsolescence. Imagine those who provided ice for the old fashioned ice box and refused to change when the modern refrigerator appeared. Don't be afraid of necessary change.

Leaders interact with followers and engage them at every level. They stay informed and aware of all activities, projects, and the various people involved. They are open to suggestions and creative ideas. Potential problems are avoided and if a problem occurs, it is addressed immediately. The leader should be accepting, approachable, and considerate. No one knows everything. Are you open to input from others?

Leaders see training disciples as a vital part of their ministry. They tailor their discipleship program to an appropriate Christian maturity and experience level. Jesus spent three years of His life training the disciples so that they would be successful after His ascension. Most churches are at their weakest in the matter of equipping their followers. How much of your time do you spend in discipleship?

Leaders know that rewards and recognition get results. Most people thrive when they are appreciated. Successful followers make leaders look good, but no leader can succeed without those who are doing the work. Do you regularly show appreciation to those you lead? Do they feel respected and appreciated?

Leaders lead through objectives. The concept of objective-based leadership means the leader inculcates the objectives of the organization into the minds of those who follow. He keeps the objectives before them and sees that everything in the organization flows accordingly. What are your objectives? Are your followers whole heartedly embracing them?

Leaders are innovators and understand that new ideas spark people to greater commitment. Are you an idea person open to new ideas or are you satisfied doing things the same way as before? A rut is a grave with the ends knocked out. Don't get into a rut. Leaders use new ideas, methods, and tools to accomplish their goals. Are you open to new ideas? Are you an innovator?

Leaders build on strengths. They need to determine their our own strengths, the strengths of their people, and the strengths of the organization and then build on those strengths. Are your strengths reflected in your leadership?

Leaders put the right people in the right positions. Matching people's abilities to performance is critical. Do you have the right people in the right positions?

Leaders stretch themselves and their followers through vision. Stagnant waters are dangerous. Moving waters are vital. Does your leadership challenge your followers and cause them to grow? Great visions challenge people to great things.

Leaders do their best and implement the best practices available. Never settle for the better when the best is available. Strive for the best people, the best ideas, the best effort, the best vision, and the best results. Are you a *best* person who strives in every way to be all that you can be and help others to be also?

Leaders deal with those who are unproductive. Often we reward effort rather than results. Effort is important in producing good results, but it is possible to produce great effort with little or no results. This is like a car spinning its wheels in the snow but going nowhere. It has been said that when the horse is dead, dismount. If something or someone isn't working, do you find out why and fix it?

Leaders leave little to chance. They plan, prepare, organize, mentor, coach, and equip to see that their efforts flourish. They understand the importance of the process and the performance. How much do you leave to chance in your leadership?

Leaders increase their expertise. A teacher must know that which he would teach. You can't give what you don't have and you can't teach what you don't know. A leader should be a role model in personal development. When he stops learning, he stops leading. Do you challenge others to learn and grow by your example?

Leaders practice accountability. Excuses and playing the blame game should not tolerated. Leadership is about making things happen. There is no substitute for discipline.

Do you demand accountability of yourself and others?

Leaders are forthright, providing open, honest, and sincere feedback to those they lead. They do not expect their followers to read their minds. They are quick to give feedback about performance. Do those you lead receive this kind of feedback and as often as needed?

Leaders understand the value of teamwork. The saying goes, "He who leads when no one is following is merely taking a walk." Leaders and followers make a team and working together fulfill common goals and objectives. Have you built a team of people who work with rather than against each other? Are you ultimately a team player?

Leaders are goal oriented in both their personal and their professional lives. This is especially true in the leadership of others. Goals are targets toward which everybody should aim. Are your goals specific, measurable, attainable, realistic, and timed with trackability?

> *Leadership is action, not position.*
> ~Donald McGannon

Leaders build on a clear set of values which they make certain are followed. Values include *ends* which represent where the organization will go and *means* which represent how it will get there. Both sets of values are of equal importance. Do you have explicitly stated values and is everyone following them?

Leaders are aware of the importance of infrastructure that supports their initiatives and programs. If the initiatives and programs outstrip the infrastructure, the organization will suffer weakness. Are you aware of the strengths and extent of your infrastructure and are you building upon it most effectively?

Leaders regularly assess the strength of various programs. Are you aware of what your weakest programs are and why? What are you doing to make the weak ones stronger and the strong ones better?

Leaders are decisive. They are decision makers who equip themselves to get the job done. When leaders have trouble making decisions, the followers are hindered. How decisive are you? What decisions give you the biggest problem?

Leaders constantly establish ambitious performance targets developing a culture of achievement and success. When performance targets are reached, they are celebrated. When they are not reached, key issues are evaluated and changes are implemented. How about your performance targets? Are they ambitious? When you miss the mark, what do you do about it?

Leaders own the mission statement. A mission statement reflects the main purpose of the organization and everything done is a direct reflection of the mission statement. What is your mission statement? Does everything your followers do fulfill the mission statement?

Leaders insist on specificity. They know that organizational objectives must be detailed and specific rather than general. How detailed and exact are your objectives?

Leaders know their success is dependent upon those whom they serve. If the needs of the church members are not being met, the lead is missing from leadership. Do you know the perspective of those you serve? Are their needs being met?

Leaders exercise candor with tact. Excellent leaders perfect their skills as tacticians. Are you striving to balance these two elements? How well are you succeeding in doing so?

Leaders respond to suggestions promptly. Suggestions should be implemented or rejected promptly. Not responding to suggestions for a prolonged period of time leads to frustration and fewer future suggestions. Do you respond promptly to suggestions?

Leaders take measured risks. They are aware that progress involves a certain level of risk-taking. An excellent leader never takes foolish risks but rather calculates and measures each risk first. How do you calculate risk and relate it to a cost/benefit analysis?

Leaders constantly talk about the direction of the organization. Effective leaders are like cheerleaders who spend much time urging others on by directing the conversation toward achieving the mission and emphasizing the direction of the organization. Are you a good vision caster?

Leaders know that followers have personal problems. If these problems are not handled, they will show up as problems in the organization. They ensure that followers receive the help they need to overcome. Suitable solutions should be provided.

Leaders understand the importance of succession. Too often when the leader steps down, inadequate attention and preparation have been given to his replacement causing the organization to flounder. It is essential that one leader build upon his predecessor's foundation and take the organization to a new level. Have you put a succession plan in place?

Leaders are capable of spotting and dealing with the major kinds of problem people in the organization:

- The arrogant who treat everyone else as peons
- The sluggards who duck their responsibility and underachieve
- The agitators who sew discord and negativity among others
- The steamrollers who are so determined to have their way they run over people
- The exploders whose volatile tempers are a source of concern and threat
- The pouters who are always upset about something
- The garbage collectors who collect all the negatives and dump them on others whenever possible
- The problematic who present a variety of problems to the organization
- The "yes...but-ers" who never take action because they always come up with some objection, reason, or excuse

How do you handle these kinds of problem people? Is your approach working?

Leaders provide a clear channel of organization and hierarchy. The organizational flowchart is not excessive or vague. Clear channels of authority and accountability are evident. When responsibility is given, the appropriate level of authority is also given to carry out the task with accountability factored in. Is your organizational flowchart clear, concise, and correct?

Leaders know that having too many or too few people reporting to one person in leadership is never good. The ideal oversight responsibility is between ten and fifteen people. Are those numbers realistic to you?

Leaders hire the right people. They recruit the finest people for their organization. Lee Iacocca said that the best leaders will make mistakes in hiring despite all efforts to avoid them, but they will correct mistakes immediately. What priority do you give to finding and hiring the best people?

Leaders understand the importance of retaining good people. Charles deGaulle said that graveyards are full of indispensable people. If you have ever tried to replace an indispensable person you know how difficult that is. Develop and use the necessary resources to retain your best people. What do you do to retain those you can ill afford to lose?

Leaders realize that the way an employee is dismissed is as important as the way an employee is recruited. This process is so important it is discussed later in this manual. How much attention have you given this important issue?

Leaders give serious attention to crisis management. Every organization will face an occasional crisis. How it is handled can make a difference in both outcome and process. If in doubt consult with people who are experts at handling crises and carefully manage the situation. Either you will manage the crisis or the crisis will manage you. Are you prepared in the area of crisis management? Here are some important things to consider.

1. Assess the cause and extent.

2. Project the course of events related to the crisis.

3. Focus on the threat to the reputation and functioning of the organization and its people.

4. Plan the most advantageous response. Consider the people affected, resources needed, and actions planned. Then reassess. Follow later with a reevaluation.

5. Implement damage control.

6. Look for opportunities provided because of the crisis and capitalize upon them.

7. Follow through and follow up.

8. Implement a strategy to prevent similar crises in the future.

My job is to get men to do what they don't want to do in order to achieve what they have always wanted to achieve.

Tom Landry

~

Leadership is action, not position.

Donald McGannon

Leaders plan for contingencies and unexpected developments. Expect the unexpected. Shrewd leaders consider what can go wrong and plan accordingly. Do you practice contingency planning?

Leaders understand the importance of expanding existing ministries and creating new ones as a necessary ingredient to growth. What new ministries would be advantageous to begin? What existing ministries need to expand?

Leaders understand that organization or reorganization is important to growth. When organizations reach a plateau, reorganization is necessary to move ahead.

Leaders lead with intentionality, design, and attention to detail. Use the "Leadership Checklist" which follows for detailed preparation and effective performance.

Leadership Checklist

This checklist has been prepared to assist a leader in providing effective leadership in the creation, organization, and execution of any program or project.

Visionary Leadership

___ Do you have a God-given vision that has inspired passion in others?

___ Has the vision possessed you so completely that it is contagious?

___ Have you communicated the vision to the most influential people first?

___ Have you cast the vision publicly?

___ Have you reinforced the vision regularly?

___ Have you used various means to keep it in front of the people?

___ Have you succeeded in creating a passionate ownership of the vision in others?

Strategic Leadership

___ Have you turned the vision into primary objectives with SMART goals?

___ Have you developed a strategic plan by breaking the vision down into a series of sequential actionable steps?

___ Is your action plan easily understood?

___ Are others challenged by it?

___ Have you developed methods to get everyone possible participating in the plan?

___ Have you developed a plan to keep people focused on the plan?

___ Have you broken the action plan into immediate, short-term, intermediate, and long-term segments if appropriate?

___ Have you organized all necessary sub-groups into the plan?

___ Have you focused on each step and specified markers to see if everyone is staying on track and achieving the desired goals and objectives?

Team-Building Leadership

___ Have you found and developed a team of people with right abilities, character, and chemistry to work on the project?

___ Do all members have a clear understanding of the vision and action plan?

___ Have you built community in your participants through social engineering?

___ Do all team members understand their specific roles in the process?

___ Do you have a plan to sustain the momentum of the team?

___ Are you prepared to fit together various personalities to prevent and resolve conflict?

Managing (Tactical) Leadership

___ Have you organized the people, processes, and resources to achieve your mission?

___ Have you developed a detailed project organizational worksheet with assignments and a clear chain of command?

___ Have you carefully anticipated potential problems that may prevent accomplishing the objectives?

___ Are you monitoring progress and correcting course as necessary?

___ How will you oversee the step-by-step, day-to-day operation of the project? Who will be responsible to whom? For what? How?

___ What type of accountability have you included? How will it work?

___ Have you prepared specific operational project controls including project worksheet, performance standards, project cost, PERT diagrams, or Gantt charts with mile-stone check points to trigger actions necessary to keep things on target?

___ Have you considered the training needs, hardware and software required, and support needed for this project?

___ How will you keep the channels of communication open for all involved in the project?

Motivational Leadership

___ How will you monitor the motivational level of each participant?

___ How will you keep motivation levels high?

___ If motivation wanes or discouragement sets in, how will you rekindle enthusiasm?

___ What motivation techniques will you use publicly? Privately?

___ Have you completed a motivational chart for the project?

Shepherding Leadership

___ How will you love, nurture, and support your people?

___ What role will prayer play in the process? How? When? Who?

___ How will you assess and meet the needs of participants?

Bridge-Building Leadership

___ How will you bring together all of the various participating groups under one leadership umbrella?

___ How will you assure the specific interests and concerns of each group are addressed?

___ How will you help the various groups keep a good attitude and a healthy perspective?

___ How will you handle disagreements and disputes?

___ How will you overcome territorial issues and a sense of entitlement?

Directional Leadership

___ When you come to an important fork in the road, how will you determine the right path?

___ How will you determine time or need for growth (pushing forward) or consolidation (assimilation)?

___ Do you have a plan for consultation if you experience a directional problem?

Completion Leadership

___ How will you celebrate the successful completion of the project?

___ How will you recognize or reward work well done?

___ How will you integrate results into future projects?

73

Recommended Scripture References

Joseph's wise leadership, Genesis 47:13-26
Moses humbly leads, Exodus 3:11
Lacked fluent speech, Exodus 4:10
Listens to advice, Exodus 18:15-27
Disgruntled with the leaders, Numbers 16:1-4
Delegated responsibilities, Deuteronomy 1:12-13
Judged equitably, Deuteronomy 1:17
No prophet like Moses, Deuteronomy 34:10-12
Strong and courageous, Joshua 1:6
Courage under pressure, Joshua 1:18
Commander of the Lord's army, Joshua 5:13-15
Organized Israelites, Joshua 7:14
Specific orders given, Joshua 8:8
Influence of good leaders, Joshua 24:31
Connection between leaders and people, Judges 5:2
Follow me, Judges 7:17-18
Humility in leadership, 2 Samuel 7:18-24
Success gave David fame, 2 Samuel 8:13
Prayer for wisdom, 1 Kings 3:5-15
Wisdom with disputing mothers, 1 Kings 3:16-28
Organization for building temple, 1 Kings 5:12-18
Reminder, there is no other God, 1 Kings 8:55-61
Advice of elders rejected, 1 Kings 12:1-11
David open to advice, 1 Chronicles 13:1
Good leadership, 1 Chronicles 18:14
Divine guidance in leadership, 2 Chronicles 31:20-21
Integrity and skill, Psalm 77:20, 78:72
Declaring God's message, Jeremiah 1:6-10, 17-19
Wealth and power poisons, Jeremiah 5:27-29
Jesus taught with authority, Matthew 7:28-29
Instructions to twelve apostles, Matthew 10:5-42

Servant leadership, Matthew 20:28; John 13:5, 14, 22;
   Acts 20:18-19; 2 Corinthians 4:5; Colossians 1:24-26
Night of prayer, important decision, Luke 6:12-16
Jesus demonstrated servant leadership, John 13:3-9
Jesus instructed the apostles, Acts 1:1-2
Distribution to widows delegated, Acts 6:1-4
Conflict between Paul, Barnabas, Acts 15:36-40
Giving encouragement, Acts 20:1
Diligent leadership required, Romans 12:8
Duties humbly accepted, Romans 12:16
Humility in leadership, 2 Corinthians 1:24
Avoid cruel use of authority, 2 Corinthians 13:10
Leaders meet secretly, Galatians 2:2
Lead gently, Galatians 6:1-2
Submit to each other, Ephesians 5:21
Obey in my absence, Philippians 2:12
Put learning into practice, Philippians 4:9
Effort on behalf of followers, Colossians 1:28-29
Fullness in Christ, Colossians 2:9-10
Model of leadership, 1 Thessalonians 2:1-16
Care expressed, 1 Thessalonians 3:1-3
Desire to be overseer, 1 Timothy 3:1
Recent convert unqualified, 1 Timothy 3:6
Servant, apostle, Titus 1:1
Instructions to underlings, Titus 1:5
Elder's credentials, Titus 1:5-9
Teach, encourage, rebuke, Titus 2:15
Deal gently, Hebrews 5:2-3
Exemplary leaders, Hebrews 13:7; 1 Peter 5:2-5
If you lack wisdom, ask God, James 1:5-6, 3:17-18
Good report about followers, 3 John 3-4
Needs rebuke, 3 John 9, 10

Management is doing things right.
Leadership is doing the right things.
~Peter Drucker

Leading Change

Motivation for Change

Motivation for change will largely be based upon the degree of dissatisfaction with the status quo. You must show the need for and the importance of the change to effectively implement it. Ministers who take over a new work often begin making changes without adequate foresight, insight, or preparation.

> *To improve is to change,
> to be perfect is to have
> changed often.*
>
> *Winston Churchill*

Steps of Change

Establish need (both internal and external motivators)

Demonstrate how the need can be met

Present the solution(s)

Convince to accept

Repeat as necessary

Climate for Change Questionnaire

Leading change is a vital part of leadership. Use these guidelines for assessment when change is required.

1. Will our people benefit from this change?
2. Will this change blend with the purpose of the church?
3. Is this change specific and clear?
4. Do the church leaders favor this change?
5. Can we try out this change before totally committing to it?
6. Are the necessary financial and personnel resources available for this change?
7. Will this change advance our program?
8. Are both short-term and long-term benefits specified?
9. Are the gains worth the cost?
10. Can we successfully implement this change?
11. Is it the right time?
12. Is God in this change?

Change Implementation Strategy [1,2]

- Create a sense of urgency demonstrating a need for change. Make the people see, feel, hear, and know that change is required.

- Sell the church leadership as well as members of important groups and enlist their support. If they are not on board, change implementation will be very difficult.

- Recruit effective leaders and make sure the right people are in the right places.

- Prepare the congregation well in advance through vision-casting and need development.

- Develop strategies to guide them through each stage of the change process.

- Design the change as "add-ons" to existing programs or activities. People will accept additions more readily than subtractions.

- Desensitize people through progressive steps.

- Can the change be labeled as an experiment to increase the level of comfort with the people involved?

- Explain the objectives of the change and how and when it will occur.

- Defuse negative reactions.

- Demonstrate the benefits of the change and provide any necessary adjustments.

- Encourage ownership in the change through participation.

- Anticipate questions, problems, and reactions and be prepared to handle them.

- Keep communication channels open through feedback.

- Demonstrate willingness to pay the price for successful realization.

- Provide recognition, appreciation, and enthusiasm to all who are involved.

- Emotional components and motivators are critical to the change process.

- Anchor the changes by connecting them to leadership development and the succession of future leadership.

- Give God the glory!

Recommended Scripture References

God speaks to Abram, Genesis 12:1-9
Change necessary, Genesis 35:2
Time to move on, Deuteronomy 1:6
Time to tear down, rebuild, Ecclesiastes 3:3
In the potters hand, Jeremiah 18:1
A new shepherd, Zechariah 1:1-6
Walk in newness of live, Romans 6:4
Changed from death to life, Romans 6:12-13
Conformed to the image of His son, Romans 12:2; Romans 8:28-30; 2 Corinthians 5:17
Paul feared making changes, 2 Corinthians 12:20-21
His workmanship, Ephesians 2:10
Will change our vile body, Philippians 3:20-21
Overcoming victory, 1 John 5:4-5

Problem Solving

Problems or unexpected difficulties may be indicators that change or improvement is needed in an area. Problem solving is an important skill as no person, family, or church exists without problems.

Problem Solving Methodology

The following is a complete strategy for efficiently and effectively working through a problem.

1. Write a concise statement which identifies the exact nature of the problem.

2. Determine the scope of the problem regarding the following aspects:

    ♦ People involved
    ♦ Programs affected
    ♦ Procedures included
    ♦ Processes affected
    ♦ Threat included
    ♦ Contamination potential
    ♦ Seriousness

3. Determine if immediate action needs to be taken to provide containment and prevent further deterioration of the situation. Possible considerations include:

    ♦ Situation rapidly deteriorating
    ♦ Contamination and enlargement risk
    ♦ Opportunity so important it should not be missed
    ♦ Can't wait for an underlying cause-analysis and more thorough consideration

    If your analysis reveals that immediate action needs to be taken, decide on the best course of action and proceed immediately. The analogy is of an emergency room doctor assessing a patient, determining that the patient is in immediate danger, and initiating critical intervention. The situation does not afford him the luxury of a long diagnostic workup and a more prolonged treatment regimentation. Stabilization is the priority.

4. If the previous step is not warranted, list the possible causes of the problem. Keep in mind that causes may be surface causes or underlying root problems and carefully consider both. Root-cause analysis requires investigation using research into underlying dynamics, antecedents, and etiology. Expertise and experience are invaluable assets. Don't hesitate to avail yourself of both through consultation with those who have more experience and mature judgment than you possess. Root-cause problem analysis leads to root-cause solutions. For instance, the Bible mentions a root of bitterness (Hebrews 12:15) indicating that problems stem from bitterness, hence the Bible calls it a root.

Some years ago I was making the rounds of the hospitals when I began experiencing chest pains, shortness of breath, and pain radiating down my left arm. When I was examined by the doctor in the emergency room, his initial diagnosis was that I was suffering a cardiac event and I was immediately admitted to the cardiac unit. After receiving test results, he announced that my heart was fine but they were running more tests. Later he diagnosed me with an intestinal disorder. I remember saying, "...but, Doc, I have shortness of breath and the pain is up here in my chest, not down here in my abdomen." He smiled and explained why I had the symptoms and how they were going to treat my condition. If he had stopped with a surface-cause analysis based upon my symptoms, he would have misdiagnosed me and correspondingly applied the wrong remedy.

Getting to the root-cause of any problem is worth the effort because it precedes the determination of the right remedy. At this point make sure to:

+ Seek God's guidance and wisdom.

+ Examine Scripture for biblical principles and answers.

+ Seek considerable and extensive input.

+ Ask thoughtful questions.

+ Borrow expertise and knowledge from others.

+ Pursue all the facts.

+ Brainstorm and analyze.

+ List all possible causes.

5. Analyze each of the causes and determine which is the most probable. Then rank order those next most probable.

6. Generate solutions based upon the determined cause(s) and select the best one. Choose the best-fit solution and the most-likely-to-work solution using the *Cost-Benefit-Fallout Technique*. The critical issue in coming to the right conclusion is having the right options as part of the process. Make sure to:

+ Investigate and gather problem causes.

+ Be aware that problems will arise and may require multiple solutions.

+ Study the scriptures using a problem-solution format.

+ Brainstorm and analyze.

+ Seek counsel and advice.

+ Develop a personal cabinet or council of experts to whom you can turn for help and input.

To assist with this step, the *How-How Technique, Brainstorming Technique*, and *Cost-Benefit-Fallout-Technique* are included on the following pages.

7. Evaluate the effectiveness of your solution and make any mid-course corrections. If your solution is not adequately resolving the problem, decide if it needs modification, needs more time to work, or needs replacement. If it needs modifying or replacement, generate alternate solutions.

8. Establish a policy for prevention of this problem in the future.

For the step above, use the *Who, What, When, Where, How and Why Technique, Why-Why Technique*, and *Mind Mapping Technique* included on the pages that follow.

Problem Solving Worksheet for Simple Problems

Identify and define the problem.

_____
_____
_____

Ask carefully crafted questions.

_____
_____
_____

Talk to the critical people.

_____
_____
_____

Get all of the facts.

_____
_____
_____

Consult knowledgeable people for input and help.

_____
_____
_____

Brainstorm and consider possible solutions.

_____
_____
_____

Implement the best solution.

_____
_____
_____

Consider possible unintended consequences of the solution.

_____
_____
_____

Monitor the solution and make any necessary mid-course changes or corrections.

_____
_____
_____

Determine how to prevent the problem from recurring. Develop policies for prevention.

_____
_____
_____

Problem Solving Worksheet for Critical and Complex Problems

Identify and define problem.

Define the scope of the problem.
 People involved
 Programs involved
 Procedures included
 Processes affected
 Threat included
 Contamination potential
 Use the *Who, What, When, Where, How, and Why Technique*

Determine if immediate action needs to be taken.
 Rapidly deteriorating situation
 Contamination and enlargement risk
 Opportunity too important to miss
 Can't wait for underlying cause analysis

Take immediate action if needed.
 Who
 What
 How

List causes of problems (Look also for the root causes.)
 Seek God's guidance and wisdom.
 Examine Scripture for biblical principles and answers.
 Seek considerable and extensive input.
 Ask pertinent questions.
 Borrow expertise and knowledge from people who know.
 Pursue all the facts.
 Brainstorm and analyze (Use *Mind-Mapping Technique*).
 List all possible causes.
 Use the *Why-Why Technique.*

Generate solutions based upon determined causes and select the best.
 Collect problem solutions from every possible source.
 Study Scripture using a problem-solving format.
 Brainstorm and analyze (Use the *Mind-Mapping Technique*).
 Seek counsel and advice.
 Develop and consult a personal cabinet of experts for assistance and direction.
 Use the *How-How Technique.*
 Use the *Brainstorming Technique.*
 Use the *Cost-Benefit-Fallout Technique.*

Evaluate the effectiveness of your solution and make midcourse corrections.

Establish a policy for prevention of problem in the future.

The Why-Why Technique

The *Why-Why Technique* is used to identify the causes of a problem. It provides a systematic method similar to a decision tree. It begins with a statement of the problem on the left side of the diagram, then moves right to the stems and from the stems to the branches at the far right by asking the question "why". The purpose of the process is to help you get to the root of the problem. The following example uses this methodology.

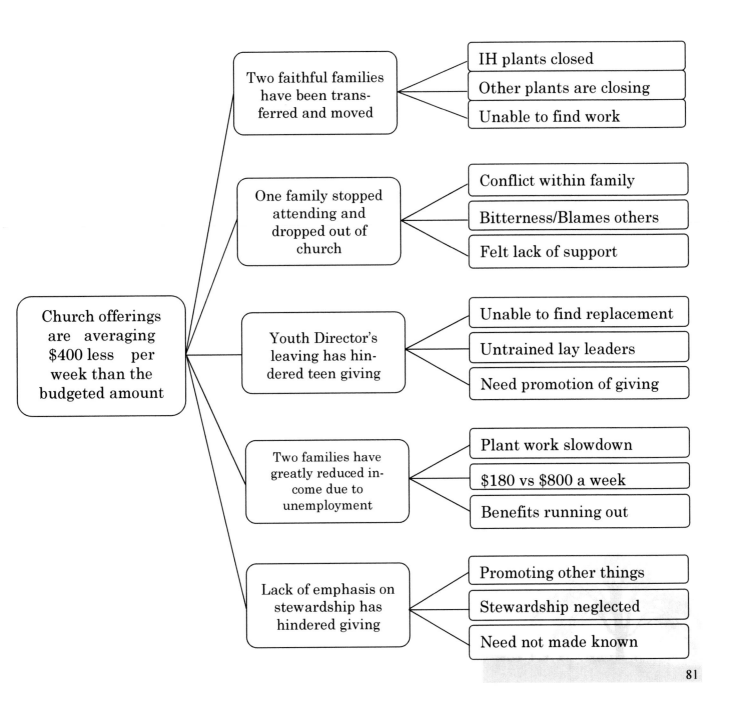

The How-How Technique

The *How-How Technique* works similarly to the *Why-Why Technique* except its purpose is to arrive at a solution instead of the cause of a problem. It also follows a decision tree format moving from left to right. The following example uses this methodology and serves as the solution(s) for the problem analyzed in the *Why-Why Technique* illustrated earlier.

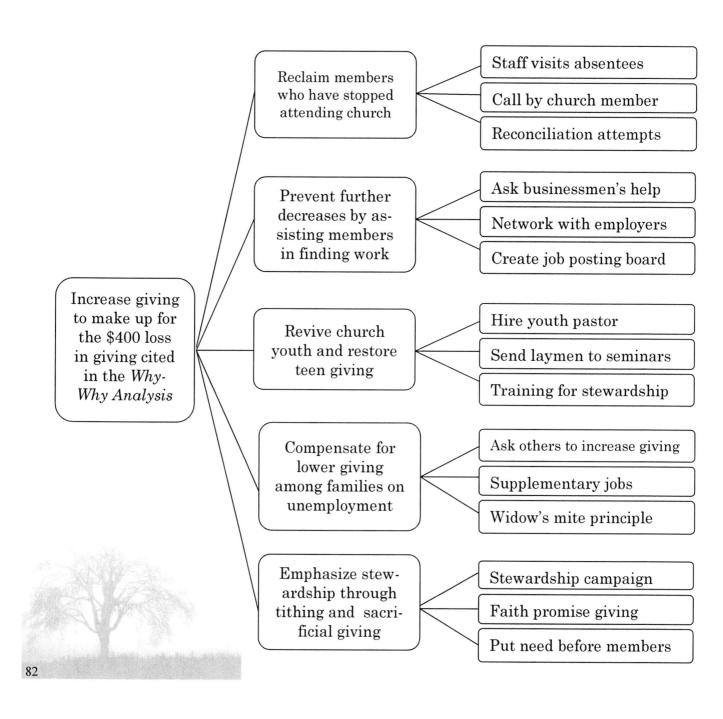

Cost-Benefit-Fallout Technique

The *Cost-Benefit-Fallout Technique* is used to evaluate proposed solutions to determine the most-likely-to-succeed or best-fit solution with an acceptable level of negative consequences. Take each proposed solution and carefully consider three elements of each. List all of the costs including the physical, financial, personal, personnel, emotional, social, organizational, and spiritual involved in implementing the solution. Then carefully consider each of these benefits using the same eight-fold criteria listed above. Finally, carefully consider the negative consequences or fallout factors in implementing each solution again following an analysis using the same eightfold criteria. Follow these steps for each proposed solution and select the one which provides the best *Cost-Benefit-Fallout Profile*. This should become your preferred or most-likely-to-succeed solution to your problem. The following form facilitates the use of this methodology.

In determining the impact of a new ministry in support of those with addictions, habits, hurts, and hang-ups, the following *Cost-Benefit-Fallout Technique* was used.

Starting a New Ministry: Celebrate Recovery (CR)			
	Cost(s)	**Benefit(s)**	**Fallout(s)**
Physical	CR is a heavy commitment Are we physically able to meet those demands?	Health	Safety of participants Relapse
Financial	Food and drink integral Materials No weddings on Fridays due to CR's use of facility	CR participants may join church CR participants may support it financially	Requires initial layout of money but will become self-sustaining
Personal	On-going commitment Do I have any habits or hang-ups that need to be addressed?	Another opportunity and support structure to right myself with God and allow others to right themselves with Him	High burn-out rate
Personnel	Training of leaders and workers Food/drink preparation Counselors and sponsors Band, soundboard, and tech operators	Leaders are trained to assist other church members who are dealing with problems	Leaders leave—retraining Labor shortage
Emotional	Extreme crisis situations a probability	Church members may benefit through participation of Christian 12 step program rather than attendance in secular program	Anonymity must be maintained
Social	Participants working through problems can be needy and require much attention anytime day or night Wolves (dating)	Influx of people, church becomes known as a helpful resource in the community	How will the church body receive this program?
Organizational	Facility use every Friday, must be set up early and cleaned afterward	Facility is being used	Use of facility by other groups may be disallowed Church members upset by smoking in the parking lot
Spiritual	Time Leaders meet for devotional time, to review previous meeting, and identify concerns	Christian 12 Step Program Reaching the unsaved Prison ministry outreach	The church is being led to do this, failure to do so is not following God's will

Assessment of Problems: *Who, What, When, Where, How, Why Technique*

This technique provides a simple profile as a basis for analysis by breaking down the answers to the following questions.

Who is causing or contributing to this problem?

Who are the people involved? How has this affected them negatively?

What is the exact nature of this problem?

What are its causes?

What relevant information is available?

What are the symptoms of the various problems?

When did this problem first appear?

When did it come to my attention?

When should it be addressed?

Where are the symptoms of the problem being manifested in the organization?

How long ago did it begin incubating?

How has this problem unfolded /developed?

How has it been addressed so far?

How has it affected various people?

How has it affected the organization?

How are the issues related to each other?

How has this problem affected functioning?

Why are we having this problem (surface causes)?

Why are we having this problem (root causes)?

Brainstorming Technique for Finding Solutions

An individual or group of people focus on a specific problem. Alternative solutions are offered verbally in a spontaneous manner as individuals think of them. The **quantity** of responses is the goal. These four rules are universally followed.

1. No judgments are made by participants during the process.
2. All ideas no matter how ridiculous, unreasonable, or impractical are encouraged.
3. Although quantity of options is what is being encouraged, the quality of ideas is the main objective.
4. Combine, piggyback, or refine ideas but never immediately discard them.

Then analyze ideas for usability, applicability, and feasibility. Rank order them by probability of effectiveness.

Biblical Examples of Problem Solving by Leaders

Joseph advised Pharaoh on the leadership issues of divine guidance, vision, strategic planning, and management principles (Genesis 41:14-57).

Moses accepted the counsel of his father-in-law Jethro who advised him on the leadership issues of prioritization, developing other leaders, delegation, and accountability (Exodus 18:13-27).

Joshua learned the leadership lessons of attitude adjustment, making good decisions, and creating positive change (Joshua 7:1-26).

Solomon practiced the leadership principles of problem solving (1 Kings 3:16-28).

Daniel wisely handled the question of eating the king's meat and drinking wine. Note his tactful approach to the one in authority, his providing a suitable option, and his suggestion of a trial run program as his proposed solution (Daniel 1:8-21).

Early church leaders exercised the leadership principles of communication, conflict management and resolution, confrontation, sustaining unity, and establishing synergy (Acts 15:1-41).

The entire book of Nehemiah is a tutorial on successful leadership. Nehemiah was not the CEO of a Fortune 500 company but a cupbearer for the king. God called him to a position of leadership. Nehemiah sought the guidance of God as he exercised his leadership skills influencing others, setting priorities, solving problems, casting vision, building people, maintaining a winning attitude, strategically planning, managing conflict, creating and maintaining teamwork, sustaining unity, establishing synergy, developing other leaders, creating positive change, persuading, motivating, managing people, establishing objectives, setting goals, delegating, and organizing.

When the wall construction reached one-half the intended height, people became demotivated and wanted to quit citing fatigue, fear, and being overwhelmed (4:6-12). Nehemiah motivated the people with an inspirational speech which resulted in their returning to work. The Nehemiah Principle teaches that momentum must be both created and recreated monthly during a project due to external and internal de-motivators (4:14). This principle is used as a basis for monthly motivational meetings in various organizations to provide inspiration and encouragement.

Handling a Serious Problem

Joe has a presenting problem of chronic lateness. *Joe's* problem could be addressed using the following process.

Define the Problem

Clearly define and present the problem so those involved have a clear understanding of the situation. Frame the problem as follows.

A (some specified thing)
> *is causing*
B (some undesirable effect)

~

A *Joe's constant tardiness*
> *is causing*
B *Serious attitude problems among the other office employees*

Define Objectives

This step involves defining the outcome you would like to achieve through the solving of the problem or making of the decision. This step is outlined as follows:

To (Action taken)
By (Date of accomplishment)
At (Whatever the cost)

~

To *ensure that Joe is prompt in all of his responsibilities and appointments*
By *the first of next quarter when management performs its yearly time study of employees*
At *no financial cost except lost time and work*

Generate Alternatives

This step involves generating as many alternative ways as possible of reaching the objectives outlined above. Be thorough in producing an extensive list of possible alternatives. Examples regarding Joe:

- Discuss the issue with Joe, determine why he is late, find solution(s).
- Explain how his problem is affecting others and enlist his cooperation.
- Deduct from Joe's salary each time he is late.
- Personally reprimand Joe for each incident.
- Devise a ladder of increasingly negative consequences.
- Tell Joe if he is late again he will be suspended without pay.
- Change Joe's work to a flex schedule.
- Demote Joe.
- Revise Joe's work to better accommodate his schedule and needs.

- Refer Joe for counseling.
- Ask Joe to develop his own action plan to handle this problem.
- Form a committee of his peers to whom he will be accountable.
- Fire Joe if he is late again.

Develop an Action Plan

This step involves two parts:

1. Analyzing each alternative generated, adding more if possible, and choosing which will be your solution.
2. Combining and modifying the chosen alternatives into a comprehensive action plan with which you are satisfied.

Resulting Action Plan for Joe:

1. Meet with Joe and state problem.
   - Recount the number of times he has been late during the last few months.
   - Point out how it is negatively affecting other employees and their attitudes.
   - Determine why he is late so often.
   - Jointly arrive at a solution to problem.
   - Devise an action plan to implement the agreed upon course of action.

2. Present a list of consequences.
   - If he's late again, he'll get a written reprimand and be docked a half-hour's pay.
   - If he is late a second time, he will receive an unpaid one-week suspension.
   - A third tardy will result in demotion.
   - If late after demotion, he will be fired.

3. Plan a meeting next month to provide him with performance-based feedback.

Troubleshoot Resulting Problems

New problems can result from previous decisions and attempted solutions. Review your action plan, anticipate potential problems which could develop during implementation, then apply the following techniques to assure the intended success of your plan.

1. Modify your action plan to avoid or minimize anticipated problems.
2. Anticipate unintended problems or obstacles through contingency planning.
3. Carefully determine how you will handle the potential problem if it occurs. Potential problems include: a) Joe may be unresponsive or uncooperative, b) he might sabotage you with other employees, c) he might become belligerent.
4. Should the action plan be modified because of these potential problems?
5. If so, how would you modify the plan?
6. If not, how would you prepare for or handle each of these problems?

Communicate

This step involves the following actions:

1. Assess people or groups which might affect the success of your action plan.
2. Ensure efficacy of your plan by providing them with adequate information.
3. Chart specific objectives for each person paired with the preferred method of communicating with them (personal visit, phone, letter, memo, or e-mail).

Person	Objective	Method
Senior Pastor	Seek advice Gain support	Personal visit
Business Manager	Provide information	Memo
Treasurer	Pay plan	Memo
Board	Seek approval for action plan	Attend next board meeting

Recommended Scripture References

Victory promised through troubles, Deuteronomy 9:1-3
No problem for boy, 1 Samuel 17:48
Problems overcome with divine help, 2 Samuel 22:30
Untouched by trouble, Proverbs 19:23
Passing through the rivers, Isaiah 43:2
The God who levels mountains, Isaiah 45:1-3
Unconfessed sin, God won't work, Isaiah 59:2
Answers to prayer may be delayed, Jeremiah 42:7
Daniel sought God's answers, Daniel 2:14-28
Worried needlessly, Matthew 8:23-27

Faith that moves mountains, Matthew 17:20; 21:21-22
Warning to those who hinder others, Matthew 23:13-15;
    Luke 11:52
Worries cause unfruitfulness, Mark 4:19
Angels rolled the stone away, Mark 16:3-4
God's miracle, John 5:2-9
The God of all comfort, 2 Corinthians 1:3-4
Will not be stumbling block, 2 Corinthians 6:3
Hindered in running race, Galatians 5:7; Hebrews 12:1
Still standing at end of struggle, Ephesians 6:13
Bearing burdens, Philippians 4:14
Waiting to make his purpose clear, Hebrews 6:13-15

Strategic Planning

Masterplanning

The role of carefully planning the future course and development of your church and ministry is essential for future success. The producing of such a plan is usually referred to as strategic planning and is an essential part of any business, church, or organization.

The roles of leadership, organization, and production are all necessary as vital elements to the flourishing organization. Such plans are based upon the mission statement, purposes, objectives, and specific goals of the organization. A good organizational strategic plan should focus on four time frames:

♦ Quarterly (90 days)
♦ Short-term planning (0-1 year)
♦ Intermediate-term planning (2-4 years)
♦ Long-term planning (5-10 years)

There are a variety of models for strategic planning, depending upon the organization's infrastructure, size, personnel, resources, and purpose. Most strategic planning focuses on achieving specific goals.

Mission Statement

Every ministry should have a comprehensive mission statement which embodies the core values and purposes of its very existence. If any ministry, activity, or action does not fit into the mission statement and is not a fulfillment or manifestation of the statement, it should either not be undertaken or discontinued if it is already in place.

Purpose

The understanding and expression of each specific purpose for the existence of your church or ministry is mandatory. The five purposes of the New Testament church highlighted in Rick Warren's book, <u>The Purpose Driven Church</u>[1], are the life's blood for the planning of any church ministry. The roles of evangelism, fellowship, worship, discipleship, and service (ministry) should be the measuring stick for determining the direction, organization, health, and programs of every part of your church.

Objectives and Specific Goals

Out of our purposes, specific objectives should be determined and from these objectives should emerge our specific goals. The goal is to produce a masterplan which is flexible and practical. The masterplan should always be kept fluid in order to allow for change and be considered a constant work in progress.

Steps in Strategic Planning

1. Seek God's will before and during every step.

2. Make certain all the right people are included in the strategic planning process.

3. Develop a comprehensive yet brief mission statement based upon the purposes of the organization.

4. Evaluate strengths, weaknesses, opportunities, and threats to the organization. The evaluation of the strengths and weaknesses should include the infrastructure, programs, personnel, resources, and organizational structure.

5. List specific objectives.

6. Carefully determine the ministry goals for the various terms previously noted. Make sure they are SMART goals which have a good fit with the mission and objectives of the organization.

7. Develop an action plan based upon strategies to reach each goal.

8. Turn the goals into projects. See the section on *Organization and Goal Setting*.

9. Plan key milestones as part of the process to monitor progress and ensure that goals will be reached and that the action plan is working to accomplish the objectives. Develop a comprehensive Gantt chart.

10. Determine and access the necessary resources and responsibilities required for the success of the plan.

11. Plan how to communicate to the necessary person the strategic plan in every feasible way as often as needed.

12. Regularly reassess the plan and its components to ensure necessary change will be made as the plan unfolds. Strategic planning is an on-going process.

13. Celebrate successes as they occur.

14. Give God the glory.

The planning materials produced by Bob Biehl in his book <u>Masterplanning</u>[2] provide excellent instruction for producing a masterplan for any organization.

Plateaus

When you engage in masterplanning keep in mind the concept of plateaus as you develop your plan. Churches tend to even off at certain levels called plateaus. If you are not aware that this is happening, you can easily find yourself stuck in a certain attendance range.

The average church in the United States is about 80 people and often has a part-time pastor. Eighty percent of churches have 200 or fewer in attendance. A good ratio of a pastor to people is one pastor for every 150 people. That is the maximum number of people that a single pastor is able to adequately care for in the role of shepherd. Consequently, when a church reaches consistent attendance beyond 150, the congregation usually hires an associate.

Churches averaging about 150 have plateaued. If an associate is added and the congregation moves forward, the two pastors can now handle up to 300 in attendance; this is a second plateau. Between 300 and 500 is the next plateau, then 500 to 800, followed by 800 to a maximum of about 1200. Growing the church beyond 1200 usually requires not only a larger staff but also a considerable non-paid lay staff leadership that can assume more responsibility and involvement in the cause. Since everything rises and falls on leadership, it is the role of the leadership through masterplanning to take the necessary steps to move the church off of a plateau to the next level.

Edgewood's Planning/Reorganization

The secret of successfully moving off a plateau and reaching a new one is reorganiza-

Church Plateaus

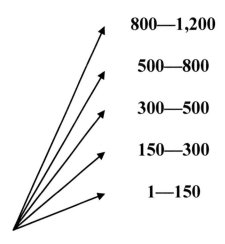

800—1,200

500—800

300—500

150—300

1—150

tion. You have to carefully plan and organize for new growth and development. Edgewood successfully moved through the plateaus by using the formula of planning and reorganization each time. Currently we are ranging in attendance between 800 and 1200, a definite plateau. Through masterplanning we are preparing to reorganize around a different staff arrangement with the implementation of ministry teams to provide leadership and development. Included in this section is an example of an action plan developed through the masterplanning process which is designed to enable the church to move from the current plateau to the next one. Since it is now being implemented it is just beginning to produce the desired results. He who has no goal will hit it every time. How high is your aim and what are you going to do to ensure you will achieve your goal?

Edgewood's 1,000-1,500 Strategic Plan

1. Reclaim people who previously attended.

2. Connect more effectively with prospects.

3. Revise assimilation plan to get or keep people on track for fellowship and growth.

4. Start Saturday evening services.

5. Get purpose-driven model fully implemented in every ministry of the church. Each of the following should be increased or the quality improved: evangelism, worship, fellowship, discipleship, and serving.

6. Strive to get everyone into a small group with top-down emphasis and frequent monitoring.

7. Hire two additional pastoral staff members to start new ministries and better oversee volunteers in existing ministries.

8. Begin single's class expansion in gym.

9. Develop multiple ministries for ladies with more opportunities to participate.

10. Increase outreach and participation in senior citizen's ministry.

11. Begin additional Sunday school classes through overlap concepts for facility maximization.

12. Promote the growth of all current ministries in the church through goal setting and tactical planning—10% in three months and 25% in one year.

13. Realign staff for maximum efficiency.

14. Improve church's website for appeal and outreach.

15. Aggressively plan and promote more outreach campaigns and events.

16. Stress evangelism continuously through modeling, projects, programs, and services.

17. Ascertain needs of our own people and of the people in the community and work to meet them.

18. Correct issues responsible for stop in attendance.
    - Format and time of services
    - Lack of connections
    - Rudeness or offensiveness
    - Wedding policy
    - Membership policy
    - Not being user friendly
    - Failure to meet the needs of people
    - Inadequate or inappropriate ushering
    - Not responding to visitors within auditorium
    - Lack of communication
    - Falling through the cracks

(Notice that this list does not include doctrine, standards, or preaching.)

19. Reorganize church with emphasis on participation and performance.

20. Use more visuals and first degree stimuli in services. These can include drama, video and other images, PowerPoint presentations, and testimonies.

21. Conduct regular progress reviews and make appropriate corrections.

22. Increase number of praise leaders on platform to mirror diversity in people represented.

23. Provide additional parking.

24. Continuously start and promote new ministries for outreach.

25. Reorganize the office area for maximum efficiency.

26. Focus more heavily on move-ins.

27. Enter building program to add additional large classrooms to accommodate increasing class sizes and new classes.

New Ministry Planning

Preliminary Questions

- Have I carefully thought through all of the aspects of my idea using the six serving men? Who? What? Where? When? Why? How?
- Have I mind-mapped my idea?
- Have I carefully considered the obstacles and potential problems of the realization of my idea?
- Have I detailed all of the necessary steps to implement my idea?
- Have I studied all the participants and players I need to consider in programming my idea?
- Have I carefully prepared for each step of the development of my idea?
- Have I developed the following charts?

Preliminary consideration chart (brainstorming and answering above questions)
Program chart (components of strategy)
Procedure chart (step-by-step plan of action)
Process chart (tracking)
Progress chart (evaluation and revision)

Planning Process for New Ministry

- Information Gathering
  Evaluate top existing programs
  Attend seminars/conferences
  Watch videos
  Read books
  Listen to CDs
  Research facts/statistics/surveys
  Discuss the ministry with consultants
  Consult with fellow leaders

- Personal Preparation
  Spiritual preparation
  Visualization
  Mental vitamins
  Motivation
  Nehemiah principle

- Purpose-Driven Planning
  Prepare a vision statement
  Write a mission statement
  Develop a purpose-driven ministry model
  Employ a user-friendliness philosophy

- Personnel Preparation
  Select and recruit sponsors/staff
  Organize sponsors/staff
  Complete vision casting and expectation building with sponsors/staff
  Allow them to give input and gain ownership of the ministry
  Train and equip sponsors/staff
  Mentor and monitor them
  Assign responsibilities to sponsors/staff (delegate)
  Schedule regular sponsor/staff meetings

- General Program Preparation
  Complete project worksheets and the Gantt chart
  Set 90 day, short-term, mid-term, and long-term SMART goals
  Use graphs for tracking progress

- Specific Program Preparation
  Brainstorm
  Cover the who, what, when, how, where, why specifics
  Determine targeting activities
  Begin scheduling

- Promotion, Preparation, Planning
  Newspapers, radio, internet
  Word of mouth

National organizations
Brochures
Invitations
Promotional announcements

♦ Meeting Preparation

Welcoming	Music
Identification	Sponsors
Personnel	Formatting
Locations	Satellites
Date/time	Videos
Groups	Subgroups
Big events	Seminars
Programs	Demonstrations
Themes	Speakers
Topics	

♦ Follow-Up Preparation

Contacts
Assimilation
Social engineering
Personal information gathering needs
Motivation profiles
Gifts/ministry
Referrals

♦ Organizational Preparation

Establish core groups
Use the key man strategy
Allow them to give input and gain ownership of the ministry
Establish commitments
Turbo activities
Pilot programming
Vision/motivation

Team organization
Monitoring

(For a detailed example of a comprehensive plan see Appendix C, *Step-by-Step Strategic Plan* as developed by the Edgewood interns. The situation given the interns was of a newly-ordained pastor who was called to a deeply troubled church. They were to develop strategically planned steps the pastor might use to turn the church around.)

Recommended Scripture References

Unity in congregation, Exodus 36:3-7
Plan to conquer, Deuteronomy 9:1
Planned ambush, Joshua 8:3-23, 1 Samuel 14:9-15, 2 Samuel 5:22-25, Luke 14:31-32
Lord's approval of journey plan, Judges 18:5-6
Hidden intentions, 1 Samuel 16:1-5
Building the temple, 1 Kings 5:12-18, 6:7
Fund raising, 2 Kings 12:4-12
Blueprint for temple, 1 Chronicles 28:11, 19
Organized worship, Ezra 3:10
Hindrances to overcome, Ezra 4:5, Nehemiah 6:1-9
Delegated building, Nehemiah 3:1-32
All plans fail except the Lord's, Psalm 127:1
Not haughty, Psalm 131:1
Character keeps on track, Proverbs 13:16
God's plan triumphs, Proverbs 19:21
Persuade with patience, Proverbs 25:15
God's counsels are faithful, Isaiah 25:1
God sees hidden plan, Isaiah 29:15
Before I formed thee, Jeremiah 1:4-5
Jesus' plan for facing accusers, Matthew 21:24-27
Strategy to destroy Jesus, Mark 15:1
Count cost before construction, Luke 14:28-30
Plan for the devil's assault, Ephesians 6:11
Uncertain of tomorrow, James 4:13-16
Redemption planned before creation, 1 Peter 1:18-20

Personal Magnetism

You only have one opportunity to make a first impression. Connecting with people must be done in a meaningful manner. They can sense when you are insincere, so strive to be genuine and transparent at all times.

Charisma

Charisma is a personal magic of leadership arousing loyalty or enthusiasm.

1. Treat all people as if they were personally sent by Jesus Christ to meet you.

2. Greet them with a pleasant, friendly smile, and continue smiling as you interact with them.

3. Give them a sincere, enthusiastic handshake and consider it a privilege of representing Christ to them.

4. Look warmly into their eyes as you meet them communicating a genuine interest.

5. Give them a genuine, heartfelt compliment or positive comment.

6. Look your best regardless of the circumstances.

7. Read their emotional state and respond with genuine emotion such as joy, sympathy, empathy, acceptance, and concern.

8. Practice mirroring of their gestures to increase their comfort and self-confidence.

9. Be a good listener and show special interest in what is important to them by providing appropriate affirmation.

10. People do not care how much you know until they know how much you care!

Likability

Likability is a quality that brings about a favorable regard. We tend to like people who:

1. Like us rather than dislike us.

2. Have similar values, opinions, attitudes, interests, past experiences, mutual acquaintances, reading habits, or hobbies.

3. Are friendly, pleasant, and at ease with others.

4. Know and use our names.

5. Are physically attractive and well-groomed.

6. Give us praise and compliments rather than criticism or sarcasm.

7. Are familiar to us and care about us.

8. Have a sense of humor. These people subtly change attitudes and behavior while avoiding exaggeration, put downs, puns, unexpected surprise, and silliness.

9. Have personally appealing qualities such as organization or creativity.

10. Make us feel significant and better about ourselves.

We need less posturing and more genuine charisma. Charisma was originally a religious term, meaning "of the spirit" or "inspired." It's about letting God's light shine through us. It's about a sparkle in people that money can't buy. It's an invisible energy with visible effects. To let go, to just love, is not to fade into the wallpaper. Quite the contrary, it's when we truly become bright. We're letting our own light shine.

~ Marianne Williamson

Motivation

Motivation Basics

Would it be a useful tool in ministry to better understand what makes people do what they do? Suppose you have a project for which a particular person seems well suited. Just dropping the project in his lap will almost guarantee failure unless he has the necessary skills and is motivated for the assignment. Knowing how to assess and motivate an individual will help set the scene for success. You will avoid frustration and experience fulfillment if you apply the principles of motivation in your ministry.

A salesman contacts you and asks to demonstrate his latest vacuum cleaner. You have recently purchased a new vacuum cleaner, but he offers a nice gift if you allow a demonstration of his product. So with your permission, he dumps dirt on your carpet and asks you to clean the area with your recently purchased vacuum cleaner. You thoroughly clean it. He then shows you the empty dirt chamber of his vacuum and begins to clean the area you have just vacuumed. He opens the dirt chamber of his machine and shows you an unbelievable accumulation of dirt extracted from your carpet by his machine. He notes your child is being exposed to dirt and bacteria as he crawls around on the dirty carpet. He offers you a special deal and a convenient payment plan. The next thing you know, you are the proud owner of a new vacuum cleaner. He motivated you to buy his product by creating a strong sense of need which triggered a powerful desire to have what he was selling. Motivation is associated with the Latin word *movere* meaning to move. Motivation occurs when we are moved by something or someone. Motives are within us and must be activated to create motivation. They generate a sense of need and want in a person to produce motivation.

Since people are motivated by their wants and needs, the stronger the wants, the greater the motivation. Unmet needs and wants are powerful motivators. Conversely, when needs are met, motivation decreases. A leader is necessarily one who motivates others toward a goal, excites, stimulates, provokes, and moves to action.

Motivators

There are twelve intrinsic human needs. The level of desire for their fulfillment in each individual is a critical factor in the motivation process. Since these are applicable to all people, learn what motivates a person and then assign a rating on a scale of 1-10 for each category. Plot these ratings on the graph found on page 99.

Need for achievement or mastery

There must be satisfaction in accomplishing something challenging, exercising talents, achieving excellence, attaining success, and becoming self-motivated. Provide new and challenging assignments.

Need for power

There must be satisfaction from influencing and controlling others, being able to lead and persuade, impacting situations, and being elevated to a position of power, leadership, and authority. Provide opportunity to influence others, make decisions, and direct projects.

Need for affiliation

There must be satisfaction from interacting with others in a friendly and sociable manner. Provide numerous opportunities for interaction and communication.

Need for autonomy

There must be satisfaction in experiencing freedom and independence operating without close supervision. Allow him opportunity to make choices, set schedules, work independently, and be given responsibility for assigned work.

Need for esteem

There must be satisfaction from receiving recognition and having work acknowledged and appreciated. Give ample feedback, public recognition, and tokens of appreciation, attention, and respect.

Need for security

There must be satisfaction from job security, a steady income, job perks, and a safe secure working environment. Create an environment in which there is predictability, eliminating uncertainty and risk.

Need for equity

There must be satisfaction from being treated fairly and ethically. This person does much comparing and is easily discouraged. Provide standards and consistency and eliminate favoritism, inequity, or partiality.

Need for self-actualization

There must be satisfaction in personal growth, self-development, and creativity. Provide new experiences to help him reach his potential and take on challenges to further develop his potential.

Need for fulfilled physical drives

These include hunger, thirst, survival, health, safety, sex, sleep, bodily comfort, and freedom from pain. Encourage him to find fulfillment of these basic needs which can easily be neglected by those busy in service to the Lord.

Emotional drives

These include pleasure, approval, curiosity, competition, respect for deity, sympathy, empathy, loyalty, devotion, love, affection, compliance, and freedom from emotional tension. Be aware of the emotions that drive people as these can affect your ministry.

Habits

These bad habits include such things as smoking, drinking, lying, stealing, cheating, and taking drugs. Be aware of the strong desires that can provide motivation to people.

Other unique needs

These include pathological and idiosyncratic peculiarities.

Since motivation is closely tied to both needs and wants, the motivator must understand what the one being motivated really wants.

Styles of Processing

People engage in several styles of processing information and situations. It is their way of approaching life. It forms the foundation for how their will is moved and how they make decisions and choices ranging from what color to paint the bedroom to what to eat for lunch. Some people use all four of the following styles of processing, therefore it is important to consider not only the styles but also the order in which the styles are used. For example, when approached by someone needing help with a project, are you most inclined to first be quiet and think about what they're saying (thinking) or do you want to sit down and talk extensively about the idea (talking)? Would you bring up objections right away (feeling) or would you pull out a piece of paper and begin jotting notes immediately (doing)?

The style of doing is characterized by a need to move forward accomplishing things without delay. The style of thinking is characterized by the need to methodically think things through, to gather sufficient information, and to take time to process. The style of feeling is characterized by the need to resolve negative feelings and to feel good about the project. The style of talking is characterized by the need to talk things out and to have another actively listen.

The Skills/Will Assessment [1]

Before application of the *Skills/Will Assessment,* the leader needs to assess the involved person's qualification, ability, and desire in accomplishing a given task. This assessment shows what kind of motivation and assistance is necessary to help someone accomplish a task. Using his *skill* level in the areas relating to the task (experience, training, and understanding) as well as his *will* (desire to achieve, incentive, and confidence) as a gauge, one can determine which approach will be most suitable. Giving someone too much or not enough direction could be the result of not knowing how to apply the *Skills/Will Assessment.*

DIRECT

1. Invest time early on in coaching and skill development.
2. Answer questions and explain.
3. Provide all of the necessary direction.
4. Allow time for learning.
5. Provide education and training in identified areas of weakness.

DELEGATE

1. Provide freedom to do the job by setting objectives not methods.
2. Remember to praise and to not ignore.
3. Provide parameters.
4. Encourage follower to involve himself in the decision-making process and to share his thinking.
5. Take appropriate risks by resisting over-management and providing more stretching tasks.

DIRECT

Low Skill
High Will

DELEGATE

High Skill
High Will

COACH

Low Skill
Low Will

ENERGIZE

High Skill
Low Will

COACH

1. Build the will by providing clear briefing.
2. Identify motivations.
3. Develop a vision of future performance.
4. Motivate using techniques taught in chapter.
5. Build the skills by coaching and training.
6. Structure tasks (defining problems, visualizing ideal outcome, identifying and brainstorming obstacles.)
7. Supervise closely with tight control and clear rules and deadlines.
8. Provide frequent feedback.

ENERGIZE

1. Identify reasons for having a low will looking at personal factors.
2. Identify task management styles.
3. Motivate the person using the techniques taught in this chapter, especially appealing to their needs as developing their wants.
4. Give feedback frequently.
5. Create personal desire for the task.

Motivational Cycles

A cycle is a series of events that recur regularly usually leading back to the starting point. This is especially applicable in the area of motivation. Your follower can be in one of three cycles: a positive productive motivation cycle, a neutral under-motivated motivation cycle, or a negative de-motivation cycle.

Negative De-Motivation Cycle

Even a high skill, high will person can get into a negative de-motivation cycle. It is important to identify the cycle in which you find a particular person at a particular time. If you find a person in the **negative de-motivation cycle**, work on confidence.

♦ Work on developing his vision of how good he can be at completing a specific task or playing a particular role.

♦ Recognize his improved performance, even if in an area not critical to his main activity. The praise and encouragement can have positive benefits in other areas.

♦ Identify and remove de-motivators.

♦ Provide encouragement and coaching with positive reinforcement.

People can be caught up in a cycle of sameness. This is represented as a **neutral under-motivational cycle** where they are merely going through the motions.

Neutral Under-Motivation Cycle

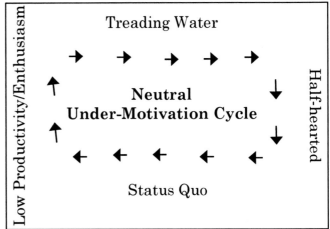

♦ Challenge the underachiever caught up in the neutral under-motivation cycle.

♦ Develop a plan to create vision and engender enthusiasm in the underachiever. Find and remove de-motivators and add incentives as motivators. Positive change is essential in motivating the underachiever.

Positive Productive Motivation Cycle

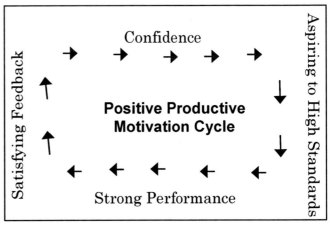

Work on praise and positive reinforcement if he is in the **positive cycle**.

♦ Identify his need for support and/or training and see that he gets it.

♦ Know what motivates your followers and use the correct motivational keys.

Personality Types

Four personality types can be illustrated by four different breeds of dogs, the pit bull, the poodle, the bloodhound, and the golden retriever. The descriptive characteristics of each personality type closely resembles the description of that particular dog. The chart below illustrates each personality type and provides full descriptions of each of the types.

The motivators and de-motivators are listed for each. From a motivational point of view, it is important to understand that the most successful pathway to motivating each type of personality is different. The most effective way to motivate each of the four different types is listed as "Needs" below.

The Pit Bull — Active task-oriented

<u>Descriptors</u>: Dominant, direct, demanding, leader, independent, active, confident, aggressive, decisive, bossy, rational, strong-willed, impatient, driven, opinionated, hard worker, courageous, unsympathetic, judgmental

<u>Motivated by</u>: Challenge & accomplishment

<u>De-motivated by</u>: Lack of action and lack of accomplishment

<u>Needs</u>: Choice instead of ultimatums, direct answers, and task orientation

The Poodle — Active people-oriented

<u>Descriptors</u>: Attention seeking, inspiring, impressing, inducing, talkative, humorous, friendly, engaging, emotional, cheerful, spontaneous, energetic, optimistic, fun-loving, exaggerates, naïve, interrupts, self-conscious, disorganized, curious

<u>Motivated by</u>: Fun, recognition, and feeling good

<u>De-motivated by</u>: Negativity and pessimism

<u>Needs</u>: Social involvement, recognition of abilities and opportunities to help

The Bloodhound — Passive task-oriented

<u>Descriptors</u>: Competent, cautious, calculating, accurate, analytical, perfectionist, orderly, scheduled, practical, musical, artistic, sensitive, inquisitive, serious, organized, moody, suspicious, hard to please, pessimistic

<u>Motivated by</u>: Information, appeals to reason, and time to think

<u>De-motivated by</u>: Lack of information and inadequate time to gather and process information

<u>Needs</u>: Details, precise planning, clearly defined tasks, and carefully calculated risks

The Golden Retriever — Passive people-oriented

<u>Descriptors</u>: Submissive, steady, security-oriented, sympathetic, kind, calm, pleasant, agreeable, flexible, responsible, diplomatic, administrative, good with people, reliable, shy, loyal, idealistic, avoids conflict, slow to act

<u>Motivated by</u>: Harmony, support, relationships

<u>De-motivated by</u>: Conflict and harsh confrontation

<u>Needs</u>: Consistency, support, own pace, time to adjust to change, and friendliness

Motivational Assessment Chart

The Twelve Intrinsic Human Needs

	Achieve/ Master	Power	Affiliation	Autonomy	Esteem	Security	Justice	Self-Actualization	Physical	Emotional	Habits	Unique Needs
10												
9												
8												
7												
6												
5												
4												
3												
2												
1												
0												

See "Motivators" on pages 94 and 95 for a complete explanation of each of the above categories.

The "Motivational Assessment Chart" should be used as follows:

1. Plot on the grid above the degree of intensity for each of the twelve motivational needs and transfer the results to the *Motivational Profile Worksheet* on the following page. Next carefully assess the things the person most wants and transfer them to the summary page. The correct assessment of the person's needs and wants is the foundation of his motivational profile.

2. Determine the principal personality characteristics of the person and apply the appropriate motivators to them based on the pit bull, poodle, bloodhound, or golden retriever designations. Few people are 100% of any of the categories. Most have a combination of the characteristics of two or three. Plug in the most prominent motivators into the profile.

3. Associated with the personality characteristics is the examination of whether the person is principally a doer, thinker, feeler, or talker. If the person is a doer, he will be primed for action. If the person is a thinker, he must be convinced by appeals to reason. If he is a feeler, he must feel good about the assignment and need to be purged of negative feelings. If he is a talker, he will need to talk out the issues involved.

4. Determine where the person is on the *Skills/Will Assessment* and apply the appropriate method of handling him based upon his need for coaching, delegation, direction, or energization.

5. Analyze where the person is in the motivational cycle—negative, neutral, or positive and apply the appropriate strategy to achieve maximum impact.

Assess all of the factors above and complete the person's motivational profile. Use it as a tool to move them toward the desired outcome. Use the techniques taught in this chapter to create desire and motivation.

Motivational Profile Worksheet

_____'s assessment of wants shows _____

_____

What are his strongest wants and desires? _____

_____

_____

_____

Personality Type

_____'s personality type is **a pit bull, poodle, bloodhound, a golden retriever.**

What style of motivation will work best for him? _____

_____

_____

_____

_____

Preferred Style of Processing and Relating

_____'s preferred style of processing and relating is   Doing
        Thinking
        Feeling
        Talking

Comments _____

_____

_____

_____

Results of Skills/Will Assessment

_____'s assessment reveals the need to: Direct (low skill and high will)
       Delegate (high skill and high will)
       Coach (low skill and low will)
       Energize (high skill and low will)

Application of the *Skills/Will Factor*: _____

_____

_____

_____

Motivational Cycle

_____ is in the: Negative de-motivational cycle
       Neutral under-motivational cycle
       Positive productive motivational cycle

The following needs have been identified: _____

_____

_____

_____

Motivational action plan: _____

_____

_____

_____

Employee Motivation On the Job

The following is a work-related self-test to discover some of the important desires which motivate us. Assess yourself or others to learn more about strengths and weaknesses, to identify important desires, and to find what motivates you or others on the job.

Please rank order these factors for your personal motivation on a 5-point scale (1=low 5=high). General categories of concern include the following:

_____ Respect for you as a person and worker

_____ Freedom to accomplish work

_____ Delegation of necessary authority

_____ Delegation of work to you

_____ Involved in planning one's own work

_____ Responsibilities

_____ Extent of supervision

_____ Nature of supervision

_____ Suitable authority being provided

_____ Detailed guidance

_____ Adequate supervision

_____ Mentoring

_____ Coaching

_____ Quality of work

_____ Job description

_____ Your personal job title

_____ Interesting job assignments

_____ New and challenging assignments

_____ Performance ratings

_____ Personal recognition

_____ Prospects of career development

_____ Opportunities for promotion

_____ Personal growth and development

_____ Personal achievement

_____ Job security

_____ Salary and benefits

_____ Social functions

_____ Working conditions

_____ Cooperativeness

_____ Getting along with coworkers

_____ Praise and recognition

_____ Company policies

_____ Job satisfaction

_____ Knowing what is going on

_____ Constructive feedback

_____ Organization's structure and process

_____ Being given clear objectives

_____ Attending high-level meetings

_____ Flexible work schedule

_____ Working alone

_____ Working with other people

_____ Being treated fairly

_____ Opportunity given to air grievances

_____ Having more authority

_____ Acquiring knowledge and skill

_____ New experiences with self-discovery

_____ Accomplishing what is challenging

_____ Freedom and independence

_____ Agreement with objectives of the organization

_____ Consistent standards with equal application

_____ Creativity

_____ Other (specify) _____

Note the factors ranked with numbers 4 or 5. These are important work motivators for you and those working under you.

Employee De-motivators On the Job
(Results of Managers' Survey)

In a survey of 4,000 managers, these reasons were given for lack of motivation in their employees. Clearly, these were considered to be powerful de-motivators.

1. They didn't know what they were supposed to do.

2. They didn't know how to do it.

3. They didn't know why they should do it.

4. Obstacles were beyond their control.

5. They didn't think it would work.

6. They thought their way was better.

7. They admitted to having a poor attitude.

8. They exceeded their personal limits and were incapable of doing the job.

9. They didn't have enough time to do it.

10. They were working on wrong priority items.

11. Because of inadequate feedback, they thought they were accomplishing what they were supposed to accomplish.

12. Job performance was sabotaged by poor management.

13. Personal problems interfered with their job performance.[2]

Motivation Strategy—Assess, Plan, Do

1. Seek understanding of how the person responds based upon his needs, wants, styles of relating, and personality type. This will help you determine the best-fit approaches to motivating him.

2. Apply the *Skills/Will Assessment* to determine what kind of direction and assistance you will need to provide him for each particular assignment.

3. Pay continuing attention to where he is in the cycles of motivation and apply the appropriate remedies if he moves into a negative or neutral cycle of motivation.

4. Create appropriate expectations so he knows what is expected of him.

5. If you are motivating an employee, use the *Employee Motivators On the Job* of work related desires and list of *Employee De-motivators on the Job* to meet his needs and to help him accomplish maximum results.

6. Show him the need and create desire within him.

7. Create vision and produce mutually agreed-upon goals.

8. Provide much positive reinforcement and timely constructive criticism.

9. Strive to satisfy his needs.

10. Always attempt to treat the person fairly.

God gives us dreams a size too big so that we can grow into them.

~Anonymous

11. Provide incentives and rewards for performance.

12. If you are moving a person toward a common goal, emphasize what is in it for him or what the benefit will be.

13. Learn what works and what doesn't, then pursue the successful tactics and avoid the unsuccessful ones.

14. Overcome barriers, discouragement, and set backs.

15. Use the *Motivational Contracting Checklist* and *Coaching Checklist*.

Motivational Contracting Checklist

Since the key to motivation is to make others want to and want to be willing to take action, contracting is an effective tool in accomplishing that process by using the following steps.

___Create two-way understanding.

___Raise expectations and provide both the means and method of attaining.

___Get commitment through agreement and contracting.

___Create goals and link them to the fulfillment of needs, wants, and desires.

___Deliver a personal challenge and break it into action steps.

___Create a supportive environment.

___Include the following motivation steps.
1. Model
2. Mentor/Coach
3. Monitor/Measure with feedback
4. Motivate
5. Multiply

___Provide inspiration and support.

___Give recognition and affirmation.

___Reassess as necessary.

Coaching Checklist

Establish trust

___Show you have their best interest at heart.

___Establish a mutual benefit relationship.

___Help them understand that if their individual goals are realized, the organization's goals will be realized.

___Show that you care about them and their reaching their goals.

Set expectations

___Be specific in instructing them concerning what they are supposed to do.

___Have them establish their own performance objectives.

___Put the goals and objectives in writing.

___Get an agreement on what they will do by when (timeline with deadlines).

Always be teaching

___Teach explicitly by pointers and tips or implicitly by stories and parables.

___Relate material in a way that is always understandable.

___Engage interest and avoid boredom.

___Collect and file stories and anecdotes to be used to evoke specific emotions for various given situations (admonishment, inspiration, tears, or laughter).

Problem solve

___Link individual performance and the organization's performance.

___Pull the team together and create team spirit and teamwork.

___Focus on the task at hand.

___Point out what they are doing wrong and help them correct it.

___Help them to realize what they are capable of doing.

___Give direction to overcome obstacles and avoid problems.

___Ask each person what kind of help he needs (time, resources, staff).

___Provide encouragement and affirm their value.

___Intervene in personality conflicts.

___Establish and maintain morale.

___Look for cause(s) of what's wrong.

___Keep small problems from getting bigger.

Serve to motivate

___Establish an environment of excellence and affirm their value.

___Apply factors gleaned from the summary page of assessment of motivators.

___Develop and maintain momentum.

___Know when to push and when to hold back.

___Know your people and what it takes to motivate each and when. Know when to nudge, excite, and invite. Know when to scold or reprimand and when to encourage or provide recognition. Practice this general formula: prod the slacker, encourage the struggler, and recognize the effort and performance of each.

Deliver discipline

___Establish rules of conduct and quality control and maintain standards by establishing consequences of behavior.

___Pull people aside for slacking, selfishness, lack of teamwork, or not sharing information.

___Discipline should be based upon trust.

___Focus on behavior not personality.

___Be even handed.

___Effective discipline leads to self-discipline.

___Make tough decisions despite your own personal inconvenience.

Recognize achievement

___Let people know they've done a good job.

___Mention names in writing and in public.

___Remember the difference between recognition (acknowledgement) and reward (benefits).

___Recognition inspires confidence, achievement, and effort.

While some use coaching and mentoring interchangeably, there is a difference. Mentors focus on the person, providing support for their individual growth, maturity, and development. Coaches focus on performance and tasks. A mentor is a friend, advisor, colleague, coach, teacher, encourager, motivator, example, model, and disciplinarian all in one.

Motivational Tips

1. Motivation comes from within and is best accomplished when people motivate themselves by accessing the right motivators.

2. Motivation is often best accomplished through the development of mutual agreements.

3. Self-discipline is an important factor in accomplishing successful motivation and is something which may be accessed by any person at any time.

4. Listening and learning about the person you want to motivate are important factors. Seek input from those you desire to motivate.

5. An optimistic and positive attitude goes a long way in assisting the process.

6. Emotions, desires, and attitudes are critical components of motivation.

7. A mutual bond of trust is very helpful.

8. By managing agreements you can manage people. Use these questions to illicit accurate information.

   Do you agree with this plan of action and are you willing to totally commit yourself to it?

   Do you have everything you need to carry out the plan? If not, what resources and support do you require?

   How can I best assist you through this process?

   What schedule needs to be developed to assess progress and refine the plan if necessary?

9. Demand results not activity. Outcome based productivity should be the focus with nothing less than satisfactory results accepted.

10. The Pareto principle states that 20% of your people will produce 80% of the work. Focus on the 20%.

11. Follow a purpose-driven model by making sure the purposes of the organization are clearly understood and acted upon.

12. Attempt to boost the self-esteem of those you need to motivate whenever possible.

13. Positive reinforcement is a powerful motivational tool.

14. Accountability is essential to the motivation process.

15. Always enlist the best people possible for any task.

16. Follow the principles of the <u>One Minute Manager</u>: Set goals, praise, and reprimand when needed.

17. Whenever possible label change as an experiment. People are more comfortable with reversible change than irreversible change.

18. Help people to feel that they are an important part of any effort.

19. Face the biggest challenges first when your energy and focus are greatest.

20. Personally set the right example. Model the behavior you want to see in others.

21. Reframe difficulties into problems to be solved.

22. Use the motivational strategy employed by Jesus Christ with his disciples: Model, Mentor, Monitor, Motivate, and Multiply.

Self-Motivation Techniques

♦ Break goals down into manageable parts.

♦ Commit to a certain number of minutes each day.

♦ Provide reminders and affirmation to yourself.

♦ Enlist assistance of others and put into place an accountability partner.

♦ Publish your plans to others for scrutinization.

♦ Put goals in writing.

♦ Establish specific deadlines.

♦ Review and adjust goals and process regularly.

♦ Link tasks to pleasurable activities.

♦ Reward yourself.

♦ Take breaks, relax, and don't overdo.

♦ Delegate when necessary.

Recommended Scripture References

Mind to work, Nehemiah 4:6
Motivated by own thoughts, Job 20:2
Lord's motivations, Psalm 20:4; 37:3-5
Examine my thoughts, Psalm 26:2
Seeking highest position, Psalm 27:4
Delight in doing God's will, Psalm 40:8
God fulfills His purpose, Psalm 57:2
Whole-hearted desire, Psalm 119:10
Follow way of truth, Psalm 119:30
Seeking greatest values, Psalm 119:36-37
Hastening to obey, Psalm 119:57-64
Vain unless the Lord builds it, Psalm 127:1
Desire to fulfill destiny, Psalm 132:1-5
Thoughts known by God, Psalm 139:1-4
The end of the lazy, the diligent, Proverbs 10:4
Knowing what is right, Isaiah 51:7
Call to discipleship, Matthew 4:20-22
Anger as bad as murder, Matthew 5:21-22
Mouth speaks from the heart, Luke 6:43-45
Jesus motivated to the cross, Luke 23:35-39
Satan's motivation, John 13:2
Outreach to others motivated by love, John 21:15-18
Ministry given of God, Acts 20:22-24
Constrained to preach, 1 Corinthians 9:16-18
All for God's glory, 1 Corinthians 10:31
Message must be preached, 1 Corinthians 15:10
Steadfast in difficulties, 1 Corinthians 15:57-58
Motivated by love, 1 Corinthians 16:13-14,
His good will, Ephesians 1:5
Walking in love, Ephesians 5:1-2
Doing the will of the Lord, Ephesians 6:5-8
Forgetting the past, pressing on, Philippians 3:12-16
Do it in His name, Colossians 3:17, 3:23-24
Faith and love motivate, 1 Thessalonians 1:3, 2:7-9
Motivated to be like Christ, 1 Thessalonians 4:11-12
God counts you worthy, 2 Thessalonians 1:11
Purpose in life, 2 Timothy 3:10
Godly life, Titus 2:8
Faith motivated, Hebrews 11:8, 27
Running to win, Hebrews 12:1-2
Desire to do right, Hebrews 13:21
Be a doer of the Word, James 1:22-25
Ready for action, 1 Peter 1:13
God searches the mind and heart, Revelation 2:23

Persuasion

Persuasion and the Ministry

Persuasion is the ability to influence people. It flows from a combination of skills which anyone can productively use. We live our lives with many influences vying for our attention, attempting to get us to see things a certain way or getting us to do what they want us to do. Some persuaders are subtle and hidden, such as lighting arrangements or the location of items on grocery store shelves to entice us to buy a certain product. Others are obvious and direct like the salesman pressuring us to buy one certain item. Understanding and using the tools and principles of persuasion can be a valuable asset to any preacher.

Godly use of persuasion is not manipulating or taking advantage of someone but the sincere and honest attempt to influence and motivate them for Jesus Christ. In Acts 26:28 King Agrippa said to the apostle Paul after he had astutely witnessed to him, *Almost thou persuadest me to be a Christian.* When you see Paul preaching and witnessing in the New Testament, you see a master persuader at work. Take the time to read the book of Philemon and examine the skills Paul employed as he attempted to persuade his good friend Philemon to accept and restore his runaway slave Onesimus. Certainly Paul never minimized nor neglected the power and influence of the Holy Spirit. Pray as if everything depends upon God and work as if everything depends upon you. By the power and wisdom of God, we should persuade men.

Seven Steps to Persuasion

1. Discover their wants and needs.
2. Build rapport. Be genuine. Be real. Help them to like you, trust you, believe you, need what you have to offer, want it now, and feel they have easy access to you and to your message.
3. Present the main idea and explain why it is important.
4. Use the ten laws of persuasion with the appropriate information taken from the *Ethos-Pathos-Logos* Chart.
5. Demonstrate the most appealing benefit and dire consequence if they fail to act.
6. Determine barriers.
   - Ask questions like "What would I have to do to convince you that taking this action would really help you?" Follow up with, "Is there any reason other than _____ to keep you from _____?"
   - Learn their values in order to relate better to them:

     Means values = things or conditions used to reach end values (cars, houses, jobs, travel, marriage)

     End values = states (love, excitement, peace, security, freedom)
   - Listen for clues about a person's means values and end values; see how he is currently striving to satisfy those needs.

     For example: End value = *Peace*

     Means to achieve peace = *Drugs*

     Show how a relationship with Christ can better satisfy those needs.

     If you notice these values in someone to whom you are witnessing, explain how Christ gives you peace in your life.

     It is your job to persuade others to accept the truth of Scripture. Preachers and teachers have similar values like social and personal morality but use different ways to achieve those goals.
   - Avoid using *don't* statements.
   - Use *might* or *maybe.*
     Example: This might make a real difference in your health.

♦ Use reverse psychology phrasing of statements.
Example: I wouldn't tell you to _____ be cause ____, or I could _____ but I won't.

♦ Start asking questions to which they can respond *yes* in order to establish a pattern of positive responses.

7. Restate the main idea. Refocus their attention upon it. Reinforce the benefits of acting on it immediately.

Research has uncovered the following ten laws of persuasion which can be universally applied to any persuasive situation.[1]

The Ten Laws of Persuasion
Specific examples included with each

Reciprocity	One feels obligated toward someone who gives him something of value such as a free set of steak knives for listening to a sales pitch.
Contrast	Place things that are relatively different together so that the differences seem greater at close comparison. The salesman proves his vacuum performs better than yours.
Friends	People are more likely to respond positively to those they perceive to have their best interest in mind. A football player allows a coach to criticize him.
Expectancy	People are more likely to respond when a respected person expects them to produce a certain result or outcome. A beloved friend expects you to purchase his product.
Association	People respond favorably when someone they like or respect such as a sports star endorses a product such as a specific brand of razor blades.
Consistency	People are more likely to have a stronger commitment when it is somehow expressed. A person who has written his testimony is more likely to stand firm in his faith because of the consistency factor.
Scarcity	Something is more valuable if scarce such as a limited edition or limited seating at events such as the Super Bowl.
Conformity	Peer pressure has power to influence in that we tend to conform to the norm of the group. (Example: "The Emperor's New Clothes")
Power	Knowledge equals both power and authority such as people taking notice of Albert Einstein's observations about things other than physics.
Time Element	Sense of urgency is felt due to a deadline such as an offer which will expire in 30 minutes requiring an immediate response.

Ultimately, persuasion comes down to these three things:

1. **Ethos (Ethical):** convincing proof of the speaker and his credibility.

2. **Logos (Logical):** convincing proof of the message or words and facts presented.

3. **Pathos (Emotional):** convincing proof of the emotions and motivational appeal.

The following page provides an overview of the contributing factors to each of these elements of persuasion.

Ethos	Logos	Pathos
Creating a favorable first impression: primarily achieved through appearance, grooming and deportment; occurs in the first few seconds of an encounter	**Refocus, reframe, or change beliefs:** appealing to a belief already held by another, slightly modifying the belief to permit the acceptance of your presentation, or changing the belief itself if warranted	**Convincing another of the benefits** to themselves, their family, or society by following a course of action
Credibility: reasonable grounds we possess for being believed	**Get and hold attention:** focusing of the mind and interest upon something or someone	**Fear of not doing it:** pain or loss of missed opportunity
Competence: capability and knowledge to perform the task at hand	**Meet needs:** making of something to be necessary, needed or wanted	**Get the camel's nose in the tent** by persuading them to take a small step first and then lead them to take a bigger step
Expertise: mastery and proficiency so as to be considered an expert	**Create wants:** create desire for a product or thing	**Creating a favorable environment** which will influence the person and the outcome
Likeability: possession of personal qualities that causes one to be highly regarded	**Effective presentation:** verbal and/or visual display of an idea or series of ideas	**Band wagon effect:** others are on board and you should be so also
Status: rank in a hierarchy of esteem	**Proofs:** evidence to back up a claim	**Emotional appeals**
Trustworthiness: quality of having the confidence of others	**Arguments:** a series of convincing statements which lead from a premise to a conclusion	**Appeal to inner motivators** like fear, hope, love, loyalty, achievement, power, or fairness
Composure: unflappability and calmness under pressure	**Framing:** the context in which something is presented or displayed	**Use of time and pressure** to motivate a choice or action
Character: reputation of moral excellence and integrity	**Word choices:** careful and purposeful selection of words for maximum impact.	**Use of their imagination**
Credentials: documents or testimonials to show entitlement, credit, or power	**Word pictures:** painting of a picture verbally through an impact-producing story	**Engaging the senses:** cause them to see, hear, feel, taste, or smell something either in reality or in their mind through mental imagery
Appearance: how we look to others	**Specific action steps** given	**Use of pain/pleasure principle**
Grooming: to look neat and attractive	**Endorsements** from others	**Creation of excitement**
Rapport building: establishment of affinity through possessing things in common	**The ability to get into their heads** to think, feel, or know what's on their minds	**Powerful testimonials from others**
Testimony: evidence or witness to authenticity and experience	**Questions convincingly answered or anticipated and answered before being asked**	**Use of favorable association**
Associations: connection with others which may enhance the person	**Comparisons:** put ideas side-by-side to make one favorable	**Counterfactual thinking:** asking someone to consider alternative realities that could become true if they made a different choice
Common ground: identification of mutual interests and relations to others	**Relevance:** germane and practical application of ideas, products, or concepts	**Union of fear with effective persuasion** to achieve maximum effectiveness
Values: the things which are most important to us	**Bold promise:** delivering what you say you will and convincing them that you will	**Use of crisis factor:** using someone's crisis to increase acceptance of your product or service
Beliefs: conviction of the truth of someone or something; confidence and trust	**Overcoming resistance:** anticipated regret of a decision or something that infringes upon our personal choice or freedom	**Impact illustrations** or mechanisms which connect with the person and create a powerful impact on them
Authority: both position and power	**Instructions** given so others will follow	
Environment: prevailing circumstances	**Convince:** to prove, or overcome by argument	
Publication: evidence of expertise	**Creation of curiosity:** arousing of interest or inquiry	
	Application of the laws of influence	
	Adding weight to the *yes* side of the equation	
	Subtracting weight from the *no* side	
	Successfully asking for what you want or need	

Contributing Factors to Successful Persuasion

The persuasion process is best illustrated by the scale of justice. On the left side of the scale is the negative which consists of all the reasons to say no or not be persuaded. On the right side of the scale are all of the reasons for deciding in a favorable way and saying yes. The successful persuasion process may be accomplished by taking enough weight off the negative side to tip the scale, or adding enough weight on the positive side to tip the scale, or a combination of both.

Scale-Tipping Persuasion Principles

A person's beliefs act as a filter through which they interpret all things. It is very helpful to the persuasion process if you understand the belief structure of the person you are trying to persuade. This knowledge will help you understand what is on each side of the scale and will provide insight into the action that must be taken to tip it.

Beliefs may be strong or weak. Very weak beliefs are easier to change; strong beliefs are very difficult to change. Most religious beliefs tend to be on the stronger side because they are often foundational beliefs upon which others may rest.

People resent having their beliefs questioned or challenged. However, beliefs may be changed more quickly when people are experiencing one of three circumstances: a crisis in their life, a significant frustration, or overwhelming stress.

These circumstances provide an imbalance in their life which causes them to be more open to a solution which will produce fulfillment and emotional release.

Cause and effect evidence tends to work better in changing beliefs.

Use questions to challenge their beliefs and present strong evidence to help them see your point on their own.

Provide proofs through Scripture, testimonies, and convincing information. There are five stages in the belief process.

Stage 1 — Rote repetition
This occurs when one parrots back what was heard with little conviction.

Stage 2 — Identification
This occurs when a person embraces a particular belief because someone else has taught it to them, such as a child who identifies himself with a particular church because his parents are members.

Stage 3 — Questioning
In this stage the person must integrate his belief into his life and must deal with the challenging questions that inevitably arise in doing so.

Stage 4 — Testing
At this stage beliefs are tested in the crucible of life, circumstance by circumstance, to see if they are true and will really work.

Stage 5 — Owning
Now the person owns the belief as his own with conviction. It has developed into a settled belief and is probably strong.

Rapport

The persuasion process usually involves people accepting you as well as your idea. Persuasion does not occur in a vacuum. To establish rapport there needs to be affinity with the person you are persuading. Look for areas of common interests to share. Be appropriately dressed and groomed to make a positive impression because you never get a second chance to make a good first impression. Trust is a very important element of rapport. It is highly unlikely we will be convinced by someone whom we do not trust.

Respect, empathy, and genuineness are excellent rapport builders. Credibility rests upon a foundation of expertise and trustworthiness.

Curiosity

The creation of curiosity is an important pathway to persuasion. Create curiosity by asking appropriate questions which will serve to pique the interest of the one you are trying to persuade. Curiosity has been called the most important emotion in the persuasion process. Consider curiosity producing questions as tools and use them much the same way as a carpenter skillfully uses his hammer or saw.

Persuasion Formula

The persuasion process has been reduced to the following formula:

Persuasion = Ethos + Logos + Pathos

It is a good idea to familiarize yourself with the processes included in the previous chart and use them as necessary to persuade. Carefully review the material in the chart under "Logos" and "Pathos" for specific techniques in persuasion.

Conveyance of Credibility

Credibility and authority can be conveyed from one person or organization to another person or organization. This is seen when a successful pastor, respected by another congregation, is asked to recommend someone to fill their pulpit or candidate for the pastorate of their church.

Anti-Persuasion Barrier

Most of us have a barrier which keeps us from being easily persuaded and protects us in a variety of ways. It acts as radar to keep out harmful or detrimental things. Much in the same way a stealth bomber easily slips through the barrier created by radar protection, so some things slip right through the anti-persuasion barrier. These include word pictures, stories, and questions.

Jesus rarely spoke without telling a story. Stories tend to slip through the anti-persuasion barrier because they affect the right hemisphere of the brain (pictorial) as well as the left (logical/verbal). Asking questions also tends to bypass the resistance provided by the anti-persuasion barrier. Indirect persuaders include statements framed in a manner such as:

> "You might want to...."
> "Would you be surprised if I told you...."
> "Imagine what would happen if...."
> "You may not know...."
> "How do you go about deciding...."
> "If you would choose...."
> "What is it that helps you to know whether...."

Certain words tend to be more powerful than others in persuasion. One of the most powerful words used in persuasion is the word *because*. Studies have shown that when someone makes a request and adds a *because* with a reason to follow, persuasion is much greater. Other powerfully persuasive words include:

Now	Why
Please	How
Results	Secrets
Proven	Benefits
Guarantee	Solution
Safety	Easy
Free	Proven
Yes	Love
Fast	**Because**

Also, when asking someone to do something, use *I need* as a vital part of your appeal. Work these words into your vocabulary and use them in the process of persuasion.

Outcome-Based Focus

As you plan the persuasive process, begin by thinking about the outcome you desire and then work backward to put together your evidence, proofs, arguments, persuasive techniques, and attention grabbers as contributors to the desired outcome.

Association

Anything positive and desirable to the person you are persuading will be beneficial to the persuasive process. Emotions are powerful movers when they are touched in a presentation. It is essential to try to include emotional appeal in your persuasion. You can find specific information on this type of appeal in the "Pathos" column on page 108.

Inner Dialogue

Most people have an internal dialogue whereby they question what you are doing or trying to do. It is helpful to keep this in mind as you begin the persuasion process. These inner dialogue questions sound like this: What are you trying to do and why? Why should I believe you? What's in it for me?

It is a good idea to address these questions in some way during the process of persuasion. Nothing takes the place of personal believability. Your presentation must be both believable and relevant.

Pleasure-Pain Principle

Far more people are motivated to avoid pain rather than to seek pleasure. It is expedient to dually emphasize the dire consequences of not acting in addition to the benefits of doing what you are asking. In business, a cost/benefit analysis can be used to cover both aspects of a presentation. This explains why more people are concerned about losing what they already have versus getting something they don't have. People tend to act in their own best interest and the pleasure-pain principle is clearly filled with self-interest. While it is true that people often want what others have, they also have a significant fear of loss and the threat of pain.

Impact illustrations are powerful convincers. They have the specific purpose of cutting through resistance and convincing the person being persuaded to take action. They draw in the listener and literally change the moment. These illustrations are sometimes called a transformation mechanism. They put people in a suggestive state and create a receptive atmosphere. They are metaphors which are a means of making sense and are physical, pictorial, persuasive, and memorable. Additionally, they are powerful because they are crafted to overcome a specific persuasion problem. A task (or powerful visual) is matched up with a concept to convince. Techniques such as found in the book How to Persuade People Who do Not Want to be Persuaded by Joel Bauer and Mark Levy beautifully illustrate these mechanisms and provide numerous examples.

Jesus used wonderful impact illustrations when He performed various miracles. Unfortunately, things such as raising the dead are not at our disposal. Some of the techniques that Jesus used include visual aids, physical activities, and power-filled illustrations.

Sensible Presentations

The more senses included in the persuasive process, the more effective the presentation. When people can see, hear, smell, taste, and touch something, it has far greater impact than any of these alone.

For effective persuasion, we remember:
    20% of what we read
    30% of what we hear
    40% of what we see
    50% of what we say
    60% of what we do and
    90% of what we see, hear, say, and do

Imagination

During a presentation if the imagination of the listeners can be utilized to vividly imagine an unfavorable outcome from saying no and a favorable outcome from saying yes, we have a powerful technique. Things vividly imagined become real to us. In fact, if we vividly imagine something, it can fool our nervous system into responding as if it is really happening. Have you ever had a vivid dream of falling off a tall building only to awaken with rapid heartbeat and respiration, your muscles tense, and sweat pouring out of your pores? The imagination activity in your dream fooled your nervous system into thinking it was really happening. If you were told to salivate, you would have trouble doing so. If you were asked to vividly imagine sucking on a lemon, the juice running into your mouth and tasting its sourness, you would probably begin to salivate quickly. Enlist the power of people's imaginations to improve your persuasive presentation.

Conclusion

Carefully prepare your presentation using some of the persuaders provided in this chapter and you will achieve maximum results. When trying to persuade, thorough preparation makes all the difference.

Recommended Scripture References

Moses lacked eloquence, Exodus 4:10
Lord's voice is powerful, Psalm 29:4
Thoughts that are eloquent, Psalm 92:5
Words aptly spoken, Proverbs 25:11
Use gentle words, Proverbs 25:15
Words like sharpened sword, Isaiah 49:2
Tongue that was taught, Isaiah 50:4
Bestowed eloquence, Jeremiah 1:6-10
Guided speech in difficult times, Matthew 10:19-20
Believe the Word, Mark 1:14-15
Gracious speech, Luke 4:22
Authority in preaching, Luke 4:32
Convincing others to sin, Luke 17:1
Eloquence of Jesus, Luke 19:48; John 7:46
Speech of ordinary men, Acts 4:13
Persuasion in teaching, Acts 17:2-4
Paul preaches and teaches, Acts 19:8
King couldn't be persuaded, Acts 26:28
Convincing others, Romans 9:1-2
Unnecessary eloquence, 1 Corinthians 2:1
Words with Holy Spirit power, 1 Corinthians 2:4
Love the best persuader, 1 Corinthians 13:1-13
Knowledgeable but untrained, 2 Corinthians 11:6
Use persuasive words, Colossians 2:4
Proclaim clearly, Colossians 4:3-4
Properly motivated, 1 Thessalonians 1:3
Through words and power, 1 Thessalonians 1:4-5
Speak your message clearly, 1 Thessalonians 1:8
Message to convince, 2 Timothy 4:2

Communication

There is unbelievable power in words, causing wars, divorces, and destruction, but also building kingdoms, inspiring men, and changing destinies. Mark Twain said using the right word is like the difference between lightning and a lightning bug. The Bible has much instruction about communication—what to do and what not to do.

Communication is one of the most significant God-given human abilities. It is often cited in relationships as being one of the most important factors in creating or sustaining problems or resolving them. All communication involves a sender and a receiver. It begins when the thoughts are formed in the mind of the communicator, encoded into language, received by the ear, and interpreted in the mind of the receiver through the process of decoding. The essentials of communication include what is said, the way in which it is said, and the way we look when we say it. If the message sent is not the message received, miscommunication has occurred. Research has revealed that there are three axioms of communication and four levels on which we communicate.

The Three Axioms of Communication

1. We are always communicating. It cannot be avoided. You may think that if you don't say anything you haven't communicated. By not saying anything, you may have sent any of the following strong messages: "I don't care," "I'm upset," "I don't like you," or "I think this is a waste of my time."

2. The message that was sent is not always the message that was received. When the message we intend to send is not clearly received by the hearer, it is not communication but miscommunication.

3. There are four levels of communication.

What you see and hear
What you think (based on beliefs)
What you feel
What you do

To illustrate the dynamics of communication, the story told in the author's article "Behind the 8 Ball: New Meanings, New Behaviors" shows how people can easily fall into a cycle of miscommunication. The couple referred to here as Dick and Jane presented during therapy as follows.

Dick and Jane were stuck in counterproductive patterns of behavior so deeply entrenched in their relationship that they were at risk to continue this way for a lifetime. Their behaviors alone were less significant than the meaning each partner assigned to those behaviors.

Dick worked the midnight shift leaving for work in the late evening and returned home early in the morning. Most mornings Jane was up and waiting for Dick to arrive home from work. Jane prepared coffee and a hearty breakfast which was on the table when he came through the kitchen door. They would talk as they ate and frequently lingered at the table as they enjoyed a second or third cup of coffee together.

Usually the following saga unfolded during the morning exchange. As they talked, suddenly Dick would leave the table, pour his coffee into the sink, and leave the kitchen. He went directly to the bedroom, closed the bedroom door, and climbed into bed refusing to say another word. He would turn his back toward the entrance so that if his wife followed him into the bedroom he would neither look at her nor respond to her in any way. Never did he offer an explanation for his seemingly rude and abrupt behavior. Jane became more frustrated and angry. She felt shut out and her increasing hostility resulted in serious anxiety symptoms.

The communication of the couple had fallen into a damaging pattern where each person misinterpreted the actions of the other.

The following **axioms of communication** were identified, outlined, and explained to the couple.

You cannot not communicate. The idea here is that we are always communicating—by our looks, our gestures, our facial expressions, our tone, our reference, or even our silence.

The message sent is not always the message received. What a person means to say may or may not be the message heard.

In all communication between two people, there is both a content and a relationship component. We can visualize communication as a set of tracks like a pair of railroad tracks. The first rail is the content, the message. The second rail is the relationship. On this track your communication affects the other person including their thoughts and feelings. Some communication makes the relationship better and stronger. Some communication makes the relationship poorer and weaker. Some communication is neutral. Care should be taken whenever possible to evaluate the communication in an effort to make the relationship stronger or at least to not make it weaker.

After applying the meaning of the first, second, and third axioms to Dick and Jane's morning ritual, the **four levels of communication** were then explained as they pertained to the couple's situation. These include **what is seen and heard, what is thought, what is felt, and what is done.**

Interaction Pattern Before Therapy

What Jane saw and heard = Dick poured out coffee, retired to bedroom without saying a word.

What Dick saw and heard = Dick lay in bed and heard her nagging.

What Jane thought = she interpreted Dick's actions as rejection and thought he did these things because he didn't love her.

What Dick thought = he thought she will never change. All she does is gripe, complain, and nag.

What Jane felt = she felt hurt and angry.

What Dick felt = he felt annoyed and frustrated.

What Jane did = she responded by following him into the bedroom nagging incessantly.

What Dick did = he avoided her as much as possible.

They were shown that once this exchange started, it followed the same predictable pattern with the same inevitable results. These can be illustrated by a horizontal figure eight pattern as seen below left.

Using the same outline structure, the counseling therapy proceeded by carefully questioning each partner about his or her interpretation about what he or she was seeing and hearing. We were trying to get through to their self-talk where these thoughts, feelings, and behaviors were occurring.

When directly questioned about why he abruptly left and went to the bedroom during those morning coffee conversations, Dick insisted that it was not because he did not love Jane, but that because he did love her he reacted that way. Dick said that in the early days of their marriage, discussions frequently became quite heated, resulting

knockdown, drag-out fights. Dick had learned the warning cues and decided rather than risk escalating the disagreement into an unpleasant confrontation, he would remove himself from the situation. This would keep him from inevitably losing control and would avoid the conflict. He strongly insisted that he did not withdraw because he didn't love Jane but withdrew because he did. In fact, he stated that in his mind, his avoidance tactic was a clear demonstration of his regard and love for her.

Jane reacted to this revelation with absolute shock. When questioned about how she would feel and react if she interpreted Dick's actions as a sign of his love for her, she responded that it would make all the difference in the world to her. Eventually the changes in their perceptions produced a new interaction pattern as illustrated below.

Interaction Pattern After Therapy

What Jane saw and heard = Dick only occasionally retired to the bedroom.

What Jane thought = Dick maintained control of his emotions by his behavior. His withdrawals showed his concern for me.

What Jane felt = acceptance and assurance.

What Jane did = Jane backed off and allowed Dick to retire without a hassle.

What Dick saw and heard = Jane not nagging him when he rushed to the bedroom.

What Dick thought = Jane was much more understanding and positive.

What Dick felt = warm feelings for Jane.

What Dick did = spent more time interacting with Jane.

in

As cited in a study done by Albert Mehrabian at UCLA, the graph below shows how communication occurs. If the primary purpose of the communication is building a relationship, making an initial impression, establishing credibility, or performing social functions, then the content of the message is not as important as body language and tone of voice.

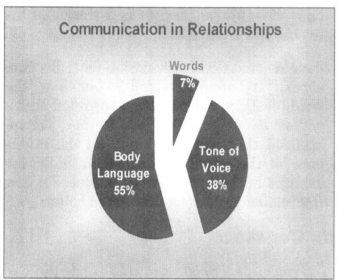

Note that under these circumstances, what we say, our actual words, accounts for only seven percent of the message conveyed. Our tone of voice or way we say it accounts for thirty-eight percent of the message conveyed. Finally, our body language and facial expression accounts for fifty-five percent of the message received.

A review of 100 studies found if the primary purpose of the communication is an informational presentation, face to face sales, negotiation, or conveyance of a message of critical importance, the words are often more important than body language.[3] Under these circumstances, the actual words of the message account for fifty-three percent of the message conveyed. The tone of voice or the way we say it accounts for fifteen percent of the message conveyed. Our body language and facial expression account for thirty-two percent of the message received.

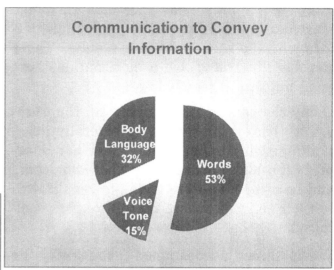

Personal Communication Inventory

Are you having trouble communicating? Are you often misunderstood or entering into conflicts with others? *The author has personally created the following communication inventory. Use of this inventory tool may help you to pinpoint where you might improve:*

Am I communicating clearly?

Is the message sent being correctly received (correct interpretation, meaning, and intention)?

Am I observing the three golden gates of communication?
    Is it true?
    Is it necessary?
    Is it kind?

Am I refraining from using a message within a message or talking in code?
    Example: "Wow, that's a flamboyant sweater!" really means, "You should dress more professionally at the office." Be sure to speak directly, but kindly; don't just hope he gets the message.

Am I avoiding faulty communication styles?
    Blaming (psychological or verbal murder where one attacks another as sick, stupid, crazy, or bad.)

Placating (psychological or verbal suicide where I treat myself as sick, stupid, crazy, or bad)

Judging (third party judging, when I go to others trying to get them to agree with me, using them as a wedge against another)

Stuffing (holding everything in with emotions bottled up to my own detriment)

Comment: Emotions that are improperly handled do not automatically go away but manifest themselves in other ways like depression, anxiety, and passive-aggressiveness.

Am I aware of my nonverbal communication (how I come across, body language, and facial expressions)?

Am I monitoring my communication processes?
   What I say
   How I say it
   How I look when I say it

Am I sharing my thoughts and feelings in an appropriate way at an appropriate time?

Is my temper under control before, during, and after I communicate?

Am I complimenting others regularly (looking for positives and expressing them)?

   Dr. George W. Crane in his book <u>Psychology Applied</u> started a Compliment Club in which members would strive to pay sincere compliments to those around them (especially those they did not get along with) on a regular basis. The results were stunning. One secretary started doing this with a boss she didn't like. In the beginning she had to work hard to find an honest compliment. After months of this, her boss ended up taking her out to lunch. They are now happily married!

Am I avoiding the communication death spiral?

   A negative comment (criticism, name-calling, or sarcastic remark) solicits a negative response; the back and forth with this kind of communication creates a whirlwind or communication "death spiral" which only serves to destroy relationships. Either avoid this verbal tornado altogether or exit it quickly if you find yourself sucked into the vortex. Respond like a fighter pilot who ejects from the plane before it crashes and burns.

Am I resolving feelings of anger toward others and not allowing them to carry over from day to day?

When involved in sticky issues, do I:
   Mirror (restate or rephrase other's words in order to clarify their meaning)?

   Switch roles (put myself in the place of the other; see the situation through their eyes; understand where they are coming from, how they feel, and why they feel that way)? This process helps change perspective and creates understanding and change.

   Exercise control of my temper and tongue?

   Constructively talk out the issue?

   Compromise where one gives to get?

   Seek out win-win solutions where both parties get something they want?

   Capitulate where one sacrifices his position for another?

   Use the sandwich approach (positive-negative-positive)? In the book of Philemon, Paul makes his plea for Onesimus, the runaway slave who stole from his master, to be forgiven and reinstated. He made this request sandwiched between compliments and praise toward Philemon.

Use word pictures? Word pictures are simply pictures painted with words. In order to be effective, it must be something familiar and understood, possess a strong emotional component, and be on-point (relevant and practical). In speaking with David about the wrong done in taking Bathsheba, Nathan used the illustration of a poor family with only one little lamb. The wealthy visitor demanded that the little lamb be sacrificed in spite of its being the only prized possession of this family. David, a former shepherd, had an emotional connection with this example resulting in his reaction that the man who took this lamb should not die but would pay back four-fold what he had taken. When Nathan said, "Thou art the man," David's heart was pricked with conviction. The word picture had effectively done its job.

Am I following all the rules for handling differences? (See next chapter.)

Do I constantly ask myself, "Will this help the relationship or situation?" Every communication potentially affects the relationship between people.

Do I refrain from assumptions? Do I expect the person to understand my needs and wants without expressing them and then become upset if he does not respond as I desire?

Part One: One person expects the other to automatically know what he needs and wants without informing the other person. In other words, he expects mind reading.

Part Two: The person then becomes upset because the expectations are not being met. The person further feels that if he tells the other what is needed and wanted followed by the person meeting that need or want, the efforts are worthless because the other person had to be told. This correlates closely with the satisfaction dissatisfaction principle. Satisfaction is closely linked to the relationship between expectation and reality.

- A person is satisfied when reality exceeds or meets expectations.
- A person becomes dissatisfied when reality does not meet expectations.

Have I considered that other people and I may use differing modes of communication?

- Circular (talking all around the problem) vs. linear (getting straight to the point) reasoning
- Feeling vs. fact-fueled responses
- Abstract vs. concrete thinking patterns

Do I make it clear when I am kidding, emotional, or persuading?

Do I consider the reason for the communication of others with me to minimize personalization? Examples:
Solving problems
Stirring up trouble
Defining power structure
Blowing off steam

Am I using communication to create distance or closeness in the relationship? Do I...
Provide positive or negative intimacy?
Express unresolved feelings?
Manipulate?
Cry for attention?
Balance the books (keep things fair)?

Am I picturing the three possible modes of expression?
Adult mode—when we communicate with control and reason in a calm, collected manner

Childish mode—when we communicate in a highly emotional, unreasonable, selfish, and demanding way like a child communicates when he doesn't get his way

Parental mode—when we communicate in a judgmental, domineering, and accusatory way

The goal is to remain in the adult communication mode as much as possible.

Am I communicating in the power of the flesh as a product of my old nature instead of in the power of the Spirit (Ephesians 4:28-32; Galatians 5:18-23)?

Communicating under the influence of our sinful nature should become distasteful to us and Spirit-controlled communication should be the goal of our every expression.

Recommended Scripture References

Listening, 2 Samuel 20:17
Lord's attentive ear, Nehemiah 1:11
Determine not to sin with one's mouth, Psalm 17:3
Interaction with God, Psalm 18:25
Keep tongue from speaking wrongly, Psalm 39:1
Ears open to hear, Psalm 40:6-8
Wise lips nourish many, Proverbs 10:20
Wise speaking, Proverbs 15:23; 25:11
Value of good words, Proverbs 20:15
Guard your tongue, Proverbs 21:23
Benefits of pure heart and speech, Proverbs 22:11
God gives boldness of speech, Jeremiah 1:6-10

Words condemn or acquit, Matthew 12:37
What comes out mouth, Matthew 15:10-20
Truth sounds unbelievable, Luke 24:9-11
Slow to comprehend, Luke 24:15-31
No other man ever spoke as He spoke, John 7:45-46
Unable to understand figure of speech, John 16:25-30
Message conveyed clearly, John 20:30-31
Misunderstanding what one reads, Acts 8:27-35
Teaching with reasoning, Acts 17:1-3
Speaking in the language of the people, Acts 22:2
Eyes used to gain attention, Acts 23:1
Understanding Spirit's influence, Romans 8:16, 26-27
Understanding enriched by Christ, 1 Corinthians 1:5-6
Message easily understood, 1 Corinthians 14:8
Treat unbelievers with tact, 2 Corinthians 2:15-16
Earn the right to be heard, 2 Corinthians 4:1-2
Acceptance with open hearts, 2 Corinthians 6:11-13
Words full of grace, Colossians 4:6
Gentle spirit as of a mother, 1 Thessalonians 2:7
Responsibility of those who hear, 1 Thessalonians 2:13
Teaching by means of speech, writing, 2 Thessalonians 2:15; 1 Timothy 3:14-15
Exemplary speech, 1 Timothy 4:12
Message must be proclaimed, Titus 1:1-3
Make teaching inviting, Titus 2:10
Faith brings understanding, acceptance, Hebrews 4:2
Hard to explain to slow learners, Hebrews 5:11
Swift to listen, slow to speak, James 1:19
Speak as to convey God's own words, 1 Peter 4:11
God's purpose in giving Scriptures, 2 Peter 1:20-21

Relationship Management/Conflict Resolution

Conflict Resolution

It is not our similarities that cause problems but rather the handling of our differences. It has been said that if two people agree on everything one of them is not needed. Whenever there is disagreement, there is the potential for conflict. Conflict is universal but is not inherently a bad thing. Sometimes conflict fosters communication, clears the air, or leads to productive solutions. There are productive and unproductive ways of handling conflict. The goal should always be for conflict to be constructive instead of destructive. In Acts 15 the church in Jerusalem experienced a potentially serious conflict over the relationship of circumcision to salvation. The conflict was resolved in a constructive manner leading to harmony and growth in the church instead of division.

Handling Differences Incorrectly

External Emotional Assault involves attacking the other person as sick, stupid, crazy, or bad. The other is then forced to give in.

Internal Emotional Assault involves devaluation of one's self so much that the feelings of worthlessness cause submission.

Third-Party Manipulation involves bringing in someone else as a hammer or a wedge.

Bottling-up involves holding the problem in or stuffing one's feelings without dealing with them.

Handling Differences Correctly

1. Use a soft or gentle beginning. *A soft answer turneth away wrath* (Proverbs 15:1).
   - Complain without being overly critical or blaming.
   - Start with something positive.
   - Use "I" statements. Avoid starting sentence with the word "you."
   - Describe what happened without evaluating or judging.
   - Talk clearly about your need.
   - Use a word picture if possible.
   - Be polite and appreciative.
   - Don't store up feelings and then blow up.
   - Use milder emotional wording instead of emotionally charged words.
   - NO name-calling.
   - End with something positive.

   Wrong response: I saw that you have written four checks this month for entertainment items. You know we don't have money for those stupid things. You're putting us in the poor house!

   Right response: Dear, I noticed there were several purchases made for items we don't normally buy. We need to talk about why we need to be more careful with our finances and look over our budget again.

2. Mend hard feelings as they develop (carefully use tone of voice and choice of words).
   - Prevent the other from becoming overwhelmed.
   - Take time out if needed.
   - Calm yourself.
   - Choose carefully your words and phrases throughout the process: I feel, I'm sorry, I appreciate, and I agree.

3. Listen with respect, empathy, understanding, and acceptance. Agree with at least part of your partner's request.

4. Collaborate/Compromise/Capitulate
   - Seek win/win solutions.
   - Use the Aikido Principle (yield to win). In Aikido one turns the opponent's

weight and momentum against him.

- Negotiate through mutual concession to a satisfactory solution.
- Yield to those of your partner's points of view and arguments that seem reasonable to you, sometimes with agreed upon terms for yielding.
- If both are yielding, work together toward resolution.
- Try developing a common way of thinking about the issue.
- Construct a realistic plan both can live with.
- Look for common feelings, goals, and understanding.
- Follow the 11-Step *Resolution Process* to follow.
- Try to consider all options.

5. Use calming techniques such as deep breathing, enjoying a hot cup of tea, using appropriate humor, and making positive statements.

Conflict Management Styles

Ken Thomas has developed an excellent model to determine and utilize conflict-handling styles. It recognizes that conflict situations are balanced by two factors:

1. The degree of assertiveness each participant manifests to satisfy his own concerns.

2. The degree of cooperativeness each participant manifests to satisfy the other's concerns.

The degree of assertiveness (on the vertical access) and the degree of cooperativeness (on the horizontal access) intersect to produce five conflict handling styles.

The two opposing forces of assertiveness and cooperativeness are plotted at right angles on the grid allowing the visual positioning of

each conflict management style. Note how avoidance, which is the most common style of handling conflict, is found in the lower left corner representing low assertiveness and low cooperativeness. Collaboration is found in the upper right hand corner representing high assertiveness and high cooperation.[1]

The five conflict-management styles are defined as follows.

Competition: When one party wants to dominate to achieve his goals, it produces a win-lose process and outcome. The philosophy of this style of conflict resolution is based on competition and dominance.

Collaboration: When both parties want to satisfy each other's concerns, it produces a win-win process and outcome. Collaboration should be the preferred style because it satisfies the needs of both parties.

Compromise: When each party is willing to give something up in order to get something in return, they engage in a give-and-take process producing a mainly-win/mainly-win process and outcome which is acceptable to both parties.

Avoidance: When one or both parties have denial, feelings of indifference, inadequacy, or a hope that the problem will resolve itself, the problem or conflict is avoided. It can produce a lose-lose process and outcome unless the problem is so trivial it is appropriate to ignore it.

Accommodation: When one party gives in to the other, it produces a lose-win process and outcome. This is capitulation.

Using the Five Conflict Styles

Each style of conflict resolution has its place. None is appropriate in every circumstance and a successful conflict manager appropriately uses each of the five. Many people have a one-size-fits-all approach and tend to use one exclusively regardless of the situation. The question is what is your preferred style and first and second backups? What is the other party's preferred style and first and second backups? It is also helpful to know how soon a person will go to his backup style if the preferred style isn't producing the desired outcome. Someone may use avoidance to handle conflict, but when backed into a corner, he may become competitive.

An excellent example of this process is a recent conflict which occurred between the executive and legislative branches of the government during a budget negotiation. The President and the leaders of Congress began the negotiation process with the President using his preferred style of compromise and the congressional leaders using a competitive style of negotiation. As the process continued, the President moved to a backup style of competition by drawing a line in the sand and refusing to cross it. He issued an ultimatum that they must accept his final proposal. When congressional leaders refused to back down, the government temporarily shut down. After several days of intense public reaction, congressional leaders moved from their style of competition to a backup style of compromise. After intense negotiations a budget was passed. Many observers felt that the congressional leaders miscalculated how quickly the President would move from a compromise position to a competitive one. This is the kind of example which can help us not underestimate the importance of using this model. The freedom to choose among these five conflict-handling styles is invaluable.

Because the potential for conflict is always present, mastering the appropriate use of each of the five styles should become an acquired skill for leaders. Here are some guidelines for the appropriate use of each of the five management styles.

Use competition when:
♦ important immediate action is required.
♦ preventing a highly competitive person from running over you.
♦ an issue is so vitally important (but unpopularly received) it must be pushed through.

Use collaboration when:
♦ the concerns of both parties are of great importance.
♦ the concerns of both parties need to be combined to satisfy both.

Use compromise when:
♦ collaboration is not possible and giving to get is required.
♦ parties have mutually exclusive goals.

Use avoidance when:
♦ the issue is unimportant or trivial.
♦ the resolution of the issue is not worth the fallout which will follow.

Use accommodation when:
♦ loyalty or equity necessitates it.
♦ getting in the good grace of another obliges it.

Handling Conflict Constructively

1. Don't fight in the heat of the moment. Cool down first.

2. Take turns talking. Don't interrupt.

3. Allow the other person to express his feelings. If you disagree, don't get defensive or intimidating. Summarize your partner's communication and feelings.

4. Be open and honest without accusing. Break the cycle of blame and resentment.

5. Consider all factors in an issue before discussion.

6. Limit discussion to the present. Never bring up past failures.

7. Eliminate these phrases:
   ♦ You never or you always....
   ♦ I can't.
   ♦ I'll try (means a halfhearted effort).
   ♦ You should...(parental statements).

8. Don't enter the death spiral. Limit discussion to the issue at hand. Think of the tremendous force and pull in the whirlwind. Avoid being sucked into it.

9. Don't name call or use personal attacks.

10. Use *I messages*, not *you messages*: "I feel hurt because..." not "You hurt me...."

11. Never counter attack even if the other person does.

12. Don't tell the other person why you think they do what they do. You are not a mind reader.

13. Ask for clarification if you don't understand something that is said.

14. Put light, not heat, on the discussion. Control your temper and tongue.

15. Remember that the resolution of the conflict is the most important thing, not winning at any cost. For example, marriage is supposed to be a win-win proposition. Watch for the "I always have to be right syndrome."

16. Agree about taboo topics that are too hurtful to handle (obesity, in-laws, politics).

17. Politely respond whenever someone accidentally or purposefully breaks these guidelines. Use an agreed-upon gesture such as making a T-sign with your hands for time out.

18. Your mate is a part of yourself. If you hurt him or her, you are hurting yourself.

19. Avoid using third parties to manipulate in a disagreement.

20. Watch trip-wire thoughts, attitudes, words, and issues. Don't allow your hot button to be pushed. Train yourself to restrain, reframe, and retrain.

21. Avoid using an ultimate traumatic episode in another's life as a sledge hammer.

22. Consider the question, "What is it like to work with me?"

23. Ask yourself, "What is it like to fight with me?"

24. Avoid these unfair fighting styles:

   The Professor lectures and patronizes.

   The Blamer puts another on the defensive, finds fault, looks for offenses, and points a finger at another.

   The Lawyer cross-examines, grills, and quizzes.

   The Demon says and does anything that causes pain.

   The Judge issues rules, laws, judgments, and verdicts.

   The Dictator uses force, threatens, and rages to win.

   The Victim whines and is suspicious.

The Dirty Fighter (hitting below the belt) breaks rules, is a hit-and-run fighter, and throws intimate confidences in the other's face.

The Distracter clowns, laughs, makes jokes, and makes fun of the issue or person.

The Passive-Aggressive does not get outwardly mad, he just gets even.

25. Appropriate the essentials of conflict resolution:
    Control
    Communicate
    Collaborate
    Compromise
    Capitulation (accommodation)

Steps of Negotiation

Control

Control your emotions, your tongue, your body language, and especially your temper. If you begin with a nasty start-up, apologize and begin again. If either of you gets overly emotional, upset, or overwhelmed, take a break for at least thirty minutes. Don't allow anger to harden into bitterness or grudge-holding (Ephesians 4:26).

Communicate

Avoid criticism, defensiveness, and all aspects of contempt including sarcasm and mockery. Treat your partner as you would a VIP. Strive to use communication to make the relationship better.

Collaborate

Brainstorm options and work toward a win-win solution. If unsuccessful, consider more options. Select the most plausible option and try it. If this proves unsatisfactory, select another option and try again. The key to successful outcomes is the generation of additional options. In most cases it is possible to find an option that will satisfy both parties.

Compromise

If a win-win situation cannot be found, use a give-and-take process where one person gives up something in order to get something in return. Working through this give-and-take process produces a satisfactory solution for both sides. With each willing to give a little to reach agreement, there is a solution. This is compromise.

Capitulate (Accommodate)

Capitulation occurs when one party is willing to sacrifice his position to give the other what he wants. This may be done out of loyalty, self-sacrifice, because the issue is of less importance, to create equity in the relationship, or as a bargaining chip in future negotiations. Love is being willing to sacrifice to meet the needs of another as Christ did for us (Ephesians 4:32).

Resolution Process

Writing down problems helps people clarify the issues and work out solutions more objectively. Use the following to find a win-win solution to a problem or disagreement.

1. Specify and define the problem or issue of disagreement.

2. State how you contribute to the problem.

3. List things you have already done which have not worked to solve the problem.

4. Brainstorm and list all possible options to resolve your problem. You are working toward a win-win process and outcome. This will best be achieved by following the Five C's of conflict resolution: Control, Communication, Collaboration, Compromise, and Capitulation.

5. Agree on one option to try.

6. List how each person will work toward the solution.

7. Set a time for another discussion to review your progress.

8. If the option you chose did not resolve the problem, choose another and further brainstorm if necessary.

9. Reinforce each other as the new pattern works.

10. Repeat as necessary.

11. If in spite of carefully following all of these steps you remain in gridlock, it is advisable to seek the help of a counselor or mediator who can bring a fresh unbiased perspective to the situation and perhaps provide additional options not yet considered.

An Example of a Successful Conflict Resolution Process

In the early 1980's, a strike of major proportions existed between the UAW and a farm machinery manufacturer resulting in the longest strike of its kind on record. During the early days of the strike the news media elicited strong comments from each side. It was clear that more control needed to be exercised over tempers and tongues. Recognizing this pattern was not contributing to the success of the negotiation, each side exclusively talked to and about the opposition in the negotiation room, fulfilling the first requirement for successful conflict resolution—control.

Discussions and negotiations continued unsuccessfully for many weeks when they were abruptly interrupted. The company representatives announced there would be no continuing negotiations because they were leaving town. When they returned the union representatives announced they were interrupting negotiations because members were taking a trip out of state. As long as they were not communicating, there was little hope of progress. When both sides returned from their respective trips, it was announced that they were eager to resume deliberations. The deliberations continued without further interruption until resolution occurred thus fulfilling the second part of conflict resolution—communication.

Issues regarding wages and benefits were initially considered to be a source of strong disagreement. Because of mutual understanding about the concerns of each other, they reached a win-win solution thus fulfilling the third important principle of conflict resolution process—collaboration.

The main sticking point was not wages and benefits but a very controversial issue of mandatory overtime. Other companies required their workers to work overtime when asked. This company had previously agreed that mandatory overtime would not be required for their workers. The company insisted, because of the strong demand for their products and the production schedules of their competitors, that they must return to a mandatory overtime policy. The union would not yield on this point. The company was determined that mandatory overtime must be reinstated. It was this issue that prolonged the strike for many months. The eventual solution was to have workers retain the option of refusing to work the overtime but having a pool of retirees who could be called to work if the regular workers refused. This permitted the company to fill the positions on the assembly line. Both sides seemed pleased with this solution. The union workers were happy because they did not have to accept mandatory overtime and retained the right to refuse to work. The company was happy because they were able to fill the jobs, keep the assembly line running, and fulfill their production schedules. This is an excellent example of fulfilling the fourth part of the conflict resolution process—compromise.

125

The final issues to be resolved included whether the employees when on strike would receive holiday pay. The company initially refused but eventually accommodated the workers. The union demanded that some employees who had vandalized a portion of the plant and were consequently fired be reinstated but the company refused. Ultimately a compromise occurred on this issue when employees were conditionally returned on probation with a proviso that they would be permanently fired if a further problem occurred. This fulfilled the fifth part of the conflict resolution process—capitulation.

Whether dealing with conflict between friends, in a marriage, or in a company, these principles of successful conflict resolution provide the framework for a successful outcome in every situation.

Confrontation
How to Confront Someone

Have you ever confronted someone? If not, you may or may not be surprised to learn that there is a certain type of person who does everything possible to avoid confrontation. Confrontation isn't necessarily a negative experience to be avoided. Occasionally, confrontation is necessary to introduce positive change in a person's life. Sometimes confrontation must occur in order for a problem to be resolved. Staying in denial of the problem or avoiding the person with whom there is a problem is *not* an ideal solution. In ministry the responsibility to address problems within the congregation frequently falls upon the pastor or missionary as the church leader. It is important that the pastor be as prepared as possible when confronting someone to avoid alienating him or her and to provide a positive atmosphere for a continued relationship.

Is confrontation biblical? Consider Nathan the prophet and King David. Do you think Nathan relished the responsibility of con-

fronting the king concerning his sin with Bathsheba? Jonah preferred running to the other end of the known world to avoid confronting the Ninevites with their sin. Confrontation is not something most people desire, but at times it is a necessity.

How we confront someone is important if we are to bring them healing and restoration. If done improperly confrontation is either unproductive at best or destructive at worst. An associate had the responsibility of confronting two ladies in his congregation about a particular problem. He was nervous and worried but met with the two ladies. They came to his office, spoke briefly, and left. The senior pastor asked about the meeting and was told, "It went splendidly. I don't know why I worried about it at all." Later at church the pastor saw the two ladies and out of curiosity the pastor asked about the meeting with the associate. The two ladies looking bewildered replied, "We just can't figure out why the associate called us in. We have no idea what he was talking about!"

The Ten Necessities of Confrontation

1. Pray for wisdom, guidance, and power.
2. Get all the facts. How?
   - Talk with the parties involved privately.
   - Stay within the circle of offense by not going outside the people directly involved in the conflict thus minimizing the spread of the problem.
3. Avoid gossip; just find facts. Make a decision to confront or not to confront. Consider the people involved, their personalities, spiritual state, the nature of the offense, consequences of the offense, or urgency. When considering confrontation, think of the analogy of a scratch. Leaving it alone, it heals; scratching may cause infection and slower healing.

4. Determine exactly how you will confront. Rehearse what you will say and how you will react.
   - How will you approach the person? Will you talk informally or set up a meeting?
   - How will you bring up the issue when you meet with them?
   - Anticipate their responses and prepare for them.
   - Decide what scripture you will use.
   - What scripture was violated?
   - What scripture has a remedy for the violation?

5. Prepare to go. Consider yourself and think about God's grace in your own life and His patience and mercy regarding your sin. Somebody wisely observed, "God only knows what any of us might do in the right situation, with the right person, at the right time, in the right place."

6. Live and practice these attitude verses:

   Brethren, if a man be overtaken in a fault, ye which are spiritual, restore such an one in the spirit of meekness; considering thyself, lest thou also be tempted.
   Galatians 6:1

   Moreover, if thy brother shall trespass against thee, go and tell him his fault between thee and him alone; if he shall hear thee, thou hast gained thy brother. But if he will not hear thee, then take with thee one or two more, that in the mouth of two or three witnesses every word may be established. And if he shall neglect to hear them, tell it unto the church; but if he neglect to hear the church, let him be unto thee as an heathen man and a publican.
   Matthew 18:15-17

7. Actually go.

8. Keep a record. Unfortunately, we live in a litigious society. Record keeping in times of confrontation has saved many pastors from lawsuits and other accusations of wrongdoing. To have a general but written synopsis of the meeting will often be enough to evidence what really happened. Take notes of important things that were said and determined. This may be done during the meeting or immediately afterwards. Keep this file for further reference.

9. Assess the outcome. Take appropriate follow-up action. Determine the next course of action.

10. Monitor the situation. Be aware of the person's church attendance and attitudes of those involved. Be sure to make contact, act friendly, shake hands, and work to restore the relationship. Let them know that you do not harbor ill will toward them.

Exploding

Explosive behavior can occur when dealing with difficult people if they become too frustrated or are provoked. Even a pleaser, if too many things build up, can explode. Hence the old adage when you get a meek man mad, look out.

Sniping

Sniping behavior can also occur if one becomes too frustrated or provoked. The sniper's attacks become more likely when his main motives are not being satisfied.

Conflict Resolution with Difficult People

Conflict resolution is necessary as we frequently encounter the same kinds of difficult people.

Perfectionist	Intimidator
Descriptors: Determined to either get the job done perfectly or not at all, nitpicker, nearly impossible to please	**Descriptors:** Determined to make things happen, accomplish his goal and get his way
Motive: Get it done rightly	**Motive**: Get it done no matter what
Agitators: Irresponsibility, sloppiness, and lack of attention to planning and detail by others intensifies his perfection-seeking behavior.	**Agitators:** Wasting time, losing focus, chasing rabbits, lack of progress or not completing the job increases his controlling and intimidating behaviors.
Pleaser	**Attention Seeker**
Descriptors: Determined to get approval and to make commitments but lacks follow-through	**Descriptors:** Determined to be the center of attention and to get people to notice him
Motive: Get approval; to be liked	**Motive**: Get attention
Agitators: Lack of approval, not being liked, and not being able to read the feelings and attitudes of others increases his approval seeking behavior.	**Agitators:** Being treated disrespectfully, being taken for granted or being unappreciated by others increases his attention seeking behavior.

Escalation of Difficult Behavior Types

1. Perfectionists are nearly impossible to please and their behavior grows stronger when the motivation to get it done rightly becomes frustrated.

2. Intimidators are dominators whose controlling behavior grows stronger when the motivation to get it done becomes frustrated.

3. Pleaser's approval-seeking behavior grows stronger when the motivation to get along becomes frustrated.

4. Attention-seeker's behavior grows stronger when the motivation to get appreciation becomes frustrated.

Principles for Handling Difficult People

1. Consider and use to your advantage the underlying motivation of difficult people.

2. Practice the trite but true adage: an ounce of prevention is worth a pound of cure.

3. Listen intently; read body language and facial expressions.

4. Practice pacing and synchronization with the voice, volume, and body language of the difficult person.

5. Find common ground and shared experience before approaching differences.

6. Practice meekness or personal control and grace when facing difficult circumstances.

7. Know and use appropriate negotiation skills and apply them at appropriate times.
8. Always look for shared or common goals and work toward them.
9. Remain flexible as much as is prudently possible.
10. Use appropriate counteractive techniques in dealing with specific behaviors exhibited by difficult people.

Intimidators

Dealing with an intimidator can be difficult. Intimidation involves the use of manipulation and control over others to achieve submission, diminish courage, and overcome resistance. The following techniques may prove helpful in dealing with the intimidator.

Counteraction Techniques

When under attack, <u>don't</u>:
♦ respond with a fit of uncontrolled anger.
♦ make excuses to justify yourself. (They don't care).
♦ roll over in submission.

When responding to attacks, <u>do</u>:
♦ stand your ground and command respect through assertiveness.
♦ interrupt their attack by calling their name over and over.
♦ focus on the major point and carefully fire back, preferably with more rapid speech.
♦ use labeling to name their emotion or action, "You're becoming verbally assaultive," or "You're losing self-control." Such labeling should be ego-alien in nature.
♦ when necessary, add a response to the label, "That's harassment and I don't like

it," or "I'm not starting with you, I don't want you starting with me."
♦ use the broken record technique of repeating a point to make your point.
♦ firmly intercede using the word *stop*.
♦ ask pointed questions and use the reversible why of asking a question to answer a question.
  1. Ask questions that make your point.
  2. Don't allow yourself to be put on the defensive through counterpoint.
  3. Move to a position of advancement instead of defense.
  4. Use assumptive questions when appropriate.
  5. Capitalize on closed questions when responding to intimidation.
  6. Don't ask in the negative.
  7. Present the positive.
  8. Answer the question with a question when needed.
  9. Use silence as a weapon when it works to your advantage.
♦ whenever possible, use the jujitsu principle. Turn their thrust against them.
♦ think strategically when watching their antics.
♦ use counter-intimidation techniques if warranted.
♦ pick and choose your battles.
♦ demand and create respect from your adversary.
♦ recognize their intimidation technique and prevent it from succeeding.
♦ win them over and experience a great reward.

Tactics of the Intimidator

Aggressive behavior	Scorn
Demands	Contemptuousness
Uncorking anger	Brainwashing
Harsh words	Humiliation
Creating fear	Harassment
Bullying	Teasing
Name calling	Embarrassment
Threats	Jumping the chain of command
Personal attacks	
Accusations	Negative associations
Blaming	
Retaliation	Creating inferiority feelings
Distortion	
One-upmanship	Insults and browbeating
Minimalization	
Arrogance	

The Perfectionist

Dealing with a perfectionist can be difficult and frustrating. The following suggestions should prove helpful as you interact with perfectionistic people.

1. Ask for their input to get their ideas about a plan or project. This will help you identify their concerns and possible hang-ups before you begin.

2. Assure them that you are concerned about getting it done as perfectly as possible.

3. Have realistic expectations about possible disagreements and nitpicking as the project proceeds.

4. Be prepared to handle possible discouragement, complaints, challenges, and negativity about the details of a project. Perfectionists will usually be difficult to please when their high standards are not being met.

5. Deal with the issue that the perfectionist's way is the best way. Sometimes the perfectionist can only see this when he is shown that another way can be as good or better.

6. Expect to provide much attention to detail when working with a perfectionist.

7. Allow adequate time to get it done rightly.

8. Insist that it does not have to be perfect for God to bless it.

The Pleaser

Dealing with pleasers can be frustrating because they quickly agree to participate in a project only to lack follow-through. The following suggestions should prove helpful when dealing with a pleaser.

1. Understand their underlying need for approval and its impact upon their commitments and responses.

2. Deal forthrightly with expectations about any commitment they are making and provide them an opportunity to limit or back away from a commitment without losing face.

3. Have realistic expectations about their performance.

4. Monitor them to ensure they are following through with their promise and motivate them when necessary.

5. Offer help or assistance if they falter.

6. Have an alternate plan if they fail to follow through.

The Attention Seeker

Dealing with attention seekers can be irritating because the appearance of their attention seeking behaviors can cause distraction leading to performance problems. The following suggestions may prove helpful when dealing with the attention seeker.

1. Expect the expression of attention seeking behaviors on their part and be prepared to redirect.

2. Provide them with a reasonable amount of attention to satisfy their need.

3. Deal with inappropriate or excessive attention getting behavior by ignoring their attempts to monopolize a conversation through your focusing on other people.

4. Ignore their less excessive or inappropriate behavior if possible.

5. Be prepared to deal with the following behaviors: excessive bragging, exaggerating, distracting, or dominating conversations.

6. If necessary, have a personal conversation with them about how their behaviors are distracting or derailing the group.

7. Provide positive feedback to them when appropriate.

Exploding and Sniping

Intimidators, perfectionists, pleasers, and attention seekers are some of the most difficult types of people to handle. Each of them may engage in exploding or sniping behavior when they are overwhelmed because increasing frustration can lead to increasing aggression.

Dealing with Explosive Behavior

1. Stay in control of your emotions, temper, and responses, or you will only add fuel to the fire and make the problem worse.

2. Let them run down by venting their anger before you respond.

3. When someone explodes in anger, use a soft, calm voice when responding and present a calm demeanor to the process.

4. Begin by asking questions about what they said during their explosive tirade. Allow them to answer the question, and then ask another. This questioning process will allow them to regain their composure.

5. Find one thing that they said, no matter how small, and agree with them on that point. Summarize what they said and express how you can understand how they are so upset because of the point with

which you agree. Then share how you will address the issue accordingly.

Dealing with Sniping Behavior

1. Snipers may be described as hurling snowballs with rocks in them at others through the use of their put downs, snide remarks, and verbal shrapnel.

2. Whether made to your face (overtly) or behind your back (covertly), the results are the same, verbal sabotage.

3. Sniper's attacks are usually a response to an unresolved or unaddressed problem. The nature of the problem may be:

   ♦ You failed to fulfill their expectations.
   ♦ You made them look or feel bad.
   ♦ You offended them.
   ♦ You insulted them.
   ♦ You slighted them.
   ♦ You beat them in some arena.

4. A primary strategy for dealing with snipers is to surface the attack. This is best accomplished by asking them these specific questions:

   ♦ "That sounded like a dig, did you mean it that way?"
   ♦ "What did you mean by that remark (or action)?"
   ♦ "Do I understand that you don't like what I'm saying?"
   ♦ "Sounds like you are ridiculing me, are you?"

5. Privately ask the sniper if you've done something to offend. If that inquiry surfaces the issue, proceed to effectively and productively deal with him about the underlying problem.

6. Seek group confrontation or denial of criticism.

   ♦ They want or need to prove their ideas are right.

- Don't reward their sniping by rolling over even if they have a point.
- Your response should neither directly contradict their allegations nor allow them to share them as objective truth.

  Ask, "Anyone else see it that way?"

  Follow up with, "I guess there is a difference of opinion, can you be more specific?"

  If the group does agree with the sniper's opinion, try to ferret out the problem.

7. If the sniper answers your questions which are designed to surface the attack with a denial, he will find it more difficult to proceed with the sniping in front of those who have heard the denial.

8. Consider the solutions to the specifics of the problem which they intended to solve, and then deal with the problem.

9. You can prevent some sniping by providing a specific time for people to bring up problems and issues for discussion or setting boundaries in advance.

10. To avoid sniping yourself:

- Disagree without being disagreeable.
- Control your emotions and tongue.
- Don't hold grudges.
- Whenever you complain, always do so with respect and offer alternate solutions with the complaint.
- Freely admit error.

- If a disagreement is about facts not opinion and you don't know the facts, stop and get them before you disagree.
- Unsolicited advice can be a big blunder.
- Serious criticism should be rendered privately.
- Defensiveness hinders progress and hurts relationships.
- Seek permission before pushing in on somebody.
- Balance the positive with the negative, presenting the positive first.
- Make people your partners.
- Show you care.
- Avoid insults at all costs and try not to offend.

Recommended Scripture References

Do to others, Matthew 7:12
These are my mother and brothers, Mark 3:31-35
Answered prayer related to forgiving others, Mark 11:25
The first last, last first, Luke 13:22-30
The cost to follow Christ, Luke 14:26
A new commandment, John 13:34
Love as Christ loved, John 15:12-17
To care for Christ's mother, John 19:26-27
Be devoted to each other, Romans 12:10
One body many members, 1 Corinthians 12:12-27
Chosen in Christ, Ephesians 1:11-12
Built together for a dwelling, Ephesians 2:19-22
Submit to one another, Ephesians 5:21-23
Paul's disciple, 1 Timothy 1:2, 18; 2 Timothy 1:2, 2:1
How to treat members of family, 1 Timothy 5:1-2
Jesus calls us brothers, Hebrews 2:11-13
Friend of God, James 2:21-23
Ask forgiveness, James 5:16
God loves his children, 1 John 3:1-3
Let us love one another, 1 John 4:7-11
Loved by God, Jude 1

Decision Making

Six Levels of Decisions

1. Routine decisions: Choose an alternative that meets the need.

2. Precedent decisions: How have we previously handled this? Does it need to be changed or established as a precedent?

3. Policy decisions: What is the policy? If there is none, should we develop one? Do we have a precedent that needs to be developed into a policy?

4. Complex decisions: Follow the decision making formula and steps.

5. Compound decisions: Create consensus among selected participants after careful discussion and consideration.

6. Deferred decisions: Discuss and decide to delay the decision until a later date (decide not to make a decision now).

Four Styles of Decision Making

The styles people use in their decision making process reflect the temperaments discussed earlier in this manual. Each of the styles is appropriate in some circumstances. Consider each person's decision-making style when dealing with him. Review the material on personality types and the decision making styles of each (pit bull, poodle, bloodhound, golden retriever). See section on motivation.

The Decision Making Process

The steps required for decision making and problem solving are very similar with some notable exceptions. All problem solving involves decision making, but all decision making does not include problem solving. In decision making you do not begin by defining the problem or by looking for root causes and solutions. Levels 1, 2, 3, and 6 are self-explanatory and levels 4 and 5 should follow the steps used in problem solving with the exceptions noted here.

Steps for Decision Making

1. Determine level of decision required.

2. Plug in appropriate decision making process.

3. If the decision is complex or compound:

   ♦ Gather all necessary information.

   ♦ Use a decision tree technique consisting of all options, the pros and cons of each option, probable outcomes of each, and the process required for each.

   ♦ Consider the best two options and compare them using a paired analysis.

   ♦ Perform cost/benefit analysis for each.

   ♦ Carefully examine the solutions from several other perspectives including gaps in information, gut reaction, process of implementation required, salability, forces for and against, feasibility, and creativity.

4. Examine the decision for the will of God. Is there anything contrary to the Word of God in these decisions? Discern the leadership of the Holy Spirit. Gather godly counsel. Examine the circumstances surrounding the decision.

5. Make your decision.

Recommended Scripture References

Heartache with wrong decision, Genesis 16:1-6
Choice of good and bad, Deuteronomy 30:15
Family's choice to serve God, Joshua 24:15
Man's choice/God's choice, 1 Samuel 16:1-13
Solomon chooses, 1 Kings 3:5
Chose truth, Psalm 119:30
Promise to follow scripture, Psalm 119:106
Man's choice, God's direction, Proverbs 16:9-10
Answering without all facts, Proverbs 18:13
Lord sees the heart, Proverbs 21:2
Immediate choice, Matthew 4:20-22
Pray before making a decision, Luke 6:12-16
Choice of eternity, John 3:36
Many turned back, John 6:66-71
King almost persuaded, Acts 26:28
Choose what is best, Philippians 1:9-10
Urged to decide, Hebrews 3:7-14
Moses' choice, Hebrews 11:24-25
Resist devil, 1 Peter 5:8-9

Personal Finance

Practice of Biblical Stewardship

It is important to practice biblical stewardship principles such as those embodied in the writings of Larry Burkett and the Crown Financial Program. Scripture teaches that everything we have belongs to God and is merely on loan for our use. Someday we will leave it all behind as Job said, *Naked came I out of my mother's womb, and naked shall I return thither. The Lord gave, and the Lord hath taken away; blessed be the name of the Lord* (Job 1:21). We cannot take our money with us, but we can send treasure on ahead through our giving. Winston Churchill said, "We make a living by what we get; we make a life by what we give."

Scriptural Giving

There are three kinds of giving taught in Scripture:

♦ The tithe which is the tenth of our increase to be set aside for God.

♦ The offering which is a special gift given to God above the tithe.

♦ Alms giving is provided directly to those in need.

All three kinds of giving should be practiced by us as faithful stewards of what God has given us. God is a giving God and if we are to be godly we must be a giving person who cares about the needs of others and delights in meeting them. The opposite of generosity is selfishness which is condemned as a sinful attitude.

God promises to rebuke the devourer for those who give. Ninety percent of what we keep with God's blessing will surely go further than 100% without it.

In the Old Testament we see the practice of giving the tithe; in the New Testament, as recorded in Acts, people brought all and laid it at the apostle's feet. A generous heart will be rewarded. God's many promises about giving are like checks signed by God made out to us.

Savings

Set aside 10% to invest in your personal savings. It's a good idea when you pay God His tithe that you also pay a tithe to your savings account. The story of the talents in Matthew 25:14-30 indicates that God expects us to be good investors of the resources which He has entrusted to us. Different servants were given different amounts of money by their master. Later when they were called into account, he rewarded those who had invested wisely and rebuked the one who had not. This principle teaches that we should both save and invest wisely based upon whatever God has given us.

Investment Suggestions

Investing your money wisely requires both knowledge and careful attention. Multiple class asset allocation of monies among stocks, bonds, cash, real estate, and possibly natural resources and precious metals provides diversification and more safety. Stocks are classified according to their market capitalization, which is the total dollar market value of all of a company's outstanding shares, whether they are domestic or international, growth or value, common or preferred. Micro-capitalization stocks have market capitalizations between 50 and 300 million dollars; small-capitalization stocks between 300 million and 2 billion dollars; mid-capitalization stocks between 2 billion and 10 billion dollars; and large-capitalization stocks over 10 billion. By investing in the stock market in large capitalization stocks you can expect an overall return of about 7% a year over the long-term. Small capitalization stocks have returned about 12% a year.

It is not a good idea to invest money in stocks for less than five years as the market can fluctuate; during a down period, if you need money, you could lose on the investment. Investing for the long-term in both larger and smaller capitalization stocks is a reasonable investment plan. An excellent article in the *Journal of Financial Planning* on the "Rewards of Multiple-Asset-Class Investing," by Roger C. Gibson, CFA, CFP, is available at http://spwfe.fpanet.org:10005/public/Unclassified%20Records/FPA%20Journal%20July%202004%20-%20The%20Rewards%20of%20Multiple-Asset-Class%20Investing.pdf. This article together with the article, "Investment Returns of Different Asset Classes Vary Greatly Over Time," which features a twenty-year look at returns of key indices located at http://www.swapmeetdave.com/Bible/Callan.htm provides excellent information before making any serious decisions about where to put your hard-earned dollars. Conservative investors can follow John Bogle's advice by putting their money in mutual funds tracking the Standard and Poor's 500 Index, the Dow Jones Averages, or the NASDAQ 100 index, or through a mutual fund group such as Vanguard Group.

In addition to books by Bogle himself, the book called *The Bogleheads' Guide to Investing* by Taylor Larimore et al. is a good book for beginners. Also investment books by Larry Swedroe, William Bernstein, and Richard Ferri should be helpful. It is a good idea for a younger person to invest more heavily in stocks and an older person less heavily. Real estate in the form of purchasing a home or owning property is most people's first and perhaps most important investment. Diversification is a must in any successful investment plan. Bonds have had a smaller rate of return over the years but are generally recommended as a part of your investment portfolio. Certificate of deposits offered by banks and credit unions offer both security and variable rates of return based upon their duration; however, monies must be locked in for a specified period and are therefore not immediately available without paying a penalty.

Savings accounts and money market funds allow you to hold your money temporarily while gaining interest. From here you can move money into other investments or you can practice dollar cost averaging putting a set amount each month into a stock or bond account. Make sure that you shop for the best rate with adequate security for your savings. Money compounds over many years and gives rich returns if invested prudently. You should seek the advice of a good financial adviser, read books on financial management and investing, subscribe to financial magazines, and then put your money to work. Your money should work harder than you do. This will only happen through intelligent, informed, and consistent financial management.

Living Within Your Means

Have a budget and stick to it. One of the major problems with not budgeting carefully is over-spending. It is primarily credit-card debt that causes problems for most Americans. Some of our expenses are fixed, including how much we spend on housing, car payments, utilities, insurance, and other specific expenditures. Discretionary spending should only be a small part of our budget. Its demands are often bigger due to excessive spending on entertainment and pleasurable activities.

Credit Card Debt

Your credit-card debt should not be over a small percentage of your total income at most and preferably be paid off entirely every month to save interest payments. You should make sure you do not take on too much debt in any form. The rule of thumb is to spend not more than thirty percent of your total budget on your housing and not more than twenty percent on all other debt. By building your savings you should be able to pay cash for purchases which will substantially save you in interest payments over the years. It is definitely to your advantage to become your own banker.

Maximizing Your Dollars

Practice the Kiplinger approach of stretching your dollars and getting the most of your money. Kiplinger Publications provides excellent suggestions on how to minimize your spending and get maximum benefit from your dollars. I suggest that you read carefully their publications and follow their advice regarding purchases, management of your money, cutting and controlling expenses, and investing. The internet site www.walletpop.com provides practical suggestions regarding cost-cutting and dollar-stretching and will provide tips to help you make the most of your money.

Purchase items when they are **on sale**. Since various items are on sale at different times, learn when items will be on sale and take advantage of these opportunities. For instance, men's clothing is placed on sale every January and July. In January the winter stock is closed out for the summer stock. In July summer stock is closed out to make room for the winter stock. Clothing stores may mark clothes down 20% to 50% and even more when they are on sale. I have personally purchased sport coats worth $250 to $300 for $20 and suits worth many hundreds of dollars for $49. When stock does not sell, it is marked down to move out quickly. Furniture and other items are on sale at select times of the year. Be a careful consumer and spend wisely.

Travel deals are available on the Internet. Cruise ships will sell unreserved cabins near sailing date for a small percentage of their normal cost. A clearing house for numerous travel agencies, http://www.travelzoo.com will advertise their bargains of unsold seats and cabins. Another site, http://www.vacationstogo.com offers a free weekly e-mail subscription which lists bargains on three classes of resorts—regular to super deluxe accommodations. These are often offered at one-tenth of the regular cost. Air fare is low when empty seats are available or travel is weak. Air travel on Tuesdays, Wednesdays, and Saturdays usually offers the best value.

A site like http://www.bookingbuddy.com searches hundreds of fares to ensure you get the lowest. You can go directly to the airline's web site and save even more. Southwest Airlines periodically offer "ding fares" at rock-bottom prices through email registration. Spirit Air has offered fares as low as $9. Priceline.com affords you the opportunity to name your own price on flights and motels. Betterbidding.com will aid in becoming a better bidder.

Become a careful consumer with **comparative shopping**. Motels rooms are offered at special rates during select seasons of the year. Savings plans are available on certain rooms. Restaurants provide coupons and discount opportunities to diners. Look at http://www.restaurant.com for coupons with many 50% discounts at select restaurants. Some restaurants offer early-evening diner specials at significant discounts. Check out http://www.bradsdeals.com for the latest coupons from various stores. Visit these sites to search for unbelievable bargains:

http://www.slickdeals.net
http://www.deals2buy.com
http://www.dealnews.com
http://www.spoofee.com
http://www.fatwallet.com
http://www.craigslist.com

The sites http://www.dealdump.com and http://www.dealighted.com offer summaries of the best bargains from some twenty eight other sites.

Condos in vacation areas can be rented reasonably from owners who are not using them during certain weeks. Check for them at http://www.tug2.net. Look at the bottom of the web page at the classifieds to find bargains for various locations and dates.

Comparison shop for items at the following sites: http://www.pricegrabber.com, http://www.nextag.com, http://www.bizrate.com, http://www.dealtime.com, http://www.shopping.com or by using search engines such as Google or Yahoo. Every kind of merchandise can be found at special prices by visiting http://shopping.geoportals.com. A comparison of numerous reviews produces a ranking of the best products together with the best prices at http://www.consumersearches.com. Consumer ratings of products can be checked at http://www.epinions.com, http://www.amazon.com, http://www.wize.com, and at merchandiser's web sites.

Watch your local newspaper ads or online sites like http://www.cars.com, http://autos.aol.com, and http://www.autotrader.com for savings on a used car. The best values will be obtained by buying a car that is a couple of years old and has depreciated between thirty-five to fifty percent off the sticker price; then plan to drive it for many years. *Consumer Reports Annual Buying Guide* provides a frequency-of-repair record for most cars with a compilation of survey results from thousands of readers who report on the reliability of the car's various mechanical systems. It pays big dividends to buy a reliable car because of the savings on repairs. Car values can be assessed by checking Kelley Blue Book (http://www.kbb.com), Edmunds (http://www.edmunds.com), and National Auto Dealer's Association (http://www.nada.com). Car appraisal guides list wholesale and retail prices of a vehicle and are usually available free on-line. Edmunds even provides a listing of the average cost of a given vehicle which is sold by private parties through classified ads. If you are pricing a new car, dealer's cost figures are available either on-line or from books available at your local bookstore or library. They include a breakdown of both the wholesale and retail costs of various options offered on the car. Car repair histories and damage reports are available through http://www.carmax.com or http://www.autocheck.com. It can be well worth the investment of a few dollars to see if a car you are considering buying has a history of damage by fire, flood, accident, or theft. You may also be able to find out if it has undergone repairs and if it was serviced regularly.

Housing for purchase is available at discounted prices if you are willing to do a few fix-up projects on your own. Use http://www.realtor.com to search for available properties in your area. Some for-sale-by-owner properties are available at lower prices and listings may be accessed through Google searches. Buying during the low point of the housing business cycle is also a clear path to savings on real estate. One can access http://www.realtytrac.com which provides listings on foreclosure properties in various markets.

You can save money by **bartering** or exchanging your services with others. If you need the services of a tradesman, you may be able to barter with him and possibly function as his helper as he does the work. This is a good way of saving money and stretching dollars.

Regarding the option to file form 4361 to exempt yourself from **Social Security**, realize that you may not be eligible for Medicare participation if you opt out of Social Security. Carefully weigh this decision because it could prove to be a very important one for your financial future.

Developing a Budgetary System

A careful system should be developed by every couple regarding how money will be managed and how financial decisions will be made in your household. Probably the person who is more competent with finances and has the available time and resources should be the one to actually write the checks or pay the bills. Determination of how purchases will be made, by whom, for how much, and what will be saved, invested or spent is critical to healthy financial functioning in any family.

Pay your bills and pay them on time. Financial integrity is its own reward. It can pay off in lower interest rates and better terms for a loan. You can live well on less with diligent preparation, planning, and management.

The *Budget Parameters* Pie Chart (below) presents a sample budget breakdown with recommended percentages for each category of expenses. The worksheet on the following page gives some helpful suggestions regarding planning and goals. A weekly financial tracking graph will enable you to determine

your current spending in each budget category.

Financial Goals for Budgeting

It is important to set goals with your money. Financial planning should include long-term goals such as paying off a mortgage and retirement. Medium-term goals should include such things as purchasing a better car, purchasing and furnishing a home, and perhaps a special vacation. Shorter-term expenses are things such as food, clothing, rent, utilities, and recreation. Make your own personal list of goals and develop your budget accordingly. Here are some helpful budgetary suggestions.

1. Your budget allocations should be based upon realistic estimates of your income.

2. Provide for the basics first, then the comforts, and finally the luxuries.

3. Solidify a plan to pay off current debts.

4. Make a savings plan, even if it is small and add to it as you pay off debts.

5. Carefully regulate your spending so as to stay within your budget.

6. Always put God foremost in your planning and budget. Stretch your dollars by shopping for bargains and carefully making purchases.

7. When you overspend in one area, it must come from another, usually from the final piece (miscellaneous) which includes personal items, entertainment, credit, school expenses, pet care, gifts, hobbies, and the ever important spending money.

If you do not manage your money, your money will manage you. There is no substitute for financial planning, management, and discipline. It will pay great dividends.

Budget Parameters

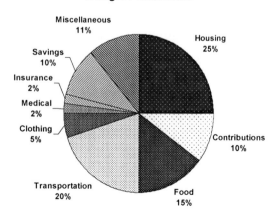

The following is the percentage range the average family spends on each category:

Housing includes rent, mortgage, utilities, phone, furnishings, taxes, maintenance, repairs, and upkeep	20 to 40%
Tithe and other contributions	1 to 3%
Food	10 to 20%
Transportation includes car payment, leasing, fuel, and maintenance	15 to 20%
Clothing	4 to 8%
Medical	2 to 5%
Insurance includes coverage for life, home, auto, and health	1 to 5%
Savings	1 to 2%
Miscellaneous	5 to 25%

Current Financial Spending by Budget Categories

Category Spending	Week 1	Week 2	Week 3	Week 4	Total
Housing					
Tithe					
Contributions					
Food					
Transportation					
Clothing					
Medical					
Insurance					
Savings					
Miscellaneous					
TOTALS					

Recommended Scripture References

Poor financial choices, Proverbs 6:1-5
Giving to the poor, Proverbs 19:17
Hoarding, Ecclesiastes 5:13-14
Silver, gold is Mine, Haggai 2:8
Good stewardship, Malachi 3:8-10
Treasures on earth or in heaven, Matthew 6:19-21
Cannot serve God, money, Matthew 6:24

Materialism, Mark 8:36
Gain world, lose soul, Luke 9:25
Parable of money management, Luke 19:11-27
Gave all, Luke 21:2
Owe no man, Romans 13:8
Giving to help other people, Philippians 4:15-19
Love of money, 1 Timothy 6:10
Eternal investment, 1 Timothy 6:17-19
Not for gain, 1 Peter 5:2

Part Two
Duties of the Minister

Introduction:
Duties of the Minister

The typical pastor may perform as many as forty functions in his ministry. The following list is an example of possible duties:

Shepherding the flock	Congregational care
Preaching	Problem handling/Management
Teaching	Musical oversight
Counseling	Ministries oversight
Leading (providing direction and vision)	Staff responsibilities/Oversight
	Coordination/Information sharing
Program/Ministry development	Dealing with boards and committees
Managing/Organizing/Oversight	Financial management
Visitation	Assimilation
Peacemaking	Intern training/Oversight
Evangelizing	Community relations/Representation
Training/Equipping	Social engineering/Connections
Stewardship/Raising money	Phoning/Correspondence
Discipleship	Motivation
Comforting/Encouraging	Personal/Professional growth
Confrontation/Discipline	Hiring/Firing/Oversight
Study/Knowledge/Biblical application	Spiritual protection
Recruitment	Consultation
Team building	Writing articles, a blog, or materials

Counseling, teaching, preaching, performing weddings and funerals, conducting visitation, involvement in financial management, and hiring are the focus of this section. These are the duties most often performed in ministry and some are areas where ministers feel under-prepared. One study found the typical pastor spends an average of eighteen hours each week engaged in some form of counseling. Understanding the basics of people, problems, interventions, and resources, knowing when to counsel and when to refer is imperative for any pastor. With so many marriages in trouble today, the pastor is often the first to be consulted by church members. The better a minister understands the dynamics of unhealthy marriages and families the more effective counselor he will become. Hurting people are everywhere and the pastor is sometimes called the poor-man's psychologist. Since he will likely divide his time among the tasks of giving thousands of sermons and lessons, performing hundreds of weddings and funerals, and doing many hours of visitation, he should strive to be the best that he can be when performing these duties.

Counseling

Essential Qualities of a Christian Counselor

A good counselor will see people as God sees them. He will recognize that they are created in His image and have purpose and value. This includes people with serious problems.

Whoso sheddeth man's blood, by man shall his blood be shed: for in the image of God made He man.
Genesis 9:6

He will recognize they are sinful and in need of help. The counselor must realize the counselee is a person made in God's image but is also a sinner. People come to him with sins and weaknesses having both known and unknown sins. Sometimes people honestly do not recognize their behavior as sinful according to God's Word.

For all have sinned, and come short of the glory of God. Romans 3:23

For God so loved the world, that he gave his only begotten Son, that whosoever believeth in him should not perish, but have everlasting life. John 3:16

He will recognize that they are capable of change. Change is always possible. The counselor should also have a reasonable expectation of personal responsibility. The counselor should not be doing all the work; if so, he is simply making the counselee dependent on him. Counselees should have assignments to complete after each session. If they show no interest in making an effort to complete the assignment or reach the goal, a reevaluation should be done.

And Jesus looking upon them saith, With men it is impossible, but not with God: for with God all things are possible. Mark 10:27

He will continually strive to live a spiritual life. One must be aware of his own weaknesses and failures. Assessing, confessing, and forsaking sin must become a habit. A good counselor will lack hypocrisy. He should be continually growing, willing to change, and striving for spiritual maturity.

If we confess our sins, He is faithful and just to forgive us our sins, and to cleanse us from all unrighteousness. 1 John 1:9

But grow in grace, and in the knowledge of our Lord and Savior, Jesus Christ. To Him be glory both now and forever. Amen. 2 Peter 3:18

He will say what he means and mean what he says. He must live rightly, be transparent, and be a person of his word. Integrity creates trust.

Better is the poor that walketh in his integrity, than he that is perverse in his lips, and is a fool. Proverbs 19:1

He will demonstrate genuine caring. Ask yourself this simple question, "Why does God gives us help?" The inevitable answer is because He cares for us.

Carefully consider this next important question and answer it for yourself before moving forward. Why do I want to help others?

Why are you really interested in helping others find biblical solutions for their problems? Some counselors are enthralled with the idea of giving advice and listening to the problems of others simply because it pumps up their ego or fulfills a need to control others. Your reason for helping others should be the same as God's. You help because you care, because you recognize the preciousness of others. In the words of John Maxwell, "People don't care how much you know until they know how much you care."

For as he thinketh in his heart, so is he: Eat and drink, saith he to thee; but his heart is not with thee. Proverbs 23:7
Even so ye also outwardly appear righteous unto men, but within ye are full of hypocrisy and iniquity.
Matthew 23:28

He will be honest about his abilities to help, and realize his limitations. Some situations require professional help and are best left to a competent counselor. For making referrals keep a list of trusted professionals. If one is going to assume the responsibility of counseling, be sure that a correct assessment is made and that there is no immediate danger of suicide.

Whoso boasteth himself of a false gift is like clouds and wind without rain.
Proverbs 25:14

He will accept a person that is hurting but not beliefs or behaviors that are sinful. A good counselor will have compassion. In other words, love the sinner but not the sin. God does this, but it is harder for us because we tend to be judgmental even though we deal with the same sins. Remember, we are all sinners saved by grace.

With all lowliness and meekness, with longsuffering, forbearing one another in love; Ephesians 4:2

He will treat others as he would like to be treated. You must practice biblical interpersonal relationships.

And the second is like unto it, Thou shalt love thy neighbor as thyself.
Matthew 22:39

One must rise above the world. Consider that being a helper presumes that you have a higher standard – a God standard.

Be not overcome by evil, but overcome evil with good. Romans 12:21

He will be discrete and confidential. Many of the things that are shared are of a personal nature and it should be understood that such information will not be shared with others. Keeping a confidence is a very difficult thing to do. It takes a lifetime to build your credibility but only a moment to destroy it.

He will attempt to understand the person's issues and be empathetic with his pain or problems. He will see the environment from which people come.

And the servant of the Lord must not strive; but be gentle unto all men, apt to teach, patient, in meekness instructing those that oppose themselves; if God peradventure, will give them repentance to the acknowledging of the truth; and that they may recover themselves out of the snare of the devil, who are taken captive by him at his will. 2 Timothy 2:24-26

He will practice humility; but for the grace of God, he could be in their shoes.

Wherefore let him that thinketh he standeth take heed lest he fall.
1 Corinthians 10:12

Crisis Intervention

A crisis occurs when an event or series of events has left a person in a temporary emotional state of disequilibrium. We try to help a person return to a state in which he can once again resolve his own problems. No counselor can solve all of the problems! Coping means to deal with, handle, or manage and indicates acceptance and standing firm in the face of these repeated challenges. In essence, the person must learn to live in the real world and must implement the methods of coping.

The development of a crisis can occur in two ways. An acute crisis is triggered by an event and occurs suddenly. A chronic crisis is created by a series of events that build up over time reaching a breaking point.

The objective in crisis intervention is to return a person to an emotionally controlled state. The first task may be to calm a hysterical person. Take control calmly but firmly saying something such as, "It sounds like something terrible has happened. I want you to stop talking for a moment. Take a couple of deep breaths. Now tell me slowly and calmly so I can understand what has happened...."

Once the person is calm, the crisis intervention counseling process can move forward. The process may take a short time or several weeks. A true crisis will probably not extend much more than four to six weeks. Anything longer is general counseling, not crisis counseling, and should be referred to a professional.

The crisis intervention guideline on the following page should be extremely helpful for the minister. The guideline gives points of reference and discussion that do not necessarily have to occur in this order. However, if the steps are followed as indicated by the acronym CRISIS (see the following page), it is likely that the counselee can be successfully led out of trouble.

Examples of Crisis Situations

Various kinds of events can trigger an acute crisis. The following events may plunge even a person who normally copes well with life into the depths of confusion and disequilibrium. Consider how one might use the **CRISIS** intervention guideline (page 146) in each of the listed situations.

Premature Birth

One may have to gently deal with the possibility of a mother not going to full term, separation from the baby (if in NICU), or the baby dying. Other members of the family may also need help in understanding and accepting the situation.

Child Abuse

As a child will certainly have trust issues, the counselor will have to carefully create a compassionate atmosphere in which the child feels safe. Without exception, all child abuse cases must be reported to the authorities. In the investigation phase, definitive signs of physical abuse must be documented. Look for obvious marks, lacerations or bruises, especially on the upper part of the body. Listen closely to what the child says and carefully observe body language. Refer to a qualified professional as necessary. One must be accurate in reporting these findings as they are serious allegations and legal action may be expected.

Status and Role Change

People encountering empty nest syndrome or becoming parents for the first time can experience serious changes. This occurs not only in lifestyle but in how a person views himself or herself and how each defines his or her role in the family or marriage.

Physical Illness Impairment

A person with a serious condition or situation such as Alzheimer's, cancer, or paralysis needs empathetic care. Help them begin to move through the stages of grief. Work to give hope, show other life options, opportunities, and possibilities for future occupation and a productive lifestyle. This type of crisis can affect entire families, so be aware that other members of the family may be in crisis as well.

CRISIS Intervention Guidelines
(by Rev. Tim Green)

Create a compassionate atmosphere
> People in crisis often feel isolated and overwhelmed.
> The goal is to help restore the person to a pre-crisis state.
> Use supportive, calming statements, and reassuring body language .
> > (Avoid judgmental statements like. "You did WHAT!?")

Retrieve the story
> Talking can be an emotional release.
> You need to know the issues so you can proceed with help. *He that answereth a matter before he heareth it, it is folly and shame unto him* (Proverbs 18:13).
> Focus only on information that is connected to the problem.

Investigate
> Past occurrences (Have they dealt with this before?)
> Present perceptions (How are they interpreting this?)
> Future apprehensions (What are they worried will happen?)

Suicidal assessment
> Ask about suicidal thoughts (frequency, intensity, duration).
> Ask about previous attempts. (If they have already tried suicide, it is easier the next time because they've already crossed a moral/emotional bridge.)
> Ask about the plan and its specifics. (If they have a specific plan, they need immediate psychiatric care!)

Intervene appropriately
> Guide in problem resolution.
> Anticipate future problems and help them develop coping skills.
> Refer to a more qualified helper if necessary.
> Have them make a phone call in your presence if necessary.

Support identified
> Family and friends
> Professional help
> God and the church body

Rape

Men should not counsel rape victims. All ministers should get professional assistance for anyone who has been raped. A local hospital or rape crisis center should be suggested. There is often a false sense of guilt associated with rape or incest so treat her with the utmost care.

Chronic Psychiatric Patient

Professionals should be consulted as soon as possible. Help them find someone with creative therapy approaches if the person feels that traditional counseling methods have not been successful. Note that the person may need medication in order to be able to think logically.

Wife or Husband Abuse

This is a silent crime and alcohol is usually involved. The victim often remains in the situation because of low self-esteem and feelings of dependence on the abuser. Because of this insecurity, the victim often goes back to the abuser and may also turn on those who try to help.

Divorce

There are many issues surrounding divorce. A few of these include spiritual guilt, false responsibility, family disapproval, social stigma, loss of friends, stress of children, self-esteem issues, housing, schedule changes, and status changes. In crisis counseling, deal only with the big issues (felt needs). Help the individual make connections for further divorce counseling or support groups for the long-term problems.

Substance Abuse

Substance abuse is usually a cover-up for an underlying issue. The substance only helps them cope with an unfulfilled life. Stress, withdrawal, and depression are typical symptoms of substance abuse.

Suicide or Attempted Suicide

Only a medically trained professional can help if the person has a genuine death wish. An individual breaking off communication and becoming ambivalent about life and death must be observed closely. The counselor must keep reinforcing the reality that their suicide would cause a great deal of pain to significant people in their life (parents, siblings, spouse, children, and friends).

Unwanted Pregnancy or Abortion

The sudden change of life plans with an unwanted pregnancy are overwhelming. There is a great amount of anxiety about the future and anger at impending loss of freedom. There may be family problems including dis-appointment of parents and financial issues. If abortion is the case, the person may need help dealing with the associated guilt.

Maturation (Stages of Life)

Consider the psychosocial stages of life and primary issues of each stage. If progress through any of these stages is not completed with adequate psychological and social development, the stages that follow become more difficult.
♦ Infancy and early childhood: trust vs. mistrust and separation anxiety
♦ Pre-puberty: behavioral changes, schooling, peer pressure
♦ Adolescence: sexual awareness, immaturity, identity, willfulness issues, independence
♦ Young adult: college, career, marriage
♦ Mid-life: productivity vs. stagnation
♦ Late adulthood/old age: meaningful life vs. despair

Sudden Unforeseen Events

Fire, flood, accidents, pregnancy, war, environmental problems, housing problems, financial issues (the stock market crash), and announcements (company closing, new boss, old flame getting married) are examples of unforeseen events which may cause great distress.

Spiritual Conflict

Salvation, demon activity, unresolved guilt, or hitting a betrayal barrier (like "God let me down") are examples of spiritual conflict.

Burnout

Families can be heavily involved in many church, school, and other community activities stretching the family thin. Some experience burn out from the job, tasks at home, a spousal role, or caring for the ill or elderly. Stress from this overextending of the family can be evidenced in various ways.

Counseling Paradigms

The ABCs of Emotion

Albert Ellis conceived this paradigm in its original form in the context of Rational Therapy (RT) as it was initially known[1]. When someone comes seeking help to deal with a particular problem, it may be helpful to consider the ABCs to help you conceptualize the real problem and the underlying problem thinking. This model is only valid when dealing with someone's irrational or unbiblical beliefs. Refer to the section on "Stinking Thinking" for a discussion of the most common unbiblical patterns of thought. Walk through the paradigm and then apply it.

Activating Event – The counselee will come to you citing a particular problem, which may or may not be the central difficulty. In most cases, the presenting problem is not the actual problem.

Belief – How is the event being interpreted? For example, a wife may believe that her husband doesn't care about her if he doesn't come right home after work. She misinterprets his action to mean that he doesn't love her.

Consequential Emotion – How do you feel about the activating event? In this situation, the wife feels unloved. Ask questions to clarify their feelings. Don't assume that you know what or how they are feeling. Get them to tell you or to tell each other.

Dispute Irrational Belief – It is helpful for the counselor to restate B, the underlying belief or interpretation of the action that contributed to the resulting emotions. In a nutshell, "So you think your husband doesn't love you because he did not come home immediately?" Don't put words in the counselee's mouth; rather try to clarify and get them to give a synopsis of their belief.

For the Christian, here we interject what has become known as truth-talk or biblical truth. This teaching is used to combat or dispute the incorrect conclusion. Teach a person to analyze their interpretation of an event and ask themselves "Is that true?" "Does he really not care about you?" "Are your feelings legitimate or correct?"

Emotional Effect – The goal is to produce an entirely different emotion because of the change in thinking or interpretation about the activating event.

Follow the Arrow – Explore why the person believes or interprets things that way. Ask, "Why do you think that way? Who taught you to interpret this event in the way you did?" Look to their childhood for clues.

Levels of Counseling

According to Larry Crabb there are three levels of counseling[2]. Each level requires the counselor to use a different tack and a certain level of expertise. The following chart may be simplistic, but it may give some guidance in the process of sifting through a person's problems.

Problem Feelings
i.e. anger; Is this prideful anger or righteous anger?
Encouragement

Problem Behaviors
i.e. stealing; Share biblical truth that stealing is wrong.
Exhortation

Problem Thinking
i.e. Root out the thinking behind the action; for the person who steals – Why do you steal if you have money? Need for excitement? Boost self-esteem? Other?
Enlightenment

These are not steps but rather a general schematic, the levels intermingle to a point. The more counseling skill that is required, the greater the value of counseling as you go down the arrow. The stages of counseling give an overview of the steps a counselor may take in order to develop biblical solutions to problem feelings, behavior, and thinking. Thinking of these stages will help the counselor to do more than just talk. By having these steps in mind while conversing, a counselor is better equipped to ask appropriate questions.

There may be a difference between Christian counseling and counseling by a Christian; they are not necessarily the same. A counselor who is a Christian may or may not have considered the scriptural basis of his advice or treatment plan. He may integrate secular material, which may be unscriptural. The Bible is the blueprint against which truth should be measured. While the Bible is the source of the truth, it is not the only source of truth; if you need brain surgery, you better choose a well-trained surgeon, not someone who has merely read the Bible. If you want to learn calculus, you better learn from a source other than scripture since it doesn't teach mathematics. The integration of psychology and scripture should use the Bible as the test—if it is unscriptural reject it. If it is true and does not go against scripture, use it for God's glory and for the benefit of others.

Guided Self-Discovery

What is Guided Self-Discovery?

This method of eliciting responses from the counselee is more than a list of questions a counselor might ask. The counselor is to be a guide in helping people discover for themselves a variety of things that may include their behavior patterns and the thinking behind them, their values, and their perspectives. Sometimes people will not come to you for the big solution to their problems; they just need help processing a situation instead of advice on how to fix things. The value of

such a method is related to the level of participation on the part of the counselee. The more a counselee thinks through a problem and takes part in reaching a solution or plan of action, the more likely he will own it. If his participation has been integral during this process, he will tend to be more inclined to take responsibility for putting the solution into practice.

What might this actually look like in conversation? The following list of questions should be helpful in guided self-discovery. Note that many of the questions are not really questions at all but rather are open-ended comments (reflecting the idea of "I wonder...") which tends to be the most productive. Another benefit of using guided self-discovery is that it will make information gathering seem less like an interrogation and more like casual conversation.

Guided Self-Discovery Comments

Tell me what's on your mind.
> Notice the word *problem* isn't even used. This gives an open-ended opportunity for them to talk.

I wonder if there is anything else on your mind. I wonder what this means to you and how you understand it.
> Help them be aware of their own perceptions.

There must be lots going on inside you. I wonder if you are ready to share some of it with me.

I wonder what alternatives you have been considering.
> Anytime there is a problem, they often try some things to fix it themselves. Find out what they've already tried.

I wonder if you have discussed this matter with other people and how you felt about what they had to say.
> It's important to know from whom they've received advice.

Have you ever successfully dealt with this problem? What did you do? When you are feeling _____, what will you be doing?
TFA – thinking, feeling, acting (doing).

What are you willing to change in order for this difficulty to be solved?
This is done only after you've identified the problem and possible actions.

How willing are you to solve this problem on a scale of 1-10 where 10 is a maximum effort?
This helps stop the blame game.

Is what you are doing working?
People often try the same things repeatedly even though they don't work.

What will have to happen for that (solution) to occur more often?

Let's assume that this problem was solved. What will that be like?
Create a vision or goal for them to live up to or accomplish.

Are there times when this problem doesn't occur?

If things were just a little better, what would be different?
View a little progress as victory; help them take incremental steps.

When this solution is working, what will be happening?
Get their general perceptions. Find out what's going on.

When this solution is not working, what will be happening? If this problem is solved, what will be different about you?
Teach that the only person you can really change is yourself. When you change yourself, you change the pattern of the problem.

Psychopathology

Christian pastors, pastors' wives, and other full-time ministers have opportunities to counsel people in their congregation. Addi-

tionally, people may come to a pastor from outside the congregation seeking some type of spiritual or emotional counsel. With severe depression and other forms of mental illness, the minister may be placing himself or the person seeking help in danger if he doesn't know what he is doing. With forms of psychosis (schizophrenia, paranoia, and bi-polar disorder) counseling tends to be ineffective because the individual is often out of touch with reality. Before counseling can be effective, the individual must be brought back to a state of reality through drug or other kinds of therapy where he can adequately reason.

It would be advisable to become acquainted with local Christian psychiatrists and counselors and have a referral list ready. One of a pastor's greatest assets may be the ability to recognize what is beyond his skill and ability.

The following is a brief overview of some of the diagnostic categories used by professional counselors.[3]

Psychosis

Psychosis is a derangement of mind characterized by a severely distorted or lost contact with reality as evidenced by delusions (false beliefs maintained despite indisputable evidence to the contrary), hallucinations (perception of objects with no reality), and disorganized (incoherent) speech and behavior. Because it involves a loss of reality, it is the most serious condition. It is associated with conditions such as schizophrenia, bipolar disorder, severe unipolar depression, drug usage, sleep deprivation, organic brain syndrome, and in some cases, severe stress which results in a brief psychotic episode.

Extreme care should be used when dealing with overt psychosis. A referral for appropriate evaluation and treatment is usually the best course of action.

Depression

Depression has been called the common cold among people today. Clinical depression is serious and needs to be differentiated from an ordinary case of the blues. The typical person has two to three days each month where they are significantly up in mood, two to three days where they suffer from a low mood (blues), and the rest of the month somewhere in between. Clinical depression is characterized by a deep depression lasting longer than two to three weeks and is diagnosed by the presence and severity of certain symptoms. Clinical depressions may be classified as mild, moderate, or severe. Any clinical depression should be a concern and if categorized as moderate or severe should be a source of great concern. While it is true that a person suffering from the blues can do a variety of things to overcome the down mood, clinical depression is an entirely different matter. One with depression has significantly altered biochemistry of the brain, notably levels of serotonin and norephinephrin.

Clinical depression may be primary or secondary. In primary depression, the depression is not the result of another medical condition; secondary depression is caused by a medical condition such as cancer or a hypoactive thyroid. There are at least ninety-one different diseases which either cause or contribute to episodes of clinical depression. It is always wise for a person suffering from depression to get a thorough medical check-up to screen for the presence of these diseases.

Depression may be unipolar or bipolar. If a person experiences severe down moods and the accompanying symptoms, it is classified as unipolar (only one way). If he has had at least one episode of mania (excitement manifested by mental and physical hyperactivity, disorganization of behavior, and elevation of mood), he is classified as suffering from bipolar depression. There are several types of bipolar illness and a number of classifications of unipolar as well.

Clinical depression can be classified as dysthymia (chronic mild depression) or major depressive illness. The differences between these two classifications is based upon the severity, the duration, and number of symptoms. Dysthymia is like having a low grade infection, except the person is afflicted with a mild case of depression lasting for at least two years. With dysthymia the person either does not have enough symptoms to be classified as suffering from major depression or may experience the symptoms for a few days at a time.

Depression can manifest itself in various ways and each individual will have a combination of individual symptoms. Anxiety and depression are different but often occur together. As many as eighty-five percent of those suffering from significant depression also suffer from anxiety. Both can manifest themselves in physiological ways. Some of the symptoms of depression are listed below.

Depression Symptoms

Sleep loss/gain
Appetite loss/gain
Feelings of being punished
Feelings of pessimism
Feelings of failure
Feelings of guilt
Feelings of self-dislike
Feelings of worthlessness
Feelings of sadness
Feelings of hopelessness
Feelings of helplessness
Loss of pleasure
Crying spells
Agitation
Loss of energy
Loss of interest in favorite activities
Irritability
Indecisiveness

Concentration difficulties
Tiredness/fatigue
Psychomotor retardation
Anxiety
Detachment
Thoughts about suicide
Loss of interest in sex

While this list is reasonably comprehensive, not all of these symptoms will be present in every person suffering from clinical depression, but the more symptoms which are present, the greater the likelihood of a serious problem. While the symptom list is thorough, the degree of severity of the symptoms is not addressed in the list. The greater the number of symptoms, the more severe the depression. The symptom list is helpful in the assessment of the probable need for treatment or referral of those suspected of having a case beyond the blues.

Clinical Depression

Eighty-five percent of all serious depressions begin with a significant loss.[4] It is not usually a minor loss but rather one that threatens their future happiness in a serious way. Depression follows a pattern and when all parts are present will likely lead to a significant depressive episode.

The depression equation is as follows:
<u>Presence of significant loss</u>
Types of loss that can lead to depression:
Loss of marriage (death or divorce)
Loss of a close friend or family member
Loss of health (chronic or serious illness)
Loss of finances (security or retirement or wealth)
Loss of job (career, livelihood)
Loss of self-worth caused by a serious blow to ones self esteem
Loss of parent (especially in children)
Loss of a boyfriend or girlfriend (typically with teens)

+ (Add) anger
(at God, at self, at the situation, at others) This anger is frequently turned inward.
+ (Add) guilt
("If only...") Guilt is often part of self-blame.
+ (Add) anxiety
(coexists often with depression)
+ (Add) entrapment
The loss cannot be resolved resulting in a feeling of being trapped with no good way out.

= (equals) depression

Treatment of Clinical Depression

Clinical depression can be a life-threatening disease. People die from it through suicide. It is always wise to know what you can and can't handle and make an intelligent referral to someone with expertise and experience. The following are some treatments which may be used.

Hospitalization
For severe depression where the threat of suicide is great, hospitalization may be essential.

Anti-depressant medications
These drugs may be necessary to restore the normal biochemistry in the brain.

Milieu therapy
This is simply a change of environment to get the person away from the situation causing or contributing to the depression.

Addressing the issues
As mentioned previously as the depression equation, addressing these specific issues will help them cope with the loss, addressing their feelings of anger, and handling the guilt.

Catharsis
The simple task of talking through their problems and emotions can begin to create healing.

Pleasurable activities
Building pleasurable activities into their life every day can be uplifting. The more reasonable and appropriate the pleasurable activities one can build into daily life the better.

Correction of thought patterns
Correcting stinking thinking will retrain the brain to use more positive thought patterns. Help the person to rid the mind of negativity.

Stress management
Relieve anxiety through stress management techniques. Stress is a major contributor to depression.

Aerobic exercise
Engaging in aerobic exercise will burn up the excess adrenaline and release endorphins, the body's natural anti-depressant.

The hostility of others aimed at the depressed person and continuing or increased stress in the life make successful treatment of depression more difficult.

Risk of Suicide

Associated with the depression may be suicidal thoughts or plans, self-flagellation (which is a form of self punishment or flogging), and self-pity.

Never take the risk of suicide lightly. If someone threatens or mentions suicide, act wisely. It is better to be safe than sorry. Most suicidal people are a threat only to themselves, but about five percent are also homicidal, meaning they intend to do others harm or to take somebody with them. Some threats of suicide do not involve a death wish but are rather a cry for help. Since it is difficult to know the difference, it is important to know the following in dealing with the possibility of suicide:

1. Take all suicide statements seriously.

2. Determine how far they have gotten into the planning. The greater the thought, the more planning, the greater the detail, the more the necessity of getting immediate treatment.

3. If a person has threatened suicide, they may be hospitalized even if they refuse to go. Hospital personnel and/or police can be helpful if a threat is made. The length of the forced hospitalization will be brief for protective and evaluative purposes and can only be continued by court order and with adequate proof of necessity.

4. Look for evidence to confirm suicidal intent such as talking about when they won't be around anymore, giving things away, parting with cherished items, or mentioning the future in such a way that leaves them out. More than a quarter of all suicides give no previous warning or indication. Even the most astute professional might not know. People will sometimes mention that the suicidal victim was previously dejected but seemed to be in better spirits shortly before they died. This is often the case because they have decided on suicide as a course of action and may evidence a better mood because they are relieved by finally seeing a way out.

5. Suicidal threats need to always be handled by the best people. Many people have been convinced that there is no threat only to find out there really was.

6. The best way to proceed with a possible suicide is to outrightly ask if there is a risk. Asking specific questions such as:
   Have you thought about suicide?
   If so, how often? How seriously?
   How would you do it?
   When would you do it?
   Where would you do it?
   The more deliberate the thought, the more serious the risk.

7. Even if someone is hospitalized and later released with the doctors feeling the threat has passed, there can be serious continuing risk. Sometimes people tell the professionals what they want to hear while concealing their true intent until they have the opportunity to carry it out. If someone is determined to commit suicide, it is almost impossible to keep him from it, short of never letting him out of your sight.

Use good judgment in determining if you can help or if they need to be referred. You can't afford for that decision to be the wrong one.

Anxiety

Anxiety is the most common form of emotional disturbance in the United States today. Approximately 28 million people are suffering from serious anxiety[5]. Many patients with various presenting problems in general practitioner's offices have anxiety-related issues. Anxiety is a painful or apprehensive uneasiness of mind over an impending or anticipated ill. It is also an abnormal and overwhelming sense of fear marked by sweating, tension, increased pulse, increased respiration, pupil dilation, and other physiological signs. Difficulty in coping is inherently part of the problem.

Types of Anxiety Disorders

♦ Panic Disorders are characterized by the physiological symptoms previously cited. Panic attacks tend to be circular in nature with the panic attack generating additional anxiety and the increased anxiety contributing to more panic attacks.

♦ Phobias are strong, irrational fears of certain objects or situations that cause the person to avoid them.

♦ Obsessive Compulsive Disorder is marked by intrusive, persistent thoughts and/or repetitive behaviors which involve anxiety and the person's attempt to control it.

♦ Post Traumatic Stress Disorder is a collection of symptomatic reactions to traumatic events.

♦ Generalized Anxiety Disorder is a general pervasive sense of anxiety not necessarily related to a particular event. It is sometimes described as free-floating anxiety.

Some anxiety disorders may be caused by medical conditions and substance abuse.

Causes of Anxiety Disorders

♦ Genetics (We do not inherit anxiety, but we do inherit our nervous systems.)

♦ Environment factors

♦ Ethnic and culture factors

♦ Symptoms caused by other psychological disorders

♦ Medical conditions

♦ Traumatic events (present or past)

♦ Excessive caffeine consumption

♦ Work or family situation

The Biology of Stress

1. Stress prompts the hypothalamus to cause sympathetic innervations of the adrenal medulla and activate the pituitary.

2. The pituitary causes the adrenal cortex to increase secretion of the glucocorticoids producing cortisol and cortisone.

3. The adrenal medulla produces catecholamine hormones epinephrine and norepinephrine.

4. Suppression of hypothalamic-pituitary-adrenal axis occurs until stress is alleviated.

5. Continued stress, worry, fear, and rumination prolong the process leading to secondary stress.

6. This leads to a repeat of the process.

Stress Remedies for Careful Instead of Care-full Living From Philippians:

1. Resolve conflicts (Philippians 4:2-3).
2. Stop anxiety and worry through taking concerns to God and turning them into prayer (Philippians 4:6,7).
3. Occupy your mind with things which are true, honest, just, pure, lovely, and of good report (Philippians 4:8).
4. Apply biblical solutions to problems (Philippians 4:9).
5. Practice thanksgiving and thanks-living (Philippians 4:4, 8b).
6. Learn contentment (Philippians 4:11).
7. Focus on others instead of yourself (Philippians 4:10b, 14, 19).
8. Have a can-do by the grace of God attitude (Philippians 4:13, 23).

It is helpful to practice aerobic exercise to burn up excess adrenaline. Take time to relax periodically. Build into your life things that you look forward to doing every day. Biblical meditation has been proven to reduce stress.

Abnormal Personality Types

It is important for the minister to be able to recognize the following abnormal personality types. Unless the minister has specialized training, he may not be equipped to help effectively. Personality disorders are characterized by these elements.

They are lifelong pervasive patterns of attitudes and actions which usually emerge during late adolescence or early adulthood. The symptoms may range from mild to severe and profoundly affect his thinking, feeling, and interpersonal relationships.

The person sees his symptoms as acceptable and consistent with his basic personality, beliefs, and self-image. This makes him rigid, inflexible, and difficult to change.

There are numerous types of personality disorders which have been identified over the years by the counseling community.

♦ Explosive Personality

A person with explosive personality tends to be unpredictable, volatile, angry, and uncontrollable.

♦ Compulsive Personality

A person with compulsive personality is compelled to move toward certain activities and is a driven perfectionist. Indicators might be that the person is a neat freak, is an activity checker or rechecker, is frustrated with self and others who don't measure up, or is a strong internal critic. He has a need to perform ritualistic actions and excessively conform to rules.

Five Areas of Perfectionism include:
Dress and appearance
Work
Home/Scholasticism
Possessions (super-organized garage)
Relationships (marriage, parenting style, communications with friends)

♦ Paranoid Personality

The paranoid personality is suspicious and distrustful. He is hypersensitive and tends to practice isolated withdrawal.

♦ Passive-Aggressive Personality

The passive-aggressive doesn't get mad, he gets even. This is done in subtle ways that frustrate, such as forgetting, dawdling, or blocking.

♦ Sociopathic Personality

The sociopath has abnormal conscience development and can do things to others that are clearly wrong without feeling any guilt. Some common indicators include:

Has very shallow emotional relationship

Is highly manipulative, exploitive (uses people)

Is self-centered (but can appear charming and friendly

Doesn't learn from punishment

Has poor impulse control

There are two distinct kinds of sociopathic personality types.
1. Anti-social sociopaths are independent and criminal.
2. Social sociopaths are non-criminal.

- Histrionic Personality

The histrionic (formerly hysterical personality) is highly emotional and loves or needs to be the center of attention. If a woman, she is likely to dress provocatively, doesn't like negativity, will skirt over real issues, is gullible, and often will match up with a sociopath. Histrionics tend toward depression.

- Borderline Personality

Those with borderline personality are often unstable both emotionally and interpersonally. They are characterized by variability of moods, instability, stressful on/off relationships, and tend to change jobs frequently.

- Anxious Personality

The anxious personality is characterized by stress, anxiety, nervousness, and leg movements. This person has trouble sitting still.

- Depressive/Dysthymic Personality

This person is down much of the time experiencing a continuing low-grade depression.

- Negative Personality

The negative personality is critical, sees the glass as half empty, focuses on the negative, and is usually cynical.

- Cyclothymic Personality

This personality has moderate up and down mood swings, is sometimes talkative and not at other times.

- Avoidant Personality

This person has been wounded in the past and consequently avoids social interaction because of feelings of inadequacy and sensitivity to being hurt again.

- Schizoid Personality

The schizoid personality is similar to the avoidant personality in that they avoid people and lack interest in social relationships. Unlike the avoidant personality, the avoidance is not precipitated by having been previously hurt.

- Schizotypal Personality

The schizotypal personality is characterized by strange, peculiar, or odd thinking and behavior, and the need for social isolation.

- Dependent Personality

The dependent personality wants to lean excessively upon other people, get others to make decisions and take responsibility for them. They tend to feel inadequate and helpless wanting others to care for them.

- Narcissistic Personality

The narcissistic personality is filled with admiration of himself and is excessively self-centered. He possesses an overly inflated grandiose image of himself and his own importance. These people are legends in their own mind.

Defense Mechanisms

Defense mechanisms are mental processes in which an individual engages to minimize his anxiety and discomfort when feeling threatened or conflicted. Unconsciously (beneath awareness) the mind attempts to find a compromise solution to a problem it is unable to resolve. These techniques prevent people from facing problems and should therefore be recognized and addressed by the minister. The following are some of the most common defense mechanisms.

- Projection—To project one's own feelings or problems onto someone else

  Example: "Thanks for the message, Pastor. Joe really needed it." or "She's such a gossip. Did you hear what she did?"

- Rationalization—To justify or excuse actions with faulty logic and explanations

  Example: The man who beats his wife says, "I beat my wife, but she deserves it. Someone's got to keep her in line."

- Introjection—To believe or do something simply because we were taught it from a very young age

  Example: One may grow up being taught the idea that human worth equals career success. This individual will attempt to excel in a career to feel important and valuable.

- Displacement—To take feelings out on someone else

  Example: A husband who has a hard day at the office may later take his frustration out on those at home.

- Denial—To deny the existence or seriousness of a problem

  Example: A person denies that he is a drug addict or that his drug addiction is causing harm to himself or anyone else.

- Distortion—To perceive situations or people unrealistically

  Example: The beaten wife says, "My husband really is a loving, kind man."

- Reaction formation—To react by switching positions to the extreme

Example: The most prejudiced people become equal rights activists or the guy who has homosexual feelings acts homophobic.

- Repression—To exclude from consciousness bad experiences which would produce anxiety and be threatening (The problems tend to appear in another form such as nervous reactions, headaches, phobias, or depression.)

  Example: A child witnesses a playmate get struck by lightning. He subsequently develops a fear of storms but doesn't recall the lightning incident because he has repressed it from his awareness.

- Phariseeism—To ignore the log in your own eye by condemning the splinter in another's eye

  Example: These are often judgmental, critical faultfinders who are attempting to take attention off their own problems.

- Devaluation—To belittle another to boost one's self-esteem

  Example: A pastor runs down another pastor because he feels threatened by his success in pastoring a larger church.

- Passive-aggression—To get even, often in subtle ways, instead of getting mad

  Example: A teen makes the family late for an important appointment because of his dawdling as a payback for his being grounded.

- Withdrawal—To avoid a problem through personal isolation

  Example: A person cancels an engagement claiming to feel ill though there is nothing wrong with him.

- Regression—To return to childish behavior

  Example: A grown adult who didn't get his way when making a purchase may have a temper tantrum in front of the sales clerk. Road rage is another example.

- Identification—To identify so much with another that one becomes like them by taking on their characteristics

  Example: A man adores Elvis so much that he acts and dresses like him.

- Undoing—To be constantly worried about actions to the point that one tries to undo what was done, having an obsession with making it right

  Example: One tries to reverse or undo his feeling by doing something that indicates the opposite feeling.

- Dissociation—To be unable to connect actions with feelings or values because of strong psychological issues

  Example: A preacher vehemently preaches against lust but seduces women.

- Somatization—To experience a physical manifestation of non-physical conflicts or issues

  Example: One worries until he physically makes himself sick.

- Sublimation—To redirect unacceptable feelings into a socially acceptable form
  Example: A person goes to the gym to pump iron when angry.

- Idealization—To overestimate the admired attributes of another person

  Example: One sees a Christian leader as perfect while ignoring his human faults.

- Sarcasm—To legitimize (negative) feelings through a more acceptable expression or sending a message in a socially acceptable form

  Example: A coworker gets in a dig about being late disguised by saying, "Nice of you to grace us with your presence."

- Compensation—To compensate for weakness or deficiency with something else

  Example: An attitude of "I'll show them" is seen when a sibling excels in one area forcing the other sibling to choose another area in which to excel.

- Magical thinking—To engage in child-like, wishful thinking

  Example: The child idealistically thinks of his parents as getting back together even though both have remarried.

- Acting out—To express feelings by outrageous behaviors

  Example: A teen gets drunk because her need for support is not being met by her absentee father who has forbidden her to drink.

- Intellectualization—To make pronouncements and put on airs to show how smart they are

  Example: A person deliberately uses words that others don't understand in order to make them look up to him.

- Sexualization—To brag about sexual prowess and conquest

  Example: The athlete in the locker room boastfully describes what he did the night before with a popular cheerleader.

- Compartmentalization—To keep one area of life separate from another

  Example: A television evangelist continues ministry with public appearances while frequently visiting prostitutes.

- Controlling—To attempt or desire total control of another person because of low self-esteem

  Example: A husband monitors his wife, keeping constant tabs on her, in order to control her every move because he fears she will connect with someone else.

- Isolation of affect—To have absence of appropriate feeling (A person thinks the feeling but doesn't actually feel it, "I guess I'm angry with him, sort of.")

Example: A girl who should have feelings of anger toward her boyfriend when she catches him with another woman and although aware of exactly what he has done to her, she lacks the appropriate feeling as a response to his unfaithfulness.

Consultation

Enlist a cabinet of competent advisors to help when in need of advice and assistance. Develop a library of the best books dealing with people's problems and their solutions.

Recommended Scripture References

Scripture makes wise, Psalms 19:7-11; 119:18, 24, 105
Lord makes known His covenant, Psalm 25:14
God's Word is good counsel, Psalm 37:30-31
God gives discernment, Psalm 119:125
Rebuke by a righteous man, Psalm 141:5
Counsel refused, Proverbs 1:29-31
Listen to counsel, Proverbs 9:9; 20:18
Take advice, Proverbs 13:10
Many counselors, Proverbs 15:22
Lord guides steps, Proverbs 16:9
Jesus the way, John 14:1-14
Experience shared, 2 Corinthians 1:3-4

Why pray ... when you can worry?

By John R. Rice

Ninety-two percent of what we worry about, will either never happen or we have no control over, so why waste the worry?

By Walter Cavert

The beginning of anxiety is the end of faith, and the beginning of true faith is the end of anxiety.

By George Mueller

Worry is a responsibility God never meant for you to assume.

By Bill Gothard

Anxiety does not empty tomorrow of its sorrows, but only empties today of its strength.

By Charles Haddon Spurgeon

The following quiz will help you appraise and better understand the stress in your life. It may also be used as a tool in counseling others.

The State of Your State		
1. Do I tend to think about the same thing much of the time?	Yes	No
Is it pleasant?	Yes	No
Is it unpleasant?	Yes	No
Is it related to other relationships?	Yes	No
Is it related to personal problems?	Yes	No
Is it related to work?	Yes	No
Is it related to home?	Yes	No
2. When something is bothering me, do I keep thinking about it?	Yes	No

3. How often do I engage in worry?	Never	Seldom	Sometimes	Often

4. When I am angry, how long does it take to get it out of my mind?

Minutes	Hours	1 day	3 days	1 week	1 month	Eternity

5. What do I do to get over my anger?		
Do I stuff it?	Yes	No
Do I get even?	Yes	No
Do I explode?	Yes	No
Do I slowly burn?	Yes	No
Do I hold a grudge?	Yes	No
Do I choose to forgive and move on?	Yes	No

6. How often do I feel tense and anxious?	Never	Seldom	Sometimes	Often

7. How long do I feel tense and anxious?

Minutes	1 hour	2-3 hours	1 day	More than one day	Weeks

8. I know when I am tense and anxious because I experience:

Heart pounding	Yes	No	Chest pain/Tightness	Yes	No
Shortness of breath	Yes	No	Inability to focus	Yes	No
Muscle tension/Twitches	Yes	No	Trouble sleeping	Yes	No
Jitteriness	Yes	No	Flushing/Blushing	Yes	No
Irritability/Impatience	Yes	No	Choking	Yes	No
Upset stomach	Yes	No	Several combined	Yes	No

The State of Your State (Continued)				
9. How often do I experience four or more of these symptoms continuously?				
	Days	**Two Weeks**	**One Month**	**More than a month**

10. When I am tense and anxious, I ...

Do nothing	Yes	No	**Stuff my feelings**	Yes	No
Talk it out	Yes	No	**Exercise**	Yes	No
Meditate	Yes	No	**Journal**	Yes	No
Think it through	Yes	No	**Pray about it**	Yes	No
Take it out on others	Yes	No	**Move on**	Yes	No

11. I frequently experience ...

Anxiety	Yes	No	**Fearfulness**	Yes	No
Hostility toward others	Yes	No	**Depression**	Yes	No
Others hostility to me	Yes	No	**Worry**	Yes	No

For the following question, please *write in the percentage for each.* Note, percentages should total **100 on each line.** Positive % + Negative % = 100%

12. What percentage of my thoughts would be positive and negative...

	Positive %	Negative%
Thoughts in general?		
Thoughts about work?		
Thoughts about home?		
Thoughts about other relationships?		
Thoughts about personal problems?		

Scoring Guide for State of Your State Quiz

#1 Most people tend to have a default thought pattern that occupies their mind. It is related to one of the categories listed but can vary at different times in their lives. When someone falls in love, thoughts tend to be preoccupied with his or her beloved. These thoughts should be pleasant not unpleasant. If your mind tends to be preoccupied with unpleasant thoughts, you need to work at changing them. You choose what you think about.

#2 Obsessively thinking about any one thing is never good.

#3 If you worry more than occasionally, it indicates you are a worrier.

#4 Anger should be resolved before the day ends. Carrying anger over to another day puts you in emotional peril.

#5 Any answer other than *choose to forgive and move on* indicates unhealthy ways of dealing with anger.

#6 If you feel tense and anxious often, you are probably maintaining unhealthy levels of adrenalin.

#7 Feelings of tension and anxiety should pass quickly. The rule of thumb is that minor issues are resolved in a day and more severe upsets resolve themselves in a time period up to three days. Tension and anxiety lasting beyond seventy-two hours indicates a potential problem.

#8 Any of these symptoms or combinations of them are stress related and therefore can be indicators of a more serious problem.

#9 If you have four or more of these symptoms continuously for two weeks or more, it can be indicative of a chronic stress reaction.

#10 Exercising, meditating, thinking it through, journaling, deciding how to deal with it, moving on, expressing your concerns to God, and praying about it are all productive ways of handling stress. Others listed are not.

#11 The things listed here tend to contribute to stress rather than alleviate it. Stress in turn contributes to each of these as well. For example, 85% of people suffering from depression also suffer from anxiety. It is a vicious cycle. Aim to reduce or rid yourself of them.

#12 If you are engaging in more than 40% negative thinking in any of the categories listed, it is a red flag. The category scoring the highest percentage is the area where change should be initiated.

Grief Counseling

The experience of grief is a conflicting mass of emotions that occurs when you reach out to someone or something that has been there for you and they are no longer there. This can be a person (in loss or death), a group of people (in loss or divorce), or an idea (happily ever after). The goal of grief therapy is to resolve the conflicts of separation, facilitate the completion of the grief tasks, and say goodbye to the pain associated with the memory of the lost relationship.

Attachments, according to John Bowlby, come from a need for security and safety; they develop early in life and are usually directed toward a few specific individuals. These tend to endure throughout one's life.

The Five Stages of Grief

There are five stages of grief. People tend to move about through the steps and do not always progress chronologically.

1. Denial is characterized by statements like "I just can't believe…" and "This can't be real." This stage usually doesn't last long.

2. Anger turned outward is characterized by feeling upset, a low frustration tolerance, and lashing out in anger. "Why did God do this to me?" is commonly asked.

3. Anger turned inward occurs when the reality of the loss is truly felt. Feelings are often bottled up inside.

4. Grief and depression allow the realization that the loved one is truly gone and enables them to grieve over the loss of the life and relationship. Not grieving causes low-grade depression.

5. Resolution and acceptance occur when one comes to terms with the loss having worked through the first four steps.

The Five Tasks of Mourning

When mourning, it is imperative that a person accomplish these five things.

1. Acknowledge and accept that a loss has occurred.

2. Acknowledge, embrace, and release the pain associated with the loss.

3. Adjust to a world that does not include the deceased or lost relationship.

4. Create an internal space for the memory of the lost relationship that then allows the griever to move on with life.

5. Turn in one's survival skills and replace them with vibrant living skills.

Manifestations of Normal Grief

Sadness, anger, guilt, self-reproach, anxiety, loneliness, fatigue, helplessness, shock, yearning, emancipation, relief, numbness, hollowness in the stomach, tightness in the chest, tightness in the throat, oversensitivity to noise, a sense of depersonalization, breathlessness, weakness in the muscles, lack of energy, and dry mouth are all normal emotional and physical manifestations of grief.

Some changes in cognition may include disbelief, preoccupation, sense of a presence, and hallucinations. Some normal behaviors during the grief process include: sleep disturbances, appetite disturbances, absent-minded behaviors, social withdrawal, searching and calling out, sighing, restlessness, crying, visiting places or carrying objects that remind the survivor of the deceased (or divorced or separated) person, or treasuring objects that belonged to the person (or place, thing, or event).

Determinants of Grief

Both the length and experience of grief is always directly related to the developmental level and conflict issues of the griever. Although grief may last a lifetime, the following categories represent some of the most important determinants.

1. Identification of who the person was and what thing or event was lost
   - origin or nature of the attachment
   - strength of the attachment
   - security of the attachment
   - ambivalence in the relationship
   - unresolved relationship conflicts

2. Mode of death (natural, accidental, suicidal, homicidal, war, childbirth)

3. Historical issues
   - complete or incomplete with other loss relationships
   - number and importance of other changes prior to this loss issue

4. Personality variables
   - age
   - sex
   - level of inhibition about expressing feelings
   - ability to handle anxiety and stress
   - mental status (personality disorders, mental health issues)
   - level of dependency or difficulty forming relationships

5. Social variables
   - ethnic, social, and religious background
   - degree of perceived emotional and social support both inside and outside of the family
   - owner of a pet
   - gains received from grieving

The Phases of Grief

The **Impact Phase** occurs in the first few weeks of the loss and is evidenced in the physical, emotional, and behavioral reactions occurring during this phase. This is an immediate reaction.

Physical Reaction
   - numbness
   - shortness of breath
   - heaviness in chest
   - empty feeling
   - nausea
   - heart palpitations

Emotional Reaction
   - shock
   - feeling of unreality
   - surrealism
   - relief (for end of suffering)

Behavioral Reaction
   - denial
   - disorientation
   - intermittent crying
   - waves of grief
   - listlessness

The **Recoil Phase** occurs as the shock and numbness wear off. The physical, emotional, and behavioral reality of the loss is felt.

Physical Reaction
   - lack of energy and fatigue
   - headaches
   - vulnerability to illness
   - tension and anxiety
   - tightness in chest
   - stomach problems

Emotional Reaction
   - anger
   - fear
   - guilt
   - regret
   - panic
   - loneliness
   - depression

Behavioral Reaction
- hypersensitivity
- avoid being home
- sleeplessness
- isolation
- obsession over loss
- overreacting

The **Acceptance Phase** occurs when the loss is accepted and the road to recovery begins.

Physical Reaction
- begin looking to the future again
- begin doing things for self again

Emotional Reaction
- begin to take responsibility for life
- begin rebuilding life

Behavioral Reaction
- begin to develop new interests
- begin experiencing personal growth
- begin moving forward

Grief Therapy

Grief Counseling Tasks

- Attentively listen and allow adequate time for talk.
- Assist in the acknowledgement and acceptance of the death, divorce, separation, or other loss.
- Help to identify and express feelings.
- Assist with skills for living without the lost relationship.
- Emphasize the need to find time to grieve.
- Help normalize behaviors.
- Acknowledge individual differences in grieving styles.
- Provide ongoing support.
- Identify defenses and coping styles.
- Diagnose any pathology associated with grief and refer to a qualified counselor.

The following tasks should be accomplished with family involvement. Information should be shared with the family at an appropriate time and in an appropriate manner. The family can support the grieving person in the following ways.

- Remember significant dates and anniversaries, especially the first year.
- Give caring assistance (provide food, cleaning, or yard work).
- Have patience with them.
- Send cards and notes.
- Pray with and for them.
- Cry with them.
- Help them reach out to other family members.

Procedures and Considerations for Grief Therapy

Understand that grief is not a disease and that the griever is not broken; they simply require a safe environment to express feelings and release pain.

- Rule out physical disease.
- Develop rapport and establish a safe place in which the work can be done.
- Re-stimulate memories of the lost relationship.
- Assess which of the tasks of grief are not completed.
- Work with emotion and lack of emotion brought up by the memories.
- Explore and defuse linking objects.
- Acknowledge the finality of the loss.
- Deal with the fantasy of ending grieving.
- Help the griever say goodbye to the person, the pain, and other hurtful memories.

Writing a Completion Letter

One way to facilitate grieving is to write a completion letter. It should state one's anger, hurt, sadness, acknowledge forgiveness, and make amends. Finish the letter with an acknowledgement of the gift the relationship held. Then say goodbye.

Some useful techniques for releasing grief emotions include: evocative language, use of symbols, writing, poetry, drawing, role playing, cognitive reconstruction, making a memory book, directed imagery, and the creation of other healing rituals.

Grief Associated Depression

Without help, one-third of depressed people will get better on their own, one-third will stay the same, and one-third will get worse. People can be unaware of their depression; that is called a masked depression. If depression begins with a loss, a crucial time for intervention is when depression is first noticed.

Recommended Scripture References

Joy of the Lord is your strength, Nehemiah 8:9-12
There is hope, Job 11:16
Dark valley, Psalm 23:4
Morning rejoicing, Psalm 30:5
The Lord is near and delivers, Psalm 34:18
Believer's death precious to God, Psalm 116:15
Laughter can follow weeping, Luke 6:21
Death swallowed in victory, 1 Corinthians 15:53
God of all comfort, 2 Corinthians 1:3-4
Death annulled, 2 Timothy 1:10
Apostle's anticipation, 2 Timothy 4:6-8
Blood of dead man, Revelation 16:3

See also the recommended scripture references under *Duties of the Minister: Funerals.*

Marriage Counseling

Exploring Marriages

Where does the counselor begin? A couple may come to you and say that they just aren't in love anymore or are unhappy with each other and their marriage. They may be tired of continuing conflict; some may be reeling from the results of an affair. Exploration of the couple's marital relationship should focus on their patterns of interaction in addition to his and her characteristics and contributions to the marital dissatisfaction. Professional therapists are trained to look beyond the symptoms, represented by the presenting problem and couple's complaints, to possible root problems which are the underlying basis of their strife.

A patient may complain of a headache to his medical doctor. A wise physician knows he must get to the cause of the symptom rather than just treat the headache. If the headache is caused by a tumor or a systemic disease such as diabetes, it needs to be diagnosed and treated. The interactional diagnoses as identified in this section provide such help to the counselor.

It is helpful to explore the areas in which problems commonly occur. Assessment tools are available which give an overview of the couple's blueprint of a marriage. *The Prepare/Enrich Marriage Inventory*[1] for premarital or marriage counseling was created for such a purpose. There are six major potential areas for marital conflict.

Six Marital Strife Hot Buttons

Realistic Expectations
People enter marriage with expectations about time use, companionship needs, personal growth, change, and romance. Discover which expectations are not being met and if those expectations are realistic.

Personality Issues
Personality issues that might affect a marriage include:
Assertiveness – willingness to ask for what you want or need appropriately
Self-confidence – ability to succeed
Avoidance – not willing to face issues, running from problems
Partner dominance – control issues

Communication
Both the quantity and quality of meaningful communication is important and reaches beyond checking schedules or talking about children. Couples need to set aside time to express their feelings to one another, to communicate wishes, dreams and desires, as well as maintaining the routines of daily life. They need to periodically discuss their relationship in the context of their needs and wants.

Conflict Resolution
How is conflict handled in the relationship? Are feelings bottled up? Is a third party sought out as judge? Does one person fade into the background? Does one try to dominate the other? Is negotiation used frequently? Help to incorporate The Five C's of Negotiation into everyday life: Control, Communication, Collaboration, Compromise, and Capitulation. See section on conflict resolution.

Financial Management
Most couples struggle with money issues related to spending, control of spending, who is the wage-earner, and who earns more. The money earned by both individuals should go into one account and not be divided by the amount of money each earned. This is especially true when one of the persons is a stay-at-home spouse.

Sexual Relationship

Eighty percent or more of all marriage counselees are having sexual problems. These problems in the bedroom could be a primary or secondary issue.

Additional areas for exploration:

Idealistic Distortion

Ignoring negative interactional patterns early in a relationship can lead to more serious problems as it evolves. A statement demonstrating the disqualification of negative signs (especially in pre-marital situations) is, "Things will be better once we get married."

Leisure Activities

When couples date they engage in a variety of leisure activities which help them get to know each other and allow bonding. After the wedding it is important to share activities that are not just part of the business of life. They need to enjoy each other's company, have meaningful conversations, and spend time together away from home.

Children and Parenting

Each parent has a different idea of how to raise a child. Parents need to train, model appropriate character and behavior, and hold the child accountable for his actions. They need to agree on rules and methods of discipline to present a unified front.

Family and Friends

What traditions will your family have? Will the husband and wife individually maintain relationships with their friends or will the couple only socialize together with others? Will there be a gal's or guy's night out?

Equalitarian Roles

Beginning a marriage each person has preconceived notions of how things ought to be and how responsibilities should be divided, including childcare, household duties, and other decision making processes.

Religious Orientation

Spiritual beliefs of husband and wife may be similar or different. These differences can affect behavior and expectations.

Couple Closeness

Doing things together, asking each other for help, sharing hobbies, and spending free time together should be a top priority. Togetherness should be maintained throughout the marriage.

Family of Origin Closeness

How does the couple regard their upbringing and background? Do they accept, reject, or modify the way their parents viewed life and marriage? Were extended families often together or consulted about important issues?

Couple Flexibility

Does the couple compromise when problems arise?

Family of Origin Flexibility

Do the families of origin compromise when problems arise?

Six Indicators for Lack of Marital Health by Dr. John Gottman

John Gottman and his team have devoted much attention to the causes and cures of couple problems. For further reading refer to their excellent resources. [2]

1. "Harsh Start-Up"

Conversations that start up with contentiousness manifested by accusations, criticism, sarcasm, and belligerence will not provide resolution of problems.

2. "The Four Horsemen of the Apocalypse of Marriage" (Relationship Killers)

Criticism focuses on blaming, name-calling, and passing harsh judgment by attacking the person rather than a specific behavior.

Contempt contaminates and poisons the relationship by showing disgust, sarcasm, and cynicism. It is displayed by eye rolling, curling the lip, and mockery. Contempt is usually fueled by continuing and longstanding negative thoughts about the spouse.

Defensiveness seeks to protect one spouse from the other by preventing or resisting criticism, arguments, aggression or threats. It usually escalates the marital strife.

Stonewalling is obstructing and being uncooperative by not responding or shutting out the partner. It only adds to the problem by deepening the chasm between the couple.

3. "Flooding"

Flooding is feeling emotionally overwhelmed with feelings which tend to produce stonewalling. The best way to avoid flooding is to disengage when the situation becomes too heated.

4. "Body Language"

Body language involves physiological reactions which produce a flight-or-fight response. The heart races, respiration increases, blood pressure rises, sweat pours out, and adrenaline freely flows. These signs of severe personal distress signal future problems.

5. "Failed Repair Attempts"

Failure to repair damage and rebuild and restore the relationship to a healthy state is the most accurate predictor of a miserable future. A couple can have all of the other five indicators in the marriage and succeed in repairing the damage caused by them, but if they suffer from failed repair attempts, they are headed for disaster. Taking a time out, using appropriate humor, apologizing, calming oneself down, and soothing each other are some good ways to stop the emotional hemorrhage.

Each spouse must take personal responsibility for making repair attempts when things become too hot.

6. "Bad Memories"

Couples who are suffering from deep-seated negative feelings will usually color every marital memory with negativity. This is similar to a drop of ink completely darkening a glass of water. Even the good times are viewed darkly. The relationship is in serious trouble if this has occurred.

Components of Marital Intimacy

Marriage is a series of relationships which individually and collectively create intimacy. Healthy marriages are like an eight-cylinder engine firing on all eight cylinders; unhealthy marriages are not firing on all cylinders. Counselors should assist the couple in understanding and developing greater intimacy in each of these eight areas.

1. Intellectual intimacy includes sharing ideas and thoughts.

2. Emotional intimacy includes warmth and closeness.

3. Social intimacy is spending time together, interacting, and doing things together.

4. Geographical intimacy is living together and sharing the same space.

5. Psychological intimacy is understanding how a partner thinks, feels, and will react.

6. Sexual intimacy is an expression of one's whole self to the other and sharing love.

7. Religious intimacy is the sharing of faith, morals, and ideals.

8. Legal intimacy is having a marriage certificate.

Pathological Marriage Interaction Patterns

In addition to identifying abnormal personality functioning in couples, it is important to recognize patterns of interaction between the two people. Consider the characteristics of oil and water separately, but it is necessary to consider their interaction when mixed together. People demonstrate certain characteristics as they interact with other personalities. The minister should be able to recognize and understand these unhealthy interaction patterns in marriages. These interactions are not gender specific. Any of the following roles may be filled by either sex.

Half Marriage

Only half of this marriage functions properly. One dominates the other in a master/slave relationship. The master or A is dominant, controlling, and demanding while the slave B is submissive and passive. Couples should be taught biblical submission, a concept which is widely misunderstood. Ephesians 5 tells us that we must love a spouse into submission and mutually submit to one another.

Attaching/Detaching Marriage

This is also called a Push/Pull marriage. One who is seeking intimacy chases the other while the other distances himself. The roles may switch over time.

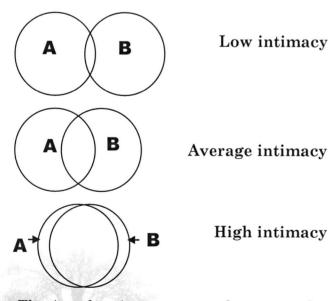

Low intimacy

Average intimacy

High intimacy

The Attacher A pursues, reaches out, and pulls closer while the Detacher B tries to push away.

Consider a woman who chases after a man until she gets him to marry her. After they are married, her interests turn to other things causing the husband to pursue her. Usually the Attacher diffuses his need by finding other interests or becoming so frustrated that he gives up trying to attach. In turn, the Detacher B then becomes the pursuer, making him then the Attacher. Often A and B switch roles after A has given up. Many business people, doctors, and ministers are detachers.

> Did You Know...Half-Marriages, Attaching/Detaching and Child Marriages account for 50% of all couples seeing a marriage counselor?

If both partners desire and produce the same amount of intimacy, there should be no problem, but if one partner desires less intimacy and the other more, you have the setup for an attaching/detaching interactional pattern. Therapy involves helping each to understand the needs of the other and to move the circles more to the middle.

Pseudo Marriage

This marriage has little or no intimacy as both partners are only going through the motions. The eight components of marital intimacy make a marriage. This couple is lacking seven of the eight components of marital intimacy. The only relationship they posses is the legal. Therapy involves helping them develop each of the seven missing intimacy components.

Neurotic Marriage

In this marriage, one is sick (mentally or physically) and the other acts as the caretaker. One suffers from depression or a debilitating illness. In these cases the healthy spouse operates around the problem. Therapy consists of creating realistic expectations, supporting the care-giving spouse, and providing suggestions to improve their situation and relationship.

Therapeutic Marriage

In this marriage one or both partners needs comfort and empathy during a period of rebound from another relationship. When the rebound phase ends, the relationship often ends with it. Therapy involves helping them transition from a therapeutic interaction where most of their conversations focus upon their past with its hurts to a more normal relationship.

Sadomasochistic Marriage

In this marriage, one partner likes to inflict pain (physical/psychological) and the other receives the pain (often because of guilt). We know that hurt people hurt people. Here are some common techniques abusers use to control and manipulate their victims.

- Physical abuse includes pushing, shoving, hitting, twisting arms, tripping, biting, punching, kicking, grabbing, beating, and throwing down.

- Emotional abuse includes putting her down or making her feel bad about herself, making her think she is crazy, or playing mind games.

- Economic abuse includes trying to keep her from getting or keeping a job, making her ask for money, giving her an allowance, or taking her money.

- Sexual abuse includes making her do sexual things against her will, physically attacking the sexual parts of her body, or treating her like a sex object.

- He uses children to give messages making her feel guilty. If there is a separation, he uses the children to send messages as a means of harassment.

- Threats are made or carried out to emotionally hurt her, threatening to take the children, to commit suicide, or to report her to welfare are common abuses.

- Using male privileges includes treating her like a servant and making all the major decisions.

- Intimidation involves putting her in fear by using menacing expressions, actions or gestures, using a loud voice, smashing things, or destroying her property.

- Isolation involves controlling what she does, who she sees, where she goes, and to whom she speaks. Successful treatment usually involves her developing an attitude that says, "I don't deserve this. You are not going to treat me like that any more." She must take the necessary actions to prevent recurrence.

Devitalized Marriage

The marriage begins rightly but gradually loses vitality and intimacy similar to a tire deflating. The relationship desperately needs revitalization which becomes the focus of counseling. It can even degrade to a pseudo marriage if successful intervention does not take place.

Dependent/Codependent Marriage

One person needs something else (example alcohol or drugs) while the partner needs the other person. Therapy consists of helping the dependent spouse become free of the dependency and the codependent spouse to overcome the need to be needed.

Child Marriage

Both partners in the marriage are always fighting, demonstrating immature behavior like two children arguing in a sandbox. Therapy involves re-parenting the partners to help them outgrow their childish ways.

Alienating Marriage

Both partners are dominant and hostile toward each other causing alienation. Treatment focuses on reducing the hostility and dominance of each partner.

Hostile-Dependent Marriage

In the hostile-dependent marriage, one or both partners exudes hostility and demandingness to cover up his or her strong dependency needs, which they despise as a sign of personal weakness. Therapy involves revealing and correcting the underlying dependency needs, removing the hostile cover up, and working through the corresponding issues. One or both spouses present an "impossible to please no matter what" profile. Helping the partners to understand the two sides within the person is a formidable task, especially if they are in denial.

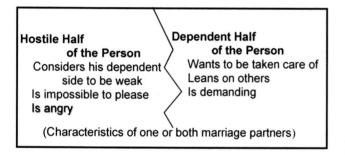

Hostile Half
of the Person
Considers his dependent side to be weak
Is impossible to please
Is angry

Dependent Half
of the Person
Wants to be taken care of
Leans on others
Is demanding

(Characteristics of one or both marriage partners)

Other Areas to Consider in Assessment and Counseling of Troubled Marriages

There are inherent differences between men and women. Men and women are different in every cell of their bodies; God made them that way. Although there is considerable overlap in both their needs and desires, there are also important differences. Women often express a strong need for their husbands to cherish them and provide them with security, romance, and attention. Men frequently express a strong need for their wives to show them respect and responsiveness. The understanding of each spouse regarding these respective needs is essential; if these basic needs are not being satisfied in the relationship, problems may develop.

Gary Chapman has identified five primary methods of expressing love, which he has called Love Languages.[3] They are receiving gifts, acts of service, physical touch, words of affirmation, and quality time. It is important to understand both your preferred love language(s) and the preferred love language(s) of your partner. It is the mismatch and the misunderstanding of the respective love languages that can cause serious problems.

The role of self-esteem of each partner in the relationship is also of great importance. Individuals with healthy self-esteem will be less threatened by differences with their partner. Healthy self-esteem also leads to healthier expressions and interaction.

The distribution of power in a relationship is vital to the counselor's assessment of the functioning and fixing of troubled marriages. A review of the eleven pathological interaction patterns (cited earlier in this section) using a power possession and distribution assessment will reveal that incorrect use of power can play a role in a troubled marriage.

Intimacy is another major area of consideration. The balance of closeness and distance preferred by each partner in a relationship is also a vital component in marital functioning. Its assessment and understanding is important in the comprehension of patterns often repeated in troubled marriages.

The same problem may have an entirely different root cause and meaning for different couples. For instance, if a wife complains she is uninformed of her husband's constant job changes, the underlying motivation might be one of self-esteem. He cannot stand the thought of her thinking less of him. It may also be motivated by an issue of power and control, and ultimately, he is trying to show her she cannot control him. The underlying motivation might also be an issue related to intimacy in that he knows his frequent job changes upset her thus creating distance between them. This allows him more independence and time alone. Counselors should be alert to the root problems and their motivations rather than merely addressing symptoms.

The Six Marital Stages

One must assess the couple's success in navigating through the various stages in their marriage. It has been said that every marriage is in reality six marriages or a marriage which progresses through six stages. Unresolved problems from a previous stage will carry over into the next stages. Each stage has its tasks which must be successfully resolved.

Tasks of Stage 1 (Newlywed Stage)
- Leave home and bond with his or her spouse. The biblical requirement is to leave and cleave, ...*For this cause shall a man leave father and mother, and shall cleave to his wife, and they twain shall be one flesh?* (Matthew 19:5)
- Develop a system of marital functioning, divide responsibilities, and settle the decisions that must be made early in the marriage. During this stage the initial blueprint is developed and implemented for the functioning of the relationship.

Tasks of Stage 2 (Arrival of Children)
- Adjust to a six-way interaction instead of two: mom to dad, dad to mom, mom to baby, baby to mom, dad to baby and baby to dad. The more children, the more dilution there will be of the interaction process thus changing the dynamic of the relationships in the home completely.
- Deal with the issues of child rearing, time taken from the marriage by the children, and the children's impact on their individual lives and marriage relationship.

Tasks of Stage 3 (School-Age Children)
- Adjust to the demands of a school schedule and of outside activities on their lives and marriage.
- Handle the increasing pressures of finances, family, and work.

Tasks of Stage 4 (Teenage Children)
- Adjust to the independence and interdependence of teenagers with the pressures and problems these years can create.
- Handle the various demands on their time, finances, and lives including conflict and stress caused by dating, driving, children's circle of friends, possible rebellion, and experimentation.
- Handle the pressures of preparing their teenagers for college or career.

Tasks of Stage 5 (The Empty Nest)
- Adjust to being alone as a couple with no children or children's activities to occupy their time and attention.
- Reestablish a marital closeness as a middle-aged couple.
- Handle mid-life crisis issues.

Tasks of Stage 6 (Retirement and Aging)
- Face old age, its pressures, possibilities, and declining health in each other.
- Prepare for the end of their relationship when one is left alone.

Goals of Marital Counseling

Each partner will understand himself or herself better and accept areas for growth.
All couples have faults and blind spots that contribute to marital tension. No issue between partners is one-sided, so each person must look to see where and how he or she is contributing to the problem.

Each spouse will understand the other better.
Understanding is often the beginning of acceptance and change. Spouses will tell others, "I just don't understand him." Knowing the reason, thinking, or motivation for a person's actions may not remedy the situation, but it helps the spouse to at least appreciate the other side of the story a little better.

The couple will understand their marital system or interaction pattern problems and accept areas for growth.

The marital system includes several things: 1) a set of expectations which can include standard of living, child-rearing, and interaction with family and friends, 2) unwritten rules, including taboos and sharing of responsibilities, 3) a mental blueprint for marriage which reflects what each spouse has learned from his or her parents. Marital interaction patterns which tend to recur may be unhealthy. Finally, each couple does specific things which contribute to marital malaise. Wise counselors notice how each partner may be causing or contributing to a problem.

Making a Marriage Healthier

It is critical for couples to have an overwhelming ratio of positive experiences to negative ones, the more the better. They need to nurture their love and relationship with pleasant time together, doing enjoyable things together, and practicing the positive little things which demonstrate their love for each other. Relationships are like plants; they must be nurtured to prosper. There is no substitute for expressions of caring and sharing. Find out what makes your spouse feel loved and appreciated by you and vice versa. An excellent exercise is to ask each partner to write down his or her specific needs which they wish their spouse to meet. Then share the lists with each other and have the partner carefully consider and spell out the ways he or she will work to meet each of the other's needs. The next step is to have each provide feedback and specific suggestions to each other about methods to meet the respective needs. Finally, each is assigned to take the list and work everyday to meet their partner's needs. Another excellent method to revitalize a relationship is to have each provide thoughtful and detailed answers to these questions.

1. I used to feel loved when you...
2. I presently feel loved when you...
3. I would feel loved if you would ...

They then discuss the things each listed and are given the assignments of doing them on a regular basis.

It is also important to resolve the resolvable problems constructively and handle the unresolvable ones in a mature and thoughtful manner. If a couple is stuck in a rut of negativity and hostility, it is crucial to seek help from a qualified counselor who will help to navigate the turbulent waters and get them unstuck. They must know, understand, and put forth the effort to meet each other's needs and to fulfill each other's desires. These steps are essential to having a healthy marriage.

Handling Marital Affairs

Infidelity is a major or contributing factor in one-third of all divorces. Every marriage counselor must be able to successfully guide a couple through marital infidelity issues if he is to be successful in repairing marital relationships. Note, Christian couples are not exempt from sexual problems including episodes and affairs.

Types of Affairs

Counselors must differentiate between episodes and affairs. Episodes are short-lived sexual experiences with little or no emotional attachment. Affairs are sexual experiences with emotional attachment; affairs are usually more serious than episodes. Emotional affairs are unhealthy emotional attachments which do not become overtly sexual but can nevertheless be a threat to the relationship.

A special caution is necessary for ministers who are counseling members of the opposite sex. The redirection of feelings and desires toward the counselor can occur in the counseling environment. The opposite can happen when the counselor gets inappropriately involved in the problems of the counselee.

Strict boundaries must be established and enforced when counseling any member of the opposite sex.

Causes of Affairs

There are numerous motivations for a spouse to enter into an affair. The following is a comprehensive list of possible reasons.

Excitement	Loneliness
Adventure	Validate desirability
Attention	Power and control
Affirmation	Variety
Revenge	Attraction
Romance	More sex
Love	Open marriage
Understanding	Desire of emotional
Companionship	closeness
Lust	Dissatisfaction with
Conquest	mate
Curiosity	Marital unhappiness
Peer pressure	Feeling of importance
Addiction	Self-esteem issues
Escape	To show a partner the
Independence	seriousness of a mari-
Bi-sexuality	tal situation
Opportunity	Make up for missed op-
Send message to spouse	portunity
Prelude to divorce	Exit (to force the partner
Opportunity	to file for divorce)
To feel special	Refusal of mate to per-
Unmet emotional needs	form desired sex acts
Opportunity	To hold on to a desirable
Entitlement	partner
Mid-life crisis	Personal inadequacy
Boredom	(Can't say no)

Correction of Affairs

Women tend to have affairs less often than men and usually do so for emotional rather than physical reasons. Their affairs are more likely to lead to the end of their marriages. Men tend to have affairs more often than women and usually for physical reasons. Their affairs are less likely than the affairs of their wives to lead to the end of their marriages. Affairs occurring near the beginning of the marriage are more likely to end in divorce than affairs occurring after many years of marriage. Affairs tear down the wall of trust in marriage and must be rebuilt brick by brick over a period of time. These steps are essential to the restoration of the marital relationship.

1. Repent of the sin of adultery. Terminate contact with the third party.

2. Address in general terms the who, what, when, and where of the affair.

3. Understand the hurt, disappointment, and anger caused by the affair.

4. Understand the motivation for or causes of the affair.

5. Forgive the offense.

6. Obtain counseling to address the relationship issues in the marriage.

7. Seek accountability to avoid future involvements.

8. Rebuild the marital relationship emotionally, spiritually, and physically.

Recommended Scripture References

Rejoice in wife of youth, Proverbs 5:18-20
Wife is a crown, Proverbs 12:4
Love covers mistakes, Proverbs 17:9
Finds a good wife, Proverbs 18:22
Prudent wife from the Lord, Proverbs 19:14
A quarrelsome wife, Proverbs 21:9, 19; 25:24
Two better than one, Ecclesiastes 4:9-12
Enjoy life with your wife, Ecclesiastes 9:9
Divorce allowed, Matthew 19:3-9
Husband and wife relationship, 1 Corinthians 7:1-7
Unbelievers/believers married, 1 Corinthians 7:10-16
Instructions to husband and wife, Ephesians 5:21-33
Elder allowed one wife, Titus 1:6
Marriage instructions to women, Titus 2:3-5
Purity, Hebrews 13:4
No fear in love, 1 John 4:18

Funerals

It is recommended that you select a good service manual to use in your ministry, particularly for weddings and funerals. A good manual will contain appropriate scripture and suggested components for various ceremonies and services. Visit a Christian bookstore and choose one which best meets your needs.

Visit the dying as often as they wish. Be aware that people can be very different in the way they desire to face their final days. Some prefer privacy and minimal contact with others. Some crave much contact with family, friends, and the church staff. One dying saint recently lamented that his church had taught him well how to live as a Christian but had never taught him how to die. Compare that with John Wesley's observation that his people died well. How to minister to the dying and their survivors is included in the section on *Grief Counseling* in this manual.

Prepare them for death (if you are actually there when they die). Offer to read scripture, pray with them, hold hands with family members around the bed, join in singing songs, offer words of support, or anything appropriate the person or family requests. When the dying one has taken his last breath, suggest to the family that a special prayer be offered to give him up to God.

Work closely with the funeral director and accommodate the family as possible in regard to the order of the service and arrangements in the church or funeral home. If you are not there when the person dies and are called later, offer to go quickly. Offer sincere condolences and read several comforting passages of scripture.

Listen as the family describes the last days and hours of their loved one; ask questions to prompt the family to talk about their loss.

Pray with the family. Demonstrate both sympathy and empathy. Make phone calls, contact the funeral home, or assist with other arrangements if asked. Ask the family if they would like a funeral dinner and offer the services of the church in preparing and serving the meal. Request an estimate of the expected attendance so you can be prepared. (If you are not asked to officiate at the funeral service, attend the visitation and offer your support and comfort the family there.)

Meet with the entire family at their earliest convenience to obtain each one's contribution to the eulogy. Work with the family in preparing the funeral sermon to include their special wishes or requests previously made by the deceased. Following are some helpful suggestions for funeral services.

Do:
- Include personal history.
- Personalize the service. Use the name of the deceased and acknowledge the family.
- Share important special memories.
- Encourage family participation.
- Show sympathy and empathy.
- Add your own personal touches.
- Tell the spiritual journey of the deceased.
- Read scripture or poems.
- Present the gospel.
- Tailor the service to meet the needs of the living.
- Assist in finding the desired music.
- Use humorous incidents as appropriate.

Do not:
- <u>Ever</u> talk about hell.
- Make the service too long.
- Ignore specific regional customs and practices.

Prepare an order of service and make copies for the funeral director, musician, soloist, sound technician, associates, and others assisting in the service.

Before the funeral, prepare your heart by thinking of the loved ones at whose service you are officiating. Treat them as you would want to be treated.

Diligently prepare the message and be compassionate in your delivery. Be prepared to handle emergencies and problems. It is their grief not yours. Show empathy and sympathy, but know that they alone can experience the full extent of their loss.

Take your place at the head of the casket for the final viewing at the conclusion of the service and be prepared to offer support and assistance as the family lingers at the casket.

Make sure to inform the funeral staff whether you will be riding with the funeral director or driving your own car to the cemetery. At the cemetery lead the casket from the hearse to the burial site. Make the committal service brief but meaningful. It is their final goodbye before leaving their loved one at the cemetery. What happens in those final moments will remain with them forever.

When you finish your committal, shake hands with members of the family seated in front of the casket and offer them flowers from the funeral spray.

If necessary, further comfort them after the services and escort them back to their car. Attend the memorial luncheon or funeral dinner and say grace over the meal before family members begin eating.

Make follow-up phone calls and visits. Pray frequently for the family during the difficult days which follow the services. After families return home, many report they feel neglected, lonely, and depressed. When the full extent of their loss sinks in and they are left with their grief, it is then that they need much assistance and support. Suggest that they become involved in a grief recovery group. If your church does not have one, refer them to a church or hospital which does.

An example of a funeral sermon incorporating all of the suggestions is included in the appendix.

Recommended Scripture References

Seat empty, 1 Samuel 20:18
Loss of David's child, 2 Samuel 12:19-23
The Lord is my Shepherd, Psalm 23
He shall strengthen your heart, Psalm 31:24
In you Lord, I hope, Psalm 38:15; 39:7
Hope thou in God, Psalm 42:5, 43:5
Hope continually, Psalm 71:15
Hope on your Word, Psalm 119:49, 81
Merciful kindness for my comfort, Psalm 119:76, 77
You are my hiding place, Psalm 119:114
Happy, hope in you, Psalm 146:5
Blessed are those who mourn, Matthew 5:4
I am the Resurrection, John 11:25
In my Father's house, John 14:1-7
Not leave comfortless, John 14:18
Now abideth faith, hope, I Corinthians 13:13
Death where is why sting? 1 Corinthians 15:51-58
God of all comfort, 2 Corinthians 1:3-4
Treasure in earthen vessels, 2 Corinthians 4:7-12
Earthly house destroyed, 2 Corinthians 5:1-10
Consolation in Christ, Philippians 12:1
Those fallen asleep, 1 Thessalonians 4:13
Comfort one another, 1 Thessalonians 4:18; 5:4
In hope of eternal life, Titus 1:1
Surrounded by a cloud of witnesses, Hebrews 12:1,2
New heaven, Revelations 21:2-4

Weddings

Weddings today require great flexibility with protocol. The preferences of the bride and groom may be more or less traditional but should be honored within reason. The planning and organization of the wedding should begin as early as possible. Great effort should be taken to adhere to the schedule set forth by the couple. Do your part to make this a very special day for all involved.

1. Schedule the wedding date as early as possible to avoid conflicts with other church activities.

2. Have an initial meeting with the couple. In addition to determining if there may be any legitimate reason why you will not be able to marry the couple, the following should be done during the meeting:

   ♦ Obtain information about the couple and their plans.

   ♦ Determine if a referral is warranted for professional pre-marital therapy.

   ♦ If a referral is not warranted, discuss pre-marital testing or counseling with *Prepare/Enrich* or an alternate assessment instrument.

   ♦ Get details of desired ceremony. A sample wedding preparation questionnaire is included in the appendix.

   ♦ Determine the level of their desired participation in the ceremony. Find out if they are writing their own vows, singing to each other, or reading a composition during the ceremony.

   ♦ Schedule the rehearsal.

   ♦ Learn details of the rehearsal dinner.

   ♦ Plan the wedding folder.

   ♦ Introduce couple to church personnel who will be involved in the wedding including the musicians, the tech person who will oversee the P.A. system and lighting, and the custodian. If these people are not currently available make sure the couple has their phone numbers and can contact them at their earliest convenience.

   ♦ Discuss fees.

   ♦ Discuss plans for the reception.

   ♦ Obtain biographical information from each partner about their courtship, engagement, spiritual history, and what attracted each to the other.

   ♦ Give a list of recommended reading materials.

   ♦ Schedule future pre-marital counseling appointments.

   ♦ Answer all questions.

3. Administer pre-marital assessments.

4. During the final pre-marital session, go over the final details of the wedding and prepare for the rehearsal.

5. Lead the participants through the rehearsal unless a wedding planner is used. Following are suggestions for the wedding rehearsal.

Complete the rehearsal in one hour as most participants are anxious to learn their roles and get on to the rehearsal dinner.

Begin by introducing yourself and welcoming everyone to the rehearsal. Ask the bride and groom to introduce all the participants of the wedding party. Go through the wedding ceremony three times.

During the first run-through, the participants remain in their seats and listen as you go through the details of the ceremony step by step.

The second time, they take their respective places and actually walk through the ceremony quickly.

In the final rehearsal, the wedding party performs as they will in the actual wedding ceremony.

At the conclusion, assemble the wedding party and cover the following:

* The importance of starting the wedding on time
* The critical role the ushers play in seating guests and their part in the wedding
* The transfer of the rings during the ceremony
* The signing of the marriage license
* Time of arrival for wedding participants
* Dressing arrangements and locations
* Minimizing anxiety during the ceremony
* Handling any contingencies which may occur in the ceremony
* The reception line, if one is used
* The scheduling of pictures to be taken before or after the wedding
* Questions

Close with prayer, then join the wedding party at the rehearsal dinner.

6. Arrive early for the ceremony and be prepared to handle unforeseen problems.

7. Perform the ceremony personalizing the service with material about the couple's history, courtship, engagement, spiritual journey, and what attracted each to the other.

Complete each part of the ceremony with sensitivity and finesse. Always be prepared and complete your task to the best of your ability.

8. Attend the reception and participate in any pictures the family may request.

9. Follow up by urging the couple to attend a newlywed class for growth and fellowship. Continue to minister to them. The best pre-marital counseling occurs six months after the wedding when they have begun to experience some of the realities of married life.

Recommended Scripture References

Cleave unto his wife, Genesis 2:21; Matthew 19:5
Loved with everlasting love, Jeremiah 34:3
Joined let man not separate, Matthew 19:6, Mark 10:9
Love as God loves, John 3:16
Love one another, John 13:34-35
Continue in Christ's love, John 15:9
Love fulfills the law, Romans 13:10
The love chapter. 1 Corinthians 13
By love serve one another, Galatians 5:13
Fruit of the Spirit, Galatians 5:22
Forbearing in love, Ephesians 4:2
Speak the truth in love, Ephesians 4:15
Love wives as Christ loves church, Ephesians 5:25
Love wife as his own body, Ephesians 5:28-33
Love as loves himself, Ephesians 5:33
Love abounds, Philippians 1:9
Knit together in love, Colossians 2:2
Be not bitter, Colossians 3:9
Abound in love, 1 Thessalonians 3:2
Love your husband, Titus 2:4
Let us love one another, 1 John 4:7

Visitation

Is any among you afflicted? let him pray. Is any merry? let him sing psalms. Is any sick among you? Let him call for the elders of the church; and let them pray over him, anointing him with oil in the name of the Lord: And the prayer of faith shall save the sick, and the Lord shall raise him up; and if he have committed sins, they shall be forgiven him. James 5:13-15

One of the major duties of the minister is to make a variety of visits. These visits may be to the healthy or to the sick, to church members or non-church members, and to homes, hospitals, or nursing homes. It is essential to prepare your heart for each type of visit.

Goals of Visitation

One of the main goals of visitation is to show empathy, making the person you are visiting feel as though they are important and not just another stop in your day. You should be able to put yourself in the position of the person you are visiting and think about what you might like to get out of such a visit.

Another goal of visiting is to create a sense of hope, reminding him that God is present and is faithful in His help, His comfort, and His love.

A minister can often help the person see the positive in his situation. Encourage him to dwell on God and His promises rather than on despair or illness.

Needs

Before the visit, it is important to have the addresses and phone numbers for the hospital and pastoral care. You should have a good sense of where you are going; checking addresses and placing a courtesy call prior to your visit might be appropriate. You should also have your clergy sticker prominently displayed in your vehicle as required when visiting the hospital. It is wise to carry a pocket New Testament with Psalms.

Verses for encouragement include Psalm 46:1; Psalm 121:1-2; Isaiah 40:31; Matthew 11:28-30; Romans 8:28-29; 2 Corinthians 12:9-10; Hebrews 4:15-16; 1 Peter 5:7.

Hospital Visitation Do's and Don'ts

1. Do get a list of your church's patients from the hospital's pastoral care department before going.

2. Do introduce yourself to the patient.

3. Do try to understand, at least to a limited degree, what is the nature of the illness.

4. Do seek to be an encouragement by being cheerful and positive; smile and use humor if appropriate.

5. Do share spiritual insights and witness if appropriate. Assure the patient that he will be in your prayers and that others in the church are praying for him. You can briefly include the gospel in a prayer.

6. Do telephone the patient later that day if a connection could not be made at the hospital.

7. Do Not open a closed door to a room occupied by a person of the opposite sex. Get a nurse to check for you or knock and wait for an invitation to enter.

8. Do Not stay long.

9. Do Not make the person agitated.

10. Do Not be intrusive by asking personal questions or for details about their illness or operation. Don't be nosy.

11. Do Not appear to be knowledgeable about something of which you are not.

12. Do Not talk about things that add mental burdens to the patient. (This would in-

clude talking about your own problems or mentioning someone else who did not recover from a similar illness.)

13. Do Not be loud.

14. Do Not ignore others in the room.

15. Do Not forget to leave something positive with them, such as *The Daily Bread* or *God at my Bedside,* a tape, or CD of a positive uplifting sermon.

Suggestions for Making Shut-in Visits

1. These visits can be more lengthy, depending on the person's condition and interest.

2. Bring a card or a gift of candy, cookies, flowers, stamps, notepaper, and pen as appropriate. You could offer a recorded sermon.

3. Listen well.

4. Share encouraging words and scripture.

5. Update them about what is happening at church. Share that they are in your thoughts and prayers. Mention that the whole church is praying for them.

6. Inquire about their needs.

7. Pray together.

Calling on Church Visitors

1. A designated church member volunteer makes phone contact within 48 hours of the church visit.

2. A letter of welcome with literature about the church is mailed.

3. A designated staff member calls within the next several days and offers a staff visit.

4. The appropriate staff member (based upon demographics) follows up with a visit.

5. The visit should include the following:
   - A warm welcome and expression of thanks for attending Edgewood
   - Questions about the visitor's background and spiritual condition
   - Presentation of the gospel, if warranted
   - Giving of pertinent literature
   - Asking and answering questions about the church or spiritual matters
   - Discussion of Sunday school classes, Class 101, and church ministries
   - Offer of making introductions to appropriate people for social connections
   - Prayer for God's blessings upon the family

6. Follow up at periodic intervals.

7. Enter person's name in assimilation program for tracking.

8. Watch to make sure the person does not get snubbed while attending services.

Recommended Scripture References

God heals thy diseases, Psalm 103:3
Learn from affliction, Psalm 119:71
Spirit sustained the infirm, Proverbs 18:14
Cup of cold water, Matthew 10:40-42
Ministry to needy, Matthew 25:36; James 5:14
Be hospitable to those who cannot repay, Luke 14:12-14
Purpose to sickness, John 11:4
Tribulation worketh patience, Romans 5:3
Hospitality practiced, Romans 12:13-18
Hospitality to stranger, 1 Corinthians 16:10-11
Refreshing visitors, 1 Corinthians 16:18
Be wise toward outsiders, Colossians 4:5
Perfected through suffering, Hebrews 2:10
Testing, trials, problems, James 1:2-4, 12; 1 Peter 1:6-7; 4:1-2
Pray for the sick, James 5:13-15
Sincere hospitality, 1 Peter 4:9

Preaching

Preparing to Preach

Preaching is the proclaiming of the Word of God. It is the most important part of the ministry; the call to full-time Christian service is often referred to as a call to preach. Perfecting one's preaching skills should be of major importance to any minister. Some very well known preachers admit to starting their careers with little skill and few results, but they worked diligently to improve and finally experienced great results. We need to do whatever is necessary to become better prepared in all of the things God has called us to do, especially the preaching of God's Word. Practice does not necessarily make perfect; but if not practiced correctly, it does tend to make permanent even our bad habits. We must do the right things in the right way to improve. The suggestions in this section should provide helpful guidance toward practice making perfect.

Paul said he was compelled to preach then further said, *...woe is unto me, if I preach not the gospel!* (1 Corinthians 9:16). Once we hear the call of God, obedience at once and in every area of our lives is expected. Paul said in 2 Timothy 4:2 that we are to preach the Word and that our lives must become the holy example of the reality of our message. Oswald Chambers said that the purpose of Pentecost was not to teach the disciples something but to make them the incarnation of what they preached so they would literally become God's message in the flesh. Jesus said near the beginning of his ministry, recorded in Mark 1:38, *...Let us go into the next towns, that I may preach there also: for therefore came I forth.* His purpose was to bring the message of life. Our duty is the same. For this kind of ministry there must be preparation.

1. Preaching involves four kinds of preparation: mental, emotional, spiritual, and physical. Spiritual preparation involves continually walking with the Lord in the Spirit and seeking God's leadership as to what He would have you to preach. Mental preparation includes study of the text and topic as you develop your message. Emotional preparation involves developing a frame of mind that fits the subject matter (a sense of awe when you preach about heaven or a sense of heaviness when you preach about judgment). Physical preparation involves staying physically fit to increase stamina and getting adequate rest, especially before delivering the sermon, so that you will be mentally alert and physically strong.

2. Develop a seed file (tangible or electronic) of sermon topics, texts, Scriptures, and illustrations. Continually update it throughout your ministry.

3. When you determine a topic and text for your message, gather material at least throughout the week (preferably longer). Keep adding to it until you are ready to develop the message. Then review all the materials and thoughts you have accumulated and condense them down to your skeleton outline. Then flesh out the rest of the message.

4. Develop a clear outline of the message.

5. Watch for and assess expressed and unexpressed needs within your congregation. Listen to people as they discuss their problems and needs with each other. Note the concerns of members who come to you for counsel. Observe the state of the congregation regarding energy, motivation, commitment, and spirituality.

6. Don't allow other ministerial work to crowd out your preparation time. Many busy pastors relegate their sermon prepa-

ration to available time left over after their other work is done each week. Preaching should be first in importance because it is the central part of your ministry. You are in a position to influence virtually every member of your congregation when you address them from the pulpit. Never take lightly that responsibility.

7. Sermons should be like carpenter's tools. They should be instruments to build, achieve desired results, meet specific needs, and fix problems.

8. Read, listen to, and watch the best preachers. Learn from their messages and deliveries.

9. Be sure to include illustrations in your messages. Spurgeon observed that illustrations are like windows that let the light in. Mark 4:34 tells that the master teacher and preacher, Jesus, never spoke without telling a story. You can't improve upon the example of Jesus Christ.

Every sermon should include an impact illustration, one that is on point to illustrate with clarity and power the main theme of the message. It should be dynamic in appeal, practical in application, and leave a lasting impression on the audience so that long after the details of the sermon are forgotten, the impact illustration will be remembered.

10. Include in your notes enough detail so that you can review your sermon, even years later, and recall what you said.

11. Good sermons make the listener learn something (appeals to the mind), feel something (appeals to emotions), and decide to do something (appeals to the will).

12. Messages should be relevant and practical and include interpretation, exhortation, illustration, and application. Never allow people to hear a message and have them leave asking "What did he say?" or thinking "So what?"

13. Demonstrate both passion and compassion as you deliver the message.

14. Always have a **saver** as part of your outline. A sermon saver is an illustration, bit of humor, anecdote, or testimony which you can use to regain the attention of the congregation if they begin to lose interest. (See examples below.) An usher once asked John Wesley if he wanted him to wake up listeners if they fell asleep during the message. Wesley responded that if people fall asleep when he was

Examples of Sermon Savers

Story	Drama	Visual aid
Illustration	Music	Testimony
Joke	Song	Object lesson
Dramatic pause	Audio	Passable visual aid object
Object lesson	Video	Co-speaker (recorded/live)
Animated gestures	Alter lighting	Enthusiasm
Voice inflection	Brain teaser	Passion
Word picture	Poem	Hand-outs
Question	Dramatic reading	Roller coaster effect (speed
Walking among audience	Shocking statement	up, slow down, turn, loop)
Audience interaction	Catchy phrase	Switch gears by doing some-
Question and answer	Appropriate sarcasm	thing totally different
Audience participation	Statistics	Special skill or talent worked
Descriptive language	Artistic illustration	into the message

preaching, the usher should wake him up.

15. Always have a specific purpose with a definite goal for each message. Evaluate if that purpose was realized and if your goal was achieved by the sermon. A person who has no goal will hit it every time. Sermons without objectives are like travelers without destinations, they have nowhere to go.

16. Abraham Lincoln once attended church with a friend. After the services the friend stated that he thought the sermon was very good. He inquired of Lincoln if he agreed. Lincoln was quiet and, when pressed, gave the opinion that it was not a particularly good sermon. When the friend inquired why he felt that way, Lincoln responded that a great sermon challenges people to do something or to be something more and that this sermon included no such challenge.

17. Never judge the effectiveness of a sermon by its flow and fluency. Sometimes a sermon which you feel was not a good effort will be used of God in unforeseen ways. One pastor mentioned that a sermon he struggled with the most turned out to be the one that influenced a member of his family more than any other.

18. Always prepare a good introduction, an excellent body of the sermon, and a strong conclusion. Read and reread sermon preparation books on homiletics, types of sermons, styles of delivery, effectiveness of preaching, and crafting the sermon. When you stop learning, you stop leading.

19. Use the sermon preparation checklist (page 189) as a tool for improvement. As an airplane pilot uses his checklist to ensure the readiness of the aircraft for flight, so the preparation checklist is a means of ensuring that your sermon is ready for delivery.

20. Good preaching is interactive in nature. Preachers should be constantly watching their audience to see if they are receiving the message. If they are not, then midcourse adjustments need to be made. Move closer to the audience, raise your voice, launch into a story, become more animated, use a long dramatic pause, modulate your tone and voice, or modify the material to ensure that the message sent is the message received.

21. Develop the habit of using first, second, and third degree stimuli in your messages. For example, third degree stimuli would be simply describing a piece of music; this is the weakest of the three. Second degree stimuli would be playing the song for the audience; a first degree stimuli would be having the musical group perform before the audience. First degree stimuli are the most powerful of the three and the most preferred. Speakers use much third degree stimuli, but you should strive to use first degree stimuli as often as you can and to use second degree when first degree stimuli are not available. This will make your messages more appealing, powerful, and effective.

22. Any time you speak you will have two kinds of competition for your audience member's attention, their external and internal perception fields. The external perception field consists of everything around them which can distract (noise, babies crying, whispering, or the hum of a fan motor). The internal perception field consists of anything going on within them which may be distracting (pain, fatigue, worry about a sick child, thinking about problems at home or work). Wise speakers realize the presence of this competition and strive to be so effective that they command the attention of their hearers in spite of these potential distractions. Make your message so compelling that they must listen to you.

23. Always try to insure that the building where you are speaking is well ventilated with temperatures not falling below 69 or above 73 degrees, adequately lighted with no shadows, and your voice is properly amplified. Paying attention to these potential external perception field distractions can make the difference between successful and unsuccessful communication. Hearing assistance devices should be available for the elderly and the hearing impaired.

24. A speaker should factor in the attention span of his hearers. Children have shorter attention spans based upon their age. If you are addressing children, you must prepare accordingly. The attention span of the adult follows a 90/20/8 minute pattern.

    ◆ 90 min. listening for comprehension
    ◆ 20 min. listening with retention
    ◆ 8 min. listening to a segment

    Therefore it is wise to break your segments into bites of 8 minutes. Include a mental break after 20 minutes with a story, demonstration, joke, change of pace, song, or film clip. The comprehension levels diminish if the message goes too long. If you watch a typical audience you will notice after 20-25 minutes their attention will wander if the speaker does not provide them a mental break and opportunity to refocus.

    The tell-tale signs of inattention are glazed over eyes, dozing, staring at the ceiling, reading, doodling, and looking at their watches. Adult's attention spans vary based upon interest in the topic, age, what's going on in their internal and external perception fields, difficulty of the material presented, and other factors. The duration of program segments of most television shows lasts approximately eight minutes before the introduction of a commercial. Keep your segments short.

25. The use of visual aids in today's visually-oriented society is highly recommended. Use of PowerPoint and other visuals is invaluable in holding and focusing the audience's attention and promoting comprehension and retention. Effective visuals should not be cluttered or distracting but should have tasteful colors with adequate contrast and an appropriate header to summarize each slide.

    Since our short-term memories can only retain five to seven items at a time, it is wise to only include about five brief items on each visual. If you include too many points, your listeners will reread the slides when they should be focusing on you. Use variety in choosing visuals. Always check for accuracy in spelling, capitalization, and punctuation. Make sure the type is large enough for the entire audience to see clearly, especially those who are older or seated in the back.

26. Practice, practice, practice. Record your sermons on audio tape and evaluate them so you can improve. Video tape your sermons so you can watch yourself as well as hear the message. Work on tone, speed, emphasis, pauses, flow, and gestures to constantly improve your preaching. Get feedback from reliable sources; strengthen your stronger areas and improve your weaker ones.

27. Billy Graham said there was no higher calling than to preach the gospel of Jesus Christ adding that he would never be willing to "step down" to run for the Presidency of the United States. If God has no higher calling than to call one to preach, believe it, practice it, and live it every day. What a privilege it is to preach the un-searchable riches of Christ!

Organization of a Good Sermon

Ways to Open a Message

- Imagination
- Quotations
- Humor
- Questions
- Personal experience
- Description
- Poem
- Statistics
- Quiz
- Dramatization
- Video clip

Body of the Message

- Will I avoid the use of religiose speech?
- Do I have first, second, and third degree stimuli?
- Will I arrest their attention?
- Will my message flow?
- Do I have a clear goal?
- Do I have examples and illustrations?
- Will I reach the intellect?
- Will I reach the emotions?
- Will I reach the conscience?
- Will I reach the will?
- Will I touch the senses?
- Do I have questions that can be asked?
- Have I asked myself *so what*?
- Will I be relevant and practical?
- Will I have credibility?
- Have I planned dramatic pauses?
- Is my message personal?
- Am I spiritually prepared?
- Am I prepared psychologically?
- Is my outline properly annotated and emphasized?
- Have I factored in the attention span of my listeners?
- Have I designed my visuals for maximum effectiveness?

Ways to Close a Message

- Ask the congregation to do something.
- Make an intellectual appeal.
- Summarize and recap.
- Tell a story.
- Use a quiz.
- Pose a question to the congregation.
- Ask for a commitment.

Winging It: Impromptu Messages

Since you will only have a few moments to organize your thoughts on any topic or scripture when you are asked to deliver an impromptu message, here are some methods to organize your thoughts for a presentation. These plans will serve you well if you commit them to memory.

1. Make your main points answer who, what, when, where, how, and why.

2. Use a problem/solution approach to your topic.

3. Use a cause/effect format.

4. Use a comparison/contrast design.

5. Use a chronological order construction.

6. Organize ideas randomly or rank ordered.

7. Develop an exposition plan of arrangement using these main points:

   - Interpretation of the verses/topic
   - Illustration of the verses/topic
   - Application of the verses/topic
   - Exhortation based on verses/topic

8. Use a lesson analysis method of organization broken down into both a doctrinal and application component.

Preaching for Interns

At Edgewood, the interns speak before our assembled staff each week. During the initial three to four months, topics are assigned immediately before they speak so they learn to master impromptu speaking. Topics assigned are easier at first then increase in difficulty. The impromptu format teaches them to think on their feet, experience the mastery of developing and organizing a message with little preparation, and makes them comfortable with spontaneous responses to questions which likely will come their way throughout their ministry.

After three or more months of impromptu speaking, they are assigned familiar topics or texts and allowed a week's preparation. As their speaking skills improve, they learn to effectively use appropriate visual aids, PowerPoint presentations, and other creative enhancements. Later they are allowed to select their own topics and texts to present messages based upon personal preferences and interests. During the two-year process, the staff gives feedback following each message with constructive criticism and suggestions for improvement. Feedback ranges from discussion of the organization, outline, and content of the message to advice about improving delivery.

The interns begin by speaking in a small room and eventually move to the church auditorium. They experience speaking in various sized rooms and different environments with the opportunity to speak at banquets, luncheon meetings, breakfast meetings, various group meetings, special events, seasonal activities, Sunday school classes, teaching in Edgewood Institute classes and eventually in the church services. After speaking some hundred times in different environments using different forms of presentation with diverse topics, they are usually vastly improved as speakers.

If an intern's message needs much improvement, the staff gives him a week to revise and deliver an improved version. The interns must constructively criticize the presentation of each visiting missionary speaker and explain how they would improve upon the presentation. The same is done with speakers they hear in other venues such as pastor's meetings. The interns are also given tapes of sermons by various speakers for review. The missionary wives follow a similar, though shorter series of steps to improve their speaking skills in preparation for their future ministries. Interns also speak to all age church groups of the church from young children to senior citizens. Participation in jail, inner city, or rescue mission ministries is encouraged. Selected books are required to be read.

> A message prepared in the mind reaches the mind.
> A message prepared in the heart reaches the heart.
> But a message prepared in the life reaches the life.

The following is a list of the assigned topics required of our missionary interns:

- Their personal testimony
- Their call into the ministry
- The importance and meaning of baptism
- How does someone know they are called into the ministry?
- What are Baptist distinctives?
- How do you know the will of God?
- How to win a person to Christ
- How do I know the Bible is true?
- How did God inspire the Bible?
- Which Bible should I use and why?
- How do you develop and maintain a closer walk with God?
- Why bad things happen to good people
- Why does God allow suffering?

- What are spiritual gifts? Which do I have?
- What is heaven like?
- Is there a hell?
- What are the Bible standards of giving?
- What is the filling of the Holy Spirit and how do I receive it?
- How do I know right from wrong?
- Three funeral messages
- Three suitable deputation messages
- Three messages for preacher's meetings
- What do I believe? Why?
- Predestination
- A Christmas message
- An Easter message
- A banquet message (after dinner speech)
- A message for senior citizens
- Ladies' meeting message
- How to win over temptation
- How to maintain integrity in ministry
- How to study the Bible
- How does God answer prayer?
- How to make a church grow
- What are the paths to ruin for a preacher and how do you resist them?
- Dealing with difficult people
- How to overcome discouragement
- What the Bible says about suicide
- Dealing with anger, your own and others
- How to keep your marriage strong
- How to raise godly children while living in a fishbowl
- Creationism/evolution: theories and proofs
- What is pride and how is it manifested in our lives?
- God's role: Problem of evil in the world
- Preaching from selected texts: John 3:3, 3:16; Romans 8:28; 2 Corinthians 5:17; Galatians 3:13; 2 Timothy 3:16; James 1:12-14

Practice Preaching Exercises

1. Get alone and practice preaching whenever possible.
2. Practice preaching spontaneously from topics selected at random.
3. Preach soundless messages using only gestures and facial expressions to develop these skills.
4. Preach while standing next to another speaker, each competing for the audience's attention.
5. Record your sermon on audio or video tape then review and evaluate it.
6. Practice preaching and teaching with audiences as often as possible. Practice opportunities may include rescue missions, street preaching, Sunday school, or devotionals.
7. Read or listen to great speakers when possible in person, on tape, radio, television, or conferences.
8. Review preaching materials continuously.
9. Ask friends and relatives to listen to you preach and give feedback.
10. Ask significant others for advice or help.
11. Build an illustration file. Keep it organized and add to it. Look for good sermon illustrations and material.
12. Develop preferred messages for special meetings and occasions.
13. Watch audiences as others speak to assess communication effectiveness.
14. Assess other speaker's presentations for content, style, interest, relevance, application, and success. Determine what could have been done to improve or correct the presentation.
15. PRACTICE. PRACTICE. PRACTICE.

Sermon Preparation Checklist

☐ Seek the Lord's leadership in what to preach.

☐ Gather information from various sources.

☐ Make a suitable outline and revise it as necessary.

☐ Identify your goals, theme, and desired results.

☐ Develop the content around your outline.

☐ Select appropriate illustrations. Illustrations are like windows which let the light in.

☐ Check the flow of the message.

☐ Determine savers and place them in appropriate positions.

☐ Bathe the sermon in prayer.

☐ Add material as you periodically meditate on the message.

☐ Think like a listener asking yourself the major questions.

☐ Prepare your heart. Your heart should always be right with God before you preach.

☐ Spend time in the Word, in prayer, and in fellowship with the Lord.

☐ Do a trial run of the sermon.

☐ Enthusiasm makes the difference. It is contagious.

☐ Be aware of the competition for your listeners' attention.

☐ Make sure you have an arresting introduction.

☐ Analyze the contents of the message. Will they learn something? Will they be moved? Will they be convicted and changed? Will they be challenged to do something?

☐ Seek appropriate feedback from honest sources following the message.

☐ It is a tragedy for people to be bored with God's Word. Make sure that doesn't happen. Be relevant, interesting, and excited.

Recommended Scripture References

God helps the poor speaker, Exodus 4:1-5
Comfort my people, Isaiah 40:1
Jesus, master preacher, Matthew 7:28
Jesus' synagogue sermons, Luke 4:14-15
Jesus preaches to sinners, Luke 15:1-2
Bold preaching, Acts 4:29
Paul's powerful preaching, Acts 9:22
Call to babbler, Acts 17:18
Many believed, Acts 19:8
Faith comes by hearing, Romans 10:17
Simple preaching, 1 Corinthians 2:1
Necessity to preach, 1 Corinthians 9:16

Open door, 2 Corinthians 2:12
I believe, I preach, 2 Corinthians 4:13
Persuade men, 2 Corinthians 5:11
Jailed for preaching, Ephesians 3:1
Bold preaching, Ephesians 6:19-20
Set for the defense of the gospel, Philippians 1:15-17
Warning and teaching, Colossians 1:28
Make it clear, Colossians 4:4
Seasoned with salt, Colossians 4:6
Preaching with power, 1 Thessalonians 1:5
Double honor for preaching, 1 Timothy 5:17
Calling to preach, 2 Timothy 1:11

Teaching

Teaching and preaching are similar; both involve verbal expression and instruction. Preaching is the proclamation of moral and spiritual instruction and is associated with a sermon. Teaching is broader in nature and application. We read in Scripture that *Jesus taught them saying....* The five Greek words used in the New Testament for teaching include the ideas of instruction, direction, training, correction, discipline, impression, admonishment, publishing, and impartation of knowledge. Every minister should strive to become a master teacher equipped not only to teach but to successfully train those in his church who desire to teach the principles and practices.

In the gospels we see Jesus teaching in the synagogue, on a hillside, by the sea, and in a house. He never missed a teaching opportunity as when encountering the woman at the well, seeing the disciples send children away, overhearing scribes questioning His authoirty, or hearing His disciples discussing who would have the greatest position in the kingdom. As His ministry was coming to a close, some of His last words are given as a commision to teach all things that He had taught during His life on earth (Matthew 28:19-20).

The Purpose of Teaching

Our purpose as Christians is to teach others what we know from God's Word and from what we have expereinced in the new life we have found in Christ. Our first goal is to point the unsaved to Jesus showing them their need of the Savior and encouraging them until they make their commitment to Him. The second goal is building a strong foundation of knowledge and understanding in them of God's Word and then to teach them how to apply it to their life situations. This foundation is necessary for a whole future life devoted to God and service to others.

The Teacher

Following are traits a teacher needs to have. The teacher...

1. Needs to have a desire to teach and to share with others his love of Christ; he sees the need to help believers grow spiritually.

2. Needs to have ability to teach. Not everyone can be a teacher. 2 Timothy 2:24 says that one of the requirements of a servant is that he is *apt to teach,* indicating he must have the necessary skills.

3. Needs to have character evidenced by traits of dependability, truthfulness, honesty, and perseverance. The life must be one of transparency and godliness. The teacher's goal should be to seek first the kingdom of God in his personal life (Matthew 6:33).

4. Needs to have a genuine love for people. He needs to be able to see them as God does, each one having worth and unlimited potential. He must have the desire to help them become all that God has planned.

5. Needs to have a love for God's Word. He must realize that to teach it he must allow God's Word to transform his life so as to be a living example of Christ. We need to have such an exemplary life (that God has produced in us) that we can say as Paul did, *Be ye followers of me, even as I am also of Christ* (1 Corinthians 11:1).

6. Needs to have had some experience in the Chrisitan life. *That which we have seen and heard declare we unto you...* (1 John 1:3). If a young Christian is put into

service without adequate knowledge, experience, and training, he will fail. He should be learning, not teaching.

7. Training/education may include:

    Christian training

    Bible college classes

    Personal Bible study (2 Timothy 2:15)

    Independent study and research

    Teacher training seminars

    Training classes provided by church

    Church attendance, taking notes and doing futher research

8. Must be a person of prayer. It is not your words but God's power that brings results (1 Corinthians 4:20). Pray in preparation and in the presentation. Pray regarding choice of material, for learners to be receptive, and that their specific needs will be met. Pray for wisdom, guidance, and sensitivity as you teach.

The Learners

With Jesus there were no unimportant people. He cared about them all. It is commonly accepted that children are the best learners. We know that most Christians accept Christ before they are 18 years of age, approximately 62%. Eighteen percent do so between the ages of 18 and 25. Only 20% of all believers accept Christ after the age of 25. Each group that is to be taught comes with special age-related needs. The teacher must know those needs and determine how to meet them. Some learners will be new Christians. Some come from other religious backgrounds. Some come with addictions to alchohol or drugs. Children come with ever changing needs as they grow and mature. Adults may face unique challenges such as single parenting, surviving the loss of a mate, or getting through a painful divorce. Many subgroups exist.

Learning Styles

Educator Bernice McCarthy has identified four basic learning styles. These represent a student's prefered way of learning. When preparing a lesson, think about providing opportunity for each of these methods to be used in each class. She finds that some learners are imaginative learners, learning by watching, sensing, and feeling. They are curious and questioning and like to share ideas. Others are analytical learners, learning by watching and listening. They expect factual and accurate information and will carefully assess the worth of what's presented. The common sense learners like to see if an idea is reasonable, usable, workable, and will test it. These people analyze and fix problems. Dynamic learners like action. They will follow hunches and are risk takers. They gravitate to situations needing flexibility and change. When a learner is actively engaged in a lesson, the more apt he is to internalize the lesson. Marlene D. LeFever, with the David C. Cook church ministries, has taken these styles and written an excellent book for Christian teachers entitled Learning Styles: Reaching Everyone God Gave You to Teach.

A Different Kind of Intelligence

Each person learns differently. Some hear a poem and remember it for years; others need to be taught a song to achieve the same results. Since we all learn differently, it logically follows that the preparation of lessons which appeals to a variety of types of intelligence will have an impact on more people. Therefore, in teaching the Bible, it is helpful to know these areas of intelligence and convey lessons through not one or two of these vehicles, but all seven whenever possible.

Here is an overview of Gardner's Multiple Intelligence Theory and how it might be used advantageously in the classroom or pulpit. People who are verbal-linguistically smart are the learners who typically do well in most academic settings excelling in reading and writing. People who are smart logically-mathematically like to ponder, calculate, and analyze. People who are bodily-kinesthetic learn better by moving around. People who are interpersonally smart learn better when able to participate in a group setting. People who are smart intrapersonally learn better when able to work alone and are given time to think and reflect. People who are smart visually-spatially learn best when able to puzzle and create visually. People who are musically smart learn best through chants and rhythms, through lyrics and song, and are excellent listeners. Gardner often adds a naturalist intelligence, an existentialist intelligence, and a spiritualist intelligence. Essentially the idea behind these kinds of smart is that people process information better if they are allowed to interact with the material in a more personal way that best suits their learning needs. Most people possess all seven intelligences and most can be fully developed. The educator would best be served when the presentation is varied to encourage the engagement of the learner.

Principles of Teaching

♦ The teacher must know the lesson or truth to be taught, must have studied well, and must have first-hand knowledge.

♦ The learner needs to attend with interest in order to learn.

♦ The language must be common to both and appropriate for the age.

♦ Teaching is exciting and stimulating effectively utilizing the pupil's mind to grasp the thought or meaning.

♦ Learning is thinking into one's own understanding a new idea or truth.

♦ The test of the teacher's teaching is the learner reproducing and applying the material taught.

Preparation for Teaching

♦ Use all tools, curriuculum, resources, books, and internet sites that are available. The teacher should be prepared beyond what is needed to teach.

♦ Prepare visuals or other learning aids. The best learning occurs when all the senses are engaged, especially seeing, hearing, and doing.

♦ It is better to present a few things well than to present a spread of many things ineffectually.

♦ Prepare well in advance of teaching to give ample time for further learning, and gathering fresh ideas for teaching and illustrations.

♦ Identify ahead of time the practical value in what is taught and its possible real life applications.

♦ Prepare thought provoking, age-appropriate questions and activities.

♦ Plan periodic reviews to refresh and remind students of what they already know and to prepare for optimal learning. For most students, a review of previously learned material will create common ground for learners and may provide fresh insight.

♦ Pray as you prepare that God may meet the needs of the learners.

Presentation

♦ Never begin a class exercise until the attention of the class has been secured. This is true of all ages. Children want to play and talk with their neighbors. Adults want to talk, comment, or catch up. Teens are more interested in interacting with their peers than in listening. Study faces to see if they are present mentally as well as physically.

- Pause if attention is interrupted and wait until attention is regained.

- Be enthusiastic; it's contagious. Stop when signs of fatigue appear as no more learning will occur.

- Adapt length of class to age of pupil, the younger the pupil, the briefer the length of class.

- Keep lesson in view. Reduce noise and keep other distractioins to a minimum. Ventilate the room to avoid stagnant air which causes sleepiness, lethargy, and inattention. Eliminate sun glare through windows.

- Maintain interest and attention. If you lose their attention, act quickly to regain it. Learn from pupils their knowledge of the subject; correct or build on that information as a starting point.

- Use illustrations appropriate to age. Don't allow the visuals to become so prominent as to become a source of distraction.

- Appeal to the interests of the age group, including use of favorite activities, songs, hobbies, and sports.

- Stimulate the pupil's mind to action. Foster in them the attitude of a discoverer and an anticipator.

- Have pupils express in their own words what they have just learned. This allows them to construct their own meaning.

- Review what was just learned and go on.

- Find the relationship of the lesson to the lives of the learner and then give it value in the practical application.

- Use short simple sentences as long sentences tend to confuse. Use clear wording. Repeat with greater simplicity if pupils fail to understand.

- Relate every lesson to former lessons allowing students to share previously attained information and how they applied it in real life.

- Each step of the lesson should lead naturally into the next.

- Lead learners to find illustrations from their own experience.

- Teach how knowledge really helps to solve problems.

- Help pupils learn to think for themselves. Help them connect truths they have learned to their lives outside of the church classroom. Help students think through problems associated with peer pressure, creationism, temptation, or major decision making.

- Use the *why* until pupil can express a reason for his opinion.

- Encourage pupils to do independent investigation. Encourage the habit of research.

- Make good use of teachable moments when incidents ocur such as somone's behavior, a comment, an unusual occurance, a community disaster, a personal problem, or a family loss or crisis. Use these as an opportunity for the class to show love, understanding, and concern. Remind them that God cares and will provide. Explain or correct misunderstanding or misconceptions. Show how bad can have a good outcome.

- Use assignments of various kinds to encourage personal research or personal application of the lesson. Personal application is the key to creating real change in a learner. Examples of extention activites could include finding a way to share your faith with someone, reaching out to someone in need, or allowing God to give you a specific task to complete. Make accountabily an integral part of the assignment and expect a report, an explanation, or sharing of task done.

♦ Always leave a teaching session on a positive note. Learners tend to remember the beginning and the end much more than the middle. They should look forward to another class.

Theory: Five Steps to Educate

Why do we teach anything? Are we simply attempting to stuff more facts into the memory banks of the brain or is there more to teaching than that? True education occurs when the following 5 steps are achieved:

Locate: Identify a problem, need, or reason for the lesson in the learner's life.

Elaborate: Take the problem to its logical end.

Illuminate: Use facts or Bible truths.

Integrate: How can the truth be applied?

Activate: Motivate to a response.

Creativity in Teaching

Students surveyed said that four out of five teachers were boring. These teachers were described as monotone, predictable, non-interactive, and lacking in animation, interest, variety, and illustration. Consider how God Himself communicates. God's style is:

Memorable—Thomas is told by Jesus to touch the nail marks in His hands and believe in the resurrection.

Unexpected—Balaam's talking donkey

Visual—Tabernacle in the wilderness and Daniel's vision

Unique—Angels speaking to shepherds

Multisensory—Celebration of the Passover

God has entrusted Christians with the most important message in the world – the truth about salvation through Jesus Christ. We have a responsibility to use the most effective means at our disposal in sharing this message with the world. Creativity in teaching allows us to take experience and knowledge and combine it in new ways to make the truth understandable and applicable.

Creativity Survey

1. Who was the most creative person you have ever known?

2. In what ways was that person creative?

3. What effect did that have on you?

4. How can you become more creative?

5. Why is it hard to be creative?

Beware of the Creativity Blocks

Attitude: I'm not creative. That won't work.

Poor Preparation: I'll just read over the lesson the night before.

Inhibitions: I don't want to look silly by singing that song in front of the class, even if it helps them remember the lesson.

Lack of Enthusiasm: I've taught this lesson a hundred times.

Minimize Importance of Lesson or Audience: They're only 3 year olds. They won't care how I teach it.

Recommended Scripture References

Teach children, Deuteronomy 4:9, 10; 11:19
Teach youth, Psalm 119:9
Understanding enlightens the Word, Psalm 119:130
Get wisdom and knowledge, Proverbs 1:1-6
Wisdom better than gold, Proverbs 16:16
Understanding a fountain of life, Proverbs 16:21
Wisdom preserves life, Ecclesiastes 7:12
My word will not return void, Isaiah 55:10-11
Scholars astonished, Acts 4:13
Phillip teaches, Acts 8:26-39
Searched the Scriptures, Acts 17:11-12
Teaching boldly, Acts 28:31
Teaching from a pure heart, 1 Timothy 1:5

Church Finance

Church Financial Management

- Teach and preach biblical stewardship principles. Materials by Larry Burkett are excellent references for biblical financial principles and practices.

- Select people who are honest, of good report, and filled with the Holy Spirit to handle and manage the church's money.

- These are job descriptions for each of the church officers who manage the money.

  Treasurer is responsible for counting and depositing the money, writing and signing the checks, preparing the financial statements, making an accounting for all church monies, and making reports to the board and congregation.

  Assistant Treasurer is responsible for performing similar duties as the treasurer and fills in when he is absent.

  Financial Secretary is responsible for keeping records and providing a statement quarterly of each individual's giving.

- Remove all potential blind spots from every aspect of the handling of money including its collection. Under no circumstances should a single individual work alone as this will prevent temptation and ensure that people have confidence in the financial management process. Scripture admonishes us to not be slothful in business (Romans 12:11). This does not mean that any one individual is not trustworthy but it helps protect him from accusation. The same two people should not be involved in any two chronological parts of the process. Three or more individuals should rotate during these processes.

- Practice the rule of twos (or more) as follows (in each other's presence):

  Two individuals should participate in the process of collecting the money.

  Two individuals should participate in the process of pooling the money.

  Two individuals should participate in the process of counting the money.

  Two individuals should participate in the process of preparing the deposit slip.

  Two individuals should participate in the signing of each check.

  Note: No one person should handle any two sequential steps.

- Pastors should not count the money or sign church checks. If forced to handle money in a very small church, always follow the rule of twos.

- Accounting for all monies in monthly detailed financial reports should be made available to the congregation.

  Every amount the church receives should be accounted for.

  Every check written by the church should have two authorized signatures. It should be recorded as to whom it was written, for what purpose, and the amount.

  Always practice an open financial policy encouraging any questions.

  The deacon board should audit the financial report and all the church finances monthly.

- Have an annual business meeting and financial report.

- Bonding of principal financial participants is up to the church board.

- Arrange budget amounts and personal accountability for each ministry of the church. The deacon board will audit these monthly.

- The church boards should have a small amount of money pre-approved for discretionary spending for convenience and emergencies. The amount will be determined by the congregation.

◆ Church trustees are required by law for nonprofit corporations.

They should be elected during the annual business meeting. They are responsible for the maintenance of the buildings and grounds of the church and execution of legal documents as required by law.

In some churches three deacons may be designated as trustees in lieu of a separate board of trustees being elected.

◆ Board members may rotate on a three-year basis or be elected annually to serve a one-year term depending on the voted preference of the congregation.

◆ Make sure all candidates elected to either board pass the test of honesty, wisdom, and are filled with the Holy Spirit as described in Acts 6:3. See standards presented in 1 Timothy 3:8-13.

◆ Since deacons and trustees will be responsible for spending the church's money, it should be required that each board member tithe. One who does not is a God robber who is dishonest with his stewardship before God described in Malachi 3:8. If he fails to tithe, he does not pass the honesty test of Acts 6:3.

◆ Use a voucher system for church transactions and for record keeping.

◆ If staff credit cards are used, make sure that these requirements are followed:

Each person must earn the privilege of having one by proving themselves during a probationary period.

There should be accountability for all finances. Receipts must be submitted to the treasurer immediately after using the card and there must be complete accountability for all credit card usage.

◆ Keep the congregation informed at all times about the church's finances. Justice Brandeis appropriately said, "Sunlight is the best disinfectant."

◆ The church should have annual campaigns to teach the principles of stewardship and to enlist new people in the practice of biblical giving.

◆ The church should teach biblical financial management classes for new and potential members as well as members who have never covered the material.

◆ It is a good idea to engage in a major church or capital improvement project every five years. This ensures that the congregation will continue practicing biblical stewardship in support of the church's movement forward. Building programs should be carefully planned and carried out. Expect accurate financial accountability.

Consider that you as the pastor may leave the church at any time but the debt will remain obligating the people for many years after you are gone; be prudent when leading the church into debt.

God's will must be determined and followed in all financial matters of the church, especially in building programs.

Fund raising is primary in importance during a building program. The church should attempt to raise as much money in advance so that a minimal amount will need to be financed, if any.

Financing may be obtained through a bank, a savings and loan, or a bond sale. The church should strive to maintain a AAA credit rating. If the church gets into financial trouble, face the creditors and work out an acceptable arrangement to pay what is owed to maintain the church's financial reputation in the community. To not pay an honest debt as promised is the sin of covenant breaking and is a serious offence before God.

♦ Insist on careful stewardship of all of the church's resources.

♦ Buildings should be carefully maintained so as to minimize future costs.

God's work
Done in God's way
Will never lack God's supplies

Hudson Taylor

Recommended Scripture References

Coming before the Lord empty-handed, Exodus 23:15
Give with a willing heart, Exodus 25:2; Exodus 35:29
Give as God has given you, Deuteronomy 16:16-17
Gave treasures to temple, 1 Chronicles 29:3-4
The temple workers provided for, Ezra 3:7
Giving out of gratitude, Psalm 54:6-7
Blessing from generous sharing, Palm 112:5-9
Honor the Lord with your wealth, Proverbs 3:9-10
Fulfill pledge, Ecclesiastes 5:4-5
People in fine homes, temple in ruins, Haggai 1:1-4
Private giving, Matthew 6:2-4
Treasures on earth, in heaven, Matthew 6:19-21
Paying your taxes, Matthew 22:15-22; Mark 12:17
Man donated tomb for Jesus, Matthew 27:57-61
Give much, receive much, Mark 4:24-25; Luke 12:48
Widow's small offering, Mark 12:41-44; Luke 21:1-4
Sharing with others, Luke 3:11
Abundance rewarded those who give, Luke 6:38
Stewardship with pure heart, Luke 11:41
Give to the poor, Luke 12:33-34
Dishonest stewardship, Acts 5:1-11
Woman helped the poor, Acts 9:36-42
Gave to fellow Christians, Romans 12:13
Proven faithful, 1 Corinthians 4:2
Pastor support, 1 Corinthians 9:7-14
Sunday giving, 1 Corinthians 16:2
Ministry profiteering, 2 Corinthians 2:17
Sowing, reaping, 2 Corinthians 9:6-7
Care for poor, Galatians 2:9-10
Share with others, Hebrews 13:16

Raising Missionary Support

The raising of the support necessary to serve the Lord as a missionary is a process which can become drawn out and discouraging. The following suggestions have been gleaned from missionaries who have enjoyed much success in raising the needed funds quickly.

1. Determine a realistic goal for your support based upon the cost of living on your field, travel expenses, shipping costs, and other miscellaneous expenses. This information can be provided by some missions groups such as BBFI. Consider the amount of support needed to accommodate changes in currency exchange rates, inflation, additions to your family, and future expansion of your ministry. Anticipate that some churches and individuals will drop your support when you are serving because of changes in the church's leadership, unexpected financial difficulties, or changes in prioritization. Unfortunately, some churches will not always be faithful in providing regular support every month; they may skip support for short or even long periods of time.

2. Prepare an appealing and professional packet of information about yourself and your ministry. Include a letter of introduction from a well-known, respected pastor, recommendations, and testimonials from others regarding you and your ministry. Do not provide an excessive amount to read as busy pastors are likely to peruse it quickly because of large volumes of mail.

3. Begin your quest for support by making a list of the churches and individuals who know you or with whom you have some connection. These should be your first and easiest contacts. This should provide you with a foundation of support on which to build and will provide encouragement as you begin your fund raising.

4. Carefully craft a paragraph of what you'll say to a pastor whose support you are seeking when you have the opportunity to talk to him. Visit church websites for information about the pastor and church. Included in this paragraph should be the following information.
   - Who you are
   - Where you are going
   - Background information about where you went to school and served your internship and the identity of your home church or sending pastor
   - Mention any connection you have with the pastor or the church like "My aunt is a member there" or "My pastor went to school with you" or "Pastor X suggested that I contact you" or "I heard about your church through ___."

   Then ask for the privilege of presenting your work to the church.

5. Offer to provide your packet of material to them. Some missionaries send out their packet before they call the church; others prefer to provide their packet after they have made contact with a church. The advantage of sending it after the phone contact is that less time and money are wasted because you do not send literature to those who do not want it and will be unlikely to read it; the disadvantage is less exposure.

6. Start inquiry calls well in advance (one year is not too soon). It is important to get into mission conferences and to start booking engagements one year in advance. Designate blocks of time to do your calling and have a specific goal for the number of calls you will make. The most successful missionaries have suggested a goal of up to 80 calls per day.

Many calls will result in no contact because of the unavailability of the pastor. Sometimes it will require a second call to connect with the pastor or designated staff member that you need to reach. Some larger churches have a designated staff member or mission's committee chair who handles missionary inquiries for support. Always be pleasant to the secretary who answers the phone. You can hear a smile on the other end of the phone and the secretary is often the gatekeeper to the pastor and may be the pastor's wife. If the pastor is not available, ask for a time when it would be most convenient to reach him; make it a point to call back at that time. It is important to schedule your calling times when you are most likely to catch pastors at their offices. Tuesdays, Wednesdays, and Thursdays are often the most opportune days as they are busy preparing on Saturday, are busy on Sunday with preaching and meetings, and take either Monday or Friday off. Wednesday afternoons may be used for preparation for the mid-week service.

Experiment with different times for calling to find the most profitable times. It is not recommended to call a pastor at home unless absolutely necessary. Continue calling until you make contact with the pastor or are told *no*. Those who try only once and give up receive few appointments; those who are persistent in calling back, up to three or four times until they reach the pastor, make many more appointments.

When calling use a spreadsheet to keep track of your calls. Keep a log of pastors called and note the time to avoid calling twice. Record what happened during the call. Make a notation of the need to call back and when.

This will be of future use when you return home on furlough. Pastors may remember your name and it will give you an opportunity to present at that time.

Your phone presentation should be short, concise, and fluid, yet detailed enough to cover all questions that a pastor might have. Most pastors receive multiple calls from missionaries every day. Respect their time. Follow up phone calls promptly with an email or letter of confirmation.

Sample Call

Good morning Pastor _____,
It's a privilege to be able to talk to you today. My name is Joshua Joyce. My wife Lani and I are missionaries to Burkina Faso. Do you have a minute to talk? (If he says yes, then continue. If he says no, ask when a convenient time would be to call back.) I am a missionary kid from West Africa. We are both graduates of Baptist Bible College in Springfield, Missouri. We were very involved in ministry at High Street Baptist Church with Pastor Eddie Lyons during our time there. After graduating we did our internship at Edgewood Baptist Church in Rock Island, Illinois, under Dr. Mel Brown. It is considered one of the best internships in the BBFI in terms of the training that you receive. We are sent out of the church there and desire to go to Burkina to start a church-planting movement with national pastors at the helm. We would also be a part of a Bible institute that is already started there. We are seeking churches in which to present our ministry and would appreciate the opportunity to come to your church, present our vision, and encourage your people in missions.

7. Ask missionaries who recently completed deputation what areas of the country yielded the greatest success in raising support. Utilize that information by calling pastors in that area.

8. Follow these helpful suggestions throughout the deputation process.

Initial phone calling

- Pray much before making your calls.
- Use your pastoral directory to provide prospects for your calling.
- Seek personal accountability with a partner if necessary to help you keep making the required number of phone calls.
- Seek encouragement in fellowship. Plan relaxation to avoid burnout.
- Systematically follow up your initial calls.
- Make sure you know the correct pronunciation of the pastor's name (ask as necessary).
- Be cordial and positive and practice attitude adjustment when discouraged.

Follow-up personal contacts

- Present briefly your God-given burden.
- When you meet with the pastor while you are visiting a church service, if he does not bring up the issue of monthly support, then bring it up yourself and inquire about the possibility of his supporting you.
- Send follow-up correspondence.
- Don't exhibit an air of entitlement or pride.
- Cultivate connections by asking those who have shown an interest in your work if they would recommend others for you to contact. Some who are impressed with your ministry may mention you to others and suggest they invite you to visit their church.
- Don't burn your bridges with pastors and churches.

9. Make sure your presentation at the church is powerful and Spirit filled; the presentation of God's Word should never be boring.

- Be prepared with an excellent message.
- Seek feedback from objective sources and hone the message until it is ready.
- Use great visuals and keep them reasonably short.
- Develop and present a video that is succinct, practical, and appropriate that will increase the audience's understanding and appreciation of your work.
- Preach your best and keep it a reasonable length.
- Seek pastoral guidance, asking if there is anything you need to be aware of before you speak.
- Mention specific needs you are praying about but don't overdo it.
- Use the KJV.
- Honor the church's convictions in your dress and presentation.
- Your wife should be ready to speak.
- Be prepared to answer questions.
- If possible, complete a survey trip so you are well informed with up-to-date personal visuals from the field.
- If you get into mission conferences you are likely to receive support.
- Listen to a recent tape of your preaching to avoid the unnoticed development of bad speech habits.
- Work in music or testimonies from your children if possible. Churches love to see family involvement if it is done tastefully.
- Share your vision and passion.

10. Have several messages prepared which will fill the particular need of the occasion (banquets, short testimonies, children's program, and men's meetings).

11. Always send a personal thank you after your visit.

12. Follow up with other contacts as necessary. If you promise something, make sure to follow through expeditiously.

13. Don't be slothful in business. It is better to be direct and open about your needs and support than to be vague or indirect.

14. Mention the pastor and the church in your presentation because it makes your presentation to them and their group personal. Paul mentioned specific churches and people regularly.

15. Offer to provide any assistance while you are there. Pastors are impressed when you offer to do anything to help their ministry such as making a visit with them, speaking to a particular group, or helping with some project they are doing.

16. Go out of your way to be friendly with the people, shake hands, be available to mix with the congregation before and after the service. *A man that hath friends must show himself friendly...* (Proverbs 18:24). Personally greet everyone when possible.

17. Work to improve all of your presentations and make them more effective.

18. Make sure your missionary display is appealing and effective; have plenty of prayer cards so you appear prepared.

19. Model your work after other missionaries who have been successful in their deputation and fund raising. Although no two missionaries are the same, their successful practices may be a help to you.

20. Incorporate persuasive principles and motivational materials; never use manipulation, deception, or exploitation.

21. Touch their hearts and emotions through poignant illustrations. Jesus never spoke without telling a story. Messages should include:

   ♦ Interpretation (Be faithful in explaining the correct meaning of the text.)
   ♦ Illustration (Illustrations are like windows which let the light shine in.)
   ♦ Application (Hearers will not automatically apply the message; you must make the application.)
   ♦ Exhortation (Sermons should challenge hearers to put the message into action.)

22. Cast your burden before them and don't be afraid to let it show. Be enthusiastic! Your presentation should be such that no one doubts your call to missions or your field. Use real field illustrations if possible to achieve maximum impact.

23. Don't bash other missionaries, mission's groups, or members of other denominations. You don't make yourself any taller by cutting other people down to size. You might offend people who have family or friends in those groups and it can keep you from obtaining support.

24. Have a cash reserve to tide you over through periods of slow bookings and weak offerings.

25. Consolidate your debts to avoid being overburdened with huge monthly payments which will put unacceptable financial pressure on you and your family.

26. Pray without ceasing.

Business Meetings

Conducting a business meeting is another duty of the minister that can be daunting. Following are suggestions to facilitate a church business meeting.

1. Document requirements for church business meetings in the by-laws which designate how they will be scheduled, by whom and when, what business will be included, where they will be conducted, who is eligible to vote, and the necessary quorum to transact business. Edgewood business meetings must be scheduled in advance to allow their announcement on Sunday in both services and on Wednesday before the actual meeting. Business meetings may be called by either of the church boards. The only Illinois state required business meeting is the annual meeting usually conducted the third Sunday in January to elect officers and provide reports to the congregation about membership, finances, and the year's activities. Other business meetings are to be scheduled as required. They are usually conducted on the church premises and require a simple majority of those members present to pass a recommendation.

   No member under sixteen years of age is permitted to participate. Members who have not attended a service or given financially to the church for the period of one year before the meeting are considered inactive and are not eligible to vote.

2. Cultivate a spirit of unity in the church stressing the importance of each participant seeking to determine what God wants the church to do, not what an individual wants. Too often business meetings are about individuals wanting their will to be done instead of God's will.

3. Emphasize that anyone will have a right to express an opinion but that the opinion must be expressed in a Christ-like way. Speaking the truth in love is admonished in Ephesians 4:12. 1 Corinthians 10:31 says, *Whether therefore ye eat, or drink, or whatsoever ye do, do all to the glory of God.*

4. Prepare the congregation regarding the issue in various ways well before the meeting. For example, mention the issue in teaching, preaching, and prayer. Thank God for orphanages which provide food, shelter, and care for homeless children if you hope to support an orphans' ministry or feeding center.

5. Before the business meeting, do any necessary research preparation and have appropriate answers to any potential question or request for information.

6. Get influential groups and individuals on board before the business meeting through formal and informal discussions and presentations.

7. Prepare for the presentation with helpful handouts, notes, PowerPoint presentations, drawings, or other visuals. If those who are knowledgeable about parts of the presentation are not required to make a formal presentation before the congregation, be sure they are available to stand and answer questions if needed as audience participants.

8. Always plan as pastor to be present to guide the business meeting and prevent unforeseen consequences.

9. Follow a standard guide such as <u>Robert's Rules of Order</u> to establish structure and procedure.

10. If someone delivers an opinion contrary to the motion, thank them, and move on without further comment.

11. If there is dissension in a meeting when the minority loses the vote, attempt to rally people around the decision of the majority. Unity is not uniformity. Even when we disagree we can do so without being disagreeable. It is a good thing when brethren will dwell together in unity (Psalm 133:1). Where the Spirit of the Lord is, there is unity.

12. Occasionally it might be wise to determine if a motion has the support to pass in advance. Consider calling for a "vote for a vote," which is the opportunity to vote about presenting the motion. The vote for a vote will tell you how much support there is and if the motion is likely to pass.

13. Be sensitive to the timing of the business meeting. It is better to wait and be sure than to rush and lose the objective.

14. Be alert to hot button issues within the congregation such as purchasing another brand of tractor when the majority of the congregation works for John Deere.

15. In sensitive situations protect the integrity of the process through disclosure and competitive pricing. Be prudent, honest, and truthful in matters of business. Financial matters should be an open book to the congregation with every amount of income and outgo accounted for. Every check written should be listed in a monthly financial statement as to how much and what it is for. A yearly financial summary should be presented at the church's annual business meeting. Any member's question should be welcomed and duly answered to promote openness and credibility.

16. Pray for God's leadership.

Managing Staff

It is the pastor who sets the example for the staff in all areas such as character, attitude, work ethic, and personality. He also is a pastor to the staff as well as to the rest of the congregation. He must be the pastor, the leader, and teacher, but also the mentor, the counselor, the motivator, and the confidant. An open door policy should be practiced to allow staff members to meet with him during the work week. Sometimes there are issues that develop or questions which arise which need immediate attention. It is the pastor who sets the positive tone and monitors the attitude of all staff members as they work together and interact in the daily routine. The staff must maintain unity, encouraging and supporting one another. Though each has his own responsiblities and duties, he must realize his specific ministry is part of the whole and the general concerns of the church are the responsibility of the whole staff.

Staff Meetings

The weekly staff meeting is of primary importance for both staff relationships and the productivity of the staff individually and collectively. A sample staff meeting schedule follows. The staff meetings present an opportunity for evaluation of the services, addressing ministry problems, input from various staff members including issues, vision casting, instruction, learning, planning, prayer, discussion, fellowship, and inspiration. Staff should pray together, have lunch together, and enjoy time together as well as address the business of the church and their respective contributions to it.

Objectives and Components

- Praise/Positive feedback/Testimonies
- Information gathering/Sharing
- Morale development
- Reviewing/Evaluating
- Team building
- Planning
- Programming
- Vision casting
- Education/Mentoring
- Problem solving
- Shepherding
- Task assignments
- Follow-up
- Accountability
- Discernment of participant's needs
- Fellowship
- Prayer

Guidelines

1. Items addressed should be necessary, relevant, time appropriate and on a need-to-know basis.
2. Meetings should start and end on time if at all possible.
3. Meetings should include all staff members.
4. Each meeting needs to follow a specific agenda.
5. Include variety.
6. Allow for breaks as necessary.

Proposed Schedule

9:00am-10:20am
Opening prayer
Praise/Positive feedback/Testimonials/Review/Evaluation
Planning for future services
Visitors/Prayer requests/Updates
Staff prayer

10:30am-12:00pm
Agenda development
Discussion of necessary items
Required activity/Action
Rotation of topics
Leadership development

Ministry growth/Assessment
Planning
Personal/Spiritual growth

12:00pm-1:30pm   Lunch

1:30pm-2:30pm
   Intern speaking/Feedback
2:30pm-???
   Meetings with individual staff members

Leading VALID Meetings

Meetings in ministry are necessary and inevitable. VALID meetings, as developed by Rev. Tim Green, are justifiable and effective with these characteristics to help your meeting be productive. A VALID meeting will:

Vision Cast
- This gives the group direction and creates member confidence in leadership.
- This creates a vehicle for group unity through shared understanding.
- This creates a motivation factor toward accomplishment.

Advance the Agenda
- Creating an agenda shows forethought and preparedness.
- The agenda keeps the meeting purposeful and on track.
- People are de-motivated by meetings that waste time and are unproductive.

Lavish Praise
- Everyone needs to know they are appreciated.
- Be specific with praise for accomplishments.
- Praise openly and in personal conversation.

Improve Relationships
- Work to improve your relationship with each member.
- Note disagreements and subsequent interpersonal dynamics.
- Seek to be a catalyst for interaction and unity.

Delegate Tasks
- This gives the group opportunity for teamwork.
- Together the team can work toward resolution of problems.
- Goal and project advancement and completion can involve the whole group.

Orienting a Staff Member

After hiring a staff member, several days should be spent orienting him to the community, the church, his fellow staff members, and his work assignments. It is important that he understands the policies and practices of the church. A detailed employment policy should be available in printed form for clarity and presentation as well as for future reference.

A comprehensive job description should be prepared for every staff member whether they are members of the pastoral staff or support staff such as custodians or secretaries. See sample job description in Appendix E. The new staff member should clearly comprehend what you want him to do, how you expect him to do it, what authority he is given, and what should be the desired outcome. Issues such as confidentiality, loyalty, faithfulness, tact, follow-through, hours, priorities, and spiritual practices should be clarified in all areas of his work assignments. He also needs to understand that there will be periodic reviews of his job experience including how often he will be evaluated, the criteria used, and the purposes of the reviews.

After the initial meetings with the new staff member, it is recommended to have weekly meetings with him during the next few months of his tenure. These sessions permit questions to be answered, opportunities for encouragement, and assistance as needed.

It is essential that any staff member gets a good start in his ministry and stays on the right trajectory; as a staff member settles into his responsibilites, the frequency of the meetings should diminish. Such meetings can taper off to monthly, then quarterly, and finally semi-annually or annually.

Evaluations of Staff

The formal evaluation of each staff member should be performed annually. The evaluation process should be conducted in private. The staff member should be asked to complete a formal self-evaluation prior to your meeting. During the meeting you will review the evaluation form together and set goals for future evaluations. If your church or organization does not have existing evaluation forms, do an internet search of various university sites for samples and create your own.

Informal evaluation of staff should occur frequently. Praise of staff members should be done publically but correction should be done in private. Every staff member should have accountability for his work to insure productive effort and the desired result.

Staff members and their wives should receive additional training and inspiration through periodic attendance at conferences, seminars, or fellowship meetings. It is also recommended that the whole staff attend occasional meetings together to foster fellowship and unity. An excellent staff is a pastor's greatest asset—take good care of them.

Staff Selection

There are five areas of assessment to consider when you are selecting any person to join your staff: consideration of the exact requirements of the job, character, competence, commitment, and chemistry. (Chemistry involves the level of cooperativeness and the ability to fit into your work environment and ministry.) The choice of an

employee who will be joining your organization is one of the most important decisions any church leader will make; consequently, the entire process should be immersed in prayer and given the priority and attention it deserves. When you are searching for, interviewing, analyzing, and selecting potential staff, we recommend you follow these principles and practices used at Edgewood:

1. Seek candidates through a network of sources who have an opportunity to know potential candidates and have had enough exposure to them to provide intelligent, accurate recommendations. Cultivate contacts with professors and mentors in select schools who are training future pastors and missionaries. Leaders of Christian organizations, fellow pastors and associates, missionaries, and friends should all be suggestion sources. This does not preclude candidates known personally to you or members of your own staff including members of their circle of friends who can provide contacts.

2. Contact and screen each potential candidate for inclusion in or exclusion from further consideration. Included below are some suggestions for the initial screening.

   ♦ A phone contact should be made. Ask if the timing is good or offer to make an appointment to phone him later for an extensive conversation.

   ♦ Introduce yourself, your ministry, and discuss details about the staff or internship position with the candidate.

   ♦ Learn about his background, interests, ministry experience, and future plans.

   ♦ The issues discussed and questions you ask should lead to exploring details regarding his Christian character including morals, values, competence for the specific position, experience, talents, abilities, cooperativeness, and insights into his willingness and ability to fit into your staff. Each area of assessment is vitally important, but the character issue is most important. You can improve his competency through training and teach him relational skills to improve his interpersonal relationships. But developing his character, if it is lacking, is a heavy commitment requiring high-maintenance and is a long-term and difficult process. This is especially true if he is content with the way he is and has little interest in improving. Dr. Bob Jones, Sr. said, "You can borrow brains, but you can't borrow character." A sample interview questionnaire follows in this section.

♦ Determine if you are interested in pursuing him or if he is not interested in your position.

♦ Allow him to ask questions.

♦ If there is mutual interest in proceeding, request a résumé and a complete set of references. A great deal can be learned through the résumé process by considering how quickly it is sent, the attitude in providing it, the care exercised in putting it together, its completeness as well as its accuracy, and the references that were provided.

♦ For interested missionary intern candidates, send a copy of the comprehensive outline of the content and training provided by the internship. Provide names and phone numbers of current interns for further information.

♦ This contact should be the first step of the winnowing process for his candidacy and should lead to either the process progressing to the next step or to his being eliminated from further consideration.

3. If he is to be considered, the next step is to request that a formal application be completed for the position and to obtain permission to check the references he has provided as part of his résumé. Do a background check through a company such as Oxford Document Management Company (www.oxforddoc.com). Oxford can provide you with a detailed investigative report of various areas of interest to you and will make it as thorough as you specify for a minimal fee. It is imperative that one of the components you include is a multi-state criminal background check to make sure there are no issues involving criminal sexual misconduct, particularly with children or teens. Note that it is wise to explain to him that you do this with all candidates for positions in the church and this does not indicate in any way any inappropriate suspicion about him on your part. Also explain the step by step personal interview and selection process to him.

Questions asked during the interview focus on a variety of areas for obtaining specific information that will provide insight. The following are sample interview questions.

♦ What kind of schedule is anticipated?

♦ What are your likes and dislikes with regard to work responsibilities?

♦ What is your philosophy of the pastor-board relationship?

♦ What other possibilities for ministry are you considering?

♦ What is your attitude toward the privacy of your home and family?

♦ How do you picture your spouse's involvement in the ministry?

♦ Briefly describe your home atmosphere growing up.

♦ How does your family feel about your being in the ministry?

- Have you ever had any difficulties with depression, moodiness, anxiety, or similar difficulties? What did you do about it? What makes you feel this way? (Note: If he answers in the positive, it does not disqualify him. It will probably make him more understanding.)
- How do you react when things do not go as planned?
- How do you respond to criticism?
- How do you feel you relate to others?
- In what areas of ministry do you feel most experienced and competent?
- What do you think are your weaknesses?
- Are you satisfied with your present education, or would you like to pursue further learning?
- What do you do in your spare time?
- Are there any points in our doctrinal system which you would not or could not affirm? If so, which and why?
- What is your philosophy of music?
- What are you convictions about alcohol, dress, and types of movies? How do you respond to those who disagree with your convictions?
- What kind of student were you? What were your favorite subjects? Your least favorite?
- Is there anything in your background we should know about? Arrests? Tickets? Moral failures?
- Are there problems in your marriage? What are they?
- What would be your expectations if you joined our staff?

Note that responses to various questions lead to follow up questions and additional questions.

4. When checking references, have a prepared list of questions to ask each referent. A sample list is included in this section. At the end of your discussion with a reference person, ask if he could give two other references who know the candidate and can provide additional information about him or his background. These additional references often prove to be very important sources. References given by the candidate are carefully selected to ensure that he will be presented in the best possible light. These additional references are not so selected and will often provide additional critical information about the candidate. Check all previous employment sources. Analyze his attitudes and behavior, relationships with bosses and employees, how he fit into the organization, how committed he was, why he left, and if the employer would rehire him.

These are sample questions asked for referents.

- What are the top three to five things that stand out about this candidate?
- What weaknesses does the candidate have?
- Would you rehire him? Yes or no and why?
- Does he have tact in dealing with people?
- Does he have ability to teach? To preach?
- What kind of leadership skills does he have?
- Does he make well informed decisions?
- Is he into athletics and sports?
- Is he a book nerd?
- Does he do well with layout and design?
- Does he know and enjoy the outdoors?
- Is he well organized?
- How is he in evangelism? worship

leading? discipleship of others? serving? assisting others? fellowshipping? interacting with others? Does he hang around after a service or does he run out the door right away?

5. If all screenings were successfully completed, invite him to officially candidate. Have him bring his family so that you can see him function in both his family and church environments. Observe how the couple relates to each other and how they handle their children in both formal and informal situations. Staff couples may spend time dining with the candidates and during a social time afterward have an additional opportunity to gather information.

On Saturday, our senior staff jointly interviews them and allows them to ask any questions they may have. This interview is conducted without the children.

They are scheduled to spend time attending functions to interact with different church groups. They speak to the Sunday school class which they will later be assigned to lead, and are introduced in the morning worship service where both the candidate and his wife will be required to give a brief testimony. We then have him preach in the evening church service.

As part of the interview we ask him to take the California Personality Inventory (CPI). This assessment contains 434 items including 20 scales measuring qualities such as dominance, independence, internal values, control, need for seeking achievement, flexibility, managerial potential, and creative temperament. It should be available for usage on-line both for test taking and scoring at Psychometrics.com. This assessment tool can reveal vital aspects of his character and leadership potential.

6. When this entire process is completed on Sunday night, the senior staff meets to discuss the couple, assess the results of the screening process, and make the decision whether to offer them the position or not. If the position is offered, we allow them a few days to pray about it and give us their answer.

7. If they refused the position, we seek another candidate. If they accept, we make arrangements for their coming, develop a timeline for the transition, and provide assistance as necessary.

Staff Corrective ACTION Checklist

For use when an employee or staff member has failed to meet specific goals or has had a significant failure in his performance.

Assess the situation and problem.
___Deal with expectations regarding the situation.
___Present your role as helper instead of critic or judge.
___Listen carefully, ask questions, and then give your response.
___Seek clarification on issues.
___Use constructive techniques in confrontation.
___Emphasize improvement planning.
___Complete a thorough two-way analysis of the situation.

Confront the problem by addressing the person responsible.
___Expectations not met should be carefully presented.
___Must create understanding of the problem and the negative consequences it is creating.
___Must make situation clear.
___Make him assume responsibility for the problem.
___Emphasize the importance of corrective action.

Take action.
___Emphasize the required change and the desired outcomes.
___Carefully determine a person's needs and wants.
___Suggest corrective measures.
___Develop a series of actions steps.
___Create goals.
___Break the solution down into a series of can-do action steps.
___Present the challenge as an opportunity.
___Implement the developmental plan and redirect course if necessary.
___Develop a specific agreed upon plan of action.
___Seek consensus, agreement, and commitment to the plan and the action steps.

Initiate a support system to ensure the plan of action is properly carried out.

On-going monitoring with feedback is necessary to make mid-course corrections.
___Assume required coaching responsibilities.
___Agree to standards to measure progress, when and how it will be assessed, and who will be involved in the process.
___Monitor the results and provide the necessary feedback with each step.

Necessary recognition and affirmation is provided.
___Provide constant encouragement when you observe the right things being done.
___Provide incentives, recognition, rewards, and praise through the process.
___Administer an appropriate reprimand when needed.

Suggest reassessment as needed. If the plan is not working, repeat the previous steps.

Dismissing an Employee

Be sure you have followed these steps before making the decision of dismissal.

1. If employee's evaluations both formal and informal have included honest candor, the issues at hand should be well defined and not surprising to him.

2. Provide accurate feedback about his shortcomings and provide opportunity for him to correct the problem.

3. This process should be recorded in the employee's personnel file and be followed up with appropriate meetings to assess progress or lack thereof.

4. It is preferable to provide the employee adequate opportunity to correct the problems before dismissal.

5. The dismissal should be handled privately with dignity. Avoid gossip or embarrassment to the employee insisting that others do the same.

6. The employee will probably feel upset, angry, stressed and perhaps afraid because of losing his position.

7. Encourage the employee and provide help in making it through the process.

8. The public reason given for the dismissal should be carefully stated so not to unnecessarily damage his future.

9. Provide adequate notice and severance unless there is a moral failure, which warrants immediate dismissal.

10. Maintain as good a relationship as possible during the process and its aftermath.

Recommended Scripture References

Work of hands rewarded, Proverbs 12:14
Work brings profit, Proverbs 14:23
Work with all your might, Ecclesiastes 9:10
Servant not above teachers, Matthew 10:24
Example of working, John 5:17
Deserve payment for labor, 1 Corinthians 9:7
Aim for perfection, 2 Corinthians 13:11
Serve whole-heartedly, Ephesians 6:6-7
Work for the Lord, Colossians 3:22-25; 4:1
Work diligently for Christian employer, 1 Timothy 6:2
Employees who are trusted, Titus 2:9-10

Part Three
The Church

Introduction
The Church

The purpose-driven model of church ministry is effective because it represents the teaching of the New Testament regarding Christ's desire and design for the ministry of His church. Evangelism, worship, fellowship, discipleship, and service are presented as the primary focus of God's purpose for its very existence. These purposes are presented with information about youth and children, small groups, team ministries, and helpful suggestions for starting new ministries in the church.

A healthy church is a growing church and our job is to allow the Great Physician to diagnose, treat, and heal the unhealthy parts as well as to promote growth, health, and wellness in the body.

The following chapters contain a succinct presentation of some important elements for producing desired results in these areas of ministry.

Love the Lord your God
with all your heart,
and with all your soul,
and with all your strength,
and with all your mind;
and, love your
neighbor as yourself.

Luke 10:27

Spiritual Life and Growth

How Friendly Is Your Church?

The Issue: Some churches are considered cold, unfriendly, and uncaring.

Have you ever gone to church, received no welcome greeting, sat through a service and walked out without exchanging even a brief pleasant conversation with anyone?

George R. Plagenz, a syndicated religious writer, sought to answer that question by looking through the eyes of a church visitor. His conclusion was that too many American churches are cold, unfriendly, and uncaring.

He based his findings on a series of visits to churches of various denominations. During each visit he used a church friendliness grading system. The point system that he used was:

♦ 10 points for a greeting ("Good morning")
♦ 100 points for an exchange of names ("I'm so-and-so... what's your name?")
♦ 200 points for an invitation to have coffee after the church service
♦ 1,000 points for an introduction to another worshiper ("I'd like you to meet So-and-so.")
♦ 2,000 points for an invitation to meet the pastor

He found that the majority of the time he could go through an entire church service without having anyone speak to him. He also attended fellowship hours where he often sat or stood alone.

Of the 18 churches he visited, 11 earned fewer than 100 points. Five got fewer than 20 points. The other two got just over 1,000 points. Some churches were certainly less friendly than others; some were luke-warm, and a select few were very unfriendly. The results should serve as a wake-up call and indicate that an important area in our churches needs improvement. Friendliness is a vital component to increasing church size. Church leaders and members should study the issue of friendliness as it relates to their own congregation. A few minutes of friendship can make all the difference. Members must be regularly reminded to greet and show an interest in others at every service or church function.

The Purpose Driven Model

Rick Warren's purpose driven model is biblical and applicable to any size church. The five levels of commitment are community (the unchurched), crowd (attenders), congregation (members), committed (growing disciples), and core (fully dedicated followers and servers). Each should be addressed by the staff and a team to provide ministry for each.

Community—Evangelism Team
Crowd—Worship Team
Congregation—Fellowship Team
Committed—Discipleship Team
Core—Serving Team

To maximize our impact in ministry to each group, we should:

1. Design programs to fulfill the purposes.
2. Examine the purpose of every program in the church and change programs as needed to best fulfill each purpose.
3. Assign every lay minister and every staff member to one of the teams.
4. Design purpose-driven ministry teams with a team pastor, a team coordinator, lay pastors, board members, and volunteers.
5. Organize specific ministries under each purpose-driven ministry team with a coordinator, assistant, appointees, and volunteers.

6. Oversee and monitor the progress and movement of each of the ministry teams to ensure that people are advancing through the five levels of commitment in the purpose driven model.

7. Build commitment of participants, developing quality at every level to accomplish the primary goal.

Promoting the Five Purposes

1. Outreach Events

   Holiday events—Holiday programs such as Halloween, Christmas, Easter, Fourth of July

   Special events—Friend Day, concerts, productions, special guests

   Other events—Bible studies, seeker groups, seminars, personal evangelism, back yard Bible clubs, Sunday school promotions, lay pastor ministry

   Outreach events should have a seeker sensitive atmosphere. Communicate warmth with genuine interest. Create a sense of belonging, making people feel welcome and wanted; give personal attention. Don't neglect follow-up.

2. Worship

   Corporate worship—drama, music, prayer, devotions, praise, communion, scripture, special music

   Individual worship—Suggest methods, materials, and motivation

3. Fellowship
   Major fellowship events planned that provide for connecting with others on a personal level, sharing with others, and providing opportunities to establishing friendships

4. Discipleship
   Personal growth ministry & opportunity
   Church-wide spiritual growth campaigns
   Small groups

5. Serving
   Understanding spiritual gifts and how God has gifted you, new ministry development, service groups, specific opportunities for service

Calendar Coordination

Plan an emphasis on each of the five purposes throughout the year. Months can be grouped together for an emphasis on each purpose or rotated monthly. In the following sections a more complete treatment of these concepts is presented.

Recommended Scripture References

Grow in spirit and character, 1 Samuel 2:26; Luke 2:52
Spiritual truth, John 6:60-69
Hope, joy, peace, Romans 15:13
Solid food, 1 Corinthians 3:1-2, Hebrews 5:11, 14; 6:1-3; 1 Peter 2:2-3
Not a child, 1 Corinthians 13:11, 13; Ephesians 4:14
Find what pleases the Lord, Ephesians 5:10
Good work begun will be completed, Philippians 1:6
Standing firm in circumstances, Philippians 1:27-30
Spiritual growth, Philippians 3:12-16
Filled with knowledge of God's will, Colossians 1:9-12
Spiritual need fulfilled in Christ, Colossians 1:15-23
Conversion, growth, Colossians 2:6-7
Mature in Christ, Colossians 4:12
Blameless and holy, 1 Thessalonians 3:13
Increase love, 1 Thessalonians 4:10
Motivated to Christian life, 1 Thessalonians 4:11-12
Growing in faith, love, 2 Thessalonians 1:3
Quest for spiritual growth, 1 Timothy 4:13
Disciplined growth, 2 Timothy 1:7; Hebrews 5:11-14; James 1:2-4
Rid of evil traits, 1 Peter 2:1-3
Live godly life, 2 Peter 1:2, 3
Distinct element of spiritual maturity, 2 Peter 1:5-9
Growing in grace, 2 Peter 3:18
Deliverance from practicing sin, 1 John 3:8-10
Health and wealth plus spiritual vitality, 3 John 2-4
Growing faith, Jude 20
Temporal and spiritual wealth, Revelation 3:15-18

Ministry Teams

Organizing/Leading Ministry Teams

When a church becomes large enough that the pastoral staff cannot fulfill their leadership roles effectively, the members of the congregation and community cannot be adequately cared for through their ministry. It points to the necessity of establishing ministry teams to provide more effective leadership, organization, oversight, and service.

Ministry teams are groups of people who commit to serve in a particular area of ministry because of interest, spiritual giftedness, or the leadership and direction of the Lord.

At Edgewood, ministry teams are organized according to the five purposes of the church; thus, we have separate worship, fellowship, discipleship, service ministry, and evangelism teams. Each team is led by a member of the pastoral staff based upon his area of ministry. The Music and Worship Pastor leads the worship team, the Administrative Pastor leads the fellowship team, the Christian Education Director leads the discipleship team, The Seniors' Pastor leads the service ministry team, and the Youth Pastor leads the evangelistic team. This arrangement is arbitrary and could easily be organized differently.

The teams must be well organized, fully functioning, and effective for God. Members of the church staff, board members, lay pastors, interested lay leaders, and participants in the various ministries should be recruited to serve on a ministry team. This arrangement is flexible and should allow some latitude in participation.

A well-functioning ministry team is important because it:

♦ allows members to effectively contribute to the leadership, development, and ministry of the congregation.

♦ provides a broader range of opportunities through the sharing of ideas and sources because none of us alone is as good as all of us together.

♦ enables the church to better implement and fulfill the five purposes of the church through laser-like focus on each purpose.

♦ fulfills the biblical mandate to equip the saints by allowing each ministry team participant to personally and spiritually grow in their knowledge and service.

♦ enables the leadership to better meet the needs of the congregation through delegation with pastors being the administrators and the members the ministers.

♦ provides for more effective oversight and development of the many ministries and ministry participants of the church.

Steps to Organize Ministry Teams

1. Recruit the potential members for the ministry team.

2. During the first meeting, introduce each team member and have each give a brief statement about himself or herself. Nametags would be helpful, especially in large groups or if some members of the ministry team do not know each other.

3. Present the purpose, objectives, and goals for the ministry team. Sell them on the importance of the ministry team and their contribution to it.

4. Provide a step-by-step agenda of what the ministry team will do and determine the best time for everyone to meet based upon member's schedules. Develop a schedule for future meetings.

5. Each team member will participate in brainstorming sessions, making suggestions of things that will develop and strengthen a particular ministry within

the domain of the team. State that all suggestions will be welcomed and that they will be sorted out later by the group.

6. Spend the necessary number of sessions required to complete the brainstorming for suggestions and recommendations. Take care not to inhibit the process.

7. After all of the suggestions have been made, lead the team in discussing each suggestion. The discussion should focus on the desirability and achievability of each suggestion.

8. Have each member of the team vote on every suggestion based upon desirability and do-ability. Use a five-point scale, with 1 being the most desirable and the most doable and 5 being the least so.

9. Tabulate the results with the suggestions ranked 1 or 2 as priorities by the participants on a list; then provide a master list of all of the suggestions that have been ranked 1 or 2. These recommendations now become the teams' projects.

10. Discuss each component of the priority list. Ask members to commit to developing a particular ministry either individually or with other team members. This commitment becomes their assignment.

11. Provide a worksheet containing the necessary steps to creatively organize and implement the recommendation.

12. Offer to meet with any team member (in person) by phone or to discuss the development of their assignment as a worksheet. Provide any guidance or support required for each team member.

13. Have each member present his or her strategic plan as developed using the worksheet in current or future team meetings.

14. Assist in the implementation of each accepted recommendation (project) by see-

ing that each team member has the necessary materials, help, and support to implement his or her assigned area.

15. Future meetings should assess follow through, and provide encouragement, assistance, and accountability to the team members.

16. As new members are recruited or volunteer for participation in the group, engage them in creative and constructive participation by allowing them to assist in the team projects or develop new recommendations which can become projects for them to develop.

17. Continue to provide whatever the team needs to function at a peak level of efficiency and fulfillment.

18. Periodically all of the ministry teams should assemble for information and awareness of each group's projects, the promotion of unity, sharing, support, and fellowship. These meetings should be scheduled at quarterly intervals unless needed more often. The meetings should be scheduled when the maximum number of members of the various ministry teams can attend.

19. The leader of each ministry team should function not only as a leader but as a facilitator to other group members. As the leaders, they should pray regularly for their team members and their respective projects.

20. The continuation of each ministry team is only sustainable by following the Nehemiah principle. The Nehemiah principle teaches us that the level of inspiration for any member of a team following a meeting will wear off within one month, hence, the reason to schedule a meeting every 30 days, at least at the beginning. After the team has been functioning well for a period of time and has successfully developed and imple-

mented the various projects undertaken as assignments, then the group may decide to meet less often.

Recommended Scripture References

Dwell in unity, Psalm 133:1-3
Teaching, preaching, healing, Matthew 4:23; 9:18-25
Faith needed for healing, Mark 6:4-6
Going two-by-two, Mark 6:7
Apostle's ministry, Mark 6:30-34
Aged widow's ministry, Luke 2:36-38
Reject minister, Luke 10:16
Joy from service, Luke 10:17
Power is of the Lord, Acts 3:12
Ministry with power, Acts 4:33
Testimony of ministry, Acts 20:17-38

Pride in ministry, Romans 11:13
No divisions, 1 Corinthians 1:10
Lord assigned each task, 1 Corinthians 3:5-9
Serving God, all win, 1 Corinthians 9:24-27
Body of Christ, 1 Corinthians 12:14-20
Treasure in earthen vessel, 2 Corinthians 4:1
I please God, Galatians 1:10
Not run in vain, Galatians 2:1-2
Bear another's burden, Galatians 6:1-2
Press toward the mark, Philippians 3:14
Holy Spirit power for ministry, Colossians 1:29
Pray for ministers, Colossians 4:3
Word came with power, 1 Thessalonians 1:4-5
Ministry not in vain,, 1 Thessalonians 2:1-6
Remain faithful, 1 Timothy 6:11-16
Fight the good fight, 2 Timothy 4:6-8
Be holy, 1 Peter 1:15-16
Holy priesthood, 1 Peter 2:5

Evangelism and Outreach

Necessity of Soul-Winning

The mode of encountering an unsaved person may vary, but seizing personal witnessing opportunities should always be foremost in the mind of any Christian.

It is important that soul-winners grasp several important concepts. How did Jesus segue into a discussion of spiritual things? Think of the woman at the well. Jesus did not just come up to her and say, "When you die, do you know if you're going to heaven or not?" He began the conversation by using present circumstances of being near the well and His knowledge of the woman to make a smooth transition into spiritual things. He said in John 4:7, *Give me to drink* because she was about to draw water. Then He piqued her curiosity and introduced her spiritual need by using the metaphor of *living water*. In John 4:10 Jesus said, *If thou knewest the gift of God, and who it is that saith to thee, Give me to drink; thou wouldest have asked of Him, and He would have given thee living water.* We do not have the Lord's omniscience, so we should try to learn something about the person by being observant and listening for any cues they give as to their beliefs, spiritual background, and spiritual needs.

Specific questions may be helpful to quickly assess a person's spiritual need. For example: Do you ever think about spiritual things? Do you attend church? Are you 100% certain that if you died today, you'd go to heaven?

While these questions are useful, it is always important to use circumstances or observations to get acquainted and to connect with a person. Then, use these circumstances or observations to springboard more naturally into a conversation about spiritual things.

A Gospel Presentation

Important steps in the Gospel presentation:

1. Show them their need.
2. Do pre-evangelism as necessary. Explain the concept of sin, repentance, and forgiveness.
3. Present the gospel. Use your personal testimony.
4. Move them closer to Christ.
5. Close with prayer and an invitation to receive Christ.
6. If they received Christ, give verses on reassurance of salvation. Discuss church attendance, baptism, and family reactions.
7. If they did not receive Christ, leave the door open for future contact. Consider leaving a tract and your business card.

Applying Persuasion Techniques

Before continuing, read the section on Persuasion. Make sure you fully understand the *10 Laws of Persuasion*. The following are some examples of how you might use persuasion techniques for a more effective presentation.

1. Reciprocity

   ◆ Create a feeling of needing to come back to the church by giving the visitor something of value.

   ◆ Give out a Father's or Mother's Day gift to all parents in attendance.

   ◆ Take someone to lunch to share the gospel.

   ◆ Give a free cassette tape, CD, DVD, or loaf of bread to visitors as a thank you for visiting.

   ◆ Give a free chart on spot removal with the gospel presentation on the back.

   ◆ Offer free or low cost quality babysitting for the afternoon to the community as a Parent's Day Out.

- Dispense tracts with valuable parenting information.

- Offer free classes such as aerobics, cooking, health, safety, or English as a second language.

- Offer free activities for children such as Halloween alternatives, egg hunts, festivals, and vacation Bible school.

2. Contrast

- Explain Christianity is the only religion without a works for salvation philosophy.

- Explain Christianity is the only religion that worships a risen founder, not a grave site.

- Explain Christianity transcends national borders like no other religion.

3. Friends

- Create church sports teams open to community participation.

- Get to know someone (acquaintance or neighbor) by inviting him or her to tea or dinner before presenting the gospel. Be truly interested in their friendship; it shouldn't seem as if you are a salesperson.

- Share with someone at work whom you know well. "I am really concerned about your future; may I share my personal experience with coming to know Christ?"

4. Expectancy

"I know you will make the right decision," or "I know you will give this careful consideration."

5. Association

Share testimonies of famous athletes, CEOs, musicians, or others to parallel the interests of those to whom you are witnessing. You might share the testimony of Joni Tada with a handicapped person or that of Chuck Colson with someone involved in politics.

6. Consistency

- Strongly encourage a new believer to take the next step of a public profession of faith or baptism.

- Strongly encourage a new believer to join you in witnessing opportunities with others. Explaining their beliefs to another will strengthen their conviction.

7. Scarcity

- Not all will enter heaven.

  Enter ye in at the strait gate: for wide is the gate, and broad is the way, that leadeth to destruction, and many there be which go in thereat. Matthew 7:13

  Because strait is the gate, and narrow is the way, which leadeth unto life, and few there be that find it. Matthew 7:14

  Not every one that saith unto me, Lord, Lord, shall enter into the kingdom of heaven; but he that doeth the will of my Father which is in heaven.
  Matthew 7:21

8. Conformity

- During the invitation tell them, "Others are coming forward now, so please, you come too."

- At camp it is often easier to make a salvation decision when others are also moved to do so in an open, intensive environment filled with the person's peers.

9. Power

- Seek the Holy Spirit's leadership and direction as you begin interaction with others.

- Have verses memorized that will be useful in the gospel presentation.

- Get to know God more intimately. Realize His purpose in reaching the lost. Seek His mind and ask His power on your efforts.

10. Time element

- Emphasize the fact that the Bible says the time to make a faith decision is now. Revelation 3:20, *Behold, I stand at the door, and knock: if any man hear my voice, and open the door, I will come in to him, and will sup with him, and he with me.* 2 Corinthians 6:2, *For he saith, I have heard thee in a time accepted, and in the day of salvation have I have helped thee: behold, now is the accepted time; behold, now is the day of salvation.*

- Emphasize that we are creatures that procrastinate and this is one decision too dangerous to put off until it is too late. We may not survive one more day as a car accident, sudden illness, or other major crisis situation is a possibility and a reality.

- Emphasize that some receive many opportunities to hear the truth, yet this could be the last opportunity to hear and act upon the truth.

Witnessing to a Catholic

There are many similarities in Catholic, Evangelical, and Baptist theology. When witnessing to a Catholic, use this to your advantage. So much time is spent on the differences that an opportunity to share the gospel is bogged down in debates on more peripheral issues that are often highly emotionally charged. You are confronting a person's way of life as well as a set of deeply ingrained and highly regarded traditions and cultural practices. Attacking a Catholic's beliefs about venerating Mary and the saints is only going to end your conversation or escalate it to an argument. Not only will your

opportunity for witnessing come to an abrupt end, but your relationship with the person probably will too. If you can present the gospel clearly and succinctly, then God's Word will have opportunity to do its job in their hearts. You can and should be persuasive, but it is the Word of God that saves, not you. Present the gospel positively and leave the door open for a future relationship with the person with whom you are sharing the gospel. If you do not take a genuine interest in the person and treat him merely as a prospective convert, he will reject your witness.

1. Introductions

- After greeting, connect with the person about his home, family, hobbies, or anything you sense that will warm up the interaction.

- Many Catholic beliefs are similar to yours. Feel free to complement the denomination's devotion to the Bible as the true Word of God, belief in the virgin birth of Christ, Christ's death, burial and resurrection, and the reality of sin.

2. Share your personal testimony.

- Explain that although you had known about spiritual things and had religious practices, you felt that something was always missing in your life. You did not know God personally, like the Bible says, as a friend.

- When you considered the possibility of sudden death and meeting God, you were not sure of your eternal standing or future.

- Tell him you share the Gospel with others because you think that there are others like yourself who know about Christ but who don't know Him personally.

3. Share Scripture Verses

- Ask if you could spend just a few minutes together looking at some Bible verses saying, "Perhaps it will be a blessing to both of us." Ask to use his Bible or show that you are reading from your own Catholic Bible. Catholics generally use the following translations:

Douay Bible includes the Books of the Apocrypha 1582 OT and 1610 NT. A more modern version, the *Douay-Rheims Bible* 1899 is also used; this is the generally accepted English Version of the Roman Church.

Jerusalem Bible (JB) 1966 (includes the Books of the Apocrypha).

New English Bible (NEB) 1970 (includes the Books of the Apocrypha).

Today's English Version (TEV) 1976 (also known as the *Good News for Modern Man*).

♦ A Catholic will distrust the King James Version of the Bible because of the historical background of the translation. If you want to try to argue the point, that is your choice. However, you will probably not be able to share the gospel without using a version he accepts. It is very important that the Catholic person have confidence in the translation.

♦ Use all or some of the following scriptures being certain to use the last. These are verses from the *1899 Douay-Rheims Bible* Version. Acquaint yourself with the differences.

These things I write to you that you may know that you have eternal life: you who believe in the name of the Son of God.
1 John 5:13

As it is written: There is not any man just. Romans 3:10

Wherefore as by one man sin entered into this world and by sin death: and so death passed upon all men, in whom all have sinned. Romans 5:12

For all have sinned and do need the glory of God. Romans 3:23

For the wages of sin is death. But the grace of God, life everlasting in Christ Jesus our Lord. Romans 6:23

But God commendeth his charity towards us: because when as yet we were sinners according to the time. Christ died for us. Much more therefore, being now justified by his blood, shall we be saved from wrath through him. Romans 5:8-9

For if thou confess with thy mouth the Lord Jesus and believe in thy heart that God hath raised him up from the dead, thou shalt be saved. For, with the heart, we believe unto justice: but, with the mouth, confession is made unto salvation. Romans 10:9-10

For whosoever shall call upon the name of the Lord shall be saved. Romans 10:13

4. Ask

"Have you ever called upon the name of the Lord?" If he claims to do this often, explain that the grammatical construction of the word *call* in this passage is not continuous action and does not have to be performed repeatedly. Explain that the one-time nature of this call is like a marriage. When people exchange vows and say *I do*, they are not married until both parties have expressed their total commitment to each other with their whole heart and soul. It is true that God has expressed his love commitment to us in the person of his Son Jesus who died on the cross for our sins. But it is also necessary for us to call upon the Lord and make a one-time, wholehearted commitment and submit to His authority over our lives just as married couples submit to one another.

5. Prayer and Invitation

Thank him for the opportunity to share and ask if you might end in a word of prayer. In your prayer say:

♦ "Thank you Lord, for _____, who was so gracious to let me share my experiences and some verses from Your Word."

- "He is a good man, a devout man."

- Because of the importance of not only believing the right things, but committing to them personally by calling on the name of the Lord, ask, "If you would like to commit yourself to God and call upon His name, ask God, not out loud but in your heart, to forgive your sin and accept you as His own."

- "I'm going to extend my hand. If you prayed in your heart to make this one-time commitment to Jesus Christ, just take my hand."

- Thank God again for the opportunity to share. End the prayer.

6. Follow-up

- If he took your hand, reassure him of eternal life.

- In either case try to make opportunity for a follow-up contact, a visit, a lunch or dinner with the family. Tell him that you will call him later and set something up. Be sure to fulfill any promise to do so.

- If time allows and he has prayed to receive Christ, use some follow-up verses such as Romans 10:11.

Tell him that one who has accepted the Lord is not ashamed. One way to demonstrate this is through baptism. If he is struggling to define his new position within the Catholic church, sees discrepancies or errors in Catholic teaching, and asks if he should continue to attend the Catholic Church, compare it to seeing a doctor that gave a bad diagnosis. Ask, "Would you go back to that doctor?"

Witnessing to Someone with No Bible Background

1. Introductions

Introduce yourself. Tell him you appreciate him taking the time to see you or talk with you. Talk about anything you have in common, things you notice about him, his family, his home, or business.

2. Pre-Evangelism

Explain that you would like to talk about salvation, which is found in the Bible. Define it as having genuine forgiveness for the things we've done wrong in life, having a personal and genuine relationship with God, and having assurance of a home in heaven after death.

3. Introduce the Problem of Sin

Everyone has heard of the 10 Commandments. The Bible says that these are a part of God's Law for man. When we lie or steal, we have broken God's law and this is called sin.

Define sin further. Sin is an archery term meaning to miss the mark. God's standard is like a bull's-eye. When we sin we miss the bull's-eye and we are not living up to God's standard.

4. Introduce the Solution of Restoration

- Ask if God will restore all who have missed the mark.

- Answer that God sent His Son to make man right with God. God chose Jesus for this task because He lived a perfect, sinless life. Jesus then would take our place and pay the price for sin.

- Illustration: If a person has many parking tickets, is summoned to court, and doesn't have the money to pay the fines, the authorities are going to send him to jail. He needs another to pay the fine for the tickets so that he won't go to jail.

- Jesus came to pay for our sins with His life. Jesus died on the cross in our place. Jesus rose from the dead because He is God in the flesh. Jesus came to earth to do this all for us. That's how much God loves you and me. Ask, "Who would be willing to die for you?"

5. Share Your Personal Testimony

6. Prayer and Invitation

Thank him for the opportunity to visit and speak with him. Ask if you might offer a word of prayer. (See the sample prayer on previous page.)

7. Follow-up
    ♦ Offer reassurance.
    ♦ Schedule personal visit.
    ♦ Encourage baptism.
    ♦ Encourage the person to begin reading the Bible.
    ♦ Assist in the acquisition of a Bible if the person does not have one.

Outreach

Trotline fishing is a metaphor for the concept of putting as many gospel hooks in the water as possible to increase your chances of catching more fish as a fisher of men. If you fish with one hook, you are not as likely to catch as many fish as if you use half a dozen poles lined up with carefully-baited hooks. A trotline contains multiple hooks as it lies in the water. The more gospel-presenting programs and opportunities you have in your ministry, the greater the probability that you will have a bountiful catch. How many gospel outreaches or hooks do you currently have? Here are some examples of proven outreach programs.

Door-To-Door Evangelism

Door to door evangelism can be one of the most difficult kinds of evangelism. Here are some suggestions to increase productivity.

Always go with a partner who can support and assist you. Jesus sent His disciples out two-by-two.

Be warm, friendly, and positive when you first meet someone at the door. Always bring a smile to the greeting.

Introduce yourself and your partner and im-

mediately state why you are there. Say, "Hello, my name is ... and this is .... We're from the ... Church and are out making some visits today to invite folks to church."

Invite them to the church and offer them a brochure which includes the gospel message.

Share your personal testimony if they are open to listening. Many will listen to your personal testimony but remember to keep it brief. If they won't allow you to go further with the visit, you have at least had the opportunity to share the gospel with them.

Ask if they are interested in knowing God personally. If they don't resist, continue with the presentation of the gospel. If they refuse, leave on a positive note so that the door is not closed to further contacts by you or someone else. Follow up the visit if appropriate.

Literature Ministry

There are many who have come to Christ because someone shared a gospel tract with them. Here are some helpful suggestions regarding the use of tracts.

Carefully select the gospel literature you will use based upon the contents and appeal of the literature.

Carry literature for the opportunity that will present itself.

Ask the person, "May I give you something special to read?" or "Here is some food for thought," or "I would be interested in your response to this."

Consider enclosing tracts in letters or when paying bills by mail. Leave one for your waitress with a tip.

Leaving a church brochure which includes a gospel message at someone's door accomplishes two purposes— provides information about the church and shares the good news of Jesus Christ.

Friendship Evangelism

By intentionally building a relationship with another, you have the chance to establish credibility and foster in them a personal interest in the message of Christ through your Christ-like example and caring.

Survey Evangelism

Survey evangelism is a door-opening method during neighborhood visiting. You explain that you are taking a survey and ask if they would mind answering a few brief questions. If allowed, you ask such questions as: Do you attend church? Are you happy in your church? Do you know what it means to know God personally? Would you be interested in knowing?

If they respond positively to the last question, tactfully present the gospel. If not, offer them some literature and move on.

Outreach Program

Capitalize upon big events and special days to provide an extra incentive for people to attend and as an incentive for your people to invite and bring others to the services. These include Friend Day, Easter and Christmas holiday programs, special guest appearances, musical programs, and concerts.

Telecare

Telecare focuses on the use of the telephone to follow up with people who visit the church, to make post-hospital or post-outpatient surgery calls, to check on absentees, to follow up counseling sessions, or to do general check-up on the spiritual well-being of your people. People are easy to reach by phone and are usually appreciative of the demonstration of care and concern.

Evangelistic Small Groups

Evangelistic groups are made up of interested people recruited to participate in a Bible study with the intention of introducing them to Christ.

Missions Committee

A missions group can be an invaluable asset to your church and its missionary outreach program. The group can:

- Make initial contacts with prospective missionaries.
- Investigate the special requests of your missionaries.
- Keep in contact with missionaries you currently support offering encouragement and discerning new and special needs.
- Entertain missionaries when they visit the church.
- Establish and maintain a missionary closet.
- Assist the staff with missionary conferences.
- Provide specific help with missionary programs.
- Perform missionary outreach ministry at home and abroad.

All of the church's programs should have an evangelistic emphasis.

Promoting Special Events

When you are anticipating a big event, preparation and systematic promotion are necessary to obtain maximum participation and results. Here are some ideas which may prove helpful.

1. Begin promoting the special event six to eight weeks in advance.
2. The early promotion should be less extensive and intensive but should increase in both intensity and frequency as the event draws closer.
3. Use many types of promotion including print, speech, posters, flyers, and word of mouth.
4. Enthusiasm makes a difference. If you expect to have your people jump an inch, be ready to jump a foot.
5. Use first degree stimuli in promotion whenever possible.

6. Use testimonials from those who have previously experienced the program or event. Satisfied customers make powerful persuaders.

7. The Sunday before your big event should have the most comprehensive and enthusiastic promotion of all. Enthusiasm is contagious.

8. The final promotion should include asking your people for a commitment to participate which can be expressed by signing up, checking a box on a card, or simply raising their hands.

9. Periodic series of emails or postal letters should be sent advertising the big event, particularly during the final week.

10. Pray for God's blessing upon the special event.

Four Reasons Why People Don't Come to Church

1. They don't feel welcome. They don't feel like it really matters to members if they are there or not. They often report that they feel ignored, unwanted, and unappreciated, and that the church is unfriendly.

2. They don't like the music.

3. They think the church cares too much about money.

4. The sermons are not relevant, practical, interesting, and don't meet their needs. The unmet needs which they report are their emotional issues, personal issues, and relational problems.

It is important for the church interested in outreach and evangelism to carefully analyze these factors as related to their services.

Backyard Bible Clubs for Children

Backyard clubs can be conducted in neighborhoods throughout your area. A host family invites neighborhood children to visit their home. Invitational flyers can be passed out throughout the neighborhood.

Jesus talked about the importance of children; we know that reaching children with the good news of the gospel is high on God's priority list. Children's hearts are tender toward spiritual things and they are eager to hear the stories of the Bible.

A new ministry or mission field often begins by reaching the children. For that reason, it is vital that one be comfortable with ministering to children in an informal setting such as a backyard or park.

Taking the message to children in someone's backyard or their neighborhood park is meeting children where they are. Jesus taught this way, out in the open, using the objects around Him as teaching tools.

Backyard Bible clubs provide a place close to home for children who don't attend church or that may be new to your ministry to learn about Jesus. It also helps Christians reach out to their own neighborhoods and build evangelistic bridges to unreached families.

A backyard Bible club can be a one, three, or five day club. It can be a morning, afternoon, or evening event. The atmosphere is welcoming and relaxed: children can attend in play clothes, perhaps even in their bare feet! Parents are usually happy to have their children "entertained" for an hour or two in their own neighborhood.

Backyard Bible clubs are usually held in someone's yard or home. The home doesn't have to be large or elaborate. There needs to be a place to tell the story, such as a large room inside or an area under a tree in the shade. There needs to be a convenient place to do a craft, a kitchen table or a picnic table in the yard. Children can work around a table while standing or sitting on the floor or lawn. Serve refreshments to the children sitting at the same table as used for crafts.

225

Utilize an area in the yard or a nearby park for active game play. You could do a Bible club in a public park, but it is best to check with local authorities for permission.

Staff

The staff needed for a backyard club depends on the number of children expected. The person hosting the club is very important. This person invites the neighborhood children to attend and usually provides refreshments. She or he makes sure their home is in order and that there are no safety issues.

The teacher is able to focus on the lesson and the students. It is important to firmly and lovingly let the children know what behavior is expected of them. It is difficult to teach children who are being unruly. Since the backyard setting can lead to rowdy behavior, the teacher and helpers must be prepared to handle disruptions. The teacher knows the schedule and how the flow of the lesson and activities should go. The teacher also delegates or leads crafts, games, and singing.

Helpers are also needed. In most cases, a teacher and two helpers should be adequate. If more than 20 children are expected, one more helper would be needed. A helper can be an adult or a mature teenager with a desire to serve.

Suggested Schedule

10 Minutes	Opening (singing, pledges, birthdays)
20 Minutes	Bible story time
20 Minutes	Bible story review game and memory verse
20 Minutes	Game time
10 Minutes	Snack time
20 Minutes	Craft time
10 Minutes	Closing

Materials

Most vacation Bible school publishing companies include a backyard Bible club component in their materials. Used VBS materials are a great source and include suggestions for crafts, refreshments, and games.

Child Evangelism Fellowship has many resources available. An example of one of the resources is a "Watermelon Party." This curriculum includes party invitations to make, a schedule, large flashcards for teaching, original songs, skits, games, and reproducible items. It uses a story about a watermelon to present the gospel; the different colors of the watermelon are used like a wordless book. We've recommended this to missionaries because the colors and the message are the same in any language; you just need to be able to get your hands on a watermelon where you are going! The snack is, of course, watermelon. It is a one-time outreach party that can be used in many settings. It is also available in Spanish.

Other materials are available from CEF including "Jesus My Friend" summer ministry kit. A 5-day club kit features five Bible lessons: Jesus Forgives the Sin of a Paralyzed Man, Jesus Cares for his Disciples in a Storm, Jesus Meets a Samaritan Woman, Jesus Heals the Centurion's Servant, and Jesus Answers a Lawyer's Questions. Hudson Taylor's missions story will keep kids coming back to hear the next adventure of this brave missionary to China. The kit also includes a teaching card booklet, multi-song visual, "Do You Know About Jesus" visualized theme song, KJV verse visual, music CD, verse tokens, and other helps.

"God is So Great" and "The Message of the Star" are Christmas outreaches (both available in Spanish). "Heaven: How to Get There" is an evangelistic outreach gospel presentation (available in Spanish).

Recommended Scripture References

Those who proclaim God's Word, Psalm 68:11
World evangelism, Psalms 96:3, 10; Isaiah 12:4-5; 45:22
Sow in tears, reap with joy, Psalm 126:5-6
Wise win souls, Proverbs 11:30
Eternity in human hearts, Ecclesiastes 3:11
Beautiful feet of evangels, Isaiah 52:7
Day when soul-winning not necessary, Jeremiah 31:34
Some will listen, some won't, Ezekiel 3:27
Jonah's warning heeded, Jonah 3:3-6
Follow me, Matthew 4:19
Let your light shine, Matthew 5:14-16
Association with sinners, Matthew 9:10-12
Keep preaching, Matthew 10:23
God's acknowledgment, Matthew 10:32-33
Parable of sower, Mathew 13:1-23; Luke 8:4-15
One lost sheep, Matthew 18:12-14; Luke 15:1-7
Great commission, Matthew 28:16-20; Mark 16:15
Sowing seed on different kinds of soil, Mark 4:3-20
Fishers of men, Luke 5:1-11
Those who acknowledge or deny Him, Luke 12:8-9
Search streets and alleys, Luke 14:16-24
Given words to speak, Luke 21:15
Harvest time is now, John 4:35-38
Lifting up Jesus, John 12:32
Ananias sent to Saul, Acts 9:10-17

Fruit of ministry, Acts 11:20, 21
Use of Scripture, Acts 13:13-52
Tactful preaching, Acts 17:21-28
Ministry of Apollos, Acts 18:24-28
All Jews, Greeks heard the Word, Acts 19:10
Personal conversion, Acts 22:1-21
House evangelism, Acts 28:30-31
Desired harvest, Romans 1:13
Unashamed of Gospel, Romans 1:16
Role of witness in salvation, Romans 10:9-10
Priestly duty to proclaim Gospel, Romans 15:16
World evangelism, Romans 16:25-27
Preacher's role, 1 Corinthians 3:4-9
One plants, another waters, 1 Corinthians 3:6-9
Faithful despite difficulties, 1 Corinthians 15:57-58
Open door opportunities, 2 Corinthians 2:12
Ministry with spiritual weapons, 2 Corinthians 10:1-5
Clear Gospel message, Galatians 1:8
Witness wherever, Philippians 1:27-30
Witness by example, Philippians 1:28-29
Gospel spreads rapidly, Colossians 1:6
Converts are joy, crown, 1 Thessalonians 2:17-20
Called to evangelize, 1 Timothy 2:5-7
Good deeds made known, 1 Timothy 5:25
Turning sinner from error, James 5:20
Lord desires all to be saved, 2 Peter 3:9

Worship

Worship is the acknowledgement of God's supreme worth. It is the expression of His perfection and worthiness. In worship one can directly address God expressing adoration, offering thanksgiving, and showing gratitude. One needs to approach the worship service with an attitude of reverential fear, awe, and wonder. Before true worship can occur, there must exist a right relationship with God obtained through the proper preparation of the heart.

Elements of Worship

Meditation:

+ Enables us to focus on God's holiness and kingdom instead of worries and cares in our lives.
+ Allows us to focus on God's goodness, faithfulness, love, and works.
+ Focuses on God's worth and worthiness.

Introspection:

+ Reveals our needs and shortcomings.
+ Exposes one's lack of respect to God and man, lack of unity, things which divide and offend as opposed to having a proper attitude toward God and His people.
+ Requires self-examination, putting earthly desires in right places (wealth, possessions, pleasure, prestige, popularity, power, money, and self-interests).

Celebration, exuberance, jubilation, and enthusiasm:

+ Is expressed as music lifts our thoughts and emotions to God.
+ Is centered on Christ.
+ Recounts blessings and benefits.

Confession:

+ Convicts of disobedience and hypocrisy.
+ Convicts of secret and willful sins.
+ Pleases Him when one eliminates from the life poor attitudes, actions and things that displease God.

Reflection and seriousness:

+ Makes us aware of His glorious presence.
+ Challenges us to seek God's direction.
+ Puts our mind on Christ and His purpose for our lives.

Renewal of commitments to God:

+ Makes one aware that the spiritual life has become dry and routine.
+ Removes hindrances which interfere in our relationship with God.
+ Restores our priority to love God and renews our commitment to follow Him.

Giving:

+ Becomes automatic as our reaction to who He is and what He has done for us.
+ Prompts acts of service to others.

Refreshes mind and body:

+ By appropriating His strength for daily living.
+ As we respond to God in acceptance of joy, peace, and freedom.

Separation from daily routine:

+ Helps us learn to wait on God.
+ Allows us to be still before Him with a listening ear.

Proclaim:

+ God's Word.
+ God's will and His purpose.
+ God's blessings.
+ God's Son.
+ God's message.

Worship requires:

+ Unity and order.
+ Holiness.
+ Corporate worship attendance.
+ Recognition of who God is.
+ Appreciation for what God has done.
+ Participation (play an instrument, sing, praise, give offering, offer thanksgiving).
+ Right relationship with God.

Worship is a meeting between God and His people. In this meeting God becomes present to His people, who respond with praise and thanksgiving; thus the worshiper is brought into personal contact with the one who gives meaning and purpose to life. From this encounter the worshiper receives strength and courage to live with hope in a fallen world. ~Robert Webber

Christ-Centered Worship

One needs to live everyday with an attitude of worship which is characterized by:

♦ Being aware of God's presence.

♦ Seeking His guidance in every situation.

♦ Cultivating an attitude of serving Him.

♦ Being constantly aware of His omnipotence, omniscience, and omnipresence.

♦ Appreciating God's nature and worth.

Priority of Worship

1. It fulfills the first and greatest commandment in loving the Lord your God with all your heart (Mark 12:30).

2. It is the first action we take as we enter His presence with thanksgiving (Psalm 100:4).

3. Praising God was the first priority of the early church (Acts 2:41,47).

4. It is the first essential when listening for the Holy Spirit (Acts 13:1).

5. Worship is an offering to God including:

   ♦ Something costly or precious.

   ♦ Giving something up.

   ♦ Surrender of self, plans, or desires.

   ♦ Accepting loss if it glorifies the Lord.

   ♦ Glorying in the Lord with praise, honor, admiration, and thanksgiving.

   ♦ Reverencing Him.

How to Worship God

1. Singing—lifting voices in sincere whole-hearted adoration

2. Speaking—prayers, praises, testimonies

3. Shouting—proclaiming God's praises

4. Confession

5. Physical expression—hands, bowing, dancing (Psalm 149:3)

6. Possessions—acts of giving, offering, surrendering, responding to God's blessings

7. Decently and in order—with clarity, enthusiasm, and energy

8. Allow the mind to be enlightened, the heart to be stirred, and the spirit to be quickened.

9. Celebrate God, His presence, His works.

Means of Worship

Shouting with a loud voice	Partaking in the Lord's Supper
Making a joyful noise	Honoring the Word of God
Praising	Being silent
Crying out	Seeking the Lord
Singing	Feasting
Playing instruments	Offering
Exalting	Sanctifying
Saying Hallelujah	Making music
Giving testimony	Offering prayer
Serving	Saying Psalms
Bowing down	Preaching
Waiting on Him	Dancing
Falling prostrate	Ministering
Lifting hands	Meditating
Clapping hands	Consecrating
Honoring with our increase	Telling His wonderful works

Recommended Scripture References

Devoted worship, Psalm 18:1-2
Love of God's house, Psalm 26:8
Giving glory to the Lord, Psalm 29:1-2
Soul thirsts for living God, Psalm 42:1-2
Exalting God above everything, Psalm 57:5
Good things from God's house, Psalm 65:4
God my refuge, Psalm 73:28
Longing for worship, Psalm 84:1-2
Rejoice all day long, Psalm 89:16
Entering courts with praise, Psalm 100:4
Joy found in God's house, Psalm 122:1
Great is our God, Psalm 145:3
Be silent before Him, Habakkuk 2:20
Offer a living sacrifice, Romans 12:1
Come near to God, James 4:8-10

Fellowship

"The state of being assimilated; people of different backgrounds come to see themselves as part of a larger...family."

wordreference.com

Most people are drawn to those with whom they share affinity or common interests. Christians should be taught to follow the practice of Jesus and to go beyond their comfort zones in order to reach out to others regardless of inclination. This kind of connection may be accomplished by social engineering or the intentional effort of bringing people together through a carefully designed plan. The following is an example of such a plan to integrate or assimilate newcomers into the church.

A Tale of Two Church Prospects

Two couples began attending a church. The first couple decided to attend a church event on their own. Although some people made an effort to welcome them, they mainly sat by themselves while others paired up fellowshipping with those they knew. This couple felt like outsiders and decided not to return to the church. The second couple was invited to the same church event but were picked up at their home by an interested couple. When they arrived at the event, they were introduced to each person attending and were included in the conversations of their host couple. At the end of an enjoyable evening, they felt a connection with many who attended the event. They were eager

Assimilation Track

STAGE	1	2	3	4	5
DESIGNATION	Curious Visitors	Convinced Prospects	Connected New Members	Committed Young Members	Continuing Mature Members
DECISION GOALS	1. Attendance	1. Attendance 2. Participation 3. Salvation	1. Attendance 2. Participation 3. Baptism/ Membership 4. Devotions 5. Relationships	1. Attendance 2. Participation 3. Devotions 4. Relationships 5. Spiritual Gift Assessment 6. Ministry and Serving	1. Attendance 2. Participation 3. Devotions 4. Relationships 5. Ministry and Serving 6. Witnessing and Reproduction
STAFF GOALS	1. Layman call 2. Staff call 3. Send letter 4. Deacon invite to church and lunch 5. Visitor reception 6. Attending worship services	1. Assign layman 2. Newcomers reception 3. Newcomers sessions 4. Staff visit	1. Adopted by family 2. New Beginnings Class 3. Class 201 4. Staff call 5. Invite to small group 6. Monitoring 7. Seminars/ workshops	1. Class 301 2. Ministry experience 3. Staff conference 4. Assign ministry 5. Follow-up/re-evaluate/re-deploy 6. Class 401 7. Contagious Christian Class 8. Ministry team position	1. Pastoral care 2. Lay Pastor training 3. Stephen's Ministry 4. Edgewood Institute classes 5. One-on-one discipleship 6. Leadership placement and training

to return to church. Which couple best represents what is happening in your church?

Fostering Fellowship

Fellowship is very personal. It is the act of sharing and caring for one another, creating a sense of connectedness to one another and to Christ Himself. In His teachings He compared our daily compassions on those in need as if we were actually caring for Him (Matthew 25:34-40).

Fellow Christians are commanded to greet, receive, love, prefer, serve, admonish, bear burdens, tolerate, forgive, comfort, edify, consider, accept, and encourage one another. It is impossible to fulfill these commandments without making contact with one another. Fellowship then becomes an important component of the Christian life. In fact, if visitors do not make at least one or two solid connections with others in the church, they will probably discontinue attending. Fellowship needs to be encouraged in most churches and in many cases needs to be engineered through programs and intentionally devised social connections. Here are some ways to foster fellowship.

1. Receptions for visitors or new members
2. Meet-the-Pastor function
3. Social mixers
4. Dinners for six or eight
5. Activities which integrate groups that wouldn't normally associate during church services allowing people to meet socially and to make new connections
6. Personal welcome including physically meeting visitors at the door, making introductions, and directing them to the information and welcome desk
7. Scheduled fellowships for entire church four to six times per year
8. Assigned partnerships
9. Each-one reach-one
10. Inviting others to dine after church
11. Women's fellowships
12. Men's fellowships
13. Family fellowships
14. Church picnics
15. Planned outings
16. Invitational events
17. Pick a clique—intentionally including others in an established group
18. Conferences
19. Introductions personally facilitated
20. Sunday school classes and small groups

Recommended Scripture References

Serve as unto Christ, Matthew 25:34-40
Good Samaritan, Luke 10:25-37
Prayer and eating, Acts 2:42
Preference one to another, Romans 12:10
Rejoice or weep with one another, Romans 12:15-16
Love your neighbor as yourself, Romans 13:8-9
Receive one another, Romans 15:5-7
Serving one another, Galatians 5:13-14
Doing good to all, Galatians 6:2, 10
Building built together, Ephesians 2:19-22
Bear with one another, Ephesians 4:1-6
Forgive one another, Ephesians 4:32; Luke 11:4
Walk in love, Ephesians 5:1
Like minded, Philippians 2:1-2
Helping others, Philippians 4:1-4
Love one another, 1 Thessalonians 3:12
Encourage one another, 1 Thessalonians 5:11
Exhort one another, Hebrews 3:13-15; 10:24-25
Follow peace with all men, Hebrews 12:14-15
Having brotherly love, Hebrews 13:1
Entertaining strangers, Hebrews 13:2
Fellowship with us and one another, 1 John 1:1-3
Love one another, 1 John 4:7-11

Discipleship

A disciple is a learner, who is following Jesus Christ, and whose life is marked by obedience, love, and fruitfulness.

~ Howard Hendricks

Essentials for Discipleship

A Firm Commitment

Discipleship begins with a decision (Mark 1:17). Seek to understand the person you are asking to make this commitment and his spiritual background.

An Ongoing Process

Jesus spent three years personally teaching and training His chosen twelve (Colossians 2:7). Discipleship is a process involving growth and maturity by design. Developing a series of personal habits and disciplines is necessary for genuine spiritual growth. Challenge your followers to be prepared to face obstacles and opposition to their spiritual growth.

Ultimate Goal

The ultimate goal is to develop spiritually mature, Christ-like, fully devoted followers of Jesus Christ.

Discipleship can be achieved individually or in a group setting. It is important to understand that the larger the number, the less personal interaction there will be. Personal discipleship programs can be tailored to fit the current maturity of the person and customized to meet his or her individual needs for genuine spiritual growth.

What qualities did Christ emphasize when He trained His disciples? You cannot improve on the way Jesus addressed the training of the twelve (See A.B. Bruce, The Training of the Twelve). A minister should evaluate discipleship materials available and select those which are doctrinally correct, appropriate to the needs of his people, and practical in application to promote effective discipleship in the congregation.

Methodology

During the three years that Jesus personally taught his disciples, he used a format which is the model all church discipleship programs should follow. He used a coaching format to successfully train them.

He did it in front of them. He modeled His message by exemplifying Godly attitudes, attributes, and actions before them in various situations (Mark chapters 1 and 2). His primary method in this phase was **demonstration**.

He did it and they did it with him. He mentored by teaching and training them in the attitudes, attributes, and actions of godly men (Mark 3:12-14). His primary method in this stage was **teaching and training.**

They did it and He was with them. He monitored their progress by assisting them as they did it and corrected them in the process until they could successfully do it (Mark 6:7-12). His primary method in this stage was **encouragement**.

They did it and He encouraged them. He motivated by encouraging, activating, and energizing His disciples as they did it (Mark 16:15-18). His primary method in this stage was **challenging** them.

They did it with others and repeated the entire process. His efforts were multiplied by their duplicating the same discipleship process with others (Matthew 28:19-20). His primary method in this stage was **commissioning** them.

Many discipleship programs fail to follow the important sequence provided in 2 Peter chapter 1 where we are told to give all diligence to this process of adding to our faith all of these things:

♦ Virtue—moral excellence or goodness

♦ Knowledge—truth and facts acquired through experience and thought

♦ Temperance—self control including the control of our desires and appetites

♦ Patience—forbearance with people and endurance of adversity

♦ Godliness—God like-ness, righteousness with reverence and piety

♦ Brotherly love—love for others

♦ Charity—God's love flowing through us

It adds that if these things are abundant in us, we will not be barren or unfruitful. Note that after faith should come virtue, the development of Christian character and values translated into Christ-like living. Then comes knowledge after virtue. Most discipleship programs try to fill a convert's mind with knowledge instead of filling their heart with virtue. Not only is the content important in discipleship but so is the order or sequence of the process and training.

Suggested Areas of Discipleship

The following are some suggestions which may be helpful as a guide for developing a discipleship program in your church.

Beliefs

Authority of the Bible
    The belief that the Bible is the Word of God and has the right to command my beliefs and action (2 Timothy 3:16)

Personal God, His existence and nature as the all knowing, all powerful creator of the universe
    The belief that God is involved in and cares about our daily lives (Psalm 121:1-2)

Lordship and Work of Jesus Christ
    The belief that Jesus Christ is the Son of God who lived a sinless perfect life, died on the cross, and bodily rose again from the dead for our salvation (John 1:12)

Assurance of Salvation
    The belief that a person comes to a right relationship with God through a personal encounter with Christ by grace through faith (Ephesians 2:8-9)

Human Nature and Sin
    The belief that human beings are sinful by nature and practice and that Christ's death not only provided for the forgiveness of sins but for the deliverance from sin (Galatians 3:13)

Eternal Perspective
    The belief in God's judgment and forgiveness, heaven and hell, the return of Christ to establish His kingdom, and the judgment of the world (John 14:1-4)

Personal Ethics and Morals
    The belief that God teaches some things are right and some things are wrong and that biblical morality is the basis for decision making and living (2 Timothy 3:16)

Church
    The belief that the church is God's primary way to accomplish His purposes on earth today (Ephesians 4:15-16)

Holy Spirit's Person and Work
    The belief that the God of the Bible is the only true God: Father, Son, and Holy Spirit (John 7; 2 Corinthians 13:14)

Identity in Christ
    The belief and understanding of being in Christ and to have Christ in us (1 Corinthians 12:13; 2 Corinthians 5:17)

Prophecy
    The belief in an application of prophetic scriptures and things to come (The book of Daniel; Revelation chapters 4 through 22)

Counteracting Opposing Viewpoints
    The belief that humanism, hedonism, and new-ageism are contrary to biblical

teaching and should therefore be counteracted (Colossians 2:8)

Virtues

Gentleness
The grace which pervades the whole person bringing kindness instead of harshness and sharpness (Philippians 4:5)

Faithfulness
The loyal and steadfast allegiance to the person of Jesus Christ and His teachings (Proverbs 3:3-4)

Joy
The inner contentment and purpose in spite of circumstances (John 15:11)

Love
The unselfish and sacrificial love and forgiveness of others; caring about another more than you care about yourself (1 John 4:10-12)

Peace
A state of untroubled well-being with the absence of strife (Philippians 4:6-7)

Self-Control
The power, through Christ, to control myself, my tongue, temper, emotions, impulses, and desires (Titus 2:11-13)

Compassion
Suffering with others so as to be moved To provide assistance, caring, and empathy (Psalm 82:3-4)

Humility
The choice to esteem others above myself (Philippians 2:3-4)

Patience
The long-suffering endurance toward others with forbearance and forgiveness (Proverbs 14:29)

Kindness and Goodness
The choice to do the right things in my relationships with others and thoughtfulness in dealing with others (1 Thessalonians 5:15)

Obedience
The choice to live in accordance with all of the teachings of Jesus Christ and His Word (John 14:15; 1 John 3:24)

Honesty and Truthfulness
The choice of speaking the truth in love and being honest in all of our attitudes and actions (The Book of Proverbs; John 14:6; Ephesians 4:15)

Forgiveness
The choice to forgive others as Christ forgave us; realizing Christ's death on the cross made it possible for God to forgive us, for us to forgive others, and for us to be able to forgive ourselves (Ephesians 4:32)

Practices

Bible Study
The study of the Bible to know the mind of God, renew my mind, and to find direction for my daily life including hearing, reading, memorizing, studying, applying, and meditating on God's Word (Hebrews 4:12)

Fellowship
The fellowship with other Christians to provide strength and growth, to accomplish God's purposes in one's life and in the lives of others (Acts 2:44-47)

Witness bearing
The sharing of my testimony, providing a witness with my life and words for Jesus Christ (Ephesians 6:19-20)

Self sacrifice
Having been bought with a price—the life, death, and resurrection of Jesus Christ—fulfill God's purpose for life (Romans 12:1)

Missions and Vision
The sharing of my time to meet the needs of others knowing that this action is as doing it to Jesus Christ Himself (Colossians 3:17)

Prayer
To have a daily prayer life, to commune with God, to intercede for others, and to make requests for my personal needs (Psalm 66:16-20)

Stewardship
Acknowledging that everything I am or own belongs to God and giving generously to His work (2 Corinthians 8:7; 1 Timothy 6:17-19)

Spiritual Gifts
The understanding of and utilization of my spiritual gifts to accomplsih God's purposes (Romans 12:4-6)

Worship
Worshiping God for who He is and what He has done for me (Psalm 95:1-7)

Single-Mindedness
The focus on God and His priorities for my life (Matthew 6:33)

Character Development
To become Christ-like in my attitudes, relationships, actions, and to glorify God in every area of my life (1 Peter 2:21)

Relationships
Biblical principles and practices related to marriage, children, friendships, and employment (Ephesians 5:18-6:9)

Endurance
The faithful continuance of obedience to Christ when circumstances and situations work against us, making it difficult to faithfully live the Christian life (1 Corinthians 10:13; 2 Corinthians 4:16-18)

Spiritual Warfare
The understanding of the enemies in our Chrisitan life, the world, the flesh, and the devil and Christ's provision for victory over each (Matthew 4:10; Romans 6:12-16; Galatians 5:16-21; Ephesians 6:10-18; 1 John 3:3-10)

Knowing and Doing God's Will
The understaning of how to determine and fulfill the will of God in our lives (Psalm 138:8; Jeremiah 29:11-13; Romans 12:2; Colossians 1:9)

Time Management and Use
The practice of using our time to maximum advantage through understanding the need to redeem the time for use effectively of our lives (John 9:4; Ephesians 5:15-17)

Discipleship should be occuring in the church services, Sunday school, small groups, and individually. The church library is an excellent resource for furthering discipleship through a carefully prepared selection of tapes, CDs, videos, books, and materials covering the various suggested areas of discipleship. By combining a variety of excellent materials within the suggested areas, each member has the opportunity to grow in grace through development of Christlikeness in His beliefs, character, and practices.

Suggested Sequence of Study Material

Leading people into Christ-like maturity is the goal of discipleship. Following is an example of one proven group discipleship sequence.

♦ Make certain that all in the group have committed their life to Christ by faith and have the assurance of salvation (1 John 5:13).

♦ The Normal Christian Life by Watchman Nee will help them understand the experience of salvation, what it means to be in Christ, and what a normal Christian life is as well as the results it provides.

♦ Sit, Walk, Stand by Watchman Nee will help them understand their position in Christ, the life they live in Christ, and their corresponding walk with Christ.

♦ Be Joyful by Warren Wiersby identifies the joy robbers which attack and hinder the Christian's life and teaches the corrective antidotes.

- So You Want to be Like Christ by Chuck Swindoll describes the disciplines which need to be accepted and practiced to live a Christ-honoring, biblically-based Christian life.

- Let Prayer Change your Life by Becky Tirabassi teaches the practice of prayer and how-to spend quality time with God every day. E.M. Bounds' excellent materials on prayer are classic.

- How to Study Your Bible by Kay Arthur teaches effective ways of independent Bible study. It will be especially helpful to have a study Bible such as the Life Application Bible.

- The Purpose Driven Life by Rick Warren teaches the importance of living life on purpose by following the biblical purposes God provides for us on a continuing basis.

Recommended Scripture References

Holy life, Psalm 15:1-5
Those who seek find, Proverbs 8:17
Stand in gap, Ezekiel 22:30
Hunger, thirst for righteousness, Matthew 5:6
Salt, light in the world, Matthew 5:13-16

Counting cost, Matthew 8:19-20
Following Jesus, Matthew 9:9
Lose life, find it, Matthew 10:39
Traits of disciple, Matthew 16:24-25; 16:25; John 8:31
Mark of a disciple, Matthew 16:24
Leave all to follow Christ, Matthew 19:28-30; Mark 10:28-31; Luke 18:28-30
Humility, Matthew 23:8-12
Calling Simon, Andrew, James, John, Mark 1:16-20
Don't look back, Luke 9:62
Cost of discipleship, Luke 14:26, 27
Walk in the light, John 8:12
Committed to one another, Romans 12:10
Testimony confirmed in convert, 1 Corinthians 1:4-6
Be found faithful, 1 Corinthians 4:2
Imitate Jesus, 1 Corinthians 4:15-16
Servant attitude, 1 Corinthians 9:19-23
Run to win, 1 Corinthians 9:24-27
Follow Christ's example, 1 Corinthians 11:1
Crucified with Christ, Galatians 2:20
Serve one another in love, Galatians 5:13
Live for Christ, gain in death, Philippians 1:21
Esteem others better, Philippians 2:3-4
Poured out drink offering, Philippians 2:17; 2 Timothy 4:6
Forget past, press forward, Philippians 3:12-16
Knowledge of God's will, Colossians 1:9-12
Mind on things above, Colossians 3:1-17
Financial priorities, 1 Timothy 6:10
Likely persecution, 2 Timothy 3:12
Faithful to run race, Hebrews 12:1-2
A chosen people, 1 Peter 2:9
Suffering, 1 Peter 5:8-9

Service

What is Ministry?

Ministry may be defined as using whatever God has given me to serve Him and to meet the needs of others. We minister in three directions: to the Lord (Acts 13:3), to believers (Hebrews 6:10), and to non-believers (Matthew 5:13). We minister to three areas of need: to the physical needs of people (Matthew 10:42), to the emotional needs of people (1 Thessalonians 5:14), and to the spiritual needs of people (2 Corinthians 5:18).

Purpose of Ministry

1. You have been created for ministry (Ephesians 2:10).

2. You have been gifted for ministry (1 Peter 4:10).

3. You have been commanded to minister (Matthew 28:18-19).

4. The church of Christ needs your ministry (1 Corinthians 12:27).

5. You will be accountable for your ministry or lack therefore (Romans 14:12).

6. You will be rewarded for your ministry (Matthew 25:23).

Now there are diversities of gifts, but the same Spirit...   1 Corinthians 12:4

My SHAPE Determines My Ministry

Rick Warren's acrostic for discovering your ministry is:

S piritual Gifts
What am I gifted to do? *But every man hath his proper gift of God, one after this manner, and another after that.*
1 Corinthians 7:7b

H eart
What do I love to do?   Revelation 17:17a

For it is God which worketh in you both to will and to do of his good pleasure.
Philippians 2:13

A bilities
What natural talents and skills do I have? *And there are diversities of operations, but it is the same God which worketh all in all.*   1 Corinthians 12:6

P ersonality
Where does my personality best suit me to serve? I *will praise thee; for I am fearfully and wonderfully made: marvelous are thy works; and that my soul knoweth right well.*   Psalm 139:14

E xperiences
How have my personal experiences prepared me to be of service to others?...*That we may be able to comfort them which are in any trouble, by the comfort wherewith we ourselves are comforted of God.*
2 Corinthians 1:4b

Consider each of these components in application to your personal life and ministry. Experimentation and assessment with other's feedback can assist you in discovering your spiritual gifts. Matching people with ministries should be of primary importance for any church leader.

Resources for discovering your spiritual gifts for serving include What You Do Best in the Body of Christ by Bruce Bugbee, Nineteen Gifts of the Spirit by Leslie Flynn, SHAPE, Finding and Fulfilling Your Unique Purpose For Life by Eric Rees, The Spiritual Gifts Inventory available free from TEAM Ministries@ www.teamministry.com, and *Uniquely You*-A Profile combining Spiritual Gifts DISC Personality Types by Mels Carbonell@ www.uniquelyyou.com available in a seven, nine, sixteen and twenty-three gifts version.

The following is a sample list of specific church ministries in our church. The list is shared with people interested in ministry after we determine their SHAPE.

Opportunities for Service at Edgewood

WORSHIP

Adult Bible Fellowship
Couple's class

Music
Worship leader
Praise band — vocal, instrumental
Praise ensemble
Special music
Choir
Composition creation
Music filing
Creative programming
Instrumental accompaniment
Equipment set up/ tear down

Recorded Media Ministry
CD duplication
Catalog messages
CD distribution

Tech Ministry
Audio
Video
Recording media
Lighting

Drama
Actors
Script writers
Set builders

FELLOWSHIP

Adult Bible Fellowship
Homebuilders class

Fellowship/Assimilation
EAT (Edgewood Assimilation Taskforce)
Telephone calling
Secretary
Assimilation coordination

First Impressions
Greeters
Welcome center
Ushers
Parking lot attendant

Website

Secretarial/Office Worker
Word processing
Printing and copying
Assist in mailings
Assist with booklets
Computer skills

DISCIPLESHIP

Adult Bible Fellowship
Administration
Teaching
Substitute teaching
Records/Secretary
Helpers/Assistant teachers
Newly wed class
Topical class
Romans classes

Sunday School
Teacher
Assistant teacher
Nursery
Superintendent
Special needs aide

Church Library
Library oversight
Review books
Processing books
Book checker
Book repair

AWANA
Commander
Director
Leader
Office Worker
Leader in training
Teachers
Game director
Bible listener
Story teller
Nurse/First aide
Community outreach
Secretary

Children
Nursery
Children's church
Super Saturday volunteer
Puppet team
Puppet script writer
Bible lesson teacher
Story teller
Backyard Bible Club
Host/Hostess
Teacher
Helper
Music leader
Special needs aide
Kids Church Krew sponsor
Children's choir
Provide snacks

Transportation
Craft leader
Organization of materials
Set up
Bulletin boards
Mailings

Discipling/Mentoring
Mentors

Women's Ministry
Bible studies
Retreats
Outreach events
Christmas party
Mother's Day banquet
Ladies Night Out

Training Events
Crown Financial
Growing Kids God's Way
Child protection class

SERVICE MINISTRY

Adult Bible Fellowship
Pastor's Bible class

Senior Citizens Ministry
Widows
Shut-ins
Nursing home
Respite support
Missions trip
Transportation

Second Winders
Meal prep
Set up and clean up
Serve meal
Programming
Activity director
Seminars
Travel activities

Helpmates

Divorce Care

Grief Share

Van Ministry
Driver

Maintenance
Carpentry
Plumbing
Electrical
Glasswork
Equipment repair
Floors — tile and carpet

Church grounds
Weeding of flower beds
Painting
Roofing
Cleaning
Snow removal

Hospitality
Shut in baskets
Christmas baskets
Housing & feeding guests
Picking up at airport
Funeral luncheons
Coordinate food drives

Men's Prayer Breakfast
Attendees
Service projects

Benevolence Coordination

Special Interests (Service)
Cake decorating
Sewing and needlework
Wood working
Linen washing
Medical nurse
Design
Electronics
Heavy equipment
Research/Development
Arts and crafts
Metal work
Photography
Videography
Mural painting
Interior design
Computer maintenance
Assemblers

EVANGELISM

The Institute

Youth
GROW-Go Reach Our World
Life Together (small group)
The Gathering (worship)
FIA (Faith in Action)

Youth Ministry
Service opportunities
Host
Snacks
Transportation
Sponsors
Mailings
Secretarial

Music
Small group leader
Youth camp chaperone
Missions trip chaperone
Graphic design
Tech team
Food prep
Supervise set up
Game director
Game helper
Research and development
Nurse/First aid
Volunteer janitorial
Electrical maintenance
Carpentry
Welding
Child care
Drama
Bulletin boards
Snack shop attendants

Evangelism

Ministry team member
Special event help
Seminar leaders
Tract ministry
Research and development
Graphic design (banners, t-shirts)
Advertising
Writing evangelistic articles
Altar response workers
Tech ministry
Videographer for testimonies
Set up and tear down for special events
Friend Day

Christmas and Easter
Community group recognition days
Comedy Night
Concerts
Website elements
Invest and Invite events
Specialty Seminars (parenting, marriage, blended family, financial, grief, death and dying, aging well, divorce, difficult children, aging parents)
Evangelism training
Outreach events
Invite cards
Church brochure
The Answer Magazine
Radio and TV
Mailings
Sporting events
  Leading
  Officials
  Statistician
Photographer

LIFEGROUPS

Adult Bible Fellowship
Ignite Bible Fellowship Class

LifeGroups
Host
Leader
Coaches
Apprentice leader

Starting Point/Group Link
Set up and tear down
Host
Leaders
Food prep and serving
Video testimonies
Lead icebreakers

Singles Ministry
LifeGroups
Faith in Action
GROW
ABF
Saturday service
"Break Down"
SALT Team (Single Adult Leadership Team)

Single Ministry Service Ops
Set up and tear down
Musicians — vocal and Instrumental
Tech — audio/video
Child care/Programming
Drama
Greeters
Ushers
Welcome Center
Leader for LifeGroup
Host LifeGroup

ADMINISTRATION

Adult Bible Fellowship

Administration
Deacons
Trustees

Celebrate Recovery
Group leadership
Leadership assistance
His Promise Band
Tech (audio/visual)
Teen ministry
Child care and programming
Food prep
Transportation
Advertising
Accountability group leaders
Secretarial needs
Jail ministry
Bible distribution
Recruitment programs
Information sharing program
Annual anniversary celeb.

Missions Committee
CASE
  Volunteer
  Fund raising events

FOOD
  Volunteers
  Promotion

Lay Pastors

Expect success.
Prepare to be blessed.

Recommended Scripture References

Serve with gladness, Psalm 100:1-2
Must be blameless, Psalm 101:6
Priority of service, Matthew 6:33
Blessings prompt service, Matthew 8:14-15
Servant attitude, Matthew 23:8-12
Joy of serving Christ, Luke 10:17
Mary and Martha, Luke 10:38-42
Jesus washes disciples feet, John 13:1-17
Love prompts to serve, John 21:15-17
Convert needs instruction, Acts 18:24-26
First serve, then minister, Romans 1:1
Call to service irrevocable, Romans 11:29
Tasks in ministry, 1 Corinthians 3:5-9
Function of Body of Christ, 1 Corinthians 12:14-20
Paul least of apostles, 1 Corinthians 15:9
Submit to each other, 1 Corinthians 16:15-16
Always rejoice, 2 Corinthians 6:6-10

Please man or God? Galatians 1:10
Serve in love, Galatians 5:13
God's workmanship, Ephesians 2:10
Talents in Body of Christ, Ephesians 4:11-13
Christ a servant, Philippians 2:7
The goal, Philippians 3:14
Energy for ministry, Colossians 1:29
Pray for those who minister, Colossians 4:3
Chosen to serve, 1 Thessalonians 1:3
Power for ministry, 1 Thessalonians 1:4-5
Pursue righteousness, 1 Timothy 6:11-16
Spirit of power, 2 Timothy 1:7
Preach the Word, 2 Timothy 4:1-5
Reward for ministry, 2 Timothy 4:6-8
Called to be holy, 1 Peter 1:15-16
You are part of spiritual house, 1 Peter 2:4-5
Serving in the Lord's name, 3 John 7
Hard work, Revelation 2:2

Youth Ministry

Introduction to Youth Ministry

Youth ministry provides an unrivaled opportunity to affect lives for eternity. Working with teenagers can be one of the most rewarding ministries within the church. Approximately 80% of people who accept Christ will do so before the age of 21. Youth ministry then becomes an exciting and compelling challenge.

A Foundation for Youth Ministry

Defining Success

What defines success in youth ministry? If you are going to have a solid philosophy on which to build a ministry, you must first determine the desired end result. Success in youth ministry may be defined by some in their numbers while others determine success by their programming. Still others say success is found in teaching. All of these things are necessary for success in youth ministry.

True success in youth ministry is found in the end product. The real question is, are your students really connecting with God? You may have great programming, but are those programs really guiding kids to God's will for their lives? You may be a great teacher, but are you personally connected to the youth so that you can help them live a life according to God's purpose? A truly successful youth ministry produces students who know, follow, and love Jesus Christ. Make disciples for Jesus Christ.

In youth ministry, as a leader, success in youth ministry is contingent on the condition of your own spirituality and your own personal relationship with Jesus Christ. You cannot lead others higher than you have already gone. You must actively demonstrate knowledge and love of Christ in your own life before you can successfully guide others in following Him. In his article "Power Leaks in Youth Ministry," Matthew Orme says, "In youth ministry, we create a gaping leak if we implement something that we don't live and breathe." Your philosophy of youth ministry needs to come from the heart of God. It must be one that is real to you.

After success is defined, plan how to accomplish that success. How do I help teenagers know Christ? How can I help them to follow Christ? How can I help them to love Christ? Asking these key questions may guide your development of a philosophy for your own youth ministry.

- Who are your students and where are they spiritually?
- Who are their parents?
- Who are the youth sponsors?
- What has worked and what has not worked?
- How much space do you have for your ministry?
- What are your needs?
- What do you want to do?
- Is God the centerpiece of your ministry?
- Who do you want your students to become?

Building A Ministry Philosophy

Philosophy is not about what we do with our students, it's about what drives our ministries. It defines our goals more clearly and allows others to have a idea of where we are headed, how we want to get there, and the reason for taking that direction.

Here are some thoughts and tools to help you develop what God desires for you.

Spend time in prayer and Bible study. This is the greatest necessity in developing God's direction for your ministry. Without God's power and direction, you are destined to fail. Seriously contemplate what God wants, then begin the process of defining how you are going to reach students.

Make sure that is it biblically based. Your philosophy may change slightly as you gain experience and knowledge but the foundational principles should remain solid. Methods change; principles never do.

Make sure it is doctrinally sound. This is true for all that we do in life, but as you develop the plan for your ministry you must make sure it corresponds with God's Word. A great example of this and one we subscribe to as a church is the purpose driven model. Everything we do in ministry revolves around five important biblical purposes: evangelism, worship, discipleship, fellowship, and ministry. For more information on this check out The Purpose Driven Youth Ministry by Doug Fields. This book will greatly help you specifically think through your objectives and the structure of your youth ministry philosophy.

Make it practically applicable. Your philosophy should not be vague or unplanned. It needs to be laid out in a fashion in which it can be measured and grasped by those around you. You are being entrusted with the greatest treasure ever given to man, the lives of our children. They need to have clear direction.

Base it upon the local church. God has ordained the church to do His work of evangelizing the world and the youth ministry is a part of that purpose. Youth ministry is not an entity unto itself. It is part of the local assembly under which it was created and ought to be viewed as a ministry that helps promote and edify the body as a whole. Community and unification within the church is crucial to our success in carrying out the Great Commission.

As you work in youth ministry, you must never forget that it is not about you; it is about God. Every life you have the opportunity to touch and every soul that accepts Christ is for His honor and glory. As you develop your philosophy of ministry, you must allow God to mold you and illuminate your heart with His wisdom so that you might reach students with the love of Christ.

Understanding and Connecting with Students

"Youth ministry that does not take seriously the charge to reach young people for Christ and establish them in His church is a self-indulgent luxury we cannot afford."[1] As stated previously in this section, we have a tremendous task before us. As our culture evolves and moves, the task of reaching the lost and the un-churched becomes increasingly challenging and difficult. What worked yesterday no longer even registers on most kid's radar. If we are going to be successful in reaching the lost, we must possess an evolving understanding of where kids are and what we must do to connect with them.

Understanding Un-churched Teens

Teens believe all religions have value. Jonathan McKee says there are five facts that must be understood about teens. Teenagers, through educational systems, through the media, and from peers, tend to think that all beliefs have moral fiber and can lead you to God. Some do not believe that there is absolute truth. Polls have shown that only one out of ten born-again teens believe in absolute truth. This religious relativism resounds throughout their culture. Teen role model Kirsten Dunst said, "I think a lot of people are losing their religion. Definitely. Even me, I know that when I grew up, I used to go to church every Sunday, and now it's become holidays. But I think as long as you have your own thing, whether it's meditation—anything that centers you in on life is good. Do I pray? Yeah, I do."[2]

They believe in God, they just don't want Him controlling their lives. There seems to be very few teenage atheists. Most kids believe that there is a God; but those same kids still want to do their own thing in life. Possessing some kind of faith is important to them as long as it doesn't go against what they want to do with their life.

Christianity is no longer viewed as being a relationship with Jesus Christ. The culture views Christianity as a heritage. "Well, my mom goes to church and my grandparents went to church, so I guess I am a Christian." This is the attitude of the un-churched teen. They don't know what it means to be a follower of Jesus Christ. Never assume that just because teens say they are Christians that they have indeed experienced the life change that only God can give.

Most un-churched teens can't tell you what they believe. Most teens have no basis for what they believe because society as a whole is missing the boat on the issue of truth. Truth, for most people, has become relative. It is what is acceptable at the time. They are so busy searching for something to meet their needs that they are willing to grasp almost anything.

The un-churched teen is searching for something to fill the void in his life. The number one priority in youth ministry is to meet the needs of people. The world is filled with students who are hurting and looking for something to fill the void in their life. You must give them what they need. Many churches send messages of disinterest to their youth."[3] We must be careful not to isolate or offend those whom we are sent to reach.

How to Reach the Un-churched

Keep informed of the current culture and be sensitive to their needs. Kids eat, breathe, and sleep their culture. From designer jeans to the latest cell phone, they are into what is going on around them. If you are going to affect their lives, you need to know what they are into. Being aware of what your kids are listening to, watching, reading, and struggling with will greatly increase your ability to reach them where they are. There are numerous books and websites devoted to studying youth culture and keeping you regularly updated.

Go where they are. One of the best ways to reach un-churched students is to go where they are. Sporting events, home visits, coaching a team, and visiting school campuses are just a few ways you can interact with students on their turf. It may be a little uncomfortable at first, but the connections you make can bring eternal results.

Seek fresh ideas, lessons, and activities. Your services and programs should always be the best they can possibly be. Try something new.

Plan programs with content that is interesting, entertaining, and relevant. Un-churched students will not come if they think it's going to be boring. We recently had a high school activity targeted specifically at the un-churched. When asked afterward what their favorite part of the evening was, most responded by saying, "definitely the service." Why? Because we planned with a purpose. They forgot about the peripheral activities and placed the focus right where we intended—Jesus Christ. Plan your program then work your plan.

Teach for growth. Always be looking for new resources and interactive ways to present God's message. Forget 35 minute lectures. Use handouts, PowerPoint, overheads, drama, short skits, or video clips. Use current issues and music to make a point. Find ways to involve your students in your lesson. The more stimuli you use, the more they will learn and retain. Most of all, keep your teaching relevant. Hit them where they live. They are looking to you for guidance through difficult circumstances. Make sure you meet their need.

Seek a life of purity. People in places of spiritual leadership are targets of Satan. He desires to trip you and destroy many lives along with your own. Although these have been previously presented, they bear repeating since youth pastors and sponsors must spend a great deal of time with youth. In youth ministry, you have to be very careful about how you treat members of the opposite sex. This applies to both men and women.

Here are the guidelines.
1. Never be alone with a member of the opposite sex.
2. Never visit a member of the opposite sex alone.
3. Never flirt with a member of the opposite sex.
4. Include your spouse or other youth sponsors anytime a member of the opposite sex is involved.
5. Spend quality time with your spouse.
6. Have an accountability partner.
7. Flee temptation.

Basic Rules to Follow With Your Teens

1. Be real and transparent. Students are looking for people who are honest, open, committed, and are genuinely interested in them.

2. The battle is a spiritual one. The foe is powerful and devious.

3. Love your students. Make it apparent that you love them. They will model your actions. They need to see that your love of God is what prompts your commitment to them. Loving your teens is more important that anything else you will do in your ministry.

4. Spend quality time with your students. Some of the most precious and memorable moments you will have with teens are just times when you are "chillin'." Make those moments happen often.

5. Allow time for them to grow and change. Some youth will grow faster than others, so be patient. Always be sowing seed and cultivating lives.

Realizing the Needs of Student Youth Personality Types[4]

Understanding youth personality types will give you greater access to understanding why they act the way they do.

In his book <u>Why Teenagers Act the Way They Do</u>, Dr. Keith Olson outlines six personality types of youth.[5]

1. The Power Oriented
2. Competitive
The power oriented personality needs to see himself in control of lives. The competitive personality uses competition in relating to others and has extreme narcissism. The primary difference between competitive and power-oriented personalities is the use of power. The power oriented personality uses power to develop skills for maturation and growth, but the competitive personality uses power against others to advance himself.

3. Aggressive
4. Rebellious
The aggressive personality attempts to push others away and set himself against others and to cause them pain and psychological injury. The rebellious personality wants to push others away or withdraw from social interacting. Unlike the aggressive personality, he is not interested in revenge. The self-demeaning personality does not believe in himself and is submissive and enters passive withdrawal.

5. Dependent
6. Conforming

The dependent personality prefers to rely on someone else who will assume responsibility or take the leadership role because he fears he will be inadequate or fail if he was to lead. The conforming-personality seeks to be accepted and liked and may sacrifice too much of himself in gaining the acceptance of others. The responsible personality is as close to the social ideal as adolescents get and is a blend of power-oriented and conforming personalities that follow through with commitments and respects authority.

Needs Teens Possess[6]

Physiological needs are the basic necessities of life.

Safety needs involve security, stability, protection, order, and freedom from fear.

Social needs are those involving the need to love and be loved, to feel accepted and to belong, and to give and receive affection.

Esteem needs are those dealing with confidence and competence, self-image, self-respect, and esteem from others.

Growth needs are those dealing with potential and being all one can become.

Some of youth's greatest issues associated with these needs are those related to loneliness, poor self-esteem, and discovering self-identity. Other major issues include poor relationships with parents, school problems, prejudice and injustice, vocational decisions, and their desire to discover God's will in their lives.

Understanding Their Behavior

There are no guarantees on how a teenager will respond. Be careful that your expectations don't exceed your student's level. By doing this you set yourselves up for discouragement and then failure.

Students will often have incongruence between what they believe and how they live. This can cause the leadership great discouragement. Try and understand that living an effective Christian life is difficult for all believers, especially your students. Their culture is very high-risk and you must provide opportunities to keep them focused on a Christ-like walk. The following are examples of assets or things that keep teens out of high-risk culture:

- Family love and support
- Positive family communication
- Caring relationships with other adults
- Regular involvement in religious, positive, and community service activities
- Reading at least 3 hours per week
- Having boundaries, rules, and consequences
- Telling the truth even when it's costly
- Standing up for what they believe
- Building cross-cultural relationships

By helping teens build in these areas, you will be better equipping them to avoid the potholes of a high risk culture and turning their focus more toward spiritual things. When the teens build up enough assets, studies show that they are less likely to engage in destructive behaviors that often prevent them from growing spiritually.

Resolving Teen Problems

There are six causes of most teen problems.

Bitterness
Bitter teenagers are critical, negative, and angry. It is usually caused by unforgiveness. Counsel them on forgiveness and the dangers of bitterness.

Lust
Students that are lustful usually carry guilt and are uncooperative. Many students (especially guys) deal with lust.

Help them understand that temptation is not sin, but when desires meet up with the bait Satan sets out, sin becomes a reality.

Materialism

Materialistic students have problems with value systems, judgment calls, and modesty issues. Teach them God's view of stewardship and how to possess a Christian worldview.

Rejection

Students experiencing rejection are usually withdrawn or act like the class clown. Give constant affirmation as warranted.

Humanism

Humanistic philosophy causes teens to be very idealistic. Eventually, idealism meets reality and it can have serious consequences in their lives. Teach them to rely on God's judgment and trust Him to lead and direct their life.

Physical problems (self-image)

Students with self-image issues are more apt to over emphasize their attire. They are usually very self critical about their appearance and can act out in numerous ways. Help them discover who they are in Christ and how He views them.

(For more information on conflict resolution please see the *Dealing With Conflict* section of this manual.)

Parents Are Your Friends

When a person begins in youth ministry, one of the most crucial mistakes to make is not involving parents in the youth department. You may feel intimidated or that they are looking over your shoulder just waiting for you to make a mistake.

Most parents are interested in what is happening with their kids and want to be supportive. Parents can be ready-made sponsors, have ideas just waiting to be tapped, and can be your most dependable help.

Check out the following ideas for a more family friendly youth ministry and more effectively connect with parents.[7]

Create an atmosphere of cooperation, by making parents your ally.

You have a role to play in the development of your students but their parent's role is absolutely critical.

Parents want to know who you are. You need to cultivate a positive relationship with the parents of your students. The more they know you, the more they will trust you. Listen to what they have to say; let them express the pains and frustration they feel. Talk to them and take time to really listen.

Families are busy. They have certain priorities and things demanding their time. Consider parents when planning a calendar for activities and youth group meetings.

Teaching family values and reinforcing parental teaching in your own lessons will go a long way in cementing strong core values in your students. Partner with parents or you risk having kids who have weak faith.

Keep communication clear.

Communicate regularly making sure your parents know what is going on in the youth ministry. Don't always expect information disseminated to students to get home. In fact, it rarely does. Stay connected with parents. Another idea for staying connected with parents is to sponsor a quarterly parents meeting. This is a great avenue for sharing information, allowing parents to lean on each other and get to know other parents. Follow this up with a monthly newsletter.

When you take the time to brag to a parent about their student, it not only affirms the student but the parent as well. It says, "Hey, you're doing something awesome with your kids. Keep it up!" Take opportunities to brag to parents about their kids and encourage them.

You are a ministry professional. They are watching you because you are an example for their kids. You need to uphold a standard of excellence in your youth ministry.

Encourage two-way communication. As a Youth Pastor you do most of the talking; it's good to give your parents an appropriate time to talk back to you. There can be many great thoughts and ideas presented by parents and their voices need to be heard.

Provide resources for the family and parents.

Look for articles, magazines, books, and videos to help parents in raising their kids. New resources are constantly being developed. You local Christian book store and the internet provide resources to help you keep abreast of these things.

Create a parent newsletter containing articles and help from numerous sources. This can be a time consuming task but if done right, it can bring you nice dividends.

Find mature parents that can share their experience and wisdom. One of your greatest assets is a parent that has been through the rigors of raising a teen and lived to tell about it. He can be an encouragement to other parents who may be struggling, hurting, and going through trials of their own.

Create programs for the whole family.

Create opportunities for parents and their families to spend time together encouraging family relationships. Have family game nights, trivia nights, or family worship services. Get creative and get families growing. Don't be afraid to invite families to your services and programs. Just because your music may be a little different or your programming may not resemble what they are used

to doesn't mean that parents won't enjoy what your ministry is doing. Have an open door policy for parents; welcome them to any service or function of the youth ministry. This may help to prevent problems and it also reduces confusion.

Ask parents to be sponsors.

Parents have a vested interest in your ministry. You are responsible for their greatest treasure, so naturally they have an interest in what you are doing. Make sure the students are comfortable with their parent working as a sponsor. You might inadvertently create undue pressure on the student, parent, or both. This may be difficult at times, but cultivating a whole family involvement is important.

Suggestions for Building Your Youth Ministry Team

For a strong team ministry, there must be sponsors who are sold out for God and focused on students. Enlisting and having strong sponsors is vital to the health and existence of any church's youth ministry. You need to seek out sponsors that have a heart for young people; people that really care and are willing to love students unconditionally. Sponsors like that are not easy to find, but when you do find them, they are worth their weight in pizza.

1. Pray.

How often we overlook this extremely important step in the Youth Ministry process. The leaders that we need are already there. We just need God's guidance to find them. Enlisting the wrong sponsors can cause you heartache and problems. What may seem like a great idea now may turn out to be a major headache in the future if God's leadership is not sought. Seek God early and often when building a sponsor team.

2. Weigh your choices.

The best leaders are not always the ones you might pick. God can use anyone who has a willing heart and a love for students. It is not a question of knowledge or ability, it is a question of the heart. One needs to understand their culture and possess youth ministry skills, but the most important thing to bring into ministry is a love for students. Pick parents who sincerely love the Lord and love working with kids.

3. Be specific in stating expectations.

Many potential youth sponsors are scared away by the thought of 20 rambunctious junior high students wildly rampaging through their house at 3:00 in the morning. When seeking ministry leaders, be sure to be specific in what you are seeking. If you need someone to help with a drama ministry, then make that known. If you need help with your praise band, then be specific. Another approach for involving people in ministry is to have ministries that are not hands-on. Not all those willing to serve have a desire to work directly with students. This is where the development of a prayer team or a resource team is vital. These people can be just as involved with youth ministry as the hands-on sponsors while staying within their comfort zone. Eventually, these people may work into a hands-on position (then you can turn those junior highers loose on their house), but until then utilize them as long as they are willing to serve.

4. Ask.

One of the most prominent reasons you don't have the sponsors you need is because you fail to ask. You are afraid you might turn someone off or maybe you just don't want to get turned down. Whatever the case, you need to be willing to ask.

Most people will at least be willing to pray about the possibility. If you don't ask, you'll never know.

Training Youth Sponsors

1. Interview as if for a regular job.

Do your homework. This step will save you numerous problems. Making sure you fully check out each potential hands-on sponsor can save you, your ministry, and your church spiritual, emotional, and possibly even financial issues in the future. A written application, a background check, and a personal interview are highly recommended. These steps can greatly diminish the possibility of an unqualified sponsor damaging the effectiveness of your ministry.

2. Schedule meetings for sponsors.

These meetings are invaluable. Meet at least once a month with sponsors for planning, training, encouragement, and camaraderie among your leadership staff. Take this opportunity to share your expectations with your staff and to express your appreciation for them.

3. Attend annual training events.

Sponsors will be more effective if you give them the training they need. Find a training event close to your area and talk to your senior pastor about paying for the event. Another option is an on-sight mini-training session with just your sponsors once each year. This can give you valuable insight into your ministry, its effectiveness, and clarification of vision. This is an excellent time to offer the Child Protection Class, which is required for all who work with youth at the church.

4. Be a team.

Working together is good, but playing together is great. Find time to spend with your sponsor team. Whether it's around the dinner table or at a bowling alley, learn to play together. Spending time together will help build a sense of unity that will spill over into your ministry efforts.

Your youth ministry team is the most valuable asset you have in your ministry. Choose them wisely, then use them to make a difference.

Keeping it Practical

Student ministry is a life-long calling. If you want to be successful, you must keep things in perspective and in balance. Use this checklist to assess your progress.

___Have I completed an annual assessment and evaluated the programs for results?

___Are goals being met?

___Have I built a strong and effective youth ministry team?

___Have I regularly checked in with my accountability partner?

___Am I staying in touch with current culture and trends in order to stay in touch with my students?

___Have I given my family the place and time they deserve in my life? Have I made sure my family knows and understands that they come first?

___Am I visible, available, and approachable at church?

___Have I participated in other ministry groups in the church?

___Am I sharing my needs and concerns with my senior pastor? Am I keeping him informed about all programs and activities?

___Am I well organized and effectively using daily planning?

___Is my ministry honoring and glorifying the Lord?

___Am I producing students who love the Lord?

Recommended Scripture References

Youthful hope, Psalm 71:5
Young man's purity, Psalm 119:9
More understanding than those older, Psalm 119:100
Counsel to youth, Ecclesiastes 12:1-7
Chosen for service, Daniel 1:3-6
Daniel chose not to defile himself, Daniel 1:8-20
Young be an example, 1 Timothy 4:12
Desires of youth, 2 Timothy 2:22

Children's Ministry

Why Children?

It has been said that children are our greatest natural resource. In them lies our future and someday our future will be in their hands. It is essential that we train them as early as possible in the way that they should go (Proverbs 22:6). The heart of the church must be in its children. Many families will come out for a children's choir program, a puppet show, an outdoor water activity, or an awards assembly. In these we find the opportunity to present the Gospel of Jesus Christ to our own children, to their friends, and to their families. The prime time to win people to Christ is when they are children. Statistics show that more than 80% of people accepted Jesus Christ as their personal Savior when they were children. This must be a pivotal ministry in every church.

It would be easy for a young pastor to delegate this important job to others like the children's director or the Sunday school superintendent and to not see it as his responsibility. Do not underestimate the importance of the ministry you have with children. They are the heart of the family. Families will leave churches over problems with their children's needs not being met or if they feel their children are being victimized in a classroom that is out of control.

There are some essential techniques every teacher should acquire, a teacher's toolbox, that when used proficiently is most successful in working with children. Its key elements include knowing your strengths and weaknesses as a teacher, being in touch with the culture of children, disciplining with dignity, and knowing how to win a child to Christ.

Me As A Teacher

Knowing who you are as a teacher can greatly empower you within the classroom.

Who I am as a teacher includes my childhood experiences, my memories of being a child in a classroom, my background, and my personal experiences. The combination of these shape who I am, not only as a person but also as a teacher. Most important is my salvation story and my personal walk with Christ. Many people who are teachers find that their spiritual gift may not specifically be teaching. However, a different spiritual gift may give you an avenue to teach a child. Identifying both your strengths and weaknesses will help you select appropriate strategies, lessons, and activities to use in your teaching. For example, if your strength is artistry, there is nothing wrong with reading a Bible story, answering some key questions, and then moving on to an artful application based on the story. Teach to your strengths and you will find that you will experience more satisfaction with the teaching experience.

The Needs of the Child Learner

In order for children to learn most effectively, there are certain needs that children must have fulfilled in order to give their complete and total attention.

Although the idea of the hierarchy has been disputed, Maslow sets forth that learners have an innate set of needs which must be met in order for optimal learning. These include the physiological needs of food, water, and sleep. Those met, feelings of safety must be felt giving way to the third need which is a sense of belonging. The work of Piaget, Eriksen, and Kohlberg lay out the various stages of physical and psychological development of children. In much the same way, James Fowler has identified the stages of faith development.[1]

Based on the idea of ages and stages, it is essential for lessons to be age appropriate. What to teach and when to teach it become key questions each children's minister must answer in the development of the scope and sequence of the children's ministry of the church.

Often children are presented with material which is beyond their understanding resulting in misunderstanding. Following are quotes from children after the presentation of a lesson.

> Noah's wife was called Joan of Ark.
> Moses went to Mount Cyanide to get the Ten Amendments.
> David was a Hebrew king skilled at playing the liar.
> Solomon had 300 wives and 700 porcupines.

Although these are funny, the misperceptions are clear. Were these ideas presented in an age appropriate manner? The following is a compilation of several sources developed as a tool which may be useful in curriculum selection and lesson planning.

Tasks of Faith

Age	Focal Engagement	Tasks of Faith (bulleted below)
2-3	3-4 minutes	

- Understand that God made everything and that He loves us.
- Understand that Jesus is God's Son.

4-5	5-10 minutes	

- Understand that the Bible is God's Word.
- Understand that God loves me and sent His Son for me.
- Understand that God provides for me and I should be thankful.
- Understand that doing wrong things makes God sad.

6-8	15-20 minutes	

- Understand that the Bible is to be a guidebook for my life.
- Understand that Jesus died for my sins.
- Understand that I need to keep God's commandments in my life.
- Understand that God is omnipresent.

Age	Focal Engagement	Tasks of Faith
9-12	30-45 minutes	

- Understand that being a Christian is a choice in the way I live my life.
- Understand service to the Lord is my privilege.
- Understand that God is omniscient.

Best Practices

Based on current brain research from the <u>Catalog of School Reform</u>,[2] the following are some best practices in the classroom in the 21st century.

1. **Absence of threat**: Children need to feel safe physically and psychologically as they learn.
2. **Meaningful content**: Students should be actively engaged in their learning.
3. **Choice**: Children can be motivated to learn when given choices or at least variety. Centers work well.
4. **Adequate time**: Students learn best when they have time to listen, participate, process, and apply.
5. **Learning style:** Children are unique. Not only do they vary in skin, hair, and eye color, but also in gender, family history, past experience, and personality shaping the learning style of the child.
6. **Enriched environment**: Children should be pulled in or invited by their surroundings.
7. **Mastery at the application level**: A student needs to see a real world application in the lesson learned.

Lesson Incorporating Best Practices

To illustrate the best practices in the church classroom, consider a lesson based on the kindness of Jesus to the woman at the well.

1. To ensure there is an **absence of threat**, greet each child by name at the door, make sure each has his or her own seat, and make sure the classroom is not threatening in any way.

2. To make sure the **content is meaningful,** use a hook that will draw the child in and give a purpose for listening. "Have you ever felt like someone was picking on you or that the whole world was being mean to you?" You are getting the child to personally connect to the woman in your story.

3. To meet the individual needs of your children, providing **choices** can be most difficult in the church classroom. This is important because the learner feels ownership of the application based on the choice made. Choices given for this story might include: a) role play of a situation where someone was being treated unfairly and another would demonstrate kindness and respect, b) mock letter written to a person you have treated unfairly or meanly because of peer pressure, c) drawing Jesus and the woman at the well writing the positive characteristics under each, and d) finding another instance in the Bible similar to the meeting of Jesus and the woman at the well.

4. To meet the need of **adequate time,** remember that as students become older, they learn more and more from each other and less and less from you. Set them up for success by planning to give adequate time for them to interact as they learn.

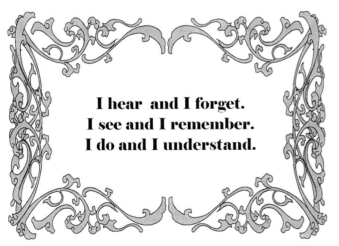

I hear and I forget.
I see and I remember.
I do and I understand.

5. To bring the story to life, an **enriched environment** can make words reality. Using an object like a rope and a bucket may start the process of making the words a reality to the learner. Using pictures or video clips to enhance the background understanding of the importance of the well may be another option to enrich the environment of the learner.

6. The most important of these is the relevance of the **real world application**. An idea for this story might be (as a class, in pairs, or individually) write an oath of kindness and three specific ways or places where it can be used.

The Classroom

The classroom itself as a physical area should be bright and colorful. It should be well organized and visually stimulating so as to beckon the students to come and learn. Others says it should resemble a home, being warm, nurturing, friendly, and comfortable. The chairs and tables should be correctly sized to match the students. The physical space should reflect its purpose. The purpose of the space is to allow children to learn about Christ and to apply that learning to their own lives.

The classroom should be cleaned on a regular basis. It should be orderly, stocked with appropriate materials, and should be free of clutter as to avoid any injuries. Walls should reflect the past and present studies of the classroom. In much the same way a small child beams when his or her work is placed on the refrigerator at home, children who attend church like to see their work on display in their classrooms. The names and pictures of the students used throughout the room give the children a sense of belonging. Every child should feel a sense of belonging, particularly those with special needs.

The expectations of the teacher should be discussed with the students and praise should be used when those expectations are met. The rules should be clearly posted for the benefit of the parents and the children. A general understanding should exist that all children can learn and that all are welcome.

In this day and age, it is especially important that teachers realize the importance of having eyes on students at all times. At no time should any classroom be left unsupervised. The result could be catastrophic.

Discipline

Discipline is one of those issues that can make or break a teacher. These are some basics that can get any teacher off to a solid start.

1. The best prevention of discipline problems is to be prepared. A well designed lesson, following the best practices, will prevent problems.

2. Say what you mean and mean what you say. Be very clear in your communications with children. They must be able to understand what you are communicating. The other part of that is to keep your word at all times. Never make a promise you cannot keep. These are errors that cause a loss in credibility. This will break your relationship with the child (or children) and cause your message to go unheard. Carefully cultivating a relationship with your students makes them more likely to respond to your teaching.

3. Be consistent. Be consistent. Be consistent. You cannot allow a behavior one week and then call the child on it the next week. Any change in your expectations should be openly discussed to maintain their confidence in your ability to be credible and fair.

4. Be fair. All children are not created equal, but your treatment of them should be as fair and equal as possible. Avoid having a favorite as this is a breeding ground for trouble.

5. Be firm but not harsh.

6. Listen and don't interrupt. Sometimes children come to church and it's the only place they feel they can be themselves. In smaller group settings, it is important to listen more than you talk. When a child shares that there is trouble at home, he may just want someone to listen to him. Sometimes being a teacher is being a guide. You may determine that another person should become involved. Do proceed carefully and weigh out all possibilities. Be aware that the child may need more help than you can give.

7. Don't use sarcasm. Younger children (ten and below) are not often capable of abstract thought, which is required to process plays on words and tones. Sarcasm is seldom a useful communication tool even with adults.

8. Never yell. A raised voice can be used to make a point in a lesson, but it should be used sparingly. Yelling at a child is never acceptable. If a child's behavior upset you greatly, remind yourself that you are the adult, count to ten, or take a deep breath. If all else fails, repeat "I am the teacher. I am the teacher. I am the teacher," over and over in your head. It works to reaffirm your authority in the classroom and give you a minute to formulate a plan of action.

9. Never intentionally embarrass a child. The child's dignity should be held intact during all interactions. Embarrassing moments can last a lifetime, none of which should be affiliated with the church in any way. Never embarrass or belittle a student.

10. Avoid being judgmental in your dealing with children. Focus instead on the choice made, the ensuing consequence, and the feeling created by that choice.

11. Be sure to think before you speak. Never tell a child he is dumb, use the word stupid, or name call. These words can crush the spirit of the child and turn him away from church for a lifetime.

12. Positive interactions with the child should far outnumber the negative interactions. Some sources say the ratio should be 3:1, while others say 12:1.

13. Deal with problems quickly and with as little distraction as possible.

14. Handle behavior nonverbally. Before you interact with a child verbally about his or her behavior, there are some nonverbal steps that can be utilized. When used skillfully, these steps will help reduce interruptions and allow more time on task.

Option 1: Ignoring the behavior

Behavior that is ignored will often be discontinued. Although this is not a true blanket statement, some children will misbehave to gain your attention. When it is clear this ploy will not work, the behavior may cease. Not all behavior should be ignored. Any behavior that causes harm to another person or interferes with the learning of the lesson must be addressed. If the behavior does not stop, move on to another option.

Option 2: Effectively using praise

In stead of focusing on a negative behavior, simply search for a behavior you want to reinforce and praise it like this: "I really like the way Samantha has placed her belongings under her chair. She is ready to learn. Thank you, Samantha. Thank you, Seth. Thank you, Ronnie. Nice job, everyone on the second row." Often the children who are being noncompliant will modify their behavior in order to receive the praise you are giving. Children pay attention to cues, and effectively using praise is a good cue for children.

Option 3: Being in close proximity

In real estate, the motto is location...location...location. In the classroom this is true as well. If a behavior is occurring at the side of the room, it is often enough to simply walk to the side of the room and teach from there. By your presence children realize they must stop their behavior. This can often be done without verbally interrupting the lesson. Making eye contact with the offender is an excellent deterrent when used with proximity.

Option 4: Removing the object

Children frequently fiddle with something during a lesson. Removing the object and placing it under the chair while teaching sends a non-verbal message that the fidgeting must stop. This is much less embarrassing to a child than the old fashioned way of stopping the lesson, forcibly removing the object and exclaiming that the object could be retrieved at the end of the day.

15. Verbal interactions are essential in a classroom. Presented are two models. These can be practiced with colleagues until they are used with comfort.

Two Structured Behavior Models

My daughter advocates using a modified Boys Town model in the classroom, both in the public schools and in the Sunday school classroom. It is essentially a coupling statement sandwiched between a child's name and a thank you. The coupling statement is just that...a coupling of an observed behavior and a desired behavior. Following are the steps for a coupling statement and examples.

Express affection. Say the child's name.
Describe the inappropriate behavior.
Describe the desired behavior (Can add rationale.)
Thank the child for compliance.

Ryan, right now you are talking and you should be singing during worship time. Thank you.

Kaitlynn, you are talking during the lesson and you need to be quiet so you and others around you can hear. Thank you.

Brendan, you are crawling on the floor and you need to sit on your chair to color the picture of Mary and Joseph. Thank you very much.

Often this simple coupling statement is enough to help the child turn his or her own behavior around.

My children's ministry director advocates using the following steps from AWANA when a child is misbehaving.

Step One (Within the classroom)
1st Warning – Call student's name, identify the behavior, tell him he has one warning.

2nd Warning – Give student a new seat near you and away from other students.

3rd Warning – Send the student to the superintendent for a time-out in an area away from the other children.

These warnings are within one class period. If a time-out is given, the parent(s) of the child will be contacted by the Sunday school superintendent, explaining that their child had a time-out and we thought they would like to know.

Step Two
If two time-outs occur in a four week period, parents will be contacted **and** the student will be asked to sit with his or her parents during the Sunday school hour the following week. The student will be invited to return to his or her classroom the next week.

Step Three
If a student is a constant disruption and does not seem to respond to the above steps, the parent(s) and child will be asked to meet with the teacher, superintendent, and the Children's Education Director. If necessary a pastoral staff member may be asked to attend. It will be determined at this time what can be done to help the student participate constructively in the classroom.

In the extreme case that a child is a constant disruption and is not responding to any intervention, that child may be asked not to return for an extended period of time.

Lessons

The lesson is the real reason for Sunday school and for children's church. It is the very heart of why the children are there. The singing, the games, the fellowship, the food, the crafts, and activities are all things that pull children in, but the change effected in the life of a child will occur because of the lesson. This lesson should be prepared with the direction of God. Pray about what is to be taught and look for guidance. If you put some of yourself into each lesson you have a greater chance of effecting change in the lives of your students. Lessons have these key components: hook, rationale, key understanding, and the application.

The Hook

Think of the beginning of the lesson in terms of the following scenario: you as the teacher are the fisherman and they as the students are the fish. The fisherman hooks the fish and pulls it in on the line. The hook in the lesson works in much the same way. You are grabbing their attention and reeling them in. The hook sets the tone for the lesson. It piques the interest of the class and creates excitement about the learning to come. This is known as an anticipatory set.

The Rationale

The rationale is the reason for the lesson, setting a clear framework within which to learn. Teaching to a more immediate need rather than a future need is a stronger reason for a lesson. The closer the lesson is to the opportunity to apply the lesson the better. Explaining clearly "what are we doing and why are we doing it" allows the learners to commit themselves to the lesson. The secret to this motivation is to make them want to learn what you want them to learn and ultimately to make them do what you want them to do. Children can be motivated by many things including need for approval, having fun, thirst for knowledge, or personal attachment.

The Key

This is the core where you deliver what they need. The key involves two very distinct parts that must be presented in unison. This includes what you say (the content) and how it is said (presentation); it is the presentation of the content.

The **content** of the lesson should connect to something they already know. Schema theory says that children remember new information much better when that information is presented in such a way that it connects to information they already possess. The idea here is that children come to us with a backpack of life experiences which they will carry with them always. All new information must somehow fit within this backpack. In this way, new learning becomes a part of who they are.

If children are learning about how Christ was kind to the woman at well, ask them to think about the last time they found someone who was in need of assistance and how they handled that situation. Presenting then the case of Jesus and the woman at the well allows the children to own that learning which becomes part of who they are as they fit it into their backpack.

The **delivery** is often as important as the content. Be cognizant of your time frame. Attention spans at various age levels will vary, but it is commonly accepted knowledge that the attention span of the child (in minutes) is approximately equal to the age of the child. If you are teaching fourth graders, you need to plan to deliver a lesson from hook to key in approximately ten minutes. Children tend also to remember the beginning and the end and not much of the middle, so make your middle count. Show your personal connectedness to your lesson and your learners.

In delivering the content, whatever you do, don't bore them. Best practices of teaching indicate that children have to be actively engaged in the learning process. The lesson should be thought-provoking and should require the learner to perform some action during or following the lesson.

Be sure your delivery is age appropriate. You would never talk to a three year old about Satan and hell! There are certain times in a child's life when they are receptive to various aspects of Christian living. Time your lessons within those windows of opportunity.

Teaching in such a way that children learn well requires that you be comfortable with noise in the classroom. This can be unsettling at first. However, when children are learning, the noise is purposeful. There are several ways to refocus the children's attention on your instruction. If children are engrossed in their learning, they may not be able to hear your cues the first time. These may be repeated several times until all children are focused back on you for extra directions or closure.

- Say "Welcome back" or have some cue word or phrase that kids can hear and to which they can respond.

- Use bells or chimes as an audible signal.

- Snap 3 times, students echo back by snapping 3 times.

- Clap a rhythm which they repeat. Only a few with hear the first one, so this is usually repeated.

- Follow directions, "If you can hear me, look up. If you can hear me, sit down. If you can hear me, touch your ear.

- Put signs up. Children put their fingers in the air to show they are in control of themselves and ready to move on.

The Application

The application is the place where the rubber meets the road much like a tire touches the pavement. It is where the "Long ago and far away..." meets the "Right here, right now." When the learner moves beyond the words of the lesson to make an action, the application begins. Make connections to real life situations that might occur within the lives of the children in your class. Be aware of the issues that your children will be facing. Be sure to use niceties. Say please, thank you, and you're welcome in class to continue the open lines of communication.

Be aware of wait time which is the amount of time that is appropriate to wait for a response from a student. Good responses require time to formulate. Children need time to complete the task given them. To illustrate this point, answer this question: How could President Abraham Lincoln have improved his presidency? Although an immediate quick response may be possible, more thought is required to rationalize and respond to this question. Proper wait time is generally accepted as 5 to 7 seconds. Counting 7 seconds on a clock gives a real sense of how long (often uncomfortable) that is.

A center or activity to further practice what was learned in the lesson is an excellent idea with which to close a lesson. This should engage the senses. Learning a lesson by watching, smelling, hearing, tasting, and touching will strengthen the lesson.

The Closing

The conclusion of the lesson should include a quick overview of what was learned and some form of a challenge. This may be something to think about, to practice, or to change. It is an independent practice activity and may even take the form of homework. A strategically placed story in the closing will leave a lasting impression.

Winning a Child to Christ

The instructional model of the church should be such that through each phase of development in the child's life he is being taught and trained in such a way that he is prepared to make a personal decision for salvation. The ultimate goal is to reach every child for Christ.

The wordless book is a good tool to use when winning a child to Christ. The Wordless Book contains no words. It is usually made of five colored pages (black, red, white, yellow, and green). It is best used this way: short, simple, and to the point.

Page 1 (The Black Page)

This page stands for sin. Romans 3:23 says we have all sinned and come short of the glory of God. Say simply that we are all sinners, guilty of sin, and someone must pay for our sin. This can also be compared to living in darkness. This page should prompt the thought, "I am a sinner."

Be careful not to say that black is sin, as some African-American children may misunderstand thinking you are saying that they are sin.

Page 2 (The Red Page)

This page stands for the blood. John 3:16 says that God loved the world so much that He gave His only begotten Son. Say simply that Christ died in our place, paying the price for our sin. This page should prompt the thought, "Christ died on the cross for me."

Page 3 (The White Page)

This page stands for cleansing. 2 Corinthians 5:17 says we become a new creature. Christ saves us and washes all of our sins away. It can be compared to bringing light into our lives. This page should prompt the thought, "I am washed whiter than snow."

In China, the color white is the color of mourning and death. Be aware of any cultural biases that might interfere with the child's understanding of the color related presentation of the gospel.

Page 4 (The Yellow Page)

This page stands for heaven. John 14:1-3 says that He has gone to prepare a place for me. Heaven is a wonderful benefit for accepting Christ.

At this point, the child should be asked these questions: if he believes that Christ came to save him, if there is any reason why he shouldn't be saved, and if he would like to pray with you. The prayer may sound like this: "Dear God, I know that I am a sinner and am lost without You. Please forgive me. I believe You sent Jesus to die for me and that He rose again. I ask Jesus to come into my life to help me to become the person You want me to be. Help me to live for You. Thank you for forgiving me. In Jesus' name, Amen."

Page 5 (The Green Page)

This page stands for growing spiritually. 2 Peter 3:18 says that I must grow in grace and in knowledge. This page should prompt

the thought, "I must grow and prosper like a plant does. I must learn more about Jesus and do the things that please Him."

Commitment to Christian Teaching

The teaching ministry of the Word of God should be taken as seriously as the preaching ministry of the pastor. It is a temptation to do only enough to get by in the context of your busy life. Your position as a Sunday school teacher is critical in the life of those you are teaching. You can either stimulate them to love the Word of God, or bore them into not coming to church and even becoming ambivalent about spiritual things. Being a Sunday school teacher is a privilege and a great responsibility that should be taken very seriously. Sunday school teachers who interact with their students closely may have a greater spiritual influence on them than the pastor or even a parent. The following are the "Ten Commandments for Teachers." Strive to keep these commandments and to bring honor to God.

Ten Commandments for Teachers

1. Thou shalt be approved. A Sunday school teacher must be a saved, separated, baptized member of his local church and approved by the pastor and department superintendent.

2. Thou shalt attend faithfully. If your students are at church more often than you are, who should be teaching the class?

3. Thou shalt be faithful in visitation and promotion. A teacher who is concerned about souls and about building a class will visit absentee students and make phone calls to check in with them.

4. Thou shalt be faithful in tithing. The Bible calls people who do not tithe robbers of God. Teach by word and by example.

5. Thou shalt be punctual. Teachers should arrive in the classroom 15 minutes before

their students. If they see you there, they will know you care.

6. Thou shalt attend teacher training and teaching staff meetings. Take advantage of opportunities to learn and share useful information about resources and teaching ideas. Encourage one another.

7. Thou shalt have a cooperative spirit. Be cooperative with the superintendent, the pastor, and other teachers.

8. Thou shalt attend activities when your students are involved.

9. Thou shalt keep your prayer life in top shape. Even the most talented teacher is not prepared to teach until he or she has spent time in prayer.

10. Thou shalt stick with it. God uses those who don't give up when things get tough.

Recommended Scripture References

Teaching your children, Deuteronomy 4:9
Child's influence, 2 Kings 5:1-3
God looks after fatherless, Psalm 10:14
Purity for a young man, Psalm 119:9
Receptive mind of children, Proverbs 4:3-4
Child known by his doings, Proverbs 20:11
Properly training child, Proverbs 22:6
Learn as a child learns, Matthew 11:25
Jesus saw value in children, Matthew 18:1-6; Mark 9:42
Fails to see importance of children, Matthew 19:13-15;
    Mark 10:13-16; Luke 18:15-17
Child praising the Lord, Matthew 21:16
Jesus has concern for sick girl, Mark 5:21-42
Value of a child, Mark 9:36-42
Christ obedient as a child, Luke 2:41-52
Children imitate parents, Ephesians 5:1
Training children, Ephesians 6:4; 1 Timothy 3:4
Children obey parents, Colossians 3:20-21
Pass faith to boy, 2 Timothy 1:5; 3:15
Believing children, Titus 1:6

Note: Child protection classes should be presented yearly to all persons teaching children and teens.

Small Group Ministry

Growing larger by growing smaller is an essential understanding in the group forum. Small groups, especially in large churches, allow people to get to know each other much better and on a more personal level. Being part of a small group can help a person feel a real sense of connectedness and belonging.

Common Components of Small Groups

Love

Love is expressed in a variety of ways in group life. First, we express love to God through prayer and worship and by giving Him praise. We express love to one another as we serve one another and care for one another in our group (John 13:34-35).

Learn

Learning about Christ and about His will for our lives is a key component of group life. The groups learn the Scripture, about one another, and about themselves (Matthew 11:29).

Serve

Service and good works are part of any vibrant, healthy, small group. Your group must decide how you will express Christian love to your community or to others in the body (James 2:17).

Reach

Groups must make decisions that ensure the group's purpose and vision are carried out. That means reaching others for Christ (Matthew 28:18-20).

Characteristics of Effective Group Leaders

♦ The burden or desire to follow and serve Christ and provide a Christ-like influence on others (1 Thessalonians 1:6; 2 Thessalonians 3:9)

♦ A strong commitment to spiritual growth and character development in one's personal life and in the lives of those close to him (Hebrews 6:1-3; 2 Peter 3:18)

♦ Commitment of obedience to God and His Word in all things and commitment to do whatever it takes to succeed (1 Samuel 15:22; Acts 5:29)

♦ A strong faith characterized by genuine vision, devotion, and tenacity (Hebrews 11:1, 6)

♦ The possession of the qualities of compassion and caring about others, their needs, and problems (Galatians 6:2; Ephesians 4:32; 1 Peter 3:8;)

♦ The ability to clearly communicate, both one-on-one and with numbers of people in a group (Acts 4:20, 26:25; Ephesians 4:15)

♦ The willingness to study and prepare thoroughly (2 Timothy 2:15; 1 Peter 3:15)

♦ The character to follow through and follow up (2 Timothy 4:5; Hebrews 6:12)

♦ Competence in the ability to lead and guide a small group (2 Timothy 2:2, 23-24)

Core Values of the Group

All groups operate according to certain values and expectations, often unspoken or unwritten. In order to foster open communication and clarity about the purpose and values of the group, it is important to put your core values in writing. Following you will find sample values that are key for small group relationships. You and your group should create your own list with the kinds of values central to your group. The important thing is that your members are committed to growing in interpersonal relationships and maturity in Christ.

Acceptance

It is important to create an atmosphere where group members affirm and encourage one another, build each other up in Christ, and help each other grow.

Availability

Group members and their resources should be available to each other. People's time, attention, insight, and material resources must be made available to each other in order to meet needs and serve one another.

Prayer

Prayer is valued in group life. The group comes together before God to praise, ask, confess, and thank the Lord for all He has done. Prayer encourages the group members to be humble, knowing that all comes from God. In prayer they also feel valued and come to understand their own worth. As you see God move to answer the prayer concerns of your members, the whole group will be encouraged.

Transparency

Openness in the relationships within the group promotes honesty and an ease of sharing feelings, struggles, joys, and hurts. Reaching the goal of authentic relationships begins with an openness with each other. The desire to be honest with each other is critical to authentic relationships. In order for trust to be built among the group members, they must speak the truth in love, so that we ...*may grow up into Him in all things, which is the head, even Christ* (Ephesians 4:15).

Confidentiality

Honest, open relationships must be guarded with an agreement of safety that what is said in the group will remain confidential, all opinions will be respected, and differences will be allowed. As part of the concept of safety, confidentiality promotes openness by promising that whatever is shared within the confines of the group will not be repeated elsewhere.

Committment

A commitment of sensitivity to the needs, feelings, backgrounds, and current situations of other group members will help build relationships in the group. In authentic relationships, accountability is voluntary submission to another group member for support, encouragement, and help in a particular area of your life. This gives that person some responsibility for assisting you in that area.

Evangelism

Evangelism is practiced to expand the community of believers through sharing your faith, using the "open chair" to invite people into the group or other types of outreach.

Multiplication

Having your group grow and eventually birth a new group enables the group to carry out the vision of seeing more people connected in Christian community and growing in their relationship with Christ.

Sample Meeting Format (90 min.)

Opening.................................... 10 min.
Icebreaker activity, singing, worshiping, sharing praises

Learning .... 30 min.
Approach, investigation, reflection, practical application

Loving...................................... 30 min.
Caring, encouraging, listening, praying, confessing

Deciding.................................... 10 min.
Defining outreach activities, scheduling Events

Doing .... 10 min.
Planning outreach, serving, closing

Organizing Your Groups

Introduce people to your church's group ministry through a process such as GroupLink which serves to mix people and organize them into groups. Andy Stanley's book, <u>Creating Community: Five Keys to Building a Small Group Culture</u>, is an excellent resource for this process.

Group Prayer

Principles of Group Prayer

♦ Prayer makes many people nervous.

♦ Include yourself in that category as you let the entire group know that you, too, have experienced some anxiety about public prayer: let them know that you will all learn together.

♦ Never pressure anyone to pray. Let the group know up front that you will not put them on the spot!

♦ Model prayer in plain language. Get rid of your "Christianese" and use words your group will understand.

♦ Encourage short prayers. Long prayers by individual group members tend to intimidate the rest of the group.

♦ Agree that all items of prayer will be kept confidential within the group.

Creative Ideas for Group Prayer

♦ The leaders are examples in prayer. Nurture a personal and vital prayer life.

♦ Hold regular leadership prayer meetings. Visionary leadership enables the leader to effect the people with whom they come in contact. Choose one day other than home fellowship night to meet. Leaders gather together to concentrate on the needs and hearts of those in the group.

♦ Each person picks a name out of a hat at the 20:20 group to pray for that particular week (with the person knowing or not knowing who is praying for him).

♦ Designate different prayer partners (again by picking from the hat) for one week to call and share needs. This would allow the people to get to know others better and to encourage younger Christians in prayer. It would increase accountability and disrupt cliques that may be occurring.

♦ The group leader needs to encourage personal prayer among the members every week as a reinforcement and reminder.

♦ Post a 20:20 prayer list. Keep track of the testimonies of answered prayer and encourage people to share about these blessings.

♦ Have prayer time dealing specifically with a topic of need (families, non-believing acquaintances, missionaries).

♦ Occasionally incorporate a special time to share testimonies of answered prayer from previous weeks' requests.

♦ Occasionally focus on a specific aspect of prayer (praise, thanksgiving, supplications, confession, or listening)

♦ Hold prayer time outside in the yard under the stars when weather is conducive.

♦ Have each person write a prayer of commitment to the Lord in response to the teaching. Have each individual put his prayer in a self-addressed envelope. Mail the prayers in a few months for the people to reflect upon after some time has passed.

♦ Encourage individuals to keep a prayer diary.

Things to Avoid When Leading a Discussion

Not making the question sound conversational	If you are asking questions that are written down, ask them in a conversational tone using your own vocabulary.
Being afraid of silence after asking a question	Don't be impatient. You must give people time to think and respond. Accept answers with a positive response.
Limiting yourself to asking questions and leading	The leader can also participate by sharing his answers and observations, but must not become a teacher or dominate the conversation.
Combining two questions into one	Be careful to ask only one question at a time.
Trying to maintain too much control	If the group takes off, don't worry as long as it is in a direction you want to go. You may need to step in from time to time to clarify the direction.
Not explaining what you expect the group to do	You are in charge. Don't hesitate to bring the discussion back if it gets too far off the topic.
Not participating when you feel the group may be wandering	The leader needs to be a participant and completely involved, even in tangents. Just don't let it go too far.
Asking a "yes or no" question	Use "how" and "why" if possible to stimulate discussion.
Asking a question that is too complex	State the questions simply and clearly.
Tending to stress your own personal application	The leader should not expect the group to be impressed deeply with the same things that impress him.
Not finishing on time	People should be allowed to stay to fellowship, but plan to end the lesson on time.
Immediately answering a question directed to you, the leader	Don't answer right away. Ask, "What does someone think?" Once the group has tried to answer, you can either affirm their answers or handle the question directly.
Being afraid to admit to the group that you don't know the answer	Don't hesitate to say, "That's a good question. I don't know." It shows honesty. Find out the answer and share it with them next week.
Launching into a lecture as soon as the discussion wanes	Don't start a sermon just because the silence is uncomfortable. Be patient. Keep asking questions.
Being afraid to show weakness	You set an example as the leader, but you are not perfect. Your group won't think less of you if you share.
Being too concerned with getting through the lesson material	There are times when you need to minister to someone in the group. Relationships are more important than finishing a study by a certain date.

Source unknown

Part Four
The Appendices

Appendix A
General Information and Methodology of Intern Training

After orientation to the community, church, and staff, each intern was given a detailed program overview with its requirements, commitments, and assignments. Each week they met with me as senior pastor for an afternoon of personal training and instruction. During this time the material contained in this manual was taught, reading assignments discussed, and assignments for the next week given. I met with them every week for the first year, then each member of the pastoral staff took turns mentoring them weekly in their respective areas of expertise for the next six to nine months; then I finished their final months' weekly meetings. The interns attended the weekly staff meetings from 9:30 am until 2 pm and fully participated in discussions and decisions. Here they were exposed to the development and implementation of programs and policies, handling of issues and problems, planning and promotion, people issues, team building and teamwork, evaluation of ministries and Sunday services. As detailed in the section on preaching, they were assigned a topic for a sermon and required to deliver it to the staff at the close of the staff meeting on Tuesday afternoons. The staff would provide feedback and offer suggestions to help improve their speaking and sermon presentation. In total they would speak to the staff about fifty times during these sessions. Next they would begin speaking to the congregation on Wednesday nights, then Sunday nights, and occasionally on Sunday morning. Whenever they spoke to the congregation, the staff would provide feedback the following Tuesday. They would have the experience of speaking approximately one hundred times during their internship experience. They also performed a wedding, a funeral, and spoke to groups of children, ladies, men, seniors, and inner city or rescue mission groups. When ready, they taught an adult Sunday school class either starting or building an existing class. Nearly all of the interns doubled their Sunday school class attendance during their tenure. They participated in outreach efforts, led neighborhood Bible clubs during the summer as an evangelistic effort, and were trained in the experience of personal evangelism including door to door visitation.

Intern wives participated in the weekly training session and were assigned appropriate topics on which to speak for several months during their final six months. They also participated in church ministries during their tenure. They were required to work in the church office for one year and be exposed to all aspects of staff ministry with their husbands.

The goal for each intern was full participation in all aspects of church administration and function. The interns were provided an open-door policy to access any member of the staff to discuss needs, problems, ministry issues, obtain advice, and get answers to their questions. Their general growth and progress were evaluated every six months. Their strengths were acknowledged and weaknesses were presented with appropriate corrective measures. During their final weeks, they were prepared for their ordination and missionary approval process. Their helpful suggestions for improvement of the internship program were incorporated.

Note that there is not included within this manual information about preparing for a particular mission field or serving in a particular culture. Nearly all of our interns were preparing to become Baptist Bible Fellowship International missionaries and had previously covered these topics in their college training.

Appendix B
Why Bad Things Happen to Good People

1. There have been numerous attempts to explain why bad things happen to good people including luck, fate, chance, or the idea that God is a weak God.

2. God has revealed Himself to us:
   - A. In creation (including the personality of man)
   - B. In history (mighty acts)
   - C. In the life and ministry of Jesus Christ
   - D. In the Bible

3. Atheists have frequently used the presence of tragedy and suffering in the world to argue against the existence of God and to attack the Christian faith. Their argument is framed as follows:
   - A. If God exists, then God is omniscient (all knowing), omnipotent (all powerful), and morally perfect.
   - B. If God is omniscient, then God knows when evil exists.
   - C. If God is omnipotent, then God has the power to eliminate all evil.
   - D. If God is morally perfect, then God has the desire to eliminate all evil.
   - E. Evil exists.
   - F. If evil exists and God exists, then God doesn't have the power to eliminate all evil, or doesn't know evil exists, or doesn't have the desire to eliminate all evil.
   - G. Therefore, God doesn't exist.

   In argumentation and debate, we disprove a position in three ways: disagreeing with the definitions, proving the premises to be false, or faulting the logic. Here all that is needed is to prove one of the six premises (A through F) to be false and the argument crumbles like a house of cards proving the conclusion (G) to be false. The fourth premise D is particularly fallacious; based upon biblical truth this article will clearly illustrate that it is a fallacy. God has reasons to permit evil which are compatible with both His nature and His love, which some have called justifying reasons. This includes the concept of God producing good out of evil as is taught in Romans 8:28 and elsewhere in the Bible. Reconsider the above argument after studying all of the points of this article and you will probably be surprised how weak the argument of the atheist actually is.

4. **God is revealed in the Bible, not as a wimp but as great and mighty.** See Job 36:26; Psalm 77:12-16; Psalm 86:10; Isaiah 40:21-31; Habakkuk 3:3-6,17-19; Romans 11:32-36; Revelation 4:11; 15:3-4.

5. **God is presented in Scripture as greater than evil, the One who will one day triumph over it and accomplish His eternal purposes.** We do not understand all of His purposes and ways because His ways are not our ways and His thoughts are not our thoughts (Isaiah 55:8). As high as the heavens are from the earth is the metaphor God uses to illustrate this difference. If God has the wisdom to know what to do and the power to be able to do it, "Then why doesn't He do something about evil?" is an often asked question.

   As we reflect on this question, consider these facts:
   - A. The difference between extrinsic (extraneous) and intrinsic (essential) almighty power is the difference between that which is possible and impossible, even for

God. He is almighty, but there are some things He cannot do such as: making a square circle, a rock too heavy to lift, existing and not existing at the same time, the number 2 not being the only whole number between 1 and 3 which is not an odd number, and going against His own nature or the nature of truth He has built into His universe. These are logical absurdities, categorical exclusives, or impossibilities by definition.

B. God is neither handicapped by the universe that He has created nor the victim of the freedom of choice He has given to man. God's omnipotence involves a world of consistent natural laws *and* human freedom, both ordained by God. A significant part of the suffering in this world is because of these two principles He has built into His creation. He is able to accomplish His perfect will yet remain true to His character and the principles He has brought into the universe. God is the cause of all causes, but is not the cause of all choices.

C. God has imposed some limits on Himself. He will not manipulate people or violate their freedom of choice, but He still has the ability to accomplish His purposes in spite of and within these limits.

D. God's purposes are according to His will. His directive will (perfect will) is distinct from His permissive will (what He permits). God is never involved in directing someone to sin although He obviously permits it. James 1:13 teaches that God is not tempted with evil and neither does He tempt any man toward evil. Allowing someone to fall while he is learning to ride a bicycle is entirely different from pushing him down to slam against the pavement. Though God does not direct us to sin, He can use even the wrongs in our lives to His ends. There is an important difference between the means and ends to God's purpose.

6. Throughout history people have associated tragedy and suffering with sin.

Suffering entered the world as a consequence of man's sin (Genesis 3:16-19). It is incorrect to think that all misery is punishment for wrong behavior. The Bible reveals numerous sources as causes of suffering: God, Satan, natural consequences of our actions, natural laws, and self-infliction. Jesus addressed the issue of people's attribution regarding the suffering of others. In Luke 13:16, He attributed a cause to Satan for a woman's suffering, and earlier in the same chapter, He addressed two recent tragedies. One involved the political leader Pilate committing atrocities and the other was a construction accident that killed eighteen people. He makes it very clear that neither tragedy occurred because of the victims' specific wrongdoings.

There were present at that season some that told Him of the Galileans, whose blood Pilate had mingled with their sacrifices. And Jesus answering said unto them, suppose ye that these Galileans were sinners above all the Galileans, because they suffered such things? I tell you, Nay: but, except ye repent, ye shall all likewise perish. Or those eighteen, upon whom the tower in Siloam fell, and slew them, think ye that they were sinners above all men that dwelt in Jerusalem? I tell you, Nay: but, except ye repent, ye shall all likewise perish (Luke 13: 1-5).

Note the strong *no* given by our Lord to the idea that these victims were worse sinners than anyone else. He also used the opportunity to demand the repentance of the accusers in verse 5.

Job suffered greatly, yet God called him a man who loved Him, eschewed evil, was perfect (complete), and upright. Though his friends judged him and accused him saying he suffered because of sin in his life and added that since his suffering was great, he must have sinned greatly. God disagreed; He rebuked them, condemning their opinions as completely false.

Two themes are repeated throughout the Old Testament regarding suffering:
   A. We frequently suffer the consequences of our bad choices and actions. The book of Proverbs is filled with such statements, and the New Testament teaches, *...whatsoever a man soweth, that shall he also reap* (Galatians 6:7).
   B. We sometimes suffer as a punishment from God as seen in the lives of Jeremiah, Isaiah, Amos, Hosea, Habakkuk, and Ezekiel. Careful examination of these Scriptures regarding judgment reveals that such punishment usually followed certain prescribed patterns:

   The prophets offer hope that God will withhold judgment if there is repentance. God specifically and repeatedly gives warning, and then He reveals that the judgment is because of their refusal to listen and respond. They knew why they were being judged. If we have been given no such warnings by God, it is highly unlikely our misery is a particular judgment. In fact, when the New Testament mentions the sin unto death, it instructs us not to pray. The Greek word also means "to inquire" (1 John 5:16). So we are not to inquire about that, probably because we do not know God's business in His dealings with others. If we examine the Bible from cover to cover (Genesis 1:1 to Revelation 22:21), we will find God gives 75 reasons (to follow) for tragedies and sufferings. Job's friends tried to play God and determine which was the cause of their friend's misery.

7. *Good* and *bad* are relative terms.
How do we know what is really good for us? Bad is, in reality, often good, or it leads to good, and vice versa. The following story is told of an old man in a village. It illustrates the role our perceptions play in how we conceive events as good or bad.

   Once there was an old man who lived in a tiny village. Although poor, he was envied by all, for he owned a beautiful white horse. Even the king coveted his treasure. A horse like this had never been seen before—such was its splendor, its majesty, and its strength. People offered fabulous prices for the steed, but the old man always refused. "This horse is not a horse to me," he would tell them. "It is a person. How could you sell a person? He is a friend, not a possession. How could you sell a friend?" The man was poor and the temptation was great, but he never sold the horse. One morning he found that the horse was not in the stable.

   The entire village came to see him. "You old fool," they scoffed, "we told you that someone would steal your horse. We warned that you would be robbed. You are so poor. How could you ever hope to protect such a valuable animal? It would have been better to have sold him. You could have gotten whatever price you wanted. No amount would have been too high. Now the horse is gone, and you've been cursed with misfortune."

   The old man responded, "Don't speak too quickly. Say only that the horse is not in the stable. That is all we know; the rest is judgment. If I've been cursed or not, how can you know? How can you judge?"

   The people contested, "Don't make us out to be fools! We may not be philosophers, but great philosophy is not needed. The simple fact that your horse is gone is a curse."

The old man spoke again. "All I know is that the stable is empty, and the horse is gone. The rest I don't know. Whether it is a curse or a blessing, I can't say. All we can see is a fragment. Who can say what will come next?"

The people of the village laughed. They thought that the man was crazy. They had always thought he was a fool; if he wasn't, he would have sold the horse and lived off the money. Instead, he was a poor woodcutter, an old man still cutting firewood, dragging it out of the forest and selling it. He lived hand to mouth in the misery of poverty. Now he had proven that he was, indeed, a fool.

After fifteen days, the horse returned. He hadn't been stolen; he had run away into the forest. Not only had he returned, he had brought a dozen wild horses with him. Once again the village people gathered around the woodcutter and spoke. "Old man, you were right and we were wrong. What we thought was a curse was a blessing. Please forgive us."

The man responded, "Once again, you go too far. Say only that the horse is back. State only that a dozen horses returned with him, but don't judge. How do you know if this is a blessing or not? You see only a fragment. Unless you know the whole story, how can you judge? You read only one page of a book. Can you judge the whole book? You read only one word of a phrase. Can you understand the entire phrase? Life is so vast, yet you judge all of life with one page or one word. All you have is a fragment! Don't say that this is a blessing. No one knows. I am content with what I know. I am not perturbed by what I don't."

"Maybe the old man is right," they said to one another. So they said little. Down deep, they knew he was wrong. They knew it was a blessing. Twelve wild horses had returned with one horse. With a little bit of work, the animals could be broken, trained, and sold for much money.

The old man had a son, an only son. The young man began to break the wild horses. After a few days, he fell from one of the horses and broke both legs. Once again the villagers gathered around the old man and cast their judgments.

"You were right," they said. "You proved you were right. The dozen horses were not a blessing. They were a curse. Your only son has broken his legs, and now in your old age you have no one to help you. Now you are poorer than ever."

The old man spoke again. "You people are obsessed with judging. Don't go so far. Say only that my son broke his legs. Who knows if it is a blessing or a curse? No one knows. We only have a fragment. Life comes in fragments."

It so happened that a few weeks later the country engaged in war against a neighboring country. All the young men of the village were required to join the army. Only the son of the old man was excluded due to his injury. Once again the people gathered around the old man, crying and screaming because their sons had been taken. There was little chance that they would return. The enemy was strong and the war would be a losing struggle. They would never see their sons again.

"You were right, old man," they wept. "God knows you were right. This proves it. Your son's accident was a blessing. His legs may be broken, but at least he is with you. Our sons are gone forever."

The old man spoke again. "It is impossible to talk with you. You always draw conclusions. No one knows. Say only this: Your sons had to go to war and mine did not. No one knows if it is a blessing or a curse. No one is wise enough to know. Only God knows."

Many things in life can be used for good or bad. Cars can provide wonderful transportation or may be destructive in accidents causing dismemberment and death; should we remove all cars to eliminate all auto tragedies? Concrete provides convenient walkways and streets, yet people severely injure themselves on the hard surfaces; should we eliminate all concrete? Wood is useful in construction and as fuel but can also become a deadly club; should we eliminate all wood? Fire is good for warming, cooking, cleansing, and lighting, yet it can rage in destructive fury; should we eliminate all fire? God has given us all of these things for our convenience and benefit; yet in the wrong hands or when used carelessly, there are painful consequences. If we want to derive the good from so many things, we must also tolerate the bad they can cause.

8. **How could God intervene and make everything good. Can He force goodness?**
Can He force men to love their wives? Can He force men to go to work? Can He force people to stop drinking? Can God violate the very freedom that He gave man, the freedom that is part of the image of God in man? Providence means "divine guidance and care" (Psalm 103:19). Is life haphazard or purpose driven? God's providence is clearly seen in the lives of so many people in the Bible like Joseph, Moses, Job, Paul, and Esther. Predestination means "to map out boundaries beforehand" (Ephesians 1:5). Although God does not override our free will, He has many ways at His disposal to influence and direct processes and outcomes. We are unable to see that which might have happened in our lives—the "what if" factor. Some hardships, painful as they may be, are used to prevent us from experiencing something far worse. **God possesses three kinds of knowledge:**

Natural Knowledge – God knows all necessary truths including laws of logic, facts, possibilities, circumstances, actions, reactions, worlds, and orders. This knowledge is essential and unconditioned; without it, God would not be God (Hebrews 4:13).

Free Knowledge – This is God's knowledge of the actual world He has created and includes His foreknowledge of everything that will happen. This knowledge is contingent on His will. Also included is God's knowledge of His own actions which He has based on His middle knowledge. (Isaiah 44:7; Ephesians 1:10.)

Middle Knowledge – This knowledge includes the events which do not in fact occur but would if the circumstances were different. God knows what every creature would do in every possible circumstance. This knowledge identifies the range of possibilities that God could create given the choices that we as free creatures would make in every possible situation. Therefore, God knows the future and all possible futures as well (1 Samuel 23:11-13; Matthew 11:23).

Based upon all of God's knowledge, He unfolds His eternal plan. Though the individual events are decided by the free choices of His creatures, God knows all possibilities and all possible outcomes. Based upon those choices, He then chooses the actualization of a specific plan based upon that knowledge. Thus, the whole complex of events is chosen by God. This concept is well illustrated in the life of Joseph. Although Joseph's brothers freely exercised their freedom of choice in their actions, as did all of the other participants, God accomplished His purpose through their decisions. Many of those decisions were wrong and sinful, but God made them, though bad, to work together for good (Romans 8:28):

- Betrayed by his brothers and sold into slavery
- Falsely accused and imprisoned by Potiphar's wife
- Forgotten by his cellmate
- Elevated by Pharaoh
- Saved his family and nation
- Revealed God's providence through his ordeal

Genesis records Joseph's instruction to his brothers regarding their decision:

Now therefore be not grieved, nor angry with yourselves, that ye sold me hither: for God did send me before you to preserve life. For these two years hath the famine been in the land: and yet there are five years, in the which there shall neither be earing nor harvest. And God sent me before you to preserve you a posterity in the earth, and to save your lives by a great deliverance. So now it was not you that sent me hither, but God: and he hath made me a father to Pharaoh, and lord of all his house, and a ruler throughout all the land of Egypt (Genesis 45:5-8).

And Joseph said unto them, Fear not: for am I in the place of God? But as for you, ye thought evil against me; but God meant it unto good, to bring to pass, as it is this day, to save much people alive (Genesis 50:19-20).

Clearly God can use different people or circumstances to accomplish His will. Esther was free to choose not to intervene on behalf of her people. If she had refused, God would have used other means. Mordecai reminded Esther of this fact when he said:

For if thou altogether holdest thy peace at this time, then shall there enlargement and deliverance arise to the Jews from another place, but thou and thy father's house shall be destroyed; and who knoweth whether thou art come to the kingdom for such a time as this? (Esther 4:14).

The metaphor of a cruise ship bound for a particular destination such as London, England, is an excellent example of God accomplishing His purposes while allowing each of us free will to make our own choices. On board the ship, people are freely moving around, living their lives as they please. They choose what to do, when and what to eat, where to go, and when to go to bed. During the process of the journey, the ship is heading for its ultimate destination of London under the direction of the captain. So God accomplishes His purposes through us or sometimes in spite of us.

God promises that He will make all things work together **for good** to those who love God and are the called according to His purpose. How can God make all things work together for good? Note that he does not say all things in themselves are good, He only promises to make them work together for good. We can observe many difficult and painful circumstances in our lives and wonder how God could possibly make these things work together for good. The best example of this is recycling. When a tin can is discarded it begins to corrode, rust, and becomes contaminated. It is scooped up and dumped into a truck to be taken to a recycling plant where it is melted down and recycled. Everything that was part of it is changed in the recycling process and out comes a new can that is shiny, bright, clean, and ready to be used. In much the same way, God takes the painful and difficult circumstances of our lives and transforms them through His recycling process. He fashions them after His purposes into a profitable, useful product (Romans 8:28). God has a way of bringing good things out of bad things. There could be no resurrection without Good Friday and the crucifixion, and again, there would have been no gain without pain.

9. **Most of the evil in this world is caused by people...not things. (Examples of this include hatred, deceit, murder, and sexual acting out.)** C.S. Lewis reminds us that four-fifths of all the evil in the world is caused by people who are exercising their free moral choice, "The only way God could eliminate these consequences would be to remove choice or eliminate mankind altogether. If we don't like the results, should we eliminate the cause?" Hugh J. McCann of Texas A&M University observes as follows. "Many of the hardships that befall humankind (including disease, ignorance, poverty) owe their existence, at least in part, to wrongful willing. The poverty of some is owed to the greed of others; suffering and deprivation may occur because of institutionalized racial or ethnic hatred. It may also be that leaders use their positions to advance their own power and prosperity at the expense of their citizenry. The cost of defense against foreign enemies may simply bring economic hardship to a nation. Who can estimate how much suffering, disease, poverty, ignorance, or threats posed by natural disasters would by now have been conquered were it not for the fact that so much of our energy and resources were diverted either to the pursuit of wrongful goals or to guarding ourselves against those who do pursue them, and mending as well as we can the harm they cause? If human wills were not so often misdirected, human life would be transformed, and the struggles against those evils, that seem to us no one's fault, much further advanced. A great deal, then, of what we are likely to view as natural evil actually falls under the heading of extrinsic moral evil."

10. **If God removed all suffering and pain would we be a better people?** Suffering and pain must have a purpose. Jesus experienced much pain and suffering even though He was God in human flesh. Suffering and love are not incompatible. The same pain that raises havoc in lives is also a gracious warning signal that something is wrong and needs correcting; thus, pain may be good or bad depending on its extent, severity, and duration. Many believe that we would be better off were we to eliminate all pain. Dr. Paul Brand wrote in <u>The Gift of Pain: Thank God for Pain</u>, that he received a several-million-dollar grant to develop an artificial pain system in attempt to assist sufferers of diseases such as leprosy and diabetes who were in danger of losing fingers, toes, and entire limbs because of their faulty pain warning system. After many years of work, repeated frustrations, and millions of dollars spent, Brand and his team abandoned their effort because a warning system for just the hand proved to be incredibly expensive, prone to frequent breakdowns, and totally inadequate to interpret the profuse sensations. He concluded that what was sometimes referred to as "God's great mistake" was actually so incredibly profound and complex that the best modern engineering and technology could not begin to imitate it. Though pain is often quite unpleasant, it is that very quality that is so necessary to save us from destruction. His continuing work with lepers caused him to see pain as a divine gift to us to prevent a "painless hell." Lepers regularly were severely burned, wounded, and even mutilated because of the absence of pain to warn them. It is that sensation of pain that warns us to remove our hand from a hot stove or withdraw our feet from broken glass. Without the warning system of pain, we would be unaware of the threat or process of injury or disease; yet the same pain that protects and helps us can be so devastating when we are ravaged by a serious disease process. Would we have been better off if our Creator had made us without a pain mechanism? Brand determined that without the overt unpleasantness involved in the pain process, the warning provided would be ignored or neglected. No wonder he co-wrote <u>Fearfully and Wonderfully Made</u> to express the profound amazement at the wonder of the working of our bodies, including pain. How would we survive without it? It is like so many things possessing duality which can be tremendously beneficial or devastatingly destructive.

11. **The purpose of life is not merely enjoyment but encompasses character building and glorifying God for our good and His purposes.** Where reason cannot wade, faith must swim.

12. **Whatever we may be forced to endure, know Christ is touched with the feelings of our infirmities.** He was tempted in all points as we are. The Lord is with us through every circumstance and will never leave us nor forsake us (Hebrews 13:5).

13. **Lazarus' sickness and death were ultimately described by Christ as being for God's glory.** Many circumstances in life somehow promote the glory or character of God in our lives or the lives of others.

14. **Some difficult circumstances are described in the Bible as being used of God to test us or prepare us to be used in some future way.** For example, the Israelites were forced to fight numerous skirmishes when they entered the Promised Land which ultimately strengthened them and honed their war skills to prepare them for the ultimate conflict against the inhabitants of the land.

15. **God uses painful circumstances to judge and discipline us much the same way we discipline our children to teach them that which is profitable and good or prevent them from experiencing some tragedy.** Hardships in our lives are used by God to transform us so that we develop Christ-likeness, especially in our character. C.S. Lewis called pain "the megaphone of God" and added "God whispers to us in our pleasures, speaks in our conscience, but shouts in our pains."

16. **Much suffering comes from a groaning world because of sin.** Thorns and thistles cause considerable pain and inconvenience.

17. **Sin cannot transform sin.** Augustine argued that evil is the absence of good not an entity in itself. He concluded that greed is the absence of generosity, hate is the absence of love, and dishonesty is the absence of honesty. Therefore, God is the author of good but cannot be held responsible for evil, which is the corruption of the good God created.

18. **God frequently uses the bad in our lives to help us to fully appreciate the good.** Ecclesiastes 7:14 tells us to enjoy the times of prosperity because they balance times of adversity.

19. **God seems to operate under a series of higher laws which are unknown or not understandable to us.** Prayer affects the eternal and is an example of the operation of these higher laws. The teaching from the Book of Job, when God answered him, revealed these principles about God's role in Job's tragedy:
   - There is a parallel between the functioning of the physical universe and the spiritual world. This analogy is strictly followed in God's response to Job.
   - Just as there are many dark and unexplained mysteries of the universe, so there are many mysteries of the spiritual universe.
   - We will never completely understand these spiritual mysteries while on this earth because God's thoughts are not our thoughts and His ways are not our ways. There is a world of difference (as far as Heaven is from earth).
   - As God followed a design for the physical universe, so He followed a design for the foundation and functioning of the spiritual (38:4-7).
   - God determined and established boundaries in each world (38:8).
   - As there are laws of nature (gravity, thermodynamics), there are also laws which govern the spiritual universe (38:33).

- God built into members of the animal kingdom certain instincts and predispositions which affect their behaviors and reactions (38:36).
- God provided directions according to His sovereignty (38:35).
- God determined food chains to sustain life (34:41).
- God prescribes time and timing according to His design. These are manifested in the various cycles of life and the universe (39:2).
- God made things according to certain purposes with definite functions and a particular nature, in other words, we are made that way to do that. Examples in the animal world would include a hippopotamus and a crocodile. Each is uniquely made to look a certain way and to live a certain way. A hippopotamus could never survive as a crocodile survives and vice versa (39:5, 29).
- God is sovereign and not subject to man's standards. He declared, ...whatsoever is *under the whole heaven is mine* (41:11).
- God challenged Job to show Him how He could do better, *Shall he that contendeth with the Almighty instruct Him? he that reproveth God, let him answer it* (40:2).
- Ultimately, God revealed that the answers to tragedy and suffering are bound up in the mysteries of the universe and the mysteries of God.

20. **When people die, we may think of it as an ultimate tragedy; yet according to Hebrews 11:35, God called people to glory because the world was not worthy to keep them.** Going to Heaven is never a loss for the one experiencing it; it is victory, a blessing, and a comfort—ultimate gain.

21. **We frequently pray as in the Lord's Prayer, "Thy will be done," then are unhappy when that prayer is answered, especially if the answer provides circumstances we do not want or like.**

22. **If there is no purpose in suffering, then it is random, senseless, and pointless which makes it more difficult to accept and endure.** Suffering that has some purpose at least provides a basis for its endurance. Suffering for suffering's sake alone adds agony on top of agony.

23. **God promises, *If we suffer, we shall also reign with Him* (2 Timothy 2:12).** This is the reward of sharing His throne. Somehow suffering is equated with eternal recognition, acceptance, and position. There appears to be something about suffering that we don't understand that makes God recognize it in this spiritual way.

24. **Psalm 37 and 73 and numerous other passages of Scripture teach us that too often we view immediate circumstances using a lens that is too small.** We need a wide-angle lens to see and understand the big picture and the ultimate outcome of God's providence. We have to look beyond this world into eternity to see God's meaning and purpose.

The following list is a comprehensive presentation of the biblical references to suffering. Although there is considerable overlap, subtle shades of meaning are important.

1. Suffering increases awareness of the sustaining power and presence of God (Psalm 68:19).
2. Suffering refines, strengthens, and perfects us (Hebrews 2:10).
3. Suffering prevents us from slipping or falling (Psalm 66:8-9).
4. Suffering allows the life of Christ to be manifested in us (2 Corinthians 4:7-11).
5. Suffering increases our dependence on God (2 Corinthians 12:9).

6. Suffering teaches us humility and keeps us from pride (2 Corinthians 12:7).
7. Suffering imparts the mind of Christ to us (Philippians 2:1-11).
8. Suffering produces perseverance and hope (Romans 5:3-4).
9. Suffering reminds us of death's inevitability and life's brevity (2 Corinthians 4:8-10).
10. Suffering can be a chastisement from God (Psalm 107:17).
11. Suffering teaches us obedience and self-control (Hebrews 5:8).
12. Suffering prevents us from sinning (Psalm 119:67).
13. Suffering is frequently produced at the hands of evil men (Psalm 37:14-15).
14. Suffering comes from our identification with Christ and His kingdom (2 Thessalonians 1:5).
15. Suffering is part of the struggle against injustice (1 Peter 2:19).
16. Suffering occurs because we participate in the sufferings of Christ (1 Peter 4:14).
17. Suffering with faithfulness and endurance produces special rewards (2 Timothy 2:12).
18. Suffering produces the opportunity for generosity and the exercise of the spiritual gifts of others (Philippians 4:12-15).
19. Suffering unites believers by producing a common purpose (Revelation 1:9).
20. Suffering produces discernment and teaches valuable lessons (Psalm 119:66-71).
21. Suffering makes us more empathic, sympathetic, and compassionate servants of God (2 Corinthians 1:5-6).
22. Suffering produces a broken and contrite spirit (Psalm 51:16-17).
23. Suffering points us to the coming of Jesus Christ (1 Peter 1:6, 13).
24. Suffering is sometimes necessary to win the lost (2 Timothy 2:8-10).
25. Suffering allows us to comfort others who are struggling (2 Corinthians 1:3-11).
26. Suffering draws us closer to Christ (Matthew 5:4).
27. Suffering helps us put material things in perspective (Philippians 3:8).
28. Suffering helps us appreciate times of peace and prosperity (Ecclesiastes 7:14).
29. Suffering tests our spirituality, character, and values by showing our reaction under pressure (Job 1:1-11).
30. Suffering gives a greater source of the grace of God (2 Timothy 1:7-8).
31. Suffering teaches us to be thankful (1 Thessalonians 5:18).
32. Suffering increases our faith (Jeremiah 29:11).
33. Suffering's tears will benefit all of Heaven (Psalm 56:8).
34. Suffering can produce an ultimate good, even bringing good out of evil (Romans 8:28).
35. Suffering in the present can prevent greater future suffering by preventing its cause (1 Samuel 19).
36. Suffering destroys counterfeit faith (Job 1:9).
37. Suffering drives us back to the basics of faith (Job 3:11).
38. Suffering provides opportunity for God to demonstrate His power (John 11:14-15).
39. Suffering helps us experience the promises of God (Luke 21:36).
40. Suffering may produce feelings of worthiness (Acts 5:41).
41. Suffering helps us remember Christ's suffering for us (Philippians 2:5-8).
42. Suffering can prove our faith to others (Hebrews 11).

43. Suffering weeds out superficial believers (Job 1:9).
44. Suffering strengthens the faith of those who endure. For example, if we always know why we suffer, our faith will not have room to grow (Hebrews 2:10).
45. Suffering can verify that we have been faithful (2 Timothy 1:4-5).
46. Suffering may prepare us for God's future purpose (Genesis 50:20).
47. Suffering results from many causes (1 Peter 2:21).
48. Suffering ultimately results from sin that twists justice and produces unpredictability and ugliness (Genesis 4:8-14).
49. Suffering teaches us that life is not merely happiness or personal fulfillment, but primarily to give honor and glory to God and fulfill His purpose (John 9:1-3).
50. Our suffering and pain may allow others to be blessed (Ephesians 3:13).
51. Suffering teaches us patience (James 1:2-3).
52. Suffering prepares us to meet Christ (1 Peter 1:7).
53. Suffering can make us more useful to God (1 Peter 1:7).
54. Suffering can turn you back to God (1 Samuel 5:6-7).
55. Suffering is sometimes a natural consequence of poor decisions and bad actions (Galatians 5:19).
56. Suffering shapes us for special service to others (Genesis 45:5-8).
57. Suffering can be an attack by Satan on our lives (Job 1:6-11).
58. Suffering can be a source of honor for those who endure it (Philippians 1:29).
59. Suffering can demonstrate our loyalty to God (Proverbs 4:9-22).
60. Suffering may manifest itself in irritations while serving others (Mark 10:38-39).
61. Suffering is not always the result of sin (John 9:2-3).
62. Suffering builds our character (Philippians 1:29-30).
63. Suffering may become an example used to help others (2 Peter 2:21, 24).
64. Suffering helps us to face reality because we know God is with us (Hebrews 5:7).
65. Suffering causes sin to lose its power (1 Peter 4:1).
66. Suffering helps the world to lose its attraction. (1 Peter 4:1-2).
67. Suffering may be caused by others, by unavoidable physical and natural disasters, by avoidable physical and natural disasters, and by ourselves (1 Corinthians 4:12-13; Hebrews 11).
68. Suffering enables us to empathize with the suffering on the cross (2 Corinthians 5:17).
69. Suffering provides awareness of others suffering in the world (2 Corinthians 1:7).
70. Suffering causes us to trust God for who He is, not what He does (Job 13:15).
71. Suffering teaches us what is important in life (Job 21:7, 15).
72. Suffering is never in vain (Galatians 3:4).
73. Suffering is a path to glory, providing the opportunity to reign with Christ (2 Timothy 2:12).
74. Suffering helps us to make reconciliation with others (Hebrews 5:8).
75. Suffering shows us where to find God through the fellowship of His suffering (Job 23:2-5; Philippians 3:10).

Appendix C
Step-by-Step Strategic Plan

The following plan was developed by a team of Edgewood missionary interns as a strategy for a new pastor who took over a deeply divided and troubled congregation. A former pastor had been accused of immorality and had been voted out of the congregation leaving slightly more than half of the membership. Many in the congregation were filled with resentment and bitterness and had sworn that they would never whole-heartedly follow a pastor again. They were experiencing deep-seated feelings of betrayal; many in the congregation were angry at others refusing to interact with them. The church was struggling financially and was deeply in debt. The departure of nearly half of the membership had left the congregation with an inability to meet its financial obligations. The new pastor was assigned the task of meeting the needs of this church and bringing healing and revival through his leadership.

I. Gather information
  A. Self-evaluation
    1. Pray for wisdom, guidance, and vision
    2. Prepare a list of Christian counselors to whom you may go for advice
    3. Develop a broad vision; give the church a new beginning
  B. Leadership evaluation
    1. Hold a meeting of the remaining deacons and trustees
      a. Give overview of the present situation
      b. Evaluate the commitment level
      c. Get a history of the past problems
      d. List and prioritize the present problems
        ~ resentment, bitterness, and distrust of leadership
        ~ financial problems
        ~ lack of leadership for existing church problems
        ~ members lost and disillusioned
        ~ church program problems
        ~ lack of vision ownership
        ~ loss of community trust and respect
    2. Hold a similar meeting of the key church leaders (Sunday school teachers, AWAWA leaders, lay pastors)
  C. Counsel evaluation

ANTICIPATED PROBLEM AND PROBLEM SOLUTION
Several deacons do not agree with the proposed problems. Those deacons with differing problems also have distrust of each other. Publicly remind them of the biblical qualities of leadership and help them to set aside their personal differences during the meeting. After the meeting, pull aside the disagreeing deacons, and attempt to help them reconcile.

    1. Seek advice from your list of Christian counselors
    2. Observe similar problems, causes, and solutions to become a problem solving specialist

II. Set SMART goals
  A. Short-term goals
    1. Make a detailed action plan within one week (evidenced by a copy of the plan containing the list of problems)
    2. Reorganize finances within ninety days (evidenced by payment plan)
    3. Develop vision within two weeks and cast it over the next year (evidenced by the development and promotion of vision)

       Use slogan   For**WARD**, On**WARD**, Up**WARD**— WARD to mean
                                               Winning others to Christ
                                               Affirming others in Christ
                                               Reaching out to others for Christ
                                               Dedicating our lives to Christ
    4. Reorganize membership/leadership of Sunday school and music programs, within six months
    5. Reorganize church programs within six months to one year
    6. Bring back lost and disillusioned membership
    7. Begin dealing with bitterness and resentment from the pulpit during the first sermons (evidenced by sermon topics and audience response)
  B. Mid-term goals
    1. Growth increase up to 300 members within five years
    2. Evaluate existing programs and build them up, adding at least one new program per year within two to five years
    3. Reorganize missions and outreach programs within the first two years (evidenced by missions giving and soul-winning)
    4. Hire additional staff member for each growth of 150 people
  C. Long-term goals
    1. Reconnect fully as a cohesive church family within five years (evidenced by overall atmosphere)
    2. Regain community trust and respect within five to ten years (evidenced by growth in membership)
    3. Continue to grow the church numerically, spiritually, and financially through the plateaus
III. Develop a specific vision (done simultaneously with goals and problem solving)
  A. Capture God's vision
    1. Know yourself
    2. Identify the values, attitudes, assumptions, and expectations that undergird your ministry
    3. Know your ministry environment
       Community, Colleagues, Congregation, Competition
    4. Know God: Study the Word and reassess your prayer life
    5. Verify the vision
  B. Communicate the vision
    1. Give your vision away in many different ways
       Sermons
       Printed materials
       Letters
       Teaching
       Meetings
    2. Set reachable goals

C. Implement the vision
  1. Inspire them
  2. Challenge them
  3. Empower them to own the vision

ANTICIPATED PROBLEM AND PROBLEM SOLUTION

An influential person is resistant to messages on resentment. He maintains a negative attitude, which spreads to others. Confront the individual on a one-on-one basis (take out for a meal) and attempt to use a biblical approach to correct his attitude. If he continues to be resistant, you and a deacon go in an attempt to correct the situation. If it still continues, bring the matter before the church and attempt to resolve the problem.

IV. Solve problems
  A. Heal the resentment, bitterness, and distrust of leadership
    1. Develop integrity
      Be transparent and vulnerable
      Live what we teach and do what we say
      Be honest and humble
      Be above reproach ("Let not your good be evil spoken of")
      Be dependable and trustworthy
      Make right decisions
    2. Develop credibility
      Keep the church growing
      Show genuine concern
          ~ Learn family links in the church
          ~ Understand their point of view
          ~ Communicate with them regularly
          ~ Be familiar with important dates in their lives
      Be a problem solver
          ~ Listen to them
          ~ Seek much input
          ~ Deal with them one-on-one
          ~ Keep leaders posted
          ~ Seek specific support
          ~ Satisfy the needs and concerns of others
    3. Use the pulpit
      Refocus congregation on:
          ~ The future, not the past
          ~ Forgiveness
          ~ Unity
          ~ Purpose and the new vision
      Bring in inspiring speakers
          ~ Revival meetings
          ~ Evangelistic meetings
  B. Organize the finances
    1. Contact all creditors
    2. Prioritize the bills
    3. Hold a business meeting
      Show the financial situation

Attempt to get commitments for tithes and one-time gifts
4. Make a payment plan
5. Incorporate a theme of giving into sermons

ANTICIPATED PROBLEM AND PROBLEM SOLUTION

We go to the bank and they are unwilling to finance. Approach the church with the situation and give this quote: "I have good news and bad news. The good news is we have all the money we need to pay the bills. The bad news is it is still in your pockets!" Then collect an offering and possibly hold fundraisers to begin paying off debts.

C. Reorganize church leadership
    1. Create job descriptions for church leadership
    2. Recruit teachers and leaders
        Visit key influencers first and meet one-on-one
        Show them the job description
        Seek specific support
        Motivate them
            ~ Ask effective questions
            ~ Do active listening
            ~ Provide clear, positive, and constructive feedback
            ~ Use the AID formula: **A**ction, **I**mpact, **D**esired outcome
            ~ Follow a GROW process: **G**oals, **R**eality, **O**ptions, **W**rap up
            ~ Use the 4 legs of motivation for evaluation and laying out a
                motivational blueprint
        Take their advice if applicable
        Request commitment to teamwork in any small way
    3. Reorganize church officers
        Hold an election to fill empty deacon slots
        Hold an election to fill empty trustee slots
    4. Reorganize program directors
        Sunday school teachers
        AWANA leaders
        Music coordinators and performers
        Nursery workers
        Ushers
D. Rebuild and grow the congregation
    1. Visit the remaining 175 members
        Pastor and five dependable deacons collectively visit six families per
            week (approximate total: 10 weeks)
        Visitation objectives
            ~ Seek specific support
            ~ Take their advice
            ~ Find a commonality
            ~ Be positive
            ~ Request commitment to teamwork in any small way
            ~ Take prayer requests
    2. Visit prospective members

This can be done after the initial 10 weeks and concurrently with visitation
to disillusioned members

Visitation objectives
~ Inform them of new church leadership
~ Find a commonality
~ Invite them to church
~ Ask if there is anything we can do for them

3. Visit disillusioned and previous members
This can be done after the initial 10 weeks and concurrently with visitation
to prospective members

Visitation objectives
~ Inform them of new church leadership
~ Find a commonality
~ Invite them to church
~ Ask if there is anything we can do for them

ANTICIPATED PROBLEM AND PROBLEM SOLUTION

There are not enough Sunday school teachers for the children based on the accepted ratio of one teacher for every seven children. Organize a schedule for needed Sunday school teachers for the next six months. Take a schedule with you when visiting church members Seek their specific support asking them to commit to one short period of time until the schedule is full. Continue this process until there are enough permanent teachers. Until the schedule is completely full, children will need to attend Sunday school with their parents.

4. Community outreach
Run article in local newspaper describing new leadership and vision

ANTICIPATED PROBLEM AND PROBLEM SOLUTION

Lack of funds for community outreach programs becomes a problem. Hold a fundraiser such as talent show, concert of church members, staff vs. youth softball game, auction, etc. Encourage church members on a weekly basis to take part in and help fund programs for growing the church. Cast the vision that God wants His church to grow!

Mail out letters to community describing new leadership and vision
Canvas the neighborhood, meeting new people, and telling them
about the new leadership and vision
Use broad media to describe new leadership and vision

E. Reorganize church programs and institute constructive change
1. Institute constructive change
Make additions only, no deletions
Show enthusiasm
Pre-sell key people
Explain reasons for changes
Discuss risks
Show anticipated results
Keep influential people on board

2. Make changes
    Evaluate the change with the checklist for yourself first:
        ~ Will this benefit the followers?
        ~ Is it compatible with the purpose of the organization?
        ~ Is it specific and clear?
        ~ Are the top 20% in favor?
        ~ Is it possible to test before making a commitment?
        ~ Are the physical, financial, and human resources available?
        ~ Is it reversible?
        ~ Is it the next obvious step?
        ~ Does it have short and long range benefits?
        ~ Is the timing right?
    Enlist the church leadership and members of important groups
    Prepare the congregation well in advance through vision casting
    Desensitize people through progressive steps (change with additions, not deletions)
    Explain the objectives of the change and how and when it will occur
    Defuse negative reactions
    Demonstrate the benefits of the change and provide any necessary adjustments
    Encourage ownership in the change through participation
    Anticipate any questions, problems and reactions, as well as be prepared to handle them.
    Keep communication channels open through feedback
    Demonstrate willingness to pay the price for successful realization
    Provide recognition, appreciation, and enthusiasm for all
    Give God the glory

3. Reorganize programs
    Children's
        AWANA (leaders, speakers, equipment, curriculum)
        Sunday school (teachers, curriculum)
        VBS (teachers, curriculum, promotion, prizes)
        Nursery (workers)
    Youth
        Youth group (leaders, activities, food, games, music)
        Camp (funds, sponsors, transportation)
        Sunday school (teachers, curriculum)
    Adults (teacher, curriculum, activities)
        College and career
        Singles
        Newlyweds
        Married couples
    Senior citizens
        Music
        Worship (leader, instruments)
        Choir
        Specials
        Instrumentals

Visitation
Shut-ins
Hospitals
Outreach—International and community missions

4. Based on the Pareto Principle, 20% of the people will do 80% of the work
20% of 175 = 35 people
This means we need 35 committed leaders to accomplish the reorganization of existing church programs

ANTICIPATED PROBLEM AND PROBLEM SOLUTION

Until we get the necessary leaders for music, the new pastor is leading the worship service. Some of the more committed leaders do not agree with the more contemporary music styles of the pastor when he starts leading "Shout to the Lord." Continue singing the old favorites and introduce one new song per month. See if this is an acceptable compromise. If it is not an acceptable compromise, modify the action plan to put off implementation of new songs until the timing is right.

F. Move the church forward into the future
1. Develop people
Delegation
Have the right motives
Determine what you can and cannot delegate
Develop job descriptions for those things you need to delegate
Recruit potential people
Provide support, encouragement, and training
Avoid reverse delegation
Further development of members into leaders
Lay pastors meetings
Institute classes
Small groups
Leader meetings (deacons, trustees, teachers)
Mentorship
Sermons/lessons
Develop leaders by being a leader
~Care about them and show genuine concern
~Model leadership
~Lead others by looking through their eyes
2. Reconnect as a church family
Church gatherings
Potlucks or picnics
Retreats or camps
Revivals
Community outreach and discipleship as a group
"If people lead others to Christ together, they will be motivated
to bring them into the church and disciple them together."
G. Regain community trust and respect
Communicate regularly our successes and progress toward goals

Appendix D
The Funeral Service for Mamie Brown

Every time that I preach a funeral sermon, I seek the Lord to determine which texts He would have me to use. I feel led today to use these three texts: 2 Corinthians 5:8-9, 2 Corinthians 12:2-4, and Philippians 1:21.

We are confident, I say, and willing rather to be absent, from the body, and to be present with the Lord. Wherefore we labor, that, whether present or absent we may be accepted of him. 2 Corinthians 5:8-9

I knew a man in Christ above fourteen years ago, (whether in the body), I cannot tell; or (whether out of the body), I cannot tell: God knoweth; such an one caught up to the third Heaven. And I knew such a man, (whether in the body), or out of the body, I cannot tell: God knoweth; how that he was caught up into paradise, and heard unspeakable words, which it is not lawful for a man to utter. 2 Corinthians 12:2-4

For me to live is Christ, and to die is gain. Philippians 1:21

May we pause for prayer. Dear Heavenly Father, I thank you for the privilege of preaching my own mother's funeral this morning. My prayer is that you would anoint me with the Holy Spirit. Put your words in my mouth, your thoughts in my mind, and the fullness of your Spirit in my heart. May I do justice in sharing the story of a life fully dedicated to Jesus Christ, and may each one of us derive comfort, strength, and peace from this message. For we ask these things in the name you could never refuse, our Lord Jesus Christ. Amen

I was reminiscing about growing up in the home of Mamie Brown. She was quite a woman! I knew that she loved me because she always showed me how much I meant to her. I appreciate the privilege of being her son. She taught me values, respect, love, and genuine spirituality.

I had grown up in Sunday school but dropped out when I was about 16 years of age. She began attending the First Baptist Church of Hammond, Indiana, about the time that I dropped out of Sunday school. She was attending there when a new young pastor Jack Hyles assumed the pulpit. She soon became one of his most ardent supporters. In fact, when a contingency in the church was attempting to vote him out, my mother was on the telephone tirelessly urging members to come to the business meeting and support this young pastor. She attended the Francis Bible Class in Sunday school and during one of the classes, she stood up and made a speech urging the ladies in that Sunday school class to support the pastor. I saw such a difference in her life when she met Christ as her Savior. Everything changed—her future, her desires, her priorities, every part of her life. She had made a profession of faith when she was a young girl but began to doubt whether she had truly committed her life to Jesus Christ. I was there at the dining room table of our home when she invited Christ to come into her life to make sure that she was genuinely saved. It was at that time that she received full assurance of her salvation, and from that moment on she never doubted.

She became one of the church's original bus captains. Early every Saturday she began visiting in the neighborhood for her bus route. She visited all day long, sometimes rushing home to eat, then returned and visited until seven or eight Saturday evening. She brought boys and girls to Sunday school by the busload. They hung on her, telling her how much they loved her because they knew how much she loved them. She constantly brought visitors to the services so they could hear the gospel and learn about Jesus Christ. During a 10 week Sunday school promotion, Pastor Hyles told me that she brought an average of seventy-five first-time visitors each week. That's the kind of Christian she was. She taught Sunday school until she was well into her 80s. I recall her visiting the girls in her class regularly to encourage them in the Lord and lead them to make commitments for Jesus Christ. Many of those girls now grown mentioned to me what an impact she had on their lives.

When she was a young girl, she wanted to be a schoolteacher but that was not possible because of the financial situation of her family. She grew up in a family of seven children. Her father was a steelworker at U.S. Steel. During the depression while in high school, her father was out of work. She was the only one working, so she would get up early in the morning and wait tables at a boarding house before she went off to high school. She gave her entire paycheck to her parents to feed the family. Her work supported and sustained her father, mother, and six brothers and sisters through a very difficult financial time in their lives. In fact, relatives have told me the family would never have made it had it not been for her.

Since she was never able to go to college to become a teacher, she attended business college and became a secretary. She excelled in her work and continued to climb the corporate ladder. Eventually she worked at company headquarters in downtown Chicago and became the secretary to the number three man in the company. I can recall her getting up early every morning, driving to the train station, and taking the South Shore from Hammond to downtown Chicago. She got off of the train and walked several blocks to her office in all kinds of weather, sometimes in snow and ice in the bitter cold. She rode the train arriving home well after dark. After her retirement she spent many hours serving the Lord each week.

At visitation last night as I talked to people who stopped by, I noted the comments people made when they talked about her. Here are some of the things folks said: she was devotedly spiritual, a tremendous achiever, an excellent money manager, a very generous person, loyal, faithful, possessed real character, had tremendous faith, and mentioned the profound influence she had on their lives. She was described as patient, dedicated, a wonderful Christian lady, outspoken, bold, sweet, friendly and forgiving. Numbers of people commented how very proud she was of her three sons. They said she mentioned us (her family) often and loved to talk about us. Someone made a comment about how stubborn she could be. Her faith was mentioned often as was her dedication to the Lord. I remember her going to church every time the doors were open and taking every opportunity to witness and serve the Lord.

When I was a teenager, I was not living for God and would often come home late at night and as I passed by her bedroom, I would see her on her knees praying for me. I believe she literally prayed me into the ministry.

She was an appreciative person, frequently expressing that appreciation to others for what they had done for her. She mentioned my uncle Lloyd and commented how he called her on the phone to check on her and how much she appreciated it. She commented how Aunt Ruth had her out to her house and cooked for her noting her thoughtfulness and the wonderful meals she prepared. She mentioned cousin Rene visiting and taking her out to eat. She so appreciated a Mother's Day card, a birthday card, a corsage, a bouquet of flowers, or some special gift. She would proudly wear the corsage and say, "This is from my son." I recall a card that I picked out for her when I was a little boy. The verse said, "Mommy I love you and love you a lot, cause you're the best mommy a kid ever got." I thought of that verse a few years ago so I sat at my computer and created a duplicate card. Inside I wrote that same verse. She called me after she received it and cried and cried. She told me how such a card meant to her as she remembered getting a card with that verse when I was a little guy.

My mother had an obsession about cleanliness! She would check to make sure that we washed our hands and she washed hers all the time. She liked to clean and was constantly cleaning something around the house. And who could forget when she was upset about something not so clean and we would hear her say "whoooooo." My mother loved three things more than anything else with the exception of the Lord and her family. She loved to grocery shop, to eat, and to go to church. I recall her going to the grocery store, going to another, and then another. She would take me to the store with her and we would go from store to store usually spending a couple hours in each store buying groceries. I would help her carry the bags to the car and into the house. A couple of years ago, we were driving through an area to attend a wedding and she said, "Mel, stop the car right now and turn in to this store. They have bananas advertised on the window for $.25 a pound!" That was so typical of her. She was a lady who loved to eat and yet she always remained slim and trim (Isn't that disgusting).

I would take her out to eat to an all-you-can-eat restaurant. She loved to eat at the Old Country Buffet; it was her favorite place. She would go through the line, fill her plate and then enjoyed eating every bite. She would return to the serving line and fill it again. When I would think she was done, she would say, "Now I have to go back for my desert." I often wondered how she could eat so much.

My father and she separated many years ago. When they were older and he developed cancer of the lung (he had recently become a Christian and then was diagnosed with cancer), he asked her if she would be willing to take care of him as he recuperated from surgery. Though they had been separated for

many years, she quickly told him yes. When he left the hospital, he went to her home and she nursed him and cared for him in a wonderful way. They became very close and were best friends until the day he died.

Not only was she forgiving, she was a generous person as well. When I was a boy, she asked me to go with her and help with a special project. We went to a store, loaded up the cart with groceries and carried them to the car. We pulled up in front of a house or apartment and we carried the groceries in. She had heard about someone who was out of work, going through a tough time, and in need of help. She took it upon herself to provide groceries for them. This example taught me the importance of giving and being sensitive to the needs of others. Winston Churchill said, "We make a living by what we receive, but we make a life by what we give."

I found the three texts mentioned earlier so appropriate in describing the life and passing of my mom. For her to live was Jesus Christ! Anybody who knew Mamie Brown, whether at work, in the neighborhood, or in any other context, soon learned how much she loved the Lord Jesus Christ. Her life was a constant example about what it meant to have a relationship with Jesus Christ. Christ was her life and it was evident that she loved Him more than anything else in the world. For her to live was Jesus Christ and to die was her gain. She often said to me, "Mel I don't fear death; I'm ready to go."

Dr. Donald Grey Barnhouse had lost his wife. His children were in the car with him as they were driving to the funeral service. He thought about how he could comfort his children about the death of their mother. Suddenly a thought crossed his mind and he said, "Kids would you rather be struck by this truck sitting beside us or would you rather be run over by its shadow?" The children responded by saying, "That's easy Daddy, we'd much rather be run over by the shadow because shadows can't hurt us." He

286

then went on to explain that that's what Jesus Christ did for us when He died in our place on the cross. He explained that Jesus took our sins upon Himself then rose again from the dead so that he could take our penalty and punishment as our Divine substitute. So instead of being struck by the truck, we only experience the shadow. Indeed, because Christ became sin for us who knew no sin, death has forever lost its sting and has no final power over us.

Dr. M. R. DeHaan used to raise bees. One day, one of the bees escaped and swooped down and stung one of his boys. When one brother saw that the other had been stung, he jumped up and ran as fast as he could with Dr. DeHaan in pursuit. When he finally overtook his son he asked why he was running. The boy replied, "Because I don't want that bee that just stung my brother to sting me." Dr. DeHaan explained this could not happen because the bee had only one stinger and when the bee stung his brother, it had no stinger left and was powerless to sting him. What a wonderful illustration about what Jesus Christ did when He took the sting of death and removed it so that when we face death, the sting would be forever gone.

Sometimes people wonder what's it like to die. Once a little boy was dying. His mother and father had not told him that he had a terminal illness that would take his life, but the little fellow figured it out and finally asked his mother if he was dying. The mom knew that she could not conceal the truth any longer, so she turned away from him and whispered a prayer, saying, "Dear Lord, you know that my son needs an answer. Please give me the wisdom to know exactly what to say." The little boy looked at his mother and said, "Mama I'm afraid to die because I've never died before. What is it like to die?" Suddenly God gave her a wonderful thought. She said, "Kenneth, you don't have to be afraid to die. Do you remember a few years ago when you were younger and you would fall asleep on the couch watching television with Mom and Dad in the living room." He said, "Yes, Mama." She said, "When you fell asleep, you'd wake up in the morning in your own room safe and secure in your own bed. When you fell asleep your daddy with his strong arms would pick you up and carry you into your room, put you in your own bed, and tuck you in. That's what it's like to die; your body will simply go to sleep and the angels will come and carry you into the arms of the Lord Jesus Christ. So you don't have to be afraid, everything will be just fine. Son, that's what it's like to die." That satisfied the little fellow; he never raised the issue or asked about it again until God called him home. His mother's explanation had removed his fear and had given him great confidence that all would be well because it was under the control of the Lord Jesus Christ.

Sometimes we look at death as if it's a terribly negative thing, but the Bible clearly teaches us that is not true. The Apostle Paul had the privilege of seeing Heaven and its wonder and was unable to talk about it for fourteen years. He was torn between two desires. On the one hand, knowing what waited for him in Heaven, he said he couldn't wait to get there. On the other hand, he said because of the ministry and the need to serve the Lord, he needed to stay here and wait. Clearly he was torn between the two, the desire to remain here and fulfill God's purpose for his life, at the same time he had an overwhelming desire to go home to be with the Lord because it's far better.

Perhaps that is well illustrated by the story of birth. When the baby is inside the mother's womb getting ready to be born, imagine if that baby could talk. It might say something like this, "I don't want to be born, I'm happy here, I've got everything I need right here in my mother's tummy. I have warmth, security, food, and comfort. I want to stay here." And we might say to that baby, "But there's a whole new wonderful world waiting for you and when you're born into it you'll see what I mean." That's a good illustration of death and Heaven. So often we think that we don't want to leave this world because we're happy here; but God would say to us that there's a whole new wonderful world waiting for us when we are born into it through death. It is a place where there's no sin, no sorrow, no suffering, no heartache, no disease, and no death—a place that He's prepared for us.

Finally, the Bible says that if we don't have the hope of life after death, then we are of all men most miserable. I couldn't officiate at funerals and give comfort to families if I did not believe these truths and be able to offer the dying and their loved ones this hope.

When Rev. John Todd was a boy, he lost both of his parents and went to live with his aunt. He was so disappointed when his aunt did not come to move him into her home. Instead she sent her servant, a man whose name was Caesar. The two of them rode together on Caesar's horse for the long ride to his new home. After dark as they rode out of the woods and saw the house in the distance, a fearful John asked Caesar if he thought his aunt would be waiting for him. Caesar assured him that she was watching and was at that moment standing with a candle at the window eagerly awaiting his arrival. When they arrived at the house, his aunt met him with a warm welcome. She served him something to eat, then tucked him into bed and sat by his bedside until he fell asleep.

Now many years had passed, she was an elderly woman and he was a minister. She wrote him a letter expressing her fear of dying and asked him for advice. He wrote to her reminding her of that day so long ago when Caesar brought him to her home to live. He talked about his fears and doubts and shared that seeing her standing in front of the window waiting and watching for him was such a comfort to him, especially when she so warmly welcomed him to his new home. He wrote that she had no reason to fear, because just as she waited to receive him home and gave him such a loving welcome, so the Lord Jesus would be waiting and watching for her to give her the warmest of welcomes to her new home, Heaven. His letter gave her great comfort and hope. I know that the Lord Jesus was waiting for my Mom to get home and warmly welcomed her to glory. What a moment that must have been when she met Jesus face to face.

So today as we lay to rest the earthly house of Mamie Brown, who lived nearly 92 years. We well know that to be absent from the body is to be present with the Lord, which is far better.

If you are here this morning and do not know for certain that you have a right relationship with God through Jesus Christ, let me urge you today to invite Jesus Christ to come into your life, forgive your sins and become your Lord and Savior.

Let us pray.

Appendix E
Hosting Meetings and Special Events

Pastors frequently are asked to host a variety of important meetings in their churches. The scope of these meetings may range from small to large numbers of people in attendance and includes conventions, conferences, fellowship meetings, seminars, preachers' meetings, revivals, and other special events. Hosting such a meeting involves extensive preparation and requires considerable attention to many details.

Ed Trenner, who has extensive experience conducting national events, produced a three-hundred point checklist, *Event Planning Checklist*. His checklist is thorough and should prove to be an invaluable help in organizing any event. This resource can be ordered through MasterPlanning Group International, PO Box 1999, Mount Dora, FL, 32756, or www.aylen.com.

Appendix F
Phone Contact — First Time Visitors

1. Introduce yourself and give a greeting.

   "Hello, my name is _____. I'm calling from the Edgewood Baptist Church. How are you today?"

2. Thank the person for attending the church service. "Thank you for being our guest at Edgewood this past Sunday."

3. Feel out their reaction to the service. "We hope you enjoyed the service."

4. Look for a bridge or point of contact to them. "Are you acquainted with anyone who attends Edgewood?"

5. Look for a non-threatening way to pursue a visit with them. "We like to get acquainted with our guests who visit Edgewood. I wonder if you would allow me and another church member the opportunity to drop by for a get acquainted visit at a time that would be convenient for you?"

6. Yes response—set up a visit. "That would be great! When would be a good time for you?"

7. No response—graciously reply with an invitation back to the church and a friendly offer of help. "Well that is alright. I'm very grateful that we had the opportunity to chat over the phone. Please worship with us again this Sunday. If there is any way that we can be a good neighbor to you, please feel free to contact us."

Suggestions:

1. Be pleasant, cheerful, and always courteous.
2. Never force yourself on someone who appears hesitant but take every opportunity to pursue and expand normal lines of communication.
3. Be careful not to appear that you are interrogating the person but do ask appropriate questions based on the course of the conversation.

Appendix G
Job Description
Administration/Assimilation Pastor

Job Responsibilities

Team Homebuilders' Class. Provide complete ministry services to members of the young married class: plan and direct retreats, lead Bible studies, plan special services and outreach activities, oversee all Young Married related home group and Bible studies, promote fellowship and service opportunities, and recruit members to the class.

Oversee the Assimilation Ministry of the Church. Plan, implement, and direct all aspects of the visitor and member assimilation into the church and its related opportunities and ministries. Foster acceptance and participation of new people by the church membership. Facilitate follow-up of visitors. Provide entry points for new people to interact with others in the congregation. Encourage participation in the church's discipleship process according to one's level of spirituality and commitment to provide the means for systematic spiritual growth.

Serve as Associate Pastor of the Church. Perform such duties as hospital visitation, counseling, preaching, missionary intern instruction, visitation, funerals, weddings, and other ministerial functions as required.

Assist Pastor Ed with Administrative Tasks.

Serve as Celebrate Recovery Staff Liaison.

Upgrade and Maintain Church Website. Integrate recent photos, current activities, schedules, and special event promotions. Provide links for prayer chains and funeral arrangements. Promote and advertise audio sermons on the site.

Insurance. Review and maintain all forms and coverage of insurance for the church including vehicle, building, health, and umbrella policies. Handle all claims and claim-related individual and group problems for the church. Assist individuals throughout a claim's processing including review of priority policy procedures and practices. Annually review all coverage and recommended updates, additions, or other changes as required. Add additional coverage as necessary for all new vehicles, buildings, and staff. Ensure optimal coverage and costs through comparative quotations. Maintain adequate records at all times.

Vehicles. Oversee purchase and maintenance of all church vehicles.

Building Use. Work with the Building Use Committee on approval and oversight of any and all uses of the church facilities including buildings, grounds, and personnel.

Equipment and Supplies Purchase. Determine the need for any one-time equipment purchases and oversee the timely and cost-effective purchase of supplies by working with the appropriate personnel using stipulated procedures.

Assist in Preparation of Operations Manual. Prepare, update, distribute a church operations manual covering all ministries of the church including process charts to the appropriate participants. Consult with staff and volunteers as needed.

Develop Informational System. Provide easy access to information systems through databases on people, projects, and ministries. These databases will not include monetary contributions.

Review and Prepare Records, Forms, Vouchers, and Letters.

Coordinate Staff Retreats and Planning Activities.

Maintain Updated Personnel Policies and Files.

Arrange for Temporary Support Staff.

Prepare Quarterly Church Operations and Activity Reports.

Coordinate Visitation Programs.

Job Requirements and Guidelines

1. Unconditionally agree with the doctrinal statement and purposes of the church.
2. Protect the reputation and integrity of others through strict confidentiality.
3. Demonstrate a high level of integrity, loyalty, and trust.
4. Display aptitude for organization, management, and people skills.
5. Create a cordial and cooperative work environment.
6. Communicate well with all groups and individuals.
7. Develop effective procedures for handling problems and complaints.
8. Be goal oriented.
9. Be adept at managing all kinds of people.
10. Practice conflict prevention and resolution.
11. Possess genuine spirituality.
12. Follow chain of command structure.
13. Be a team player.
14. Accept new challenges as opportunities.
15. Desire personal and professional growth and commit to pursue it.

Appendix H
Staff Evaluations

Please take the appropriate time to evaluate yourself based upon the criteria given below. We will review your analysis together during out face to face session. Each criterion is related to performance and provides knowledge of exactly what you have to do to improve.

1. What have you done well in your position this year?

2. Leadership involves succeeding in each of these areas. Please evaluate yourself in each.
   - Energy expended and passion for your job
   - Your performance engendering commitment and motivation, managing and relating to others among those under or associated with your ministry
   - Success in making difficult choices and providing constant improvement in the performance of your areas of responsibility and in those under you
   - Success in establishing and achieving or exceeding personal and professional goals in your ministry

3. What are your vision and goals for your area of ministry for the next year?

4. What do you need to do to improve the performance in/of your ministry? How can I help you?

Appendix I—Sample Forms

Why-Why Technique
How-How Technique

Purpose: Arrival at a solution to the problem

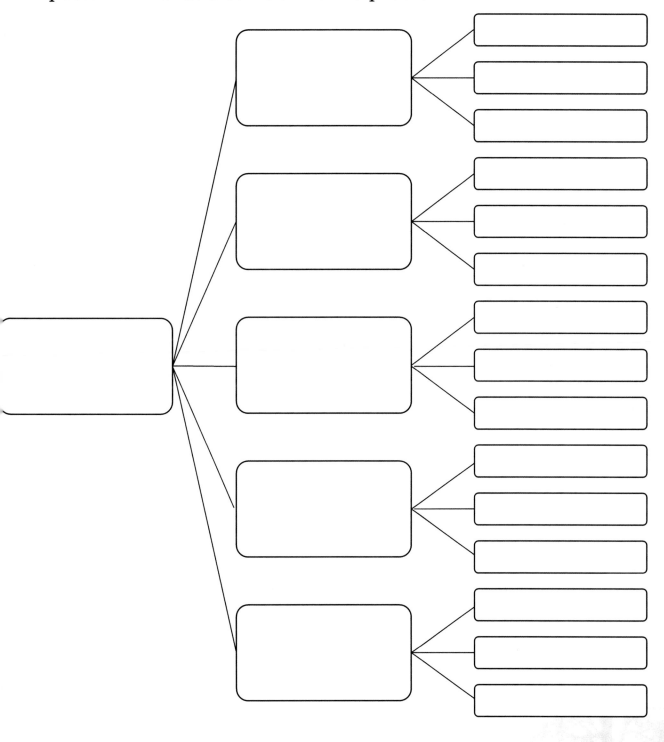

Individual Activity Parental Permission and Release of Liability Form

Edgewood Baptist Church
2704 38th Street, Rock Island, Illinois 61201
(309) 786-7913

Student's name _____

Address _____ City _____ St. ____

Medical insurance company_____ Policy # _____

Medical conditions or allergies *(Include food allergies.)*

_____

Current medications *(Please give details of when each medication must be taken.)*

_____

Emergency contact _____ Phone (____) _____

Address _____

(Please see other side for liability agreement and signature.)

<u>Description of activity or event and dates involved:</u>

Activity description: _____

Departure and return times and locations:

_____

_____

Activity leaders: _____

How to contact us if needed: _____ Cell: _____

Listed below are the activities we have planned to offer to the students during the activity. Please sign next to any activities in which you <u>DO NOT</u> wish your child to participate.

Activity / Event_____

Activity / Event _____

Activity / Event _____

Activity / Event _____

RELEASE OF LIABILITY FORM

(To be signed by the parent(s) or legal guardian of a teen
participating in a ministry-sponsored or organized function)

I/we hereby agree as follows:

I/we, the undersigned parent or legal guardian, hereby consent to my/our teen, _____
_____, taking part in the above mentioned activity.   *(First)*
          (Last)

I/we certify that my/our teen is able to participate in the above activities including transportation to and from the activities. If my teen has a medical condition that may be relevant to a physician in the event of an emergency, I have listed such conditions below. In the event an emergency occurs, I may be reached at the telephone number listed below. If I cannot be reached, I hereby authorize the Ministry administration or Ministry official to make emergency medical decisions for my teen. If there are any activities I do not want my teen to be involved in, I have listed them previously.

I understand that all reasonable safety precautions will be taken at all times by Edgewood Baptist Church, and I/we shall not hold the Ministry nor any of its officers or agents liable in any way for any occurrence in connection with the activities described above, even if such activities result in injury, death, dismemberment, injury to reputation, emotional distress or other damages to my/our teen or the teen's family, heirs, or assigns. I/we shall save and hold harmless the Ministry and its officers and agents from any claim by me, my family, estate, heirs, or assigns arising out of my/our teen's participation in this activity.

In consideration of my/our teen being allowed to take part in the activities described above, I/we hereby personally assume all risks in connection with the activities, for any harm, injury, or damage that may befall my/our teen while traveling to and from the Ministry and participating in the activities themselves, including all risks connected therewith, whether foreseen or unforeseen.

I/we shall exempt and release the Ministry and its officers and agents from all liability whatsoever for personal injury, property damage or wrongful death caused by negligence. I/we expressly agree that this release, waiver, and indemnity agreement is intended to be as broad and inclusive as permitted by the law of the State of Illinois and that if any portion thereof is held invalid, it is agreed that the balance shall, notwithstanding, continue in full legal force and effect. This release contains the entire agreement between the parties hereto, and the terms of this release are contractual and not a mere recital. The parties shall resolve any dispute arising under this agreement only through negotiation, mediation, or binding arbitration.

I/we further state that I HAVE CAREFULLY READ THE FOREGOING RELEASE AND KNOW THE CONTENTS THEREOF AND I SIGN THIS RELEASE AS MY OWN FREE ACT. This is a legally binding agreement that I have read and understand.

Date: _____

_____   _____
Parent or Legal Guardian   Parent or Legal Guardian

Congratulations On Your Upcoming Wedding!

We want your wedding at Edgewood to be a special event. Planning and preparation are the keys to experiencing a wonderful wedding day. We look forward to assisting you in order to make your day a success.

12. Lighting requests _____

13. Who will dismiss audience? _____
    Will there be a receiving line? _____
    If yes, what order? _____

14. Costs:

Church
    Auditorium _____
    Gymnasium _____
    Crown Fellowship Hall _____
    Side Room _____
Janitor
    Auditorium _____
    Gymnasium _____
    Crown Fellowship Hall _____
    Side room _____
Musicians
    Singers _____
    Keyboard _____
    Other _____
Sound/Lighting Tech _____
Minister _____
    (Fee includes pre-marital counseling, wedding detail
    preparation, and ceremony.)

Payment to <u>individuals</u> should be made at the <u>rehearsal</u> in order to diminish the number of details for the wedding day.

NO SMOKING OR DRINKING OF ALCHOLIC BEVERAGES IS ALLOWED IN THE CHURCH BUILDING OR ON THE CHURCH PROPERTY.

Wedding of: _____

His address: _____

Phone: _____
Dad's name: _____
Mom's name: _____
Step-dad's name (if applicable): _____
Step-mom's name (if applicable): _____

Her address: _____

Phone: _____
Dad's name: _____
Mom's name: _____
Step-dad's name (if applicable): _____
Step-mom's name (if applicable): _____

1. Date of ceremony _____
   Formal _____ Semi-formal _____ Informal _____

2. Place ceremony will be held (auditorium, side room) _____

   Estimate of attendance _____
   Officiating pastor _____

3. Date of rehearsal _____ Time: _____
   Rehearsal dinner _____ Time: _____
   Who is invited _____

4. Will there be music?
   Organ _____ Piano _____ Electronic keyboard _____
   Name of player _____
   Soloist (s) _____
   Songs _____
   _____

5. Will all be present for rehearsal? _____

6. Single ring _____ Double ring _____

7. Will reception be held in the church?
   Gym _____ Crown Fellowship Hall _____

8. Plans for decorations? _____

   Will there be flowers? _____
   Delivered by? _____
   Time: _____ Carpet _____
   Candelabra _____ Who will light _____
   Unity candle _____ Who will light _____
   When will the above be delivered? _____
   Photographer _____
   Videographer _____

9. Brides attendants (indicate order): _____
   Maid of honor _____
   Bridesmaids _____
   _____
   Flower girl and/or ring bearer _____

10. Groom's attendants (indicate order):
    Best man _____
    Groomsmen _____
    _____
    Ushers _____
    _____

11. Wedding colors: Ladies _____ Men _____

Will CD/taped music be used? _____
Where placed in the ceremony? _____
_____

Evaluation of Service Form

Component of Service	Rating Scale: 1=Poor							10=Superior		
Energy level of the service	1	2	3	4	5	6	7	8	9	10
Flow of the service	1	2	3	4	5	6	7	8	9	10
Start/End on time	1	2	3	4	5	6	7	8	9	10
Music	1	2	3	4	5	6	7	8	9	10
Worship	1	2	3	4	5	6	7	8	9	10
Evangelism	1	2	3	4	5	6	7	8	9	10
Discipleship	1	2	3	4	5	6	7	8	9	10
Fellowship	1	2	3	4	5	6	7	8	9	10
Serving	1	2	3	4	5	6	7	8	9	10
Friendliness	1	2	3	4	5	6	7	8	9	10
Attendance	1	2	3	4	5	6	7	8	9	10
Visuals	1	2	3	4	5	6	7	8	9	10
Announcements	1	2	3	4	5	6	7	8	9	10
Visitors	1	2	3	4	5	6	7	8	9	10
Temperature	1	2	3	4	5	6	7	8	9	10
Sermon	1	2	3	4	5	6	7	8	9	10
Relevance	1	2	3	4	5	6	7	8	9	10
Practical application	1	2	3	4	5	6	7	8	9	10
Staff example	1	2	3	4	5	6	7	8	9	10
Efficiency of personnel	1	2	3	4	5	6	7	8	9	10
Overall effectiveness	1	2	3	4	5	6	7	8	9	10

Suggestions/Comments:

_____

_____

_____

_____

_____

_____

Worship Planning Sheet

Date:_____

Sermon title:_____

Sermon theme:_____

Sermon purpose:_____

Sermon text:_____

___Prelude

___Call to worship

___Hymns

___Choruses

___Responsive reading

___Silent meditation

___Drama

___Greeting of visitors

___Missionary moment

___Pastoral prayer

___Offering

___Offertory

___Doxology

___New song

___Children's program

___Children's choir

___Scripture

___Benediction

___Testimony

___Choir anthem

___Special music

___Baptism

___Communion

___Baby dedication

___Reception of members

___Sermon

___Announcements

___Open praise/prayer

___Other

Prelude:_____

Announcements:

_____
_____
_____
_____

Hymns:
    1._____
    2._____
    3._____

Choruses:
    1._____
    2._____
    3._____
    4._____

Special music:
    1._____
    2._____

Responsive reading, p. _____
Scripture reading, _____
Benediction:_____
Postlude:_____
Other:_____

_____
_____

Order of service:
    1._____
    2._____
    3._____
    4._____
    5._____
    6._____
    7._____
    8._____
    9._____
    10._____
    11._____
    12._____

Questions:
Does this service glorify the Lord?
Is it Spirit-filled?
Is it Christ-centered?
Is it edifying to believers (inspiring, instructing, involving)?
Is it appealing to visitors (convincing, comfortable, clear)?
Will it motivate people to be more Christlike and obedient?

Edgewood Baptist Facility Use Form

Thank you for completing this form. The information provided will help us to better serve you.

1. Request date: _____ 2. Event date: _____ 3. Event time period: _____

4. Responsible person: (Name) _____ (Phone number) _____

5. Number of participants: (Adults) _____ (Children) _____

   Room number(s) requested:_____

6. Kitchen requested: (Gym) _____ (Basement) _____ (None) _____

7. Purpose of event: _____

8. Beverage and food involved: _____

9. What supplies needed? (Indicate approximate quantity needed. Disposable items are available at cost for non-church events.)
   Disposable table cloths _____
   Disposable table service for _____ persons.
   Other: _____

10. What equipment do you need? (Please circle.)

    Tables   Video/TV
    Chairs   Portable chalk or white board
    Extension cords   Overhead projector
    Portable screen   Game equipment
    Audio equipment
    Other: _____

11. Elevator use requested: No _____ Yes _____ (Get key from church secretary)

12. Building/Room key arrangements: (Check correct item below.)
    _____ Responsible person has own key to enter and lock up
    _____ Responsible person will get key from church secretary
    _____ Other: _____

13. Other support needed from custodian? _____

14. Other pertinent information? _____

Custodial Fee For A Wedding, Wedding Reception, Or Open House:
Auditorium - $80
Crown Fellowship Hall - $60
Multi-Purpose Facility - $120

15. Have you received a copy of the facility use guidelines?
    Yes   _____
    No   _____

Guidelines For Facility Use

(Thank You For Being Good Stewards)

General

1. The church secretary will maintain an advance notice reservation schedule and will have keys available for check out by the leader of the group using the center. Reservations must be made 24 hours in advance.

2. All requests will be documented on the Edgewood Facility Use Form.

3. The use of this facility is a privilege and must always be scheduled with the church office. Occasionally a group may be asked to forfeit its reservations for a special church function.

4. The leader of each group is responsible for contacting the custodian to receive information about the maintaining of the security, lighting, heating/cooling, and cleanup of the center, or must have the custodian present to handle these areas of responsibility.

5. Responsible person must be an Edgewood member and must be 21 years of age. Use by individuals less than 21 will only be allowed if an adult (21 or older) is present at the activity.

6. Groups outside the church requesting facility use must request through the deacon board and must fill out the *Edgewood Baptist Facility Use Form*.

7. Standing reservations, such as reserving the facility for the third Saturday each month, must be approved by the deacon board.

8. Willful damage or destruction of equipment will be at the expense of the parties involved.

9. Any group or individuals that abuse this privilege may be denied further use of the facility.

10. Activities with children involving beverage and/or food will be restricted to the Crown Fellowship Hall or the gym.

11. All youth activities must be sponsored and adequately supervised by responsible adults. Required adult/child ratio: 1 adult/10 children, but a minimum of 2 adults for any activity.

12. No beverages are allowed in the sanctuary or foyers at any time.

13. No equipment, tables, or other supplies shall be borrowed or removed from the premises without obtaining permission from the church office in advance.

14. We will have respect for those around us and will not offend them either by deed or word.

15. All who use these facilities will honor the Lord Jesus Christ by their actions, words, and attitudes. No profanity or obscene gestures will be tolerated. There will be no smoking, use of alcohol, or dancing on the premises.

16. The facility must be left as it was found. Anyone using the building after 5:00 p.m. on Saturdays will be held responsible for setting it up, if needed, for Sunday school.

17. For security reasons, at least one male shall be present during all ladies' functions to monitor access to the facilities. This requirement is the responsibility of the person in charge of the planned activity.

Gym

1. All equipment that is used will be returned to the proper storage area: balls to the racks, AWANA equipment to the proper storage crate, and tables to the storage room.

2. Those engaging in physical activities will wear basketball-type shoes only that are of a type that do not leave dark scuff marks.

3. The facilities and equipment will never be used in a manner for which it was never intended such as intentionally bouncing balls off the walls or light fixtures and kicking the walls or doors.

4. Coordinate with the church custodian before adjusting the gym thermostat.

Kitchen

1. Any group or individuals using this facility will always clean up trash and sweep floor before leaving.

2. Any group or individuals that use the kitchen, utensils, or dishes will clean all used items, counters, and appliances as well as return them to their respective storage locations. Take all trash to the dumpster.

3. To avoid injury no small children are to be in the kitchen once cooking has begun.

4. Replace aluminum foil in the ovens when you are through using the kitchen.

5. Leftovers should not be placed in the church refrigerator.

Endnotes

Part 1: Personal Preparation

Attitude

1 David D. Burns, *Feeling Good Handbook* (New York: William Morrow, 1989), 8-11.

2 Warren W. Wiersby, *Be Joyful* (Colorado Springs: Cook Communications, 2005), 129.

Vision

1 Michael E. Gerber, *The E-Myth* (New York: Harper Business, 1986), 12-21.

George Barna's research and writings on vision are essential reading.

Leadership

1 John Zenger and Joseph Folkman, *The Extraordinary Leader* (New York: McGraw-Hill, 2002).

2 Jack Welch, *Winning* (New York: Harper Business, 2005).

3 Jeffrey A. Crames, *Jack Welch on Leadership* (New York: McGraw-Hill, 2005).

There are more than one thousand books on leadership and even more on management practices. Many cover similar ground. Books by Jack Welch, Peter Drucker, and John Maxwell do a good job of distilling down the material to both the essential and practical applications.

Leading Change

1 John P. Kotter, *Leading Change* (Boston: Howard Business School Press, 1996).

2 John P. Kotter and Don S. Cohen, *The Heart of Change* (Harvard Business School Press: 2002). *John Kotter is the foremost authority in leading change in an organization.*

Strategic Planning

1 Rick Warren, *The Purpose Driven Church* (Grand Rapids: Zondervan, 1995).

2 Bob Biehl, *Masterplanning* (Nashville: Broadman and Holman, 1997).

Motivation

1 Max Lansberg, *The Tao of Coaching* (Santa Monica, California: Knowledge Exchange, 1997).

2 Ferdinand F. Fournies, *Coaching for Improved Work Performance* (New York: Liberty Hall Press, 1987), 77.

Persuasion

1 Robert B. Cialdini, *Influence: Science and Practice* (Columbus, Ohio: Allyn and Bacon, 2008).

Books by Kevin Hogan on persuasion and influence are excellent reviews of research articles on persuasion.

Communication

1 Judee K. Burgoon, David B. Buller, and W. Gill Woodall, *Nonverbal Communication* (New York: McGraw-Hill, 1996), 140.

Relationship Management/Conflict Resolution

1 Ken Thomas, "Toward Multi-dimensional Values in Teaching: The Example of Conflict Behaviors" (Academy of Management Review, July 1977).

2 Warren W. Wiersby, *Be Joyful* (Colorado Springs: Cook Communications, 2005), 129.

Part 2: Duties of the Minister

Counseling

1 Albert Ellis and Robert Harper, *A Guide to Rational Living* (Santa Monica, California: Wilshire Books, 1975).

2 Larry Crabb, *Basic Principles of Biblical Counseling* (Grand Rapids: Zondervan, 1975).

3 *Diagnostic and Statistical Manual of Mental Disorders-DSM-IV-TR* (Arlington, Virginia: American Psychiatric Publishing, 2000).

4 Aaron T. Beck, A. John Rush, Brian F. Shaw, and Gary Emery, *Cognitive Therapy of Depression* (New York: Guilford Press, 1987).

5 Diagnostic and Statistical Manual of Mental Disorders-DSM-IV-TR (Arlington, Virginia: American Psychiatric Publishing, 2000).

There are over 300 schools of counseling. The best philosophy is found in Larry Crabb's book, Effective Biblical Counseling, where he presents four approaches to biblical counseling and recommends the fourth ("Spoiling the Egyptians") which uses scripture as the basis for counseling adding techniques which are not unscriptural from other sources.

Marriage Counseling

1 David Olson, *Prepare/Enrich* (Minneapolis: Life Innovations, 2009).

2 John Gottman and Nan Silver, *The Seven Principles for Making Marriage Work* (New York: Three Rivers Press, 1999).

3 Gary Chapman, *The Five Love Languages: How to Express Heartfelt Commitment to Your Mate* (Chicago: Northfield Publishing, 1995).

John Gottman has extensively written about marriage problems based upon his life's work examining couples in his research department at the University of Washington. His books are thorough and practical. William Hiebert and Robert Stahmann's books on marital assessment and counseling are excellent.

Preaching

Haddon Robinson and Warren Wiersby's books on preaching are filled with helpful information. Jack Hyle's book, Teaching on Preaching, has many helpful suggestions.

Teaching

Thomas Armstrong's Seven Kinds of Smart and Howard Gardner's Multiple Intelligences: New Horizons in Theory and Practice are excellent resources on multiple intelligences. Thomas Armstrong in his book Multiple Intelligences in the Classroom has applied specific techniques for teachers to use productively in the classroom. Bruce Wilkenson's Seven Laws of the Teacher and Seven Laws of the Learner are also invaluable resources.

Part 3: The Church

Youth Ministry

1 Bo Boshers, Scott Larsen, and Larry Landquist, *Reaching Kids Most Youth Ministries Miss* (Loveland, Colorado: Group Publications, 2000), 5.

2 Kirsten Dunst quoted (Rolling Stone, May 23, 2002).

3 Jonathan McKee, *www.thesource4ym.com/howdoi/staffutu.asp*

4 Ken Sapp, *www.vanishingcookies.com/kensapp/ym/ym_youth_personality_types.html*

5 G. Keith Olson, *Why Teenagers Act the Way They Do* (Loveland, Colorado: Group Publications, 1987).

6 Doug Fields, *Purpose-Driven Youth Ministry* (Grand Rapids: Zondervan, 1998) 268.

7 Doug Fields, *Purpose Driven Youth Ministry* (Grand Rapids: Zondervan, 1998) 277.

Children's Ministry

1 James W. Fowler, *Stages of Faith* (San Francisco: Harper, 1995).

2 Mark Buechler, *Catalog of School Reform* (Portland: Northwest Regional Educational Laboratory, 2002).

Index

About the Author

Dr. Mel Brown attended Purdue University, graduated from Evangel College (B.A.), Baptist Bible College (B.Th.), Western Illinois University (M.S.), and Northern Illinois University (Ed.D.) graduating with top honors is his academic pursuits. His undergraduate studies include emphasis in communications, theology, and business; his graduate studies were in the field of counseling with specialization in clinical psychology and marriage and family therapy. He interned at Pine Knoll Psychiatric Hospital in Iowa and served his residency at Marriage and Family Counseling Center, Rock Island, Illinois. He has trained counselors at all levels of experience.

He has pastored three churches with congregations ranging in size from small to large. He has served as senior pastor of the Edgewood Baptist Church, Rock Island, Illinois, for over forty years.

Dr. Brown has lectured in colleges and universities throughout the Midwest, has taught for Moody Bible Institute and served as director of their Quad Cities extension program. He has served on the board of directors of various community and learning organizations, and is the recipient of eighteen academic and professional awards.

The two year training program he established at the Edgewood Baptist Church for pastors and missionaries has received critical acclaim and international recognition.

CPSIA information can be obtained at www.ICGtesting.com
Printed in the USA
LVOW022034151111

255126LV00003B/5/P